The Protection of Traditional Knowledge on Genetic Resources

The Protection of Traditional Knowledge on Genetic Resources

Frantzeska Papadopoulou

Law Faculty, Stockholm University and Business School, Linnaeus University, Sweden

Edward Elgar
PUBLISHING

Cheltenham, UK • Northampton, MA, USA

Published by
Edward Elgar Publishing Limited
The Lypiatts
15 Lansdown Road
Cheltenham
Glos GL50 2JA
UK

Edward Elgar Publishing, Inc.
William Pratt House
9 Dewey Court
Northampton
Massachusetts 01060
USA

A catalogue record for this book
is available from the British Library

Library of Congress Control Number: 2017959522

This book is available electronically in the **Elgar**online
Law subject collection
DOI 10.4337/9781786437433

MIX
Paper from responsible sources
FSC® C013056

ISBN 978 1 78643 742 6 (cased)
ISBN 978 1 78643 743 3 (eBook)

Typeset by Columns Design XML Ltd, Reading
Printed and bound in Great Britain by TJ International Ltd, Padstow

Contents

Acknowledgements

I am very grateful to the Law Faculty of Stockholm University for financing the research that formed this book, and for supporting my research plans in any way possible during recent years. My colleagues at Stockholm and Linnaeus University, as well as extended international colleagues, have contributed with their input in various ways, forming me as a researcher and giving a character to this book. I am also very thankful to the team of editors working with my book for their professionalism, patience and support. Last but not least, a special thanks to my family: my husband Björn, and my children Manos, Nicole and Amalia; without their support this book would not be possible.

Abbreviations

ABS	Access and Benefit Sharing
AK	*Ancistrocladus korupensis*
ASEAN	Association of Southeast Asian Nations
BGVS	Bedrift Geneesmiddelen Voorziening Suriname
BIO	Biotechnology Industry Organization
BMS	Bristol-Myers Squibb
CABI	Centre for Agriculture and Biodiversity International
CARIFORUM	Forum of Caribbean States
CBD	Convention on Biological Diversity
CC	Creative Commons
CGEN	Genetic Heritage Management Council
CGIAR	Committee of Plant Genetic Resources
CGRFA	Commission on Genetic Resources for Food and Agriculture
CI	Conservation International
CLR	compensatory liability regime
COP	Conference of the Parties
CoTeRGAPA	Technical Council of the Ministry of Agriculture, Rural Development and Fisheries on Agrarian Genetic Resources, Fisheries and Agriculture
DGP	Department of Genetic Heritage
DNA	deoxyribonucleic acid
EC	European Community
EPC	European Patent Convention
EPO	European Patent Office
EU	European Union
FAO	Food and Agriculture Organization
FTA	Free Trade Agreement

GATT	General Agreement on Tariffs and Trade
GEF	Global Environment Facility
GI	geographical indication
GNU	Gnu's Not Unix (Operating System)
GPL	general public licence
GR	genetic resources
GRR	Genetic Resources Recognition
HIV	human immunodeficiency virus
ICBG	International Cooperative Biodiversity Groups
ICESCR	International Covenant on Economic, Social and Cultural Rights
IFPMA	International Federation of Pharmaceutical Manufacturers and Associations
IGC	Intergovernmental Committee on Intellectual Property and Genetic Resources, Traditional Knowledge and Folklore
ILO	International Labour Organization
INPI	National Institute of Industrial Property
IP	intellectual property
IPR	intellectual property right
IRRI	International Rice Research Institute
ITLOS	International Tribunal for the Law of the Sea
ITPGRFA	International Treaty on Plant Genetic Resources for Food and Agriculture
IU	International Undertaking
IUCN	International Union for Conservation of Nature
MBG	Missouri Botanical Gardens
MGR	marine genetic resource
MINAE	Ministry of Environment and Energy of Costa Rica
MTA	material transfer agreement
NCI	National Cancer Institute
NGO	nongovernmental organisation
OAU	Organization of African Unity
PCT	Patent Cooperation Treaty
PGRFA	plant genetic resources for food and agriculture

PIC	prior informed consent
PLT	Patent Law Treaty
PVP	plant variety protection
RGGV	Register of Plant Genetic Resources
SCP	Standing Committee on the Law of Patents
SPLT	substantive patent law treaty
STSTBA	Scientific Body
TK	traditional knowledge
TKGR	traditional knowledge on genetic resources
TRIPS	Trade-Related Aspects of Intellectual Property Rights
UDHR	Universal Declaration of Human Rights
UNCED	United Nations Conference on Environment and Development
UNHCR	United Nations High Commissioner for Refugees
UNCLOS/ LOSC	United Nations Convention on the Law of the Sea
UNCTAD	United Nations Conference on Trade and Development
UNEP	United Nations Environment Programme
UN FAO	Food and Agriculture Organization of the United Nations
UPOV	International Union for the Protection of New Varieties of Plants
US	United States
USPTO	United States Patent and Trademark Office
VPISU	Virginia Polytechnic Institute and State University
WIPO	World Intellectual Property Organization
WTO	World Trade Organization

1. When arrows from the jungle aim at the heart of modern intellectual property rights

1.1 INTRODUCTION

Issues pertaining to the ownership, management and transfer of natural resources have historically been of central importance in international law. Concerns about environmental degradation have enriched the discussion on the ownership and management of valuable natural resources, introducing legal obligations related to their preservation and sustainable use. Genetic resources are no exception to this, and in the past decades, international negotiations, international conventions and a vivid debate have all attempted to find a way to combine the conservation and sustainable use of such resources while at the same time securing the fair and equitable sharing of the benefits arising from their use. This really is an era of green developmentalism, in which nature is subject to extensive commodification, on the basis of which both environmental and conservationist concerns and the sharing of benefits are addressed.

The advent of biotechnology has contributed in this direction, opening up space for new, revolutionary uses of genetic resources and constituting the basis for the development of commercial products mainly in the areas of agriculture and pharmaceuticals. Intellectual property rights (IPRs) and the exclusive rights they provide to the results of R&D in the field, aside from increasing the commercial potentials of these products, have also brought to the surface another new parameter in the already established natural resources discussion, namely that of the value of know-how regarding their applications. In the field of genetic resources, such know-how is very often embodied in what is called traditional knowledge (TK). TK-related applications provide valuable leads to researchers in the agricultural and pharmaceutical fields and thus become a necessary intangible asset accompanying tangible genetic resources – for the purposes of this book, named 'traditional knowledge on genetic resources' (TKGR). The net effect of these recent developments is an increasing interest in IPRs and access to TKGR.

Today, biodiversity constitutes one of the major sources of inspiration, as well as a major source of raw material, for a number of different industries, such as agriculture, biotechnology, food, cosmetics and pharmaceuticals. Growing consumer interest in 'green products' is reorienting scientific interest towards the search for novel natural substances. TKGR-based biotechnological research presents considerable advantages; for example, success ratios in trials concerning the search for valuable genetic resources increase from 1 in 10,000 samples to 1 in 2. In fact, the use of TKGR could increase efficiency in screening plants for medicinal properties by more than 400 per cent. Obviously, both the higher success ratios obtained by employing TKGR in preliminary research and shorter development times for new products reduce costs, leading to higher profitability.[1]

The challenges posed to the IPR system with regard to the protection of TKGR concern well-known questions, namely how (if at all) to protect subpatentable innovation and when and under which circumstances an emerging valuable subject matter justifies the introduction of a new entitlement, either under one of the established IPRs or under the scope of *sui generis* rights. These questions are of course more than familiar to the IPR world, and the protection of TKGR would in fact be a typical IPR question were it not for that fact it has become a symbol of North/South inequality.

Since the discussion takes place in the framework of IPRs, it needs to address whether the TKGR is in fact a new subject matter worthy of protection, or whether its protection entails a further enclosure of the public domain. It is furthermore debatable whether an exclusive right (already existing or *sui generis*) is a necessary measure for TKGR, or whether other means of protection, such as measures against unfair competition or liability rules, are equally appropriate.

The transfer of TKGR from the South to the North is not a new practice. The value of TKGR trade has been recognised since ancient times, marking international relations and constituting the background of wars and political decisions. These practices flourished even more during colonial times. Economic colonialism was in some cases based on the transfer and exploitation of TKGR. During colonial times, scientists, breeders and botanists from the colonising world collected and transferred useful and rare plant genetic resources to their home countries. At the time, plant genetic resources were considered 'common resources'.

---

[1] Prakash, G., *Science and the Imagination of Modern India*, Princeton: Princeton University Press (1999), pp. 201–27.

With a few exceptions of restricted access, such as in the notable cases of rubber, quinoa and cacao,[2] genetic resources were shared by and accessible to all. In the twentieth century, the regulatory structures changed dramatically, initiating a process of gradual commodification of genetic resources that has lasted for decades.[3] As observed above, technological innovation laid the ground for the development of industries, commercially exploiting genetic resources and associated know-how.

The emerging interest in TKGR access and exploitation has brought to the surface a number of unfortunate market failures originating in the special characteristics of TKGR trade and in the weaknesses of the legal framework.[4] It is developing countries, with expanding populations and limited scientific and technological development, that contain valuable biodiversity. One of the main concerns of the developing world has been that scientists from technology-intensive countries have accessed genetic resources that were later adapted into commercially viable valuable forms, protected by patents or other IPRs and eventually sold back to developing countries, often at prohibitive prices.[5] In this respect, TKGR holders tend to overestimate the contribution of their resources and of

---

[2] Monson, J., 'From Commerce to Colonization: A History of the Rubber Trade in the Kilombero Valley of Tanzania, 1890–1914', History, Vol 21 (1993), pp. 113–30.

[3] During the latter part of the twentieth century, the discussion on commodification of an endless list of subject matter came to be of major interest. With market freedom on the one hand and the risk of dehumanisation on the other, the evaluation of liberatory economic rhetoric became more and more relevant. Obviously, with commodification theories applied to the market in babies for childless couples, in body parts and in human beings, it was only logical to expect they would reach TKGR too. See Radin, M., Sunder, M., 'The Subject and Object of Commodification', Stanford Law School Public Law and Legal Theory Working Paper Series, Research Paper No 97 (2004).

[4] A long list of patents granted on what was previously considered traditional medicine or agriculture is presented in McGown, J., 'Out of Africa: Mysteries of Access and Benefit Sharing', Edmonds Institute in Cooperation with African Centre for Biosafety (2006).

[5] Tolan, S., 'Against the Grain: Multinational Corporations Peddling Patented Seed and Chemical Pesticides are Poised to Revolutionize India's Ancient Agricultural System. But at What Cost?', *LA Times*, 10 July 1994, p. 18. See also Wolfgang, L., 'Patents on Native Technology Challenged', Science, Vol 15 (1995), p. 1506. Another interesting article is Roht-Arriaza, N., 'Of Seeds and Shamans: The Appropriation of the Scientific and Technical Knowledge of Indigenous and Local Communities', Mich J Int L, Vol 17 (1996), pp. 936–7.

their traditional knowledge in the development of the end products.[6] On the other hand, they usually have very minor experience with IPRs, if any, and only limited possibilities to offer a realistic prognosis of their future commercial value. The general mistrust of the system just described is strengthened by the fact that IPRs protect the end products originating in the developed world while providing limited or no protection for the initial contribution, no matter how crucial it is – as in the case of TKGR. Developing countries very often express concern that the current intellectual property (IP) system does not provide any protection against acts of misappropriation of TKGR-related innovation, excluding it indirectly from the scope of protectable subject matter.[7]

Developed nations focus more on the ability to maintain their right to unrestricted access to genetic resources while defending the current structure of the IPRs system and the protection this affords their technological achievements. An argument often employed to defend this position is that technology transfer is dependent on the existence of strong IPRs and enforcement mechanisms. For the developed world, technological applications that contribute the necessary modifications of a substance in order to turn it into a commercial product are recognised as the core value of the innovation, while the value of genetic resources and TK is considered to be limited simply to that of a raw material.[8]

The increasing commercial interest in TKGR and the belief that it is possible to protect it (or its derivatives) by means of the IPR system

---

[6] See for instance Marden, E., 'The Neem Tree Patent: International Conflict over the Commodification of Life', BC Int L & Comp L Rev, Vol 22 (1999), pp. 279–95.

[7] On the challenges faced by the modern IPRs, see Levin, M., 'Intellectual Property Rights in Transition: Legal Structures and Concepts in Adaptation to Technological Challenges. Towards an Intellectual Property System for the 21st Century. A Nordic-European Research Programme' in Wahlgren, P. (ed), *Intellectual Property*, Scandinavian Studies in Law Vol 42, Stockholm: Stockholm Institute for Scandinavian Law (2002), p. 83 ff.

[8] On the importance of TKGR for pharmaceutical research see Schmitt, E.K., Moore, C.M., Krastel, P., Petersen, F., 'Natural Products as Catalysts for Innovation: A Pharmaceutical Industry Perspective', Current Opinion in Chemical Biology, Vol 15 (2011), pp. 1–8. See also Patwarhan B., Annant Mashelkar, R., 'Traditional Medicine-Inspired Approaches to Drug Discovery: Can Ayurveda Show the Way Forward?' Drug Discovery Today, Vol 14 (August 2009), pp. 804–9, referring to the Tanga project in Tanzania under which 4000 AIDS patients were treated with herbs prescribed by traditional healers. Very interesting results were reported with regard to the reduction of opportunistic diseases accompanying HIV infection.

raises the question of whether it is possible for traditional knowledge to be commodified, and thus become valuable to a broader public, without posing a threat to the social structures that sustain it and the livelihoods of indigenous peoples that depend on it. One of the fundamental assumptions behind the strategies to protect TKGR is that indigenous peoples represent a coherent and authentic voice, while the protection of their traditional knowledge is projected as their sole and maybe final chance to fight Westernisation. Little attention is paid to the changing conditions of the everyday lives of indigenous communities or to their respective diverging approaches with regard to bioprospecting and TKGR protection.

The protection of TKGR has gradually become one of the major challenges of twenty-first-century international law,[9] as well as of the international IPRs system. TKGR is one of those few subject matters whose protection lies at the crossroads of a broad spectrum of diverging rights and institutional frameworks, raising a wide range of issues, from land rights to human rights, plant genetic resources regulation, environmental regulations and IP protection.[10]

The complexity of the subject matter and the multiple interconnecting actors do not facilitate clear-cut solutions to the TKGR market failures. At the same time, several international organisations have included TKGR protection in their respective negotiations and agreements. TKGR is thus subject to a complex regime that is of importance to multiple individual legal institutions, with overlapping rules. As a result, the international legal framework regulating the legal status of TKGR provides for a number of potential layers of protection, consisting mainly of:[11]

- The 1961 International Union for the Protection of New Varieties of Plants (UPOV), concerning breeders' rights over new plant varieties that they breed intentionally. Plant breeders' rights are a new form of IP protection for plant varieties.[12]

---

[9] Dutfield, G., *Intellectual Property Rights, Trade and Biodiversity*, London: Earthscan (2000), p. 62 ff.

[10] For an elaboration of the process of bioprospecting and where it leads to, see Posey, D., Dutfield, G., *Beyond Intellectual Property: Toward Traditional Resource Rights and Indigenous Peoples and Local Communities*, Ottawa: IDRC (1996), pp. 5–64.

[11] Listed in chronological order.

[12] International Convention for the Protection of New Varieties of Plants, Paris, 2 December 1961, as Revised at Geneva on 10 November 1972, 23 October 1978 and 19 March 1991 (UPOV Doc 221(E), 1996).

- The UN Food and Agriculture Organization (FAO), which has elaborated two key international agreements: (1) the 1983 International Undertaking on Plant Genetic Resources; and (2) the 2001 International Treaty concerning the regulation of access to plant genetic resources.[13]
- The Convention on Biological Diversity (CBD), regarding the conservation of biodiversity, the sustainable use of its components and the fair and equitable sharing of the benefits arising therefrom. The CBD also makes reference to indigenous communities' rights.[14]
- The World Trade Organization (WTO) Agreement on Trade-Related Aspects of Intellectual Property Rights (TRIPS), setting minimum international standards for the protection of IPR.[15]

The background, and in some cases a side effect, of the complex TKGR regime is the internationalisation of TKGR access and the legal status of TKGR.[16] Despite the plethora of potentially relevant legal institutions in the field, to this day the legal regime related to the protection of TKGR remains unclear and difficult to apply.[17] The international instruments

---

[13] FAO (1987), Extract of the twenty-second session of the FAO Conference, Rome, 5–23 November 1983. Resolution 8/83 – International Undertaking on Plant Genetic Resources and Annex. CPGR/87/ Inf 3 FAO, Rome. International Treaty on Plant Genetic Resources for Food and Agriculture through FAO Resolution 3/2001.

[14] The CBD was signed at the Earth Summit in Rio de Janeiro, Brazil, in 1992 and entered into force on 29 December 1993. It is the first global agreement to cover all aspects of biological diversity: the conservation of biological diversity, the sustainable use of its components and the fair and equitable sharing of benefits arising from the use of genetic resources. For the text of the Convention see http://www.cbd.int.

[15] Agreement on Trade-Related Aspects of IPR Art 1(1), 15 April 1994, Marrakesh Agreement Establishing the World Trade Organization, Annex 1C, 33, ILM 1197, 1198 (1994) – Results of the Uruguay Round, Vol 21 33 LLM 1197, 1201 (hereinafter the TRIPS Agreement).

[16] See Rosendal, K., 'Impacts of Overlapping International Regimes: The Case of Biodiversity', Global Governance, Vol 7 (2001), pp. 95–117, discussing the phenomenon of overlapping rules and institutional regimes in this particular case.

[17] The limitations of the current IPR system with regard to the protection of traditional knowledge, as well as the side effects of the lack of a clear-cut legal entitlement and potential remedies for this, have been debated and negotiated in various forums, such as UNESCO, WHO, WIPO, UNEP, UNCTAD, FAO, CGIAR, World Bank, and COP, but also in a number of NGOs. The decentralised

mentioned above create the preconditions and lay the ground for the introduction of a new legal entitlement, but do not go as far as to actually establish one.[18]

Currently there is no specific legal entitlement protecting TKGR on the international level. National legislative and regulatory initiatives of relevance have attempted to embody the general principles provided for under the international regime and address their interaction with the current IP system, but have not demonstrated satisfactory results.

Post-CBD reports and negotiations in the field have focused either on the practical aspects of a *sui generis* right for the protection of TKGR or on the specific adjustments necessary in order to accommodate this 'new' subject matter under the realm of traditional IPR. Such approaches are certainly fully legitimate if the focus is the drafting of a ready to use legal tool to accommodate TKGR trade in the short run. Whether this is the natural, correct or most efficient approach may be disputed, however.

The lack of a concrete entitlement is an undeniable complication in a world where the exploitation of TKGR – bioprospecting – is an established practice. However, the lack of conceptual clarity complicates both the application of the vague legal system and the development of a viable long-term solution for the protection of TKGR. In fact, the lack of conceptual clarity concerns not only terminology related to TKGR, such as 'traditional knowledge' and 'genetic resources', but also terminology of central importance to the general legal system, such as that of property, common resources and open access.

This book investigates the need of a legal entitlement covering TKGR *ab initio*. While the dominant part of the relevant literature considers the natural place of TKGR protection to *ipso facto* lie under the realm of private property rights,[19] this book tests a number of variations of possible protection frameworks.

One of the starting points of the approach chosen relates to the fact that this is not the first time we have searched for an appropriate legal entitlement for natural resources and associated know-how. In fact, some

---

approach to the negotiations concerning the protection of TKGR presents obvious weaknesses in terms of coordination and coherence.

[18] Both the CBD and the ITPGRFA refer to the principle of protection of traditional knowledge and to fair and equitable sharing of the benefits arising from the use of genetic resources, but neither introduce a legal entitlement covering traditional knowledge.

[19] See also Reichman, J., 'Of Green Tulips and Legal Kudzu: Repackaging Right in Subpatentable Innovation', Vanderbilt L Rev, Vol 53 (2000), pp. 1743–98.

of the particularities of TKGR were also present in the evolution of land rights,[20] as well as in the case of deep-sea resources.[21] It is thus possible to draw parallels from past experiences of resource allocation when considering the protection of TKGR.

Despite the fact that the elaboration of an appropriate form of entitlement for TKGR might give us the impression of deja vu regarding the old traditional concerns of resource allocation, it presents certain particularities that may not be overlooked. The management of TKGR via the grant of a legal entitlement suggests two objectives: access and conservation. The TKGR regulation should thus 'reward' the holders of TKGR and promote further conservation, while on the other hand facilitating access to TKGR of interest and allowing its inclusion in sequential innovations.[22]

Both the CBD and the FAO instruments have put in place a general legal framework that aims to regulate the transfer and trade of TKGR. The FAO framework proposes a communitarian regime covering a predetermined range of plant genetic resources, while the CBD opts for an expressive commodification based on a clear statecentric approach. By means of its Access and Benefit Sharing (ABS) provisions, the CBD creates a set of economic incentives for the conservation of biological diversity.[23]

Regional and national implementation initiatives have attempted to interpret and elaborate on the provisions of the CBD, introducing layers of new potential legal entitlements and a list of different groups of rightholders, ranging from ministries to governmental authorities and indigenous peoples' representatives. National legislation provides for detailed schemes of contractual structures (bioprospecting agreements), designed to regulate access to TKGR. These agreements are very often developed under licensing agreement models that would normally presuppose the existence of some form of legal entitlement on the traded

---

20 Regulated by human rights norms. See for instance UN Human Rights Committee, *Ominayak and the Lubicon Lake Band v. Canada* (1990), Annual Report of the Human Rights Committee, UN Doc A 45/40, Bd. II AP A (1990).

21 See for instance the 'common heritage of mankind' principle, to be discussed later in this book.

22 In the case of TKGR, the protection framework seems to be burdened with another task: environmental protection in the form of conservation and sustainable use of biodiversity.

23 Siebenhuner, B., Dedeurwaerdere, T., Brousseau, E., 'Introduction and Overview to the Special Issue on Biodiversity Conservation, Access and Benefit Sharing and Traditional Knowledge', Ecological Economics, Vol 53 (2005), pp. 439–44.

subject matter. What is, however, miraculously lacking both in the text of the CBD and in the subsequent implementation initiatives is a specification of the nature and structure of the traded entitlements. The only right expressly provided for on the international level is that of state sovereignty over national genetic resources. Although the recognition of national sovereignty is a notable development and bears an impact on the status and thus the trade of TKGR, it certainly cannot offer a satisfactory legal framework.

IPRs have become the natural resort for such an analysis, not just because the forthcoming entitlement has been placed under their scope, but also because they have a major impact on TKGR trade since they grant exclusive rights on end products and processes encompassing such subject matter. Moreover, major actors in the TKGR market, on the users' side, are dependent upon IPRs for their continued activities.[24] This twofold IP approach – on the one hand, the possibility to patent end products and the impact of this on the realisation of 'fair and equitable sharing of the benefits' arising out of the TKGR trade; on the other, the possibility to protect the starting material (TKGR) with *sui generis* IPRs – actually creates new pressures for the current IP system and poses fundamental challenges to its further development and future role.[25]

The overarching goal of this book is to present and evaluate alternative forms of entitlements for the protection of TKGR by testing the following:

- The scope and content of the constraints and requirements placed on the elaboration of a TKGR entitlement on the basis of the binding international agreements.
- The national and regional initiatives in the elaboration of such an entitlement, the choices made, the outcome and the extent to which available flexibilities were taken into account.
- The possibility to proceed to a systematisation of the principles and objectives important in the process of elaboration of a new entitlement, in this case on TKGR.

---

[24] Well-known examples are obviously the pharmaceutical industry and the biotech industry. See also Maskus, K.E. 'Intellectual Property and the Transfer of Green Technologies: An Essay on Economic Perspectives', WIPO Journal, Vol 1 (2009), pp. 133–7.

[25] See in this respect Oguamanam, C., 'Localizing Intellectual Property in the Globalization Epoch: The Integration of Indigenous Knowledge', paper presented at the fourth Annual Doctoral Students Conference of the Association of Pacific Rim Universities, Mexico City, Mexico (24–29 August 2003).

To what extent would the present objectives and principles assist in the process, and what outcome would they have for TKGR protection?

1.2 THE EVALUATION FRAMEWORK

Evaluation of the already tested alternative forms of protection for TKGR, as well as the proposal of an 'ideal' legal entitlement for the specific subject matter, should be based on certain prespecified objectives. Efficiency seems like a natural starting point, since one of the main purposes of this entitlement is the frictionless operation of the TKGR market.

On the other hand, taking into consideration the objectives that should be attained by means of the upcoming entitlement, the special characteristics of TKGR as a subject matter and the interests of its potential rightholders, a pure efficiency-based analysis would provide a restricted perspective. As a result, this book chooses to proceed to a discussion and evaluation of alternative forms of protection on the basis of a combination of the Coasean model on economic efficiency and a theory of equity and justice. Efficiency and equity are terms that have been employed in a number of different theories and models. For the purposes of this book, the use of 'equity and justice' is based on Rawls' theory of fairness as justice.[26]

In his article 'The Problem of Social Cost',[27] Ronald Coase made a groundbreaking contribution to the law and economics literature. According to the Coase Theorem, where market transactions are costless, rearrangements of rights will always take place if these lead to an increase in the value of production. In Coase's world of zero transaction costs, parties negotiate and reach agreements that maximise the total output of the transaction, being both efficient and wealth maximising.

[26] Rawls, J., *The Law of the Peoples*, Cambridge, MA: Harvard University Press (2001); Swygert, M., Yanes, K.E., 'A Unified Theory of Justice: The Integration of Fairness into Efficiency', Wash L Rev, Vol 73 (1998), pp. 249–324. In their article, Swygert and Yanes propose a combination of the Coase Theorem and of the Rawlsian model on fairness. Although this model has been criticised in literature, and while the methodological framework of this study is not solely restricted to the said model, Swygert and Yanes' contribution will serve as a starting point upon which to build a combination model of efficiency and equity: see in particular pp. 304–24 of their article.

[27] Coase, R.H., 'The Problem of Social Cost', J Law Econ, Vol 3 (1960), pp. 1–44.

Thus governmental intervention should in fact 'copy' the outcome of the negotiation in a marketplace with no transaction costs.

Rawls, on the other hand, conceptualised the principle of social justice and the effects this should have on the evolution of the legal system. In his book *A Theory of Justice*,[28] Rawls envisages a situation where participants in a would-be society are gathered under a 'veil of ignorance'.[29] While they know everything about human history, conditions and nature, they know nothing about their own situation. These members of the society are called to develop the principles of governance on the basis of their mutual interest. The fact that they are bargaining while unaware of whom/what they represent makes them intuitively empathetic towards the needs and interests of others, because those 'others' could easily be themselves.

With regard to international justice, Rawls provides for a somewhat nuanced methodological approach in the introduction of a fairness perspective in the Law of Peoples.[30] The Law of Peoples is a political perception of right and justice applied in international relations. To arrive at his elaboration of the Law of Peoples, Rawls once again employs the principles of the 'original position' and the veil of ignorance, this time applicable to peoples and not individuals.

Both the Coase Theorem and Rawls' theory build upon a hypothetical model of consensus resulting from bargaining. Coase bases his theoretical model on a costless bargaining scheme. Rawls' consensus model, meanwhile, relates to society's constitutional framework and the recognition of human or fundamental rights, as well as principles of encouraging liberty and at the same time addressing inequalities. In order to ensure that personal interest does not prevail, individuals participating in the Rawlsian bargaining model are covered by a veil of ignorance with regard to their economic and social situations.

A major difference between the two models is the importance of rational empathy in the Rawlsian model, and its total absence in the Coase Theorem.[31] Rawls' veil of ignorance presupposes that individuals will take into consideration the importance and need of a 'security net for

---

[28] Rawls, J., *A Theory of Justice*, Oxford: Clarendon Press (1972).

[29] Rawls (1972).

[30] Rawls, J., 'The Law of Peoples', Critical Inquiry, Vol 20 (1993), pp. 36–68.

[31] Adelstein, R., 'Equity and Efficiency in Markets for Ideas', Conn J Int L, Vol 17 (2001–2), pp. 1–14.

all'.[32] The rational individuals in Rawls' original position would opt for the most efficient use of available resources in order to create the highest expected outcome. Risk aversion will thus have a balancing effect. Individuals would be willing to accept a lower expected possible outcome in order to ensure any positive outcome.[33] Rawls' concept of 'constructive empathy' is more than an emotion – rather, it is a rational choice.[34] Thus, constructive empathy is not a result of pity and compassion but rather a strategic choice, and in this regard the two models are in fact complementary to each other.[35]

1.2.1 Efficiency: The Coasean Approach

1.2.1.1 The Coase Theorem

The appropriate institutional framework for the allocation of entitlements has been one of the most debated subjects in the field of law and economics. The path-breaking contribution of Ronald Coase, in 'The Problem of Social Cost',[36] and the subsequent massive literature stemming from both proponents and opponents to his Theorem, has been and still is one of the major intellectual platforms in the field. The Coase Theorem provides that in a world of zero transaction costs, rights will be rearranged in view of increasing production value. Originally, the Coase Theorem was formulated to address the issue of negative externalities, but during the past five decades it has been applied to a number of distinct areas of law, from the market for hepatitis-free blood to declarations of war to IPRs.[37]

---

[32] Dworkin, R., 'Rawls and the Law', Fordham L Rev, Vol 72 (2003–4), pp. 1387–92.

[33] For an analysis risk of aversion see Bosch-Domenech, A., Silvestre, J., 'Does Risk Aversion or Attraction Depend on Income?', Economics Letters, Vol 65 (1999), pp. 265–73.

[34] Merritt, G., 'Justice as Fairness: A Commentary on Rawls' New Theory of Justice', Vand L Rev, Vol 26 (1973), pp. 665–86.

[35] Individuals are thus willing to give up part of the wealth surplus in order to guarantee that their actual welfare will not fall under a specific level.

[36] Coase (1960), pp. 1–44.

[37] For a 'critique' of the application of law and economics to IPRs see Rahmatian, A., 'A Fundamental Critique of the Law-and-Economics Analysis of Intellectual Property Rights' in Dinwoodie, G. (ed), *Methods and Perspectives in Intellectual Property*, Cheltenham: Edward Elgar (2013), pp. 71–114. For clear support, see Lands, W.M., Posner, R.A., 'An Economic Analysis of Copyright Law', in Posner, E.A. (ed), *Law and Economics*, Aldershot: Ashgate (2000), pp. 325–63, where law and economics is applied to copyright law.

Coase's contribution was initially expressed as an opposition to the classic (and, at the time, well established) Pigouvian approach to the necessity of governmental intervention.[38] Coase claimed that an initial assignment of entitlements is irrelevant to overall welfare. According to Coase, all involved agents will seek to conclude mutually advantageous bargains. In other words, Coase assumes that the parties are rational – an assumption that also constitutes one of the Theorem's weaknesses, since rationality is a subjective concept.[39]

The vagueness in the Theorem's formulation has allowed for a number of interpretations and reformulations. According to Stigler, the Theorem established that under perfect competition, private and social costs will be equal;[40] Cooter, meanwhile, considered that resource allocation is efficient regardless of the structure of liability law, provided that bargaining is frictionless.[41] Farell reformulated Coase's hypothesis, saying that since nothing obstructs efficient bargaining, people will negotiate until they reach Pareto efficiency.[42] Notwithstanding the subsequent reformulations and interpretations of both followers and opponents, all seem to agree on a number of common fundamental assumptions. Hoffman and Spitzer summarised the major common assumptions as follows:[43] two agents in the bargaining; perfect information of the agents; competitive markets; zero transaction costs; costless litigation; profit-maximising producers; no wealth effects; pursuit of mutually advantageous bargaining.

A fundamental assumption of the Theorem – and the major source of its flexibilities and, at the same time, its alleged weaknesses – is zero transaction costs. Coase did not provide for any further definition or

---

[38] The 'conflict' between the Coase Theorem and the Pigouvian approach has been challenged. See Simpson, B., 'Coase v. Pigou Reexamined', J Legal Stud, Vol 25 (1996), pp. 53–97. Coase presented a view that was in direct conflict with Pigouvian legal tradition. He claimed that in the absence of transaction costs, those who are responsible and those who suffer from negative externalities will negotiate an efficient allocation of resources, independent of the initial assignment of rights among them.

[39] Elsten, J., 'More than Enough', Univ Chicago Law Rev, Vol 64 (1997), pp. 749–61.

[40] Stigler, J., *The Theory of Price*, New York: The Maximilian Co. (1966), p. 113.

[41] Cooter, R., 'The Cost of Coase', J Legal Stud, Vol 11 (1982), pp. 1–33.

[42] Farrell, J., 'Information and the Coase Theorem', J Econ Persp, Vol 1 (1987), pp. 113–29.

[43] Hoffman, E., Spitzer, M., 'The Coase Theorem: Some Experimental Tests', J Law Econ, Vol 21 (1982), pp. 73–98.

clarification of this term; this has been a strong focus of both followers and opponents.

Transaction costs have been defined as the costs of bringing bargainers together, of maintaining and revising the agreement and of the capital required to affect the agreement.[44] They include costs spent on getting a large number of people together to bargain and costs of excluding freeloaders.[45] They are also identified as the costs that occur when trading partners attempt to identify and contact one another (identification costs), when contracts are negotiated (negotiation costs) and when the terms of the contracts are verified and enforced (enforcement costs).[46] Dahlman reiterates that there are three classes of transaction costs: those of search and information; those of bargaining and deciding; and finally those of policing and enforcement. These are in fact all due to the parties' lack of information.[47] According to Demsetz, the level of transaction costs varies from one case to another. Product standardisation is a transaction cost-reducing factor since buyers need not examine the goods in person, and feel comfortable with allowing others to buy and sell for them.[48] Naturally, a high level of uncertainty and infrequent transactions are both factors that could lead to increased transaction costs.[49] The level of transaction costs can also vary depending on the nature of the transaction in question, uncertainty, rare exchanges and the level to which investments are transaction-specific.[50]

In some cases, transaction costs are so low that it is more desirable to allow the market to solve the deficiencies. According to Daly,[51] this happens in cases where a limited number of parties are bargaining and

---

[44] Toumanoff, P., 'A Positive Analysis of Market Failure', Kyklos, Vol 37 (1984), pp. 529–38.

[45] Toumanoff (1984), pp. 529–38.

[46] Mishan, E.J., 'The Postwar Literature on Externalities: An Interpretative Essay', J Econ Lit, Vol 9 (1971), pp. 1–16.

[47] Dahlman, C.J., 'The Problem of Externality', J Law Econ, Vol 22 (1979), pp. 141–8.

[48] Demsetz looked into the transaction costs in the New York Stock Exchange and concluded that the securities that were most traded entailed fewer transaction costs: Demsetz, H., 'The Cost of Transacting', Quarterly J Econ, Vol 82 (1968), pp. 33–50.

[49] Williamson, O., 'Transaction-Cost Economics: The Governance of Contractual Relations', J Law Econ, Vol 22 (1979), pp. 233–61.

[50] Williamson (1979), pp. 233–61.

[51] Daly, G., 'The Coase Theorem, Assumption, Application', Economic Inquiry, Vol 12 (1974), pp. 203–13.

where competition prevails in the market. Farell adds that market-originated solutions are preferable where there is private information, the government would be unable to make use of the information in question, there is a lack of artificial barriers that could block voluntary private contracts and the negotiating parties are limited in number and easily identified.[52]

1.2.1.2 Implications of the Theorem

Coase claimed that in a market of zero transaction costs, the initial allocation of entitlements would not be important with regard to economic efficiency since the entitlement would in any case end up with the party valuing it the most. Rational parties will always bargain in order to achieve Pareto-optimal allocation of resources.[53] Obviously, Coase did not consider his world of zero transaction costs and perfect competition to be a reflection of the real world and real markets. He was rather making an *e contrario* statement: in the real world, the initial allocation of entitlements is important and has an effect on the allocation of resources, since transaction costs are not negligible.

The Theorem sheds new light on the role of private negotiations in the rule-making process. When comparing different policy solutions, one should take into account deficiencies in the system that can be resolved by means of private bargaining. According to Farell, when evaluating an institution, one needs to examine the outcomes of the institution per se before investigating which defects can be remedied by negotiation.[54]

Consequently, when introducing a new legal entitlement it is of importance to work with the certainty and predictability of the legal rule as well as with its substance. Transaction costs might obviously concern one party more than the other, since the party suffering less is the one that can more easily trade around an inefficient rule. In the well-known and often employed example of pollution, the polluter is to be held liable since he or she is the one who holds the private information on the level of pollution.[55] Another policy alternative might be to assign the entitlement to the party that values the right most. Obviously, this is the

---

[52] Farell (1987), pp. 113–29.

[53] Pareto optimality is named after the Italian sociologist and economist Vilfredo Pareto (1848–1923) and is a situation in which economic resources and output are allocated in such a way that any change to make an individual better off would entail that someone else would be worse off.

[54] Farell (1987), pp. 113–29.

[55] Randall, A., 'Market Solutions to Externality Problems, Theory and Practice', Am J Agric Econ, Vol 54 (1972), pp. 175–8.

solution that would be reached by the parties should transaction costs be zero. When the entitlement is assigned to the party most desiring the right, then there is no bargaining incentive in the market.

The Coase Theorem has been subject to harsh critique and a series of attempts to illustrate its shortcomings and weaknesses over the years. It has, however, managed to prevail. Calabresi, one of the scholars who initially criticised it, reconsidered his views and stated that the conclusions Coase reaches remain the same in the short as well as the long term.[56] Demsetz became a proponent of the Theorem in 1972,[57] presenting his application of the Coasean model according to which the long-term effects of a change in the assignment of property rights do not nullify the conclusions reached by Coase.

The Coase Theorem had a significant impact on the seminal dichotomy between liability rules and property rules. Calabresi and Melamed,[58] as well as Kaplow and Shavell,[59] seem to draw the same conclusion regarding the doubtful equivalence of these two alternative forms of entitlement. Kaplow and Shavell conclude that possessory interests are best protected by property rights, while liability rules prevail in cases of harmful externalities.[60] Demsetz provided that in markets with positive transaction costs, the initial allocation of the liability rule would in fact have an impact on resource allocation.[61] Consequently, allocation of the rule of liability should take into account which party can avoid the costly interaction at the lowest cost. A normative interpretation of the Theorem indicates that legal rules minimising transaction costs are to be preferred as more effective.[62]

---

[56] Calabresi, G., 'Transaction Costs, Resource Allocation and Liability Rules: A Comment', J Law Econ, Vol 54 (1968), pp. 13, pp. 49–70.

[57] Demsetz, H., 'When Does the Rule of Liability Matter?' J Legal Studies, Vol 1 (1972), pp. 13–28.

[58] Calabresi, G., and Melamed, A. Douglas, 'Property Rules, Liability Rules, and Inalienability: One View of the Cathedral', Harv L Rev, Vol 85 (April 1972), pp. 1089–128.

[59] Kaplow, L., Shavell, S.M., 'Property Rules versus Liability Rules: An Economic Analysis', Harv L Rev, Vol 106 (1996), pp. 713–90.

[60] Kaplow, Shavell (1996), pp. 723–54.

[61] Demsetz, H., 'Toward a Theory of Property Rights', Am Econ Rev, Vol 57 (May 1972), pp. 347–59.

[62] Polinsky, A.M., *An Introduction to Law and Economics*, Boston: Little Brown and Company (1989), pp. 25–45.

Ayres and Talley developed their own normative interpretation of the Theorem, focusing on private information as transaction costs.[63] Ayres and Talley consider that when two parties have private information about how much they value an entitlement, endowing each party with a partial claim to the entitlement can reduce the incentive to behave strategically during bargaining by inducing greater disclosure.[64]

1.2.2 Fairness as Justice and Rawls

1.2.2.1 The *Theory of Justice*

Equity and justice considerations have traditionally played an important role with regard to the structure and application of legal rules. Recently, justice and equity as objectives have been considered in relation to earlier stages of the law-making process, as for instance in the process of allocating scarce resources and addressing society's inequalities. Rawls' *A Theory of Justice* was a major contributor to the development of a model on equity applied in the field of institutional choices and changes.[65]

Rawls builds on the well-established theoretical framework of the social contract.[66] He considers that just, obligatory and stable principles for ordering the basic structure of society are more likely to be arrived at if the affected person views the process as an effort to reach agreement. Thus, each person is awarded an equal share in formulating principles and, by accepting the benefits of the agreements, assumes a duty to accept their obligations. According to Rawls, individuals gather under societal frameworks in order to promote their mutual advantage. Society should not limit its endeavours to advancing its members' benefits but should in general be 'regulated by a public conception of justice'. Members of a society should accept the 'fundamental principles of justice' and should also know that others accept the same principles.[67]

Rawls intended to take the Contractarian Theory a step further by considering not only forms of government, but also the basic principles

---

[63] Ayres, I., Talley, E., 'Solomonic Bargaining: Dividing a Legal Entitlement to Facilitate Coasean Trade', Yale LJ, Vol 104 (1995), pp. 1027–1117.

[64] Ayres, I., Talley, E. (1995), pp. 1027–1117.

[65] Rawls (1972).

[66] On natural law and justice see Weinreb, L., *Natural Law and Justice*, Cambridge, MA: Harvard University Press (1987), pp. 224–67.

[67] See also Christie, G.C., 'The Importance of Recognizing the Underlying Assumptions of Legal and Moral Arguments: Of Law and Rawls', Australian J Legal Philosophy, Vol 28 (2003), pp. 39–52.

that will rule on these forms. Although Rawls himself did not attempt to apply his model to private relations, the proponents of his theory did.[68] The classical social contract theory presupposes the achievement of consensus between individuals in a society.[69] Rawls contributed by developing the preconditions and negotiating the environment for such a consensus.[70] He assumes that individuals are gifted both with rationality and intuition, and are able to select the option that better furthers their objectives. Individuals' rational reflection will thus lead them to understand the desirability of ranking principles, in order to later maximise their collective preferences.

Individuals participating in this fundamental bargaining process are to be found in the 'original position'. They are to act without envy, in order to maximise social goods without being influenced by destructive motives and feelings. In order to guarantee the absence of envy, Rawls limits the individuals' knowledge of their own situation.[71] In the original position, participants have their common sense, self-interest and knowledge of each of the general facts about human nature and society.[72] Nevertheless, as no one knows if he/she is poor or rich, black or white, male or female, strong or weak, sick or healthy, or any other particular facts regarding their own circumstances, actors are bargaining 'under a veil of ignorance'. Rawls considers that inherited or acquired characteristics, such as wealth, intelligence and strength, should not be relevant in this initial bargaining position. He assumes that people are incapable of envy and that they have no mutual interest in each other.[73] Finally, Rawls

---

[68] A classic example of an attempt to broaden the Rawlsian model is that of Swygert and Yanes, who applied Rawls to private contractual relations.

[69] For the relation between Kant's contract theory and Rawls', see Ripstein, A., 'Private Order and Public Justice: Kant and Rawls', University of Toronto, Legal Studies Research Paper No. 894431 (2006).

[70] See also, Mikhail, J., 'Rawls' Linguistic Analogy: A Study of the Generative Grammar Model of Moral Theory Described by John Rawls in "A Theory of Justice"' (PhD Dissertation, Cornell University, 2000), Georgetown Public Law Research Paper No 766464 (1 May 2000), discussing the issue of moral institutions on the basis of a linguistics approach.

[71] People are usually influenced by their own situation and seek to gain as much as possible, a situation that disfavors any consensus. Rawls (1972).

[72] See also Apreda, R., 'Underlying Counterfactual Conditionals in Rawls' "Justice as Fairness" – How the Overlapping Consensus Becomes Functional to the Original Position', Universidad del CEMA Documento de Trabajo No 238 (June 2003), pp. 1–19.

[73] Rawls (1972), p. 144.

presupposes that there are some 'primary goods, including wealth, liberty and power, which rational men would certainly desire'.[74]

Obviously, the 'initial bargaining position' is a metaphorical situation aimed at reflecting principles of neutrality and impartiality. These theoretical assumptions are certainly not new phenomena and are also found in the works of Locke and Kant.[75] Rawls continues with the crystallisation of two fundamental principles ruling his model: those of equal liberty and distributive justice.[76] Equal liberty covers the freedom of conscience, liberty of the person, political rights, speech, assembly and association.

Rawls builds upon the principle of efficiency. When goods are distributed and individuals are no longer willing to trade goods they have received for goods held by others, the distribution is efficient. Rawls clarifies that the principle of efficiency cannot give any indication of whether the distribution is fair or not, but tries to explore whether the application of this second principle will lead to a distribution that is both efficient and just. Rawls is thus attempting to consider systems in which the operation of the principle of efficiency would produce a just distribution, having as a starting point the fact that 'the principle of efficiency cannot serve alone as a conception of justice'.[77]

Rawls proceeds with a direct reference to the obligations and duties of individuals in society. He makes a distinction between moral duties and moral obligations. Moral duties include the duty of mutual respect and the duty to avoid causing unnecessary suffering. In line with the Rawlsian 'principle of fairness', individual obligations originate in the basic principle that an individual should not gain from the cooperative effort of others without contributing his or her fair share.[78]

---

[74] Rawls (1972), p. 62.

[75] Locke, J., 'Second Treatise on Civil Government: Essays by Locke, Hume, and Rousseau', in Baker, E. (ed.), *Social Contract: Essays by Locke, Hume, and Rousseau*, New York: Oxford University Press (1962), pp. 3–143. With regards to the work of Kant see Murphy, G.J., 'Hume and Kant on the Social Contract', Philosophical Studies, Vol 33 (1978), pp. 65–79.

[76] Rawls (1972), pp. 11, 60. See also Locke, J., 'Of Property', in May, L., Brown, L. (eds), *Philosophy of Law*, Oxford: Wiley-Blackwell (2009), pp. 251–8. According to the priority principle, liberty in Rawls' work is the first principle to be satisfied. Thus, justice cannot be applied before liberty is.

[77] Rawls (1972), p. 71.

[78] This is the principle of reciprocity or mutual benefit.

1.2.2.2 The international dimension of fairness

Applying Rawls' Theory of Justice at the international level would have as an effect the equal distribution of primary social goods among individual members of a global society, unless unequal distribution would benefit the least favoured in this world.[79] Nevertheless, Rawls did not support the extension of the scope of his original theory to also cover the regulation of international society, and proposed instead a nuanced moral theory, presented in his contribution on the Law of Peoples.[80] Rawls rejects liberal imperialism in his consideration that such a principle imposes liberal standpoints on all peoples, treating those peoples instrumentally and without respect for their own way of honouring liberal ideals.[81]

In the theoretical framework of the Law of Peoples, the fictional forum of 'original position' exists, but the parties are no longer 'free and equal individuals'; rather, they are 'free and equal peoples'.[82] Rational representatives of liberal peoples are being 'situated symmetrically' subject to a veil of ignorance that excludes knowledge of territorial size, population, strength of people, level of economic development or natural resources.[83] Peoples in the 'Society of Peoples' would thus be able to agree upon the following principles of justice: freedom and independence of Peoples; observation of treaties and undertakings; the duty of non-intervention; the right to self-defence; the obligation to honour human rights; observation

---

[79] Rawls, J., *The Law of Peoples*, Cambridge, MA: Harvard Univerity Press (2001), pp. 1–54.

[80] With regard to a defence of Rawls' approach to international justice see Reidy, D., 'A Just Global Economy: In Defense of Rawls', J Ethics, Vol 11 (2007), pp. 193–236. For an interesting application of Rawls' theory to international environmental issues see Shelton, D., 'Describing the Elephant: International Justice and Environmental Law', in Ebbesson, J., Okowa, P. (eds), *Environmental Law and Justice in Context*, Cambridge: Cambridge University Press (2009), pp. 55–76. See also Twinning, W., 'Law, Justice and Rights: Some Implications of a Global Perspective', in Ebbesson, J., Okowa, P. (eds), *Environmental Law and Justice in Context*, Cambridge: Cambridge University Press (2009), pp. 76–115.

[81] Among the many critiques of the application of Rawls' theory, one that stands out is Elkins, D. 'Responding to Rawls: Toward a Consistent and Supportable Theory of Distributive Justice', BYU J Public Law, Vol 21 (2007), pp. 267–323.

[82] Rawls (2001), pp. 11–85.

[83] Pettit, P.N., 'Rawls' Peoples' in Martin, R., Reidy, D. (eds), *Envisioning a New International Order – Essays on Rawls' Law of Peoples*, Oxford: Blackwell (2005), pp. 38–55.

of restrictions in the conduct of war; and assistance to peoples living under unfavourable conditions.

Rawls' choice to focus on 'peoples' as major players rather than 'states' is motivated by the will to avoid being attached to the traditional idea of sovereignty. Rawls presents five different types of domestic societies:[84] 'reasonable liberal peoples', 'decent peoples', 'outlaw states', 'societies burdened by unfavourable conditions' and 'benevolent absolutism'. According to Rawls, only the first two categories qualify for respect and tolerance (and thus interaction with other peoples) in order to agree upon the creation of rules of cooperation. In his international view of fairness, the liberal and decent peoples agree on the design and functioning of a global institutional order, based on the rules of good conduct, obedience and cooperation. Rawls regards liberal democratic peoples as corporate moral agents, as persons in the moral sense of the term. The fact that representatives of equal peoples and not persons determine the content of the Law of Peoples brings Rawls' theory into contrast with the dominant cosmopolitan standard of global justice. According to cosmopolitan critique, Rawls treats individual persons unequally.[85]

Rawls claims that parties have a 'duty of assistance' in his international justice theory, but he fails to justify this claim satisfactorily because, given the size of omission and indifference of developed countries to assist developing countries, this would actually classify developed countries as 'outlaw states' under the Rawlsean theory of the peoples.[86] In fact, such outlaw states are denied equal respect and tolerance and thus are not accepted as equal partners in the elaboration of international rules.

Rawls presents two major general requirements for global or international economic relations.[87] According to the first principle, well-ordered peoples are obligated, as a matter of justice, to take affirmative steps to aid those burdened societies unable to constitute and sustain themselves as well-ordered peoples. According to the second, trade and economic relations between well-ordered peoples are to be free and fair, and therefore mutually advantageous for all well-ordered peoples over the long term. These two principles are the major objectives that the international community must meet in terms of justice. It deserves to be noted that the principle of free and fair trade entails a commitment to

---

84 Rawls (2001), pp. 113–21.

85 See Beitz, C.R., 'Rawls's Law of Peoples', Ethics, Vol 110 (2000), pp. 669–96.

86 Rawls (2001), pp. 105–13.

87 Rawls (2001), pp. 113–21.

transactional justice without, however, requiring the limitation of international economic inequalities.

According to Rawls, apart from these two fundamental obligations, peoples may take on additional obligations by means of treaty making or customary practice.

The duty of assistance is the well-ordered peoples' obligation to assist burdened societies to become well-ordered peoples. The characterisation 'well-ordered' does not, however, presuppose 'liberal and democratic people'.[88] Well-ordered people cannot be too poor; thus, material wealth is considered sufficient to sustain the rule of law and a stable government.[89] Wealthy states are under the obligation to discharge the duty of assistance prior to committing to national projects or any other obligations. Thus, well-ordered peoples that do not satisfy their duty of assistance are in violation of the first principle of international justice. However, Rawls fails to address the moral implications of this violation.

Rawls states that well-ordered peoples are to refrain from monopolising markets, forming cartels and acting as oligopolies, or in any other way bringing any frustration to free and fair international or global trade and economic relations. Furthermore, trade with or between 'burdened peoples' will likely involve unequal bargaining positions.

1.2.3 A Dualistic Approach

While Rawls' theory has attempted to explain the regulation of the relationship between individuals and the state, or among peoples and international justice, the Coase Theorem focuses on the regulation of relationships between individuals. Where regulation of individuals is needed, it should be formulated on the basis of the result that free bargaining of the parties would attain in a market with no transaction costs.[90]

---

[88] It requires, however, that peoples are decent, in that they are organised through a genuine scheme of social cooperation between members as persons or moral agents.

[89] In this respect, Rawls emphasises that wealth does not *guarantee* a well-ordered society.

[90] See Tuori, K., *Critical Legal Positivism*, Aldershot: Ashgate (2002), pp. 154–99 and Swygert, M.I., Yanes, K.E., 'A Unified Theory of Justice: The Integration of Fairness into Efficiency', Washington L Rev, Vol 73 (1998), pp. 249–327, available at SSRN: http://ssrn.com/abstract=81948. For a critique of Swygert and Yanes' approach, see Korobkin R.B., Ulen T.S., 'Efficiency and Equity: What Can Be Gained by Combining Coase and Rawls?', Washington L Rev, Vol 73 (1998), pp. 329–49.

Obviously, there are no explicit equity considerations in the Theorem. However, integration of such a perspective is not incompatible with the spirit of the Coasean model. Coase himself has underlined the importance of governmental interference in cases where the market does not fulfil the Theorem's assumptions. Though the Coasean model guarantees the efficiency output for transactions, it has in some cases been deemed inappropriate, especially where parties present a considerable disparity in bargaining power. Thus, in general, the regulation of such transactions may not be based on the agreement those parties would have reached in the absence of transaction costs.[91]

In this respect, intervention by means of governmental regulation would not aim at the restitution of the transaction's efficiency, but more at safeguarding of its equity. Legal restrictions to freedom of contract are introduced to remedy the inequity in the parties' bargaining power that would inevitably lead to inequitable assignment of the wealth output. In cases where there is a considerable disparity of bargaining power between the parties, no real negotiation can take place, let alone a Coasean negotiation.[92]

Though the Law of Peoples is interesting and the principles presented in it could partly be applied to the protection of TKGR, it is mainly Rawls' Theory of Justice and the methodological framework it introduces that will be employed in this book. The Rawlsian 'veil of ignorance',[93] under which the parties will have to negotiate, could change the conditions under which Coasean negotiations take place, integrating an equity perspective into the efficiency analysis. One of the problematic issues arising when discussing TKGR protection is the fact that TKGR rightholders award TKGR a greater value than appropriate, expecting to remedy North/South inequality by means of TKGR protection, proceeding to an evaluation of the fairness aspect of an otherwise efficient entitlement. Such an attempt to employ the 'veil of ignorance' changes the prerequisites under which the Theorem will apply, since the parties are fully informed about the costs and benefits of the transaction but are

---

[91] For an interesting combination of the objectives of efficiency and equity, see Mattei, U., *Comparative Law and Economics*, Ann Arbor: University of Michigan Press (1997), pp. 13–25.

[92] See in this respect Kessler, F., 'Contracts of Adhesion: Some Thoughts about Freedom of Contract', Columbia L Rev, Vol 43 (1943), pp. 629–42, stating that where there is a disparity of bargaining power there is no real negotiation. It is the stronger party that is dictating the terms and conditions of the agreement; the weaker party has a 'take it or leave it' choice.

[93] Rawls (1972), pp. 102–5.

unaware of which party to the agreement they will represent. In this model, providing for the hidden identities of the parties, the veil of ignorance will guarantee a level of equity and fairness at the core of the system.[94] On the whole, this dualistic approach is in line with the two fundamental objectives of the CBD: the importance of 'sustainable use' of TKGR while guaranteeing 'fair and equitable sharing' of the benefits arising thereof. This combined model may thus be applied to evaluate the alternative forms of protection and regulation of TKGR exploitation.

---

[94] Distributive arrangements.

2. Towards a horizontal and vertical institutionalisation of TKGR trade

2.1 BETWEEN BIOPROSPECTING AND BIOPIRACY: MARKING THE FINE LINE

Bioprospecting as a concept, but also as a promoted policy scheme, was officially introduced in the late 1980s under the initiative of nongovernmental organisations (NGOs) and US-based academics. One of its primal goals was to overcome problems faced in the implementation of conservation programmes. In this emerging traditional knowledge on genetic resources (TKGR) trade environment, yet another term, 'biopiracy', gradually emerged to describe the unlawful bioprospecting practices of developed countries and their industries, at the same time giving a name to the principal form of market failure in the bioprospecting market.[1] Biopiracy concerns were further strengthened by the impact of international intellectual property rights (IPRs).[2]

Bioprospecting and, thus, also biopiracy concerns are not phenomena that appeared for the first time in the past few decades. TKGR has played an important role in international diplomacy since ancient times, and has in certain cases influenced the evolution of history. Egyptian pharaohs planned and carried out military and diplomatic interventions in order to gain access to genetic resources from other parts of the world, with ships

---

1 Aoki, K., 'Neocolonialism, Anticommons Property, and Biopiracy in the (Not-so-Brave) New World Order of International Intellectual Property Protection', Ind J Global Legal Stud, Vol 6 (1998), pp. 11–58. Another valuable approach is that presented in Coombe, R., 'Protecting Cultural Industries to Promote Cultural Diversity: Dilemmas for International Policy-Making Posed by the Recognition of Traditional Knowledge', in Maskus, K.E., Reichman, J. (eds), *International Public Goods and Transfer of Technology under a Globalised Intellectual Property Regime*, Cambridge: Cambridge University Press (2005), pp. 559–614. Coombe discusses the anthropological perspective and how that can influence the protection of TKGR and the fair and equitable sharing of benefits.

2 See also Cameron, X., Makuch, Z., *The UN Biodiversity Convention and the WTO TRIPS Agreement*, Gland: World Wide Fund for Nature (1995).

sent to the Gulf of Aden searching for cinnamon;[3] Sumerians were reported to have conducted expeditions which had as a major goal the collection of new crop seeds.[4]

Predecessors of the Columbian Seed Exchange and the transfer of seeds that occurred during colonial times involved informal patterns of transcontinental crop diffusion.[5] According to Brush,[6] it was in the prehistoric New World that maize, beans, avocados and chilli pepper migrated from Mesoamerica in the Northern Hemisphere to South America, while tomatoes and tobacco were transferred in the opposite direction. In the prehistoric Old World, on the other hand, wheat and cabbage crops moved to Asia from the Mediterranean, while rice and stone fruits (e.g. peaches and apricots) transferred to the Atlantic region.[7]

Towards the end of the fifteenth century, crop and seed exchange became more systematic and more intense.[8] Regular communications between Europe, Africa and the New World were established, and crop exploration was given official status. Plant explorers accompanied expeditions to foreign countries even in times of war, allowing for the collection and exchange of medicinal, industrial and food crops. Crop exchange thus played an important role in international relations and the evolution of international trade relations of the time.[9] However, the systematic collection and documentation of TKGR's potential usages and value only began during the late seventeenth and the eighteenth centuries.

Botany gradually became an important part of colonial history. The aim of European scientists – and even of priests with botanical interests – travelling in Central and South America, Asia and Africa was to procure

---

[3] Mooney, P.R., *Seeds of the Earth: A Private or Public Resource*, London: International Coalition for Development Action (1979).

[4] Mooney (1979), p. 167.

[5] Crosby, A.W., *The Columbian Exchange: Biological and Cultural Consequences of 1492*, Westport: Greenwood Publishing Co (1972), pp. 208–22.

[6] Brush, S., 'The Demise of Common Heritage and the Protection of Traditional Agricultural Knowledge', paper prepared for the Conference on Biodiversity, Biotechnology and the Protection of Traditional Knowledge, St Louis, MO (4–5 April 2003).

[7] Zohary, D., Hopf, M., *Domestication of Plants in the Old World: The Origin and Spread of Cultivated Plants in West Asia, Europe, and the Nile Valley*, 3rd edition, New York: Oxford University Press (2000), pp. 241–53.

[8] See also Kloppenburg, J., *First the Seed – The Political Economy of Plant Biotechnology 1492–2000*, Cambridge: Cambridge University Press (1988), p. 155.

[9] Brockway, L.H., *Science and Colonial Expansion: The Role of the British Royal Botanic Gardens*, New York: Academic Press (1979), pp. 215–19.

valuable plants, as well as associated local knowledge, for cultivation, processing and use in further research. According to some theories, crop domestication was in fact possible because crops' wild ancestors were removed from their original habitats to grow in other environments.[10]

While colonisers initially had gold and silver in mind in their quest to find the 'riches' of the new colonies, they learned to appreciate the new 'green gold'. Sugar, tobacco, indigo, ginger, gums, aloes, brazil wood and guaiacum were soon valuable assets. During the eighteenth century, sugar was the largest cash crop imported into Europe from the Americas, while quinine (Peruvian bark) was the most valuable commodity shipped from America to Europe. Gradually, drug prospecting became one of the major motives of Europeans travelling to newly acquired colonies,[11] with the goal of acquiring what would be not only a valuable asset upon their return home, but also a necessary tool for their survival while in the tropics.

Thorough study of data available in Europe regarding the fauna and flora in the part of the world they were about to visit was essential preparation for the bioprospectors of the eighteenth century. On accepting the post of physician to the governor of Jamaica, Hans Sloane[12] – later the president of the Royal Society of London – collected all available information concerning plants in tropical areas, in order to ensure that he would recognise valuable plant genetic resources when he encountered them. Upon arrival, and like other bioprospectors of his time, he turned to local populations in order to gather information and traditional knowledge concerning the 'products of nature'.[13] Another documented example is that of the Dutch physician Philippe Fermin (1729–1813), who reported with regard to indigenous communities in Suriname, 'they know the virtues of

---

[10] Hawkes, J.G., *The Diversity of Crop Plants*, Cambridge, MA: Harvard University Press (1983), p. 109.

[11] Europeans with major interests in TKGR were generally physicians. At the time botany was quite closely connected to medicine and an important part of medical education.

[12] Sloane, H., 'A Voyage to the Islands [of] Madera, Barbados, Nieves, S. Christophers and Jamaica (1707)', in Schiebing, L., Swan, C. (eds), *Colonial Botany, Science, Commerce and Politics in the Early Modern World*, Pennsylvania: University of Pennsylvania Press (2005), pp. 100–19.

[13] For instance, in the West Indies, Nicolas Louis Bourgeois (1710–76) served as a secretary of the Chamber of Agriculture and tried to win indigenous peoples' friendship, then offered money and finally used coercion. Another interesting example is that of Europeans who, trying to learn of an antidote for poisoned arrows, threatened to wound indigenous people with the same arrows.

plants and offer cures that put to shame physicians coming from Europe ... but, I could never persuade them to instruct me'.[14]

'Bioprospectors' of the eighteenth century employed threats and coercion when indigenous peoples were reluctant to share TKGR.[15] In some cases, TKGR was protected by means of secrecy regarding sacred indigenous and local population practices. European trading companies of the time, on the other hand, guarded their investments in plant genetic resources through strictly guarded monopolies.[16]

This era of 'colonial bioprospecting' is often described as a period of time characterised by an endless quest for knowledge and truth, facilitated by open communication and sharing of the major advances of science. Obviously, such a description leaves an important part of the story untold. 'Colonial bioprospecting' was not subject to access regulations, property regimes, IPRs or other forms of entitlements on TKGR. It was, however, dominated by relations of conquest, coercion, commerce, slavery and privately imposed and enforced monopolies.

In modern times, TKGR continues to be important with regard to both farming practices and traditional medicine. Plant genetic resources are the major source of food for a vast part of the world's population. Just 15 food crops provide 90 per cent of the world's food energy intake, while as few as three of these – rice, maize and wheat – are the staple foods of 4 billion people.[17]

It has been claimed that 80 per cent of the people in developing countries rely on traditional medicine for their primary healthcare needs, while about 85 per cent of traditional medicine involves the use of plant extracts.[18] In India, no fewer than 8000 plant species are used as traditional medicines. In that list we find pharmaceuticals against malaria,[19] and against childhood leukaemia (*Chatharantus roseus*).[20]

[14] Schebinger, L., Swan C., (eds), *Colonial Botany, Science, Commerce and Politics in the Early Modern World*, Philadelphia: University of Pennsylvania Press (2004), pp. 83–100.

[15] Sloane (2005), p. 83.

[16] The importance of holding TKGR and controlling the flow of seeds and crops is best illustrated by the history of Manaus and rubber cultivations.

[17] UNFPA (United Nations Populations Fund) Footprints and Milestones: Population and Environmental Change – The State of World Population (2001), p. 17.

[18] Farnsworth, N.R., 'Screening Plants for New Medicines', in Wilson, E.O. (ed.), *Biodiversity*, Washington, DC: National Academy Press (1988), pp. 212–16.

[19] Quinine, known for its medical properties.

[20] A plant grown in Madagascar.

During the period 1983–94, 78 per cent of new antibacterial medicines and 61 per cent of new anticancer medicines in the United States were of natural origin. Pharmaceuticals of plant origin represent a considerable share of 42 per cent of sales, amounting to US$17.5 billion.[21]

Modern international law is based on the fundamental principle of a state's sovereignty over its genetic resources. The need to formalise the principle came as a consequence of decolonisation: former colonies wanted to make sure that they had control of the resources found under their jurisdiction. The principle was officially recognised in a UN General Assembly Resolution.[22] It deserves to be noted, however, that sovereignty has been circumvented a number of times in the field of environmental law.[23]

Although the value and importance of TKGR through history has not been contested, what remains unclear to date is the legal status and thus the institutional framework of the basis on which transfers and trade of TKGR may occur. The legal status of TKGR has been closely related to land rights both because of its nature and also of the identity of the rightholders – the indigenous communities.

There have been three major eras with regard to the legal identity and status of TKGR. The first stretches from the ancient years through colonialism and ends with the FAO Global Plan for plant genetic resources in the 1980s, under which TKGR enjoyed a status comparable to that of *terra nullius*, or simply of lacking an official regulatory framework for exchange. The second is marked by the FAO International Undertaking, which gave TKGR the legal status of 'common heritage of mankind'. The third and final is that of expanding commoditisation of TKGR, promoted directly by the Convention on Biological Diversity (CBD) and indirectly by means of international intellectual property (IP) conventions.

---

[21] Laird, S., ten Kate, K., 'Biodiversity prospecting and forest conservation: has it lived up to its promise?', in Pagiola, S., Bishop, J., Landell-Mills, N. (eds), *Selling Forest Environmental Services: Market-Based Mechanisms for Conservation*, London: Earthscan (2002), pp. 241–86.

[22] UN General Assembly Resolution 1803 (XVII), 14 December 1962, Permanent Sovereignty over Natural Resources, reprinted in 2 ILM 223 (1963).

[23] See for instance, Principle 21 of the Stockholm Declaration stating that states should ensure that the activities within their jurisdiction do not cause damage to the environment or other states or areas beyond the limits of their jurisdiction. This tendency is also present in the text of the CBD, reaffirming national sovereignty while at the same time burdening states with extensive responsibilities.

The CBD and Food and Agriculture Organization (FAO) instruments provide for the horizontal institutionalisation of the TKGR trade and the Trade-Related Aspects of Intellectual Property Rights (TRIPS) and International Union for the Protection of New Varieties of Plants (UPOV) instruments for the vertical, since they perceive TKGR as part of their protected innovations and not as a subject matter to be protected per se. In practice, patentability criteria such as novelty and inventive step exclude TKGR from the scope of the patent system. On the other hand, a 'processed' version of TKGR, in which substances are purified and isolated so that the product can be distinguished in kind, is nowadays patentable. Consequently, companies that manage to isolate and purify a substance – even if this was originally a TKGR substance – can apply for a patent and enjoy exclusive rights. The imbalances in this respect that are incorporated in the IP system became even more apparent after the entry into force and national implementation of the TRIPS Agreement.

2.2 THE LEGAL STATUS OF TKGR

Transfer of TKGR from tropicals and subtropicals to Europe during colonial times was an internal affair between colonies and the 'mother country', and posed minimal legal and political challenges. However, the demise of colonialism on the one hand, and the continuing exploration of new areas' potentials on the other, have led to debate regarding the legal status of TKGR.[24] Terms such as *res nullius*, *res communis*, 'common heritage of mankind' or 'rights subject to state sovereignty' have often been employed to describe the legal status of TKGR.[25]

2.2.1 TKGR in the Sphere of *Terra Nullius*

Land has been not only the source of natural resources, but also a prerequisite for the spiritual and religious survival of indigenous communities. TKGR developed as a direct consequence of this cultural and

---

[24] See also Mgbeoji, I., 'Beyond Rhetoric: State Sovereignty, Common Concern, and the Inapplicability of the Common Heritage Concept to Plant Genetic Resources', Leiden J Int L, Vol 16 (2003), pp. 821–37.

[25] See also Gepts, P., 'Who Owns Biodiversity and How Should the Owners be Compensated?', Plant Physiology, Vol 134 (4) (2004), pp. 1295–1307.

practical interrelation between the land and its inhabitants.[26] Consequently, the history of ownership and the legal status of TKGR have been closely related to the history of land rights. European colonisation entailed extensive expropriation of indigenous lands, as well as the imposition of private rights over land, and other proprietary structures that greatly interfered with the indigenous land culture. Since indigenous communities had no control over their lands, control over access to and use of their TKGR was also impossible. Therefore, as long as indigenous lands were treated as *terra nullius*, TKGR, as a direct extension, enjoyed the same status.

During colonial times, initial landholders were deprived of their lands either by means of questionable purchases in which lands were exchanged for nominal trades or by simply invoking their *terra nullius* status. This differentiation in colonial policy was mainly dependent on the structures and particularities of the indigenous community to be expropriated. Indians of North America quickly adapted to European trade habits; entering into agreements with the chiefs of the tribe was the easiest and most direct way of acquiring lands. Aboriginals of Australia, on the other hand, did not accept any commercial arrangements with colonialists, and as a consequence the legitimacy of their lands' transfer into the hands of the colonisers had to be based on the proclamation of their *terra nullius* status. Land classified as *terra nullius* was free for anyone to put claims upon.

Lawyers in England were in fact persuaded that settlers were allowed to occupy uninhabited land.[27] For the proponents of the *terra nullius* principle, there was just one obstacle to overcome: indigenous communities' presence in the areas. According to colonisers' predominant view at the time, Aboriginals of Australia were limited in number and should not be awarded title to the vast areas they inhabited. They were considered to be 'savages', walking around naked with no shelter or developed agriculture, and thus incapable of being land proprietors.[28] The association between agriculture and land rights had a lengthy history in

---

[26] For the link between land rights and IPRs see Carbone, J., 'Back to the Future: Intellectual Property and the Rediscovery of Property Rights and Wrongs', St Louis ULJ (2002), pp. 629–54.

[27] Wood, T., *An Institute of the Laws of England*, London (1724), reprinted in 2006 by the Lawbook Exchange referenced in the High Court of Delegates, London: Cambridge University Press (1971).

[28] One of the major characteristics of Aboriginals that Captain Cook reported back to Britain was that they did not even have 'cultivation', the lack of which was a clear sign of lack of civilisation.

medieval and early modern philosophy, with major proponents including Locke, Grotius and Smith.[29] In the late eighteenth century, many believed a society without agriculture to be a society without property rights to land, and the legal fiction of *terra nullius* persisted and legitimised land acquisition.[30] The theory of *terra nullius* was put into practice over a long period of time before actually receiving official recognition. During the first years of colonisation, all disputes arising between Aboriginals and settlers were used as proof of the former's total ignorance with regard to their right to property.[31]

Terra nullius was uncontested by settlers but also by those indigenous who lacked legal standing. The discovery doctrine legitimised the expropriation of indigenous communities' lands;[32] 'settlers' had the authority to control the possession and use of indigenous lands, as well as the management and exploitation of natural resources.[33] The strengthening of the international human rights movement during the 1970s and the altered economic and social conditions of that time brought an end to land expropriation practices, and the inoperability of the discovery and

---

[29] According to Adam Smith, all civilisations go through four different stages: 'hunting, pasturage, farming and commerce'; hunters know nothing about property; and pastoralists invent property rights on their animals, while farmers need and invent property rights on their lands. See Brewer, A., 'Adam Smith's Stages of History', Discussion Paper No 08/601, Department of Economics, University of Bristol (March 2008), pp. 1–24.

[30] Naturally, the application of the 'terra nullius' doctrine led to conflicts between countries claiming rights on land. There are three well-known cases in this regard: the case of the island of Palmas of 1928, between the United States and the Netherlands; the case of Clipperton Island in 1931, between France and Mexico; and the case of Eastern Greenland in 1931, between Norway and Denmark. For the application of the 'terra nullius' doctrine to these cases see Mahmoudi, S., *The Law of the Deep Seabed Mining*, Stockholm: Almquist & Wiksell International (1987), pp. 90–3.

[31] See also Roos J., 'Aboriginal Land Rights, a Continuing Social Justice Issue', Australian eJournal of Theology, Vol 8 (October 2006), pp. 1–8.

[32] Amiott, J., 'Environment, Equality and Indigenous Peoples' Land Rights in the Inter-American Human Rights System', Envtl L (2002), pp. 873–903. See also Benedict, C., 'The Status and Rights of Indigenous Peoples in Canada' in *Rudolph Bernhardt Encyclopedia of Public International Law*, Vol II, Oxford: Oxford University Press (1995), pp. 405–42.

[33] *Johnson v. M'Intosh*, 21 US 543 (1823), where it was stated that the discovery of America gave the European nation the 'exclusive right to extinguish the Indian title either by purchase or by conquest'.

terra nullius doctrine was gradually declared.[34] The landmark case in the field is that of *Mabo v. Queensland* (1992),[35] which stated that Aboriginal title survived European colonisation and continues to exist, subject to the sovereignty of the Crown.[36]

State sovereignty over plant genetic resources and thus over TKGR has been an inherent element of statehood. A number of domestic legislative acts regulating access to forests, wildlife and parks were also introduced during colonial times.[37] Historically, states have never been under an obligation to grant free access to their genetic resources. During the colonial years, important colonisers such as France, the United Kingdom and the Netherlands adopted elaborate and stringent methods to protect their 'valuable' plants.

Well-known historical examples include the indigo dye trade monopoly enjoyed by the French. Export of indigo seeds from French Antigua constituted a capital offence.[38] The government of Ethiopia, one of the few countries to have escaped formal colonialism, embargoed the export of coffee germplasm. Black peppercorns were not to be transferred from India, while Ecuador was reluctant to supply cocoa germplasm to other cocoa-producing states. For a while, Peru and Bolivia stipulated that quinine trade was a government monopoly.[39] The Dutch, in order to maintain their monopoly in the supply of nutmeg, destroyed all nutmeg and clove trees in the Moluccas except for those on three islands where they placed their plantations.

Naturally, these stringent attempts to preserve monopolies in TKGR trade were accompanied by other states' attempts to break those 'green' monopolies. In some cases, states sponsored criminal activities such as the smuggling of plants. In order to break the Brazilian monopoly in the rubber trade, the British helped Henry Wickham smuggle 70,000 rubber

---

[34] On the national level, the Aboriginal Land Rights Act of 1976 gave Aborigines the right, for the first time, to claim land they can prove they traditionally owned. This was further liberalised by the Native Title Act (1994).

[35] *Mabo v. Queensland*, 107 ALR 1 (1992). See also Schillhorn, K., 'The Status and Rights of Indigenous Peoples in Australia', Heidelberg J Int L (1999), pp. 463–96.

[36] A subsequent interesting case in the field is *The Wik Peoples and Thayorre People v. The State of Queensland & Ors*, where it is affirmed that native title coexists with pastoral interests.

[37] Examples of such legislative acts are the Ugandan Forest Act and the Kenyan Forest Act, both of 1942.

[38] Kloppenburg (1988), p. 154.

[39] See Whitt, L., *Science, Colonialism and Indigenous Peoples*, Cambridge: Cambridge University Press (1999), pp. 1–29.

seeds in a boat that eventually reached the British colonies in Asia. This enabled the gradual collapse of the Brazilian rubber trade and, in turn, of the Brazilian economy.[40]

Regulating and benefiting from plant genetic resources and associated traditional knowledge is not a new phenomenon. However, the changes in international politics and diplomacy, the demise of colonisation and the appearance of new international structures changed the framework under which TKGR transfer and protection may be achieved. The lack of international conventions regulating such transfer in colonial times, and preceding them, cannot be considered equivalent to 'free and unregulated' exchange in practice.[41]

2.2.2 International Transfer of TKGR: A 'Common Heritage of Mankind' Practice?

The informal institutional patterns on the basis of which TKGR was transferred and traded for thousands of years declined mainly for political reasons. The need for an institutional framework regulating the access and transfer of plant genetic resources was initially motivated by concerns related to food production and security, as well as the conservation of agricultural biodiversity and genetic resources.[42] The forum for this institutional change was the FAO.

2.2.2.1 Common heritage or common concern of mankind?

One of the first times the principle of 'common heritage of mankind' appeared in international law was during the negotiations concerning the legal status of deep seabed mining resources.[43] In the late nineteenth century, scientists discovered large quantities of polymetallic nodules on

---

[40] Oldham, P., 'Biopiracy and Bioeconomy' in Glasner, P., Atkinson, P., Greenslade, H., *New Genetics, New Social Formations*, London and New York: Routledge (2007), pp. 114–37.

[41] See also Bosselman, K., 'Plants and Politics: The International Legal Regime Concerning Biotechnology and Biodiversity', Colorado Journal of International Environmental Law and Policy, Vol 18 (1995), pp. 111–48.

[42] Global Plan of Action for the Conservation and Sustainable Utilization of Plant Genetic Resources for Food and Agriculture, FAO.

[43] See Mahmoudi (1987), pp. 119–69. For an elaborate presentation of the origins and meaning of the term 'common heritage of the mankind' see Mahmoudi, S., 'Common Heritage of Mankind, Common Concern of Humanity', in Beurier, J.-P., Kiss, A., Mahmoudi, S. (eds), *New Technologies and Law of the Marine Environment*, London: Kluwer Law International London (1990), pp. 215–23.

the deep seabed. Access to these new mineral resources was finally a clear and imminent possibility, but did entail one difficulty: the deep seabed did not fall under the jurisdiction of any state. As a result, before access was attempted, a new legal regime had to be established. The regime adopted was that of the 'common heritage of mankind'.[44] The Antarctic Treaty referred to the interests of 'science and mankind',[45] while the Non-Proliferation Treaty discussed 'the devastation that would be visited upon all mankind by a nuclear war'.[46] Furthermore, the UN General Assembly provided that uses of outer space should be performed on the basis of the 'common interest of mankind as a whole'.[47]

The term 'common' stands for something that is shared by all,[48] and this obviously raises similar issues of representation to those discussed with regard to 'mankind'.[49] Finally, 'heritage' concerns property that

---

[44] Guntrip, E., 'The Common Heritage of Mankind: An Adequate Regime for Managing the Deep Seabed?', Melb J International Law (2003), pp. 376–405. UN Doc A/6695 (1967). See also White, M., 'The Common Heritage of Mankind', Case Western Reserve Journal of International Law, Vol 14 (1982), pp. 509–42; Tenenbaum, E., 'A World Park in Antarctica: The Common Heritage of Mankind', Virginia Environmental Law Journal, Vol 10 (1990), pp. 109–36; Blaser, A., 'The Common Heritage in its Infinite Variety: Space Law and the Moon in the 1990s', J Law and Technology, Vol 5 (1990), pp. 79–99. See also Wolfrun, R., 'The Principle of the Common Heritage of Mankind', Heidelberg J Int Law, Vol 43 (1983), pp. 369–82.

[45] Preamble to the Antarctic Treaty, 1 December 1959 (1961) 12 UST 794, TIAS No 4780.

[46] Preamble to the Treaty on the Non-Proliferation of Nuclear Weapons, 12 June 1968 (1970) 21 UST 483, TIAS No 6839.

[47] UN Assembly Resolution of 1959. UNCLOS, opened for signature 10 December 1982, 1836 UNTS 3 (entered into force 16 November 1994). Goldie, L., 'A General International Law Doctrine for Seabed Regimes', Intl Lawyer, Vol 7 (1973), pp. 796–819. See also Trotti, J., 'Compensation versus Colonization: A Common Heritage of Mankind Approach to the Use of Indigenous Medicine in Developing Western Pharmaceuticals', Food and Drug Law Journal, Vol 56 (2001) pp. 367–82; Cocca, A.A., 'Mankind as the New Legal Subject: A New Juridical Dimension Recognized by the United Nations', *Proceedings of the 13th Colloquium on the Law of Outer Space*, Brussels (1971), pp. 211–14. See also Gorove, S., 'The Concept of Common Heritage of Mankind: A Political, Moral or Legal Innovation', San Diego LR, Vol 9 (1972), pp. 390–402; GA Res 2749 (XXV); UN Doc A/C1/544 (1970); GA Res 2467 A (XXIII) (1968).

[48] According to *Webster's New World Dictionary of the American Language*, the word 'common' refers to something belonging to a community at large or to the public.

[49] In this regard it is important to investigate whether it is the state that would be competent to 'manage' the common resources.

belongs to a person or that is reserved for him or her by reason of birth; it is something handed down from one's ancestors or the past, as a characteristic, culture, tradition, etc.[50] In order to apply this rather traditional definition of 'common heritage', one would need to show that the ancestors of 'mankind' were vested with some property or interest rights to the resources in question.[51] This makes the concept almost inoperable.[52]

A legal regime ruled by 'common heritage of mankind' in fact entails a number of pre-determined characteristics: resources falling under 'common heritage of mankind' are such that no state can claim sovereignty upon; all states have the responsibility of managing the said territory; all states share in the benefits from the exploitation of the territory or its resources; and all countries must use the territory for exclusively peaceful purposes.[53] According to the United Nations Convention on the Law of the Sea (UNCLOS), the International Authority will be vested with the mandate to protect the rights and interests of mankind. Thus, a *sine qua non* for the application of the 'common heritage of mankind' principle is the establishment of an international management authority that will represent the rights of mankind and exploit the resources in question to its benefit, in order to distribute them later on to mankind. However, resources covered by the 'common heritage of mankind' regime are either of such a nature that no real commercial exploitation has yet occurred, or have a very limited scope and thus do not allow for sufficient collection of past experiential data.

The principle of 'common concern of humanity', on the other hand, has a clearer meaning and increased acceptability. The status of resources as 'common concern to humanity' regulates obligations relating to their preservation and protection against threats, and not so much the sharing of rights.[54] Environmental concerns affect all of humanity and threats to the environment cannot be limited by national borders. Thus, global collaboration is necessary. While the principle was initially applied to

---

50 *Webster's Dictionary*, p. 23.

51 Gorove (1972).

52 Crabb, J., 'The Environment and Values of the Legal System of Congo-Kinshasa', Wis L Rev, Vol 4 (1966), pp. 1124–34.

53 In addition, some legal bodies add the fifth characteristic that all countries have a shared responsibility for the preservation of the unique or irreplaceable resources of the territory in question for future generations. See Tenenbaum, E. (1990), p. 114.

54 Mahmoudi (1990), pp. 220–2.

natural resources such as minerals, oils and forests, its scope was soon expanded to also cover sea, air, soil, ecosystems and biodiversity.

Contrary to 'common heritage of mankind', 'common concern of humanity' does not relate to proprietary rights or rights of access to the resources. 'Common concern of humanity' inspired a number of principles included in the negotiations preceding the adoption of the CBD. In particular, in its preamble, the CBD stipulates developed countries' obligations to assist both financially and by means of technology transfer in relation to developing countries' environmental law-related obligations.

2.2.3 Transposition of 'Common Heritage of Mankind' to Genetic Resources

The Human Genome Project gave rise to an extensive discussion on the legal status of the genome. The choice between a communitary/commons or an exclusive rights regime led to vivid debate. Scientists compared the human genome to the Wild West, or the Oklahoma territory that was appropriated by private entities at a frantic pace.[55] At the same time, a considerable part of the doctrine expressed the wish to include human genetic resources under the realm of the 'common heritage of mankind' principle. The proposals were so concrete as to include a draft text of a United Nations Convention on the Application of the Common Heritage of Humankind to the Human Genome Project.[56] Though such a convention was never signed, the arguments presented provide valuable input with regard to the transposition of the 'common heritage of mankind' principle to plant genetic resources.

The legal framework of plant genetic resources access and transfer was more a result of lengthy negotiations. Developing countries' complaints regarding uncompensated access to TKGR found a response in the International Undertaking on Plant Genetic Resources, passed by the Food and Agriculture Organization in 1983, which deemed all plant germplasm the 'common heritage of mankind'.[57]

---

[55] See Sturges, M., 'Who Should Hold Property Rights on the Human Genome? An Application of the Common Heritage of Humankind', Am U Int L Review (1997–8), pp. 219–61.

[56] Sturges (1997–8), pp. 253–60.

[57] See Jurgensen, T., 'Of Plants, Patents and Breeders' Rights: Some Proposals for International Unification of Proprietary Protection of Plant Biotechnology', J Agric Taxn & L, Vol 12 (1991), pp. 291–314.

The FAO hosted three international technical conferences – in 1967, 1973 and 1981 – to discuss the technological advances in the field of plant genetic resources. Technological developments in the field were the starting point for discussion of the regime governing access to plant genetic resources, regulating use and benefit-sharing mechanisms. The blurry status of genetic resources and the application of a *res nullius*-based regime did not provide the stability and transparency desired in order to serve the fundamental FAO principles of food security and conservation. Thus a change in the applicable legal status was deemed necessary. The official institutionalisation of TKGR exchange was initiated in 1983 under the auspices of the FAO Global Plan. The objectives of the Global Plan were to ensure safe conservation of plant genetic resources and promote their availability and sustainable use, while at the same time providing a flexible framework for sharing benefits and burdens.

Thus, the legal concept of 'common heritage of mankind' was officially transposed to plant genetic resources for food and agriculture for the first time in the 1980s, during negotiations that preceded the establishment of the FAO Committee of Plant Genetic Resources (CGIAR). The principle was further confirmed in the 1983 FAO Conference establishing the CGIAR and adopting the International Undertaking of Plant Genetic Resources, where it was clearly stated that 'plant genetic resources are a heritage of mankind and consequently should be available without restriction'.[58]

2.2.3.1 The International Undertaking on Plant Genetic Resources for Food and Agriculture

The International Undertaking on Plant Genetic Resources for Food and Agriculture was the first comprehensive international agreement dealing with the question of the right to access plant genetic resources for food and agriculture (PGRFA). It was adopted by the FAO Conference in 1983,[59] its primal goal being the harmonisation of matters regarding access to PGRFA. The International Undertaking (IU) is an international agreement primarily concerned with the exploitation,[60] preservation, evaluation and documentation of plant genetic resources,[61] as well as

---

[58] FAO (1987), Extract of the Twenty-Second Session of the FAO Conference, Rome, 5–23 November 1983. Resolution 8/83 – International Undertaking on Plant Genetic Resources and Annex. CPGR/87/ Inf 3. FAO, Rome.

[59] Resolution 8/83.

[60] Article 3 of the International Undertaking.

[61] Article 4 of the International Undertaking.

with their availability for the purposes of scientific research, plant breeding or genetic resources conservation.[62] It provides for the establishment of international networks and gene banks,[63] supplied with a global information system, all coordinated by the FAO.[64]

Article 6 of the IU underlines the importance of international cooperation in order to accomplish the objectives of the Undertaking, and pinpoints the need to participate in the establishment or strengthening of developing countries' capacities in the field.[65] Resolution 4/89 provided for the first official interpretation of the Undertaking.[66] According to it, plant breeders' rights are not incompatible with the provisions of the IU.[67] Access to plant material could be restricted in compliance with the national and international obligations of the source country. The implementation of Farmers' Rights would, according to the Resolution, be best achieved by the effective conservation, management and use of plant genetic resources for the benefit of both present and future generations of farmers.[68] In addition, it was underlined that the term 'free access' is not equivalent to uncompensated access.[69]

In the Preamble of Resolution 5/89, it had already been stated that plant genetic resources are the 'common heritage of mankind', to be preserved and to be freely available for use. The Resolution continued by stressing the importance of the farmers' contribution in the conservation of genetic resources, and that they – especially farmers from developing countries – should benefit from the improved and increased use of the natural resources they have preserved. Finally, Resolution 3/91 provided for an interesting interpretation of the legal status of PGRFA, stating that although genetic resources are the 'heritage of mankind', they are always subject to respective states' sovereignty over their resources.[70] Obviously, this double-sided status of plant genetic resources leads to certain complications, since it is difficult to know who owns the resources and

62 Article 5 of the International Undertaking.
63 Article 7 of the International Undertaking.
64 Article 7(e) of the International Undertaking.
65 Article 6.1 of the International Undertaking.
66 Adopted in November 1989.
67 Plant Breeders' Rights as provided for under the UPOV Convention.
68 The Resolution referred to the establishment of an International Fund that would support the conservation and management of plant genetic resources: see Article 4.
69 Article 5(a) of the Resolution.
70 Article 3 of the Resolution.

whose interests/decisions are to prevail. As has been discussed previously, the legal principle of 'common heritage to mankind' presupposes a lack of national sovereignty.

One of the important points of Agenda 21 was the strengthening of the FAO Global System on Plant Genetic Resources. The need to harmonise it with the outcome of the CBD negotiations was also highlighted. The adoption of the CBD was followed up by Resolution 3 of the Nairobi Final Act, which requested clarification of the regime applicable for access to *ex situ* collections,[71] as well as the status and meaning of Farmers' Rights. The 1993 FAO Conference progressed further and proceeded to negotiations for the revision of the IU in view of the content of the CBD.[72]

In the revision of the IU,[73] technical,[74] economic,[75] and legal aspects of the status of plant genetic resources were discussed. The legal aspects related to the regulation of access to plant genetic resources, states' sovereign rights and what these entailed for access regulation, property rights versus IPRs regarding plant genetic resources, and the forms of benefit sharing arising from the use of the said genetic resources.[76]

Most developed countries chose either to reject the principles of the Undertaking or to underline reservations to provisions dealing with the absence of breeders' rights. Critics of the Undertaking elaborated that the said agreement polarised nations instead of providing for a compromise, thus failing to incentivise TKGR conservation. No less than eight UPOV member countries protested at the FAO Conference that the text of

[71] *Ex situ* collections at the time of the adoption of the CBD remain outside its scope.

[72] Resolution 7/93.

[73] CPGR-Ex1/94/5 Supp, September 1994.

[74] The technical aspects discussed were the identification of plant genetic resources for food and agriculture and the tracing of their geographical origins by modern genetic analytical techniques.

[75] Among the economic aspects were the value of plant genetic resources for food and agriculture and the economic analysis of plant genetic resource conservation and erosion.

[76] Lettington, R.J.L., 'The International Undertaking on Plant Genetic Resources in the Context of TRIPs and the CBD, Bridges Between Trade and Sustainable Development, International Center for Trade and Sustainable Development', Year 5, No 6 (July–August 2001), pp. 11–13.

the IU was in conflict with existing law, both with regard to national breeders' rights legislation and to the UPOV treaty.[77]

The common heritage rule of the Undertaking was in fact accused of endangering developed countries' private property systems. However, the IU was not able to prevent industrial countries from providing for IP protection for plant genetic resources while at the same time failing to provide any sort of compensation for developing countries.[78] It thus gradually became obvious that the IU was not a satisfactory legal instrument, which could on the one hand cover all alternative parameters of access and transfer of plant genetic resources while on the other providing a viable long-term solution.

2.2.3.2 The International Network of *Ex Situ* Collections under the auspices of the FAO

The International Network of *Ex Situ* Collections[79] was established in accordance with Article 7.1(a) of the IU in order to regulate the status of genetic resources held in *ex situ* collections.[80] The designated germplasm would be held 'in the trust of the international community', no ownership would be claimed and no IP protection would be sought over the designated germplasm and related information.[81] In the Preamble of the Agreement, it was made clear that the germplasm in question will have been donated or collected on the understanding that it will remain freely available, especially for developing countries.

---

[77] See also Bordwin, H., 'The Legal and Political Implications of the International Undertaking on Plant Genetic Resources', Ecology LQ, Vol 12 (1985), pp. 1053–69.

[78] Correa, C., 'Biological Resources and Intellectual Property Rights', EIPR, Vol 14 (1992), pp. 154–7. See also Eshbach, R., 'A Global Approach to the Protection of the Environment: Balancing State Sovereignty and Global Interests', Temp Int'l & Comp LJ, Vol 4 (1990), pp. 271–80; Rackleff, K., 'Preservation of Biological Diversity', Colo J Int'L Envtl L & Pol Y, Vol 3 (1992), pp. 429–78, p. 405, where it was stated that world leaders are starting to recognise plant genetic resources as global commons.

[79] The status of *ex situ* collections has always been rather unclear. The need to determine their legal situation led to the said initiative.

[80] Twelve centres of the Consultative Group on International Agricultural Research decided to sign agreements with the FAO placing most of their collections under the FAO policy mechanisms.

[81] The standard agreements between the collection centres and the FAO, placing collections under the auspices of FAO, were signed in October 1994. They have been revised and developed in connection with the revision of the International Undertaking as well as the negotiations that led to the adoption of the ITPGRFA.

Article 1 provides that the material transfer agreements (MTAs) shall be construed in line with the provisions of the CBD and the International Understanding (now ITPGRFA). The list of plant genetic resources found under the International Network will be catalogued,[82] published by the centres and revised every two years.[83] According to Article 3, each Centre is bound to hold the designated germplasm 'in trust for the benefit of the international community, in particular developing countries', while it should not claim any legal ownership over the designated germplasm or any IPR over that germplasm or related information. The designated germplasm will be managed and conserved in line with the international gene bank standards.[84]

Samples of the material as well as related information will be made available to users – either directly or through the FAO – for the purposes of scientific research, plant breeding or genetic resources conservation.[85] Article 9 states that access to this material shall be available without restrictions.[86] In the event of such a transfer, the Centre shall ensure that all subsequent uses proceed in accordance with Articles 3(b) and 5(a) of the Agreement.[87] The recipient of the designated germplasm will not be able to seek any property or IP rights on the said material.[88] Although this might seem a rather straightforward rule, it may in fact be subject to divergent interpretations. A question of major interest is thus whether the recipient of genetic material may in fact apply for IP rights on a processed version of the material, or when the material is part of a broader invention.

---

[82] The term used hereinafter in the agreement is 'designated germplasm'.

[83] Article 2 of the Agreement places collections of plant germplasm under the auspices of the FAO.

[84] Article 5(a) of the Agreement.

[85] Article 9 of the Agreement.

[86] In the joint statement of FAO and CGIAR Centres in respect of the Agreement, it is made clear that 'no restriction' shall not mean *contra* the objectives of the Convention on Biological Diversity. The rights of the countries of origin should be respected.

[87] According to the Joint Statement of FAO and the CGIAR Centers on the Agreement Placing CGIAR Germplasm Collections under the Auspices of FAO, the Centres are free to provide access to material through material transfer agreements as long as they can guarantee that they will remain in the public domain.

[88] However, the Centre will not be held responsible for the monitoring of the recipient's compliance to the said obligations.

2.2.3.3 Codes of conduct

Apart from the legally binding international agreements developed under the FAO agenda, codes of conduct were adopted in order to provide a set of principles under and by which genetic resources would be held as well as transferred to third parties.

2.2.3.3.1 Code of Conduct on Plant Biotechnology In 1991, the Commission on Genetic Resources for Food and Agriculture (CGRFA) requested the preparation of a draft Code of Conduct on Plant Biotechnology, with the objective of maximising the positive effects of biotechnology and minimising the negative ones. The objectives of the Code of Conduct on Plant Biotechnology are to promote the use of biotechnology, especially in developing countries, and facilitate access to the material and the flow of relevant information while minimising the environmental risks of the said technologies. Article 4 underlines the fact that the Code is voluntary and dependent upon the collaborative actions of governments.[89] The Code of Conduct states the need to proceed with the transfer of appropriate biotechnology to developing countries and to the benefit of local farming communities.[90] Governments should create the conditions necessary for facilitated access to a genetic resources framework in which both formal and informal innovators shall be rewarded.[91] The grant of IPRs should not unduly restrict access to plant genetic resources for farmers, breeders and scientists.[92] Farmers, especially in developing countries, should be guaranteed the right to reuse the seed of the previous season, including that originating from protected varieties.[93]

2.2.3.3.2 The International Code of Conduct for Plant Germplasm Collecting and Transfer The Code of Conduct for Plant Germplasm (Germplasm Code),[94] adopted in November 1993, is a voluntary code based upon the principle of national sovereignty over plant genetic resources.[95] The Germplasm Code is in compliance with the CBD and

---

[89] The Code should be implemented in harmony with the CBD, the International Plant Protection Convention and other international agreements on biosafety.

[90] Article 7.1.3 of the Code of Conduct.

[91] Article 9.1 of the Code of Conduct.

[92] Article 9.2 of the Code of Conduct.

[93] Article 9.3 of the Code of Conduct.

[94] CPGR/93/1.

[95] Article 3.2 of the Code of Conduct of Plant Germplasm Collecting and Transfer.

the ITPGRFA.[96] One of its objectives is to promote the sharing of benefits derived from plant genetic resources, and related information, between the donors and users of the germplasm.[97] Moreover, the Code recognises the rights and needs of the local communities that manage and preserve plant genetic resources to facilitate their compensation,[98] as well as to avoid situations in which benefits derived from plant genetic resources by these local communities and farmers are undermined by the transfer or use of others.[99]

Article 3.2 states that 'the conservation and continued availability of plant genetic resources is a common concern of humankind'.[100] Permits to collectors are granted through an institutional framework,[101] which has been established by the relevant governments.[102] In addition, the issuance of a permit shall be subject to certain conditions that the recipient must respect, such as the provision of indicative plans of the field mission, the types of material to be collected, reference to both species and quantities, notification to the host country of the need for assistance (if necessary), participation of national scholars and scientists and supply of all other information the source country might consider necessary.[103]

The issuing authority shall then examine the application and notify the potential recipient of its decision as soon as possible.[104] If the permit is granted, the applicant shall be informed of all limitations or restrictions

---

[96] Preamble of the Code of Conduct of Plant Germplasm Collecting and Transfer.

[97] Article 1.7 of the Code of Conduct of Plant Germplasm Collecting and Transfer.

[98] Article 1.8(a) of the Code of Conduct of Plant Germplasm Collecting and Transfer.

[99] Article 1.8(b) of the Code of Conduct of Plant Germplasm Collecting and Transfer.

[100] The term 'common concern of humankind' is a concept linked to the 'common heritage of mankind' and could create concerns in relation to the benefit-sharing obligation established in the CBD, as discussed in section 2.2.1.

[101] According to Article 6.2, governments should designate an authority responsible for issuance of the permits after informing the recipients of the relevant regulation and legislation.

[102] Article 6.1 of the Code of Conduct of Plant Germplasm Collecting and Transfer.

[103] Articles 7.1(a)–(g) of the Code of Conduct of Plant Germplasm Collecting and Transfer.

[104] Article 8(a) of the Code of Conduct of Plant Germplasm Collecting and Transfer.

to the collecting rights granted, as well as of all relevant legislation.[105] According to Article 10.1, the collectors should respect the local communities and their customs and values, and should demonstrate a kind of gratitude; however, the article does not specify in detail what form this gratitude might take.[106]

2.2.3.3.3 International Treaty on Plant Genetic Resources for Food and Agriculture The lengthy negotiations of IU revision were finally concluded by the adoption of a new legal instrument, namely the International Treaty on Plant Genetic Resources for Food and Agriculture (ITPGRFA).[107] The Preamble underlines the importance of realisation of Farmers' Rights, by means of the ITPGRFA access and benefit-sharing provisions. The objectives of the ITPGRFA are strikingly similar to those of the CBD, namely 'the conservation and sustainable use of plant genetic resources for food and agriculture and the fair and equitable sharing of the benefits arising out of their use'.[108]

According to Article 9, Farmers' Rights constitute recognition of the contribution of generations of farmers from all over the world.[109] The ITPGRFA drafts a list of these rights: the protection of traditional knowledge (TK) relevant to plant genetic resources; the right to equitably participate in sharing benefits arising from the utilisation of plant genetic resources; and the right to participate in decision making at the national level on matters related to the conservation and sustainable use of the resources in question. Article 10, meanwhile, proclaims the sovereignty of states over their plant genetic resources while at the same time pinpointing the importance of a multilateral system that facilitates access and benefit sharing.[110]

---

[105] Article 8(c)–(h) of the Code of Conduct of Plant Germplasm Collecting and Transfer.

[106] Article 10.1 of the Code of Conduct of Plant Germplasm Collecting and Transfer.

[107] International Treaty Concerning the Regulation of Access to Plant Genetic Resources, United Nations Food and Agriculture Organization, Resolution 3/2001 (2001). Treaty adopted through FAO Resolution 3/2001.

[108] Article 1.1 of the ITPGRFA.

[109] Part III of the ITPGRFA.

[110] See also Lawson, C., 'Intellectual Property and the Material Transfer Agreement under the International Treaty on Plant Genetic Resources for Food and Agriculture', EIPR, Vol 5 (2009), pp. 244–54. For an interesting illustration of how the ITPGRFA introduces a liability regime see Hensson-Apollonio, V., 'Case 10. The International Treaty on Plant Genetic Resources for Food and Agriculture: The Standard Material Transfer Agreement as Implementation of a

The multilateral system solely covers the PGRFA listed in Annex 1 of the Treaty.[111] As a rule, it includes crops that already exist in the public domain and those that exist under the control of the Contracting States.[112] However, all other interested holders are free to participate.[113] For instance, CGIAR, with its *ex situ* collections, is part of the system. While the ITPGRFA provides for a list of 64 crops and forages that could fall under the scope of the Multilateral System, not all of them are in fact included. Taking into consideration the difficulties in achieving consensus, the negotiating parties decided that some of the listed genera would be automatically included and the rest would remain outside of the Multilateral System until they are voluntarily included by the member states.

Article 12.3 enumerates the 'rules' governing access to plant genetic resources under the Multilateral System. Access is not possible for chemical, pharmaceutical and industrial uses.[114] Material, related passport data and non-confidential descriptive information is to be accessed free of charge.[115] The recipients will not be able to claim any IPR or other rights on the material in the form in which it was accessed from the Multilateral System.[116] On the other hand, access to plant genetic resources protected by IPR shall be proceeded with in conformity with all relevant international agreements.[117] Access to the plant genetic material is to be made available 'expeditiously' and 'free of charge' or for 'minimum costs involved' under Standard Material Transfer Agreements (SMTAs), which contain the provisions of Article 12.3(a), (d) and (g) as well as benefit-sharing provisions.[118] The terms of the SMTA will apply

---

Limited Compensatory Liability Regime', in G. Van Overwalle (ed), *Gene Patents and Collaborative Licensing Models*, Cambridge: Cambridge University Press (2009), pp. 289–93. See also López Noriega, Isabel et al, 'Assessment of Progress to Make the Multilateral System Functional: Incentives and Challenges at the Country Level' in Halewood, M., et al (eds), *Crop Genetic Resources as Global Commons: Challenges in International Law and Governance*, London: Earthscan and Bioversity International (2013).

111 Article 11.1 of the International Treaty.

112 According to Article 11.3 of the International Treaty, the contracting states will take all appropriate measures to encourage that third parties holding genetic resources enter into the Multilateral System.

113 Article 11.2.

114 Article 12.3(a).

115 Articles 12.3(b) and 12.3(c).

116 Article 12.3(d).

117 Article 12.3(e).

118 Benefit-sharing provisions can be found in Article 13.2(ii).

to all subsequent transfers of the material.[119] In the case that a contractual dispute arises, the contracting parties will be able to seek recourse under their respective legal systems.[120] It is important to note that SMTAs are in fact private contracts between individual recipients and providers.

The International Treaty encompasses a rather detailed plan for the sharing of benefits under the PGRFA's Multilateral System of exchange. Article 13.2 states that benefit sharing shall be conducted through the following mechanisms: exchange of information; access to and transfer of technology; capacity building; and finally, sharing of monetary and other benefits of commercialisation.[121]

Contracting parties are encouraged to proceed to an exchange of information concerning technologies and research results regarding the concerned plant genetic resources. Technologies for the conservation, characterisation and evaluation of the resources will be made available to the other parties under the Multilateral System. Particularly with regard to developing countries, a set of measures will be set forward for the establishment of partnerships in research, as well as commercial joint ventures related to the material exchanged. Technologies that enjoy IP protection will be made available to developing countries under fair and most favourable terms.[122] While it is positive that the TRIPS Agreement includes an explicit technology transfer provision, it may not be interpreted in such a way as to entail that the obligation to transfer technology is by any means equivalent to setting aside the IP-related obligations and the IP system in general. Closely related to technology transfer is the capacity building of participating states, especially of developing countries. Scientific and technical education on the conservation and sustainable use of genetic resources for scientists from developing countries is also to be prioritised.[123] Commercial benefit sharing is envisioned under the framework of the ITPGRFA as a form of cooperation between the public and private sector. According to Article 12.3(d)(ii), the recipient of material that will proceed to the commercialisation of a product, incorporating material accessed under the Multilateral System, shall be paid an equitable share of the benefits. There are a variety of payment mechanisms and levels of payment, as well as a number of exemptions of

---

119 Article 12.4.

120 Article 12.5.

121 See also Mekouar, M.A., 'A Global Instrument on Agrobiodiversity. The International Treaty on Plant Genetic Resources for Food and Agriculture', FAO Legal Papers Online No 24 (2002).

122 Article 13.2(b) (iii).

123 Article 13.2(b).

certain categories of commercialisation,[124] to be determined by the governing body.[125]

2.2.3.4 'Common heritage' or 'common concern' of mankind for TKGR?

Both the Convention on Biological Diversity and the FAO Treaty on Plant Genetic Resources have as a starting point the sovereignty of states over their plant genetic resources. While the CBD is traditionally considered to have shifted the legal status of TKGR from 'common heritage' or 'common concern of mankind' to that of national sovereignty, the change had in fact already occurred by means of the introduction of the International Treaty on Plant Genetic Resources for Food and Agriculture (ITPGRFA). Article 10 of the ITPGRFA provides that in 'their relationships with other States, the Contracting Parties recognise the sovereign rights of States over their own plant genetic resources for food and agriculture, including that the authority to determine access to those resources rests with national governments and is subject to national jurisdiction'. While state sovereignty and common heritage are in principle mutually exclusive principles, a form of reconciliation was attempted in the field of plant genetic resources.[126] A very good illustration of the conflict between these two principles, relevant also for TKGR, is that of Amazon protection. While industrialised countries have expressed the view that the Amazon should fall outside the sovereign rights of Brazil and be managed under a common heritage of mankind regime,[127] Brazil has not accepted any interference in its rights

[124] That becomes relevant when commercialisation is carried out by small farmers.

[125] The governing body for this Treaty is established by means of Article 19 of the International Treaty. Its functions and mandate are described in Articles 19.3(a)–(n).

[126] See Schrijver, N., 'Permanent Sovereignty over Natural Resources versus the Common Heritage of Mankind: Complementary or Contradictory Principles of International Economic Law?' in Denters, E.M.G., Peters, P., de Waart, P.J.I.M. (eds), *International Law and Development*, Cambridge: Cambridge University Press (1988), p. 401, Correa, C.M., 'Sovereign and Property Rights over Plant Genetic Resources', FAO Background Study Paper No 2; Commission on Plant Genetic Resources – First Extraordinary Session, Rome (7–11 November 1994).

[127] McClearly, R.M., 'The International Communities' Claim to Rights in Brazilian Amazonia', Political Studies, Vol 39 (1991), pp. 691–707. See also in this respect Goldenberg J., Durham, E.R., 'Amazonia and National Sovereignty', International Environmental Affairs, Vol 2 (1992), p. 22. Since the Amazon

over the region, which in fact represents 42 per cent of Brazilian territory. Consequently, although Brazilian development policy may endanger both the conservation and the sustainable use of genetic resources, as well as the traditional knowledge and indigenous communities of the Amazon region – with the possibility, in turn, of detrimental effects for the global environment and biodiversity – third-party countries may not intervene and assert a collective extraterritorial jurisdiction over Brazilian Amazonia.

2.3 TKGR COMMODIFICATION IN PRACTICE[128]

2.3.1 Commodification as a Means to an End in Environmental Policy

Addressing concerns related to environmental risks and biodiversity loss is, in Western legal tradition, increasingly a matter of addressing ownership of lands and genetic resources. The starting point for this approach is that the benefits of owning and exploiting a genetic resource also constitute the incentives for conservation. Environmental policy in the Western world as late as the 1960s was based on the perception that 'man is given dominion over all creatures and things'.[129]

The advocated 'green developmentalism' promotes the commodification of natural resources as a main remedy for environmental degradation and biodiversity loss.[130] The dominant approach to modern environmental conservation policy is to deal with environmental degradation by greening the economy and attempting to mainstream the economics of biodiversity in order to support development. This is also the approach

---

region produces 50 per cent of the world's oxygen and a substantial part of the world's fresh water and biodiversity, countries have expressed their concerns for its management.

[128] Commodification is the process whereby an object – whether tangible, such as seed, or intangible, such as knowledge about the seed – is turned into a commodity, that is, something that acquires economic worth and can be bought and sold. See Gepts (2004), p. 1304.

[129] Contrary to the oriental approach in which humans are the mere trustees or stewards of the environment. See McHarg, I., 'Values, Process and Form' in Lee, J., *The Fitness of Man's Environment* (Washington: Smithsonian Institute Press, 1968), p. 213.

[130] McAfee, K., 'Selling Nature to Save It? Biodiversity and Green Developmentalism', Environment and Planning D: Society and Space, Vol 17 (1999), pp. 134–54.

that was adopted in the drafting of the CBD. Biodiversity holders are to be compensated for caring for and contributing to the conservation of biodiversity and genetic resources by sharing the benefits which arise out of the commercialisation of products originating from their biodiversity.

2.3.2 Commodification in TKGR Protection

The evolution of TKGR's legal status, from the 'commons' through its gradual commodification, was influenced by a number of different factors. The adoption and implementation of the TRIPS Agreement, UPOV and CBD were of course of major importance in this respect.[131] TKGR is in practice treated as a commodity nowadays, and thus the evolution of a legal framework to accommodate new needs has been necessary.[132]

Several examples of TKGR commodification reveal the need to provide for a complete legal framework regulating its status and transfer, and to this day influence the implementation of the CBD.

The neem tree (*Azardirachta indica*) is known in Sanskrit as 'Sarva Roga Nivarini' or 'cure for all ailments', and is closely connected to Indian culture. In some regions, the new year begins with eating the tender shoots of the neem tree; in other areas, the tree is worshipped as sacred. Indians use neem tree bark to clean their teeth, and neem leaf juice is used to prevent psoriasis and other skin disorders. Furthermore, neem extract is used as an antidote to malaria and neem oil is used as a

---

[131] For a very interesting discussion on the transfer of subject matter from the commons to IP protection and the challenges this imposes for the international IP system, see Levin, M., 'The Pendulum Keeps Swinging – Present Discussions on and around the TRIPS Agreement', in Kur, A., Levin, M. (eds), *Intellectual Property Rights in a Fair World Trade System: Proposals for Reform for TRIPS*, Cheltenham: Edward Elgar (2011), pp. 3–61.

[132] The disadvantages of the commodification of TKGR by means of the CBD and the persistence in preserving the 'commons' nature of TKGR. See Donovan, E., 'Beans, the Patented Fruit: The Growing International Conflict over the Ownership of Life', Loy LA Intl & Comp L Rev, Vol 25 (2002–3), pp. 117–42, discussing in detail objections to the patentability of enola beans, in one of the known cases of alleged biopiracy. With regard to the process of commodification of seeds see Ewens, L., 'Seed Wars: Biotechnology, Intellectual Property and the Quest for High Yield Seeds', Intl & Comp L Rev, Vol 23 (1999–2000), pp. 285–310; Fidler, D., 'Neither Science Nor Shamans. Globalization of Markets and Health in the Developing World', Ind J Global Legal Stud, Vol 7 (1999), pp. 191–223.

female contraceptive. In 1959, a German entomologist reported that neem trees had been spared during a locust swarm that devoured all other foliage.

In the 1990s, a group of American researchers managed to find a way to alter the active ingredient, creating a storage-stable version of neem extract. The US Patent Office granted Patent No 5124349 to W.R. Grace & Co, an agricultural chemical company, for this particular derivative of the neem tree.[133] Finally, in 1994 the Environmental Protection Agency registered Neemix, Grace's stabilised azadirachtin solution for use on food crops. For anti-biopiracy activists all around the world, the neem patent became one of the major illustrations of market failure and of the weaknesses of the patent system's granting a patent on something that is already known. The lack of any consideration for cultural perspectives in the patent system was underlined.[134]

Another relevant case is that of the rosy periwinkle, a plant native to the island of Madagascar, which has been used to develop two pharmaceuticals for the treatment of Hodgkin's disease and juvenile leukaemia. Eli Lilly – the patent owner of the two pharmaceuticals, Vinblastine and Vincristine, which originate from the rosy periwinkle – is estimated to have earned US$100 million per year from the products, but no compensation was awarded to Madagascar or to the local communities, who were in fact the owners of TKGR on the rosy periwinkle.[135]

The cases of basmati rice and turmeric have considerably enhanced the TKGR discussion. In 1996, the US-based company RiceTech was granted a patent on seeds and plants related to basmati rice.[136] After opposition from India, the patent claims were restricted.[137] Turmeric, meanwhile, is used in India for cooking, as a dye and in cosmetics, as well as for its medicinal purposes. In 1995, a US patent was granted to two Indian

---

[133] The patent covered a method of creating stabilised azadirachtin in solution and the stabilised azadirachtin solution itself.

[134] For the neem tree story see Marden, E., 'The Neem Tree Patent: International Conflict over the Commodification of Life', Boston College International and Comparative Law Review, Vol 22 (1999), pp. 279–95.

[135] Karasov, C., 'Who Reaps the Benefits of Biodiversity', Environmental Health Perspective, Vol 109 (2001), pp. 582–7. On the value of agricultural economy see Maskus, K.E., 'Intellectual Property Rights in Agriculture and Interests of Asian-Pacific Economies', The World Economy, Vol 29 (2006), pp. 715–42.

[136] US Patent No 5, 663, 484.

[137] Re-Examination Certificate C1, issued on 29 January 2002, cancelling claims 1–7, 10 and 14–20 of the original basmati patent. An important part of the discussion was dedicated to the use of the name 'basmati'.

researchers working for the University of Mississippi on the use of turmeric in wound healing.[138] Opposition proceedings by the Indian Centre for Scientific and Industrial Research led the patent to be revoked,[139] on the basis of lack of novelty.[140]

Additionally, karela (bitter gourd) juice has been used in India for the treatment of diabetes. A herbal mixture containing karela and other ingredients was the basis for a patent granted to a New Jersey-based company.[141] Meanwhile, the Enola beans patent was granted on a plant variety of a yellow fieldbean.[142] Indeed, there is an endless list of seeds, plants and other genetic material selected from traditional medicinal and agricultural practices and made the subject of some form of IP protection in Western countries: pozol,[143] *Phyllanthus amarus*,[144] hoodia cactus,[145] quinone,[146] tamate,[147] arogyapaacha;[148] all these plants are representative

---

[138] US Patent No 5, 401, 404.

[139] Re-Examination Certificate B1, issued on 21 April 1998, cancelling all claims in the original patent.

[140] Prior art evidence in the form of ancient Sanskrit texts was presented.

[141] US Patent No 5, 900, 240, issued on 4 May 1999.

[142] US Patent No 5, 894, 079.

[143] Pozol is a traditional drink used by the Maya in Mexico for nutritional purposes and for the prevention of intestinal ailments. In 1999, Quest International, a Dutch corporation and the University of Minnesota were granted a patent for the active component in pozol. Recognition of the indigenous populations and 'fair and equitable sharing' of the benefits arising from the commercialisation of the resources in question never occurred.

[144] Phyllanthus amarus is a medicinal plant used in India to treat jaundice. Tests showed that the active substance of the plant can cure Hepatitis B and E. A patent was awarded to the Fox Chase Cancer Center.

[145] Hoodia cactus is an appetite suppressant used by the San of Southern Africa to ward off hunger on long hunting trips. The commercialisation of Hoodia by an American company brought some form of compensation to the local communities.

[146] The quinoa patent was granted to two researchers from Colorado State University. The researchers came into contact with the plant genetic resources in question after contact with Bolivian indigenous communities who gave them those plants and seeds. The public attention that this case attracted led to the final abandonment of the rights by the patent owners.

[147] Tamate is a small cylindrical tomato used by Amazonian Indians to cure some forms of cancer. The active ingredient in tamate, lycopene, was isolated and sold as a cancer treatment.

[148] The arogyapaacha plant is used by the Kani in South India for medicinal purposes. On the basis of the plant's active ingredient, an antistress and antifatigue sports drug named Jeevani was developed. The appropriation and use of the genetic material was performed on the basis of a cooperation agreement

cases of green trade practices such as the ones described above. They are examples of how TKGR can be of value to third parties, and thus of value to indigenous communities outside and above their traditional uses, in a global trade environment.[149]

2.4 THE INSTITUTIONAL FRAMEWORK OF THE CBD AND COMMODIFICATION OF TKGR IN INTERNATIONAL LAW

The gradual de facto commodification of TKGR motivated and enhanced changes in the institutional platform. Clearly, a major contribution to this end was the entry into force of the CBD. However, in parallel to the implementation of the Convention, which sets the objectives and general principles of the institutional framework covering TKGR trade, countries were also faced with the challenges of implementing the TRIPS Agreement. This international IP agreement constitutes a central parameter to discussions on TKGR protection, as it has both direct and indirect impacts on the implementation of the CBD objectives. The direct impact relates to the boundaries set by the Agreement regarding the adjustments to which 'traditional IPR' might be subject in light of the protection of TKGR.[150] The indirect impact relates to changes in the extensive protection of inventions, in particular in the biotechnology field, with regard to TKGR.[151]

The adoption of the CBD and its entry into force in 1993 signalled a major change of attitude with regard to the protection of natural resources. Previous conservation conventions were concerned with the

---

between the indigenous community, the Tropical Botanic Garden and Research Institute of India and Arya Vaida Pharmacy, an Indian pharmaceutical company. Part of the agreement was the establishment of a trust fund that would allow for the profits of commercialisation to be shared.

[149] See also Cottier, T., Panizzon, M., 'Legal Perspectives on Traditional Knowledge: The Case for Intellectual Property Protection', Journal of International Economic Law, Vol 7 (2004), pp. 371–99.

[150] For the concept of biodiversity, see Bowman, M., 'The Nature, Development and Philosophical Foundations of the Biodiversity Concept in International Law', in Bowman, M. and Redgwell, C. (eds), *International Law and the Conservation of Biological Diversity*, London: Kluwer Law International (1996), pp. 5–32.

[151] Kloppenburg, J.R., 'Seed Wars: Biotechnology, Intellectual Property and the Quest for High Yield Seeds', BC Intl Comp L Rev 285, Vol 23 (1999–2000), pp. 285–310.

rational use of 'common' resources and the protection of endangered species, and omitted to address the protection of natural resources on the basis of a globally comprehensive regime. In this respect, one of the major steps forward, achieved by means of the CBD, was the internationalisation of issues such as the conservation and sustainable use of such resources.[152] To this day, there is no real consensus as to the Convention's effects.

More than 150 countries eventually signed the Convention, although some 20 states expressed major reservations regarding the final text.[153] The CBD was considered to be 'generic and open to interpretation', or 'too vague to be threatening'.[154] Although specific provisions of the Convention caused these reactions on the part of states – even those which signed it – it could be concluded that there was general consensus with regard to the general principle of reciprocity, meaning that countries contributing to the conservation of TKGR should also be participating in the sharing of the benefits.

2.4.1 Background and Negotiations Preceding the Convention

The CBD is certainly not a convention adopted in a vacuum.[155] The need for an international convention providing for the protection of biodiversity had been expressed in a number of different international fora. One of the first such initiatives was the World Conservation Strategy, adopted by the International Union for Conservation of Nature (IUCN),

---

[152] Boyle, A., 'The Rio Convention on Biological Diversity', in *International Law and the Conservation of Biological Diversity*, The Hague: Kluwer Law International (1996), pp. 33–55. See also Powers, M., 'The United Nations Framework Convention on Biological Diversity: Will Biodiversity Preservation Be Enhanced through its Provisions concerning Biotechnology Intellectual Property Rights?' Wisconsin Int LJ, Vol 12 (1994), pp. 103–24, stating that the objectives of the CBD could in fact be achieved in harmony with IPRs.

[153] 'Nations Forge Biodiversity Convention that is "Flawed", Rio Support Doubtful', Int Envtl L Rep (BNA) (3 June 1992), p. 346; 'Vote on Proposal to Protect Biotech Patents Delayed to Ensure No Conflict with Rio Treaty', Intl Env L Rep (BNA) (17 June 1992), p. 398.

[154] 'Industry Officials Call Biodiversity Treaty Vague, See Little Impact on Competitiveness, Other Areas', Intl Env Rep (BNA) (29 July 1992), p. 511. See also 'Two Successful Weeks at Rio', Nature (18 June 1992), p. 253; USA, Declaration Made at the United Nations Environmental Programme (UNEP) Conference for the Adoption of the Agreed Text of the CBD, printed in 31 ILM (1992), p. 848.

[155] See Downes, D., 'The Convention on Biological Diversity: Seeds of Green Trade?', Tul Envtl LJ, Vol 163 (1994–5), pp. 163–80.

United Nations Environment Programme (UNEP) and World Wildlife Fund in 1980.[156] In 1982, the World Charter for Nature was validated as a formal resolution of the United Nations General Assembly, which provided for the conservation of the earth's 'genetic viability'.[157]

The objectives of the CBD were initially presented in the Stockholm Declaration,[158] and subsequently introduced in international agreements.[159] An illustrative example is Principle 21 of the Stockholm Declaration, recognising the rights of nations to exploit their resources. Principle 21 has been reaffirmed in a number of other international instruments, such as the resolution authorising the Earth Summit,[160] hereinafter the UNCED Resolution.[161]

2.4.1.1 The Stockholm Declaration

The UN General Assembly of 1970 adopted a series of principles that would later appear in a number of other relevant international agreements, including the Convention on Biological Diversity. Some of the major principles were: (1) development plans should be compatible with sound ecology; (2) environmental policies should avoid the risk of adverse effects on the developing countries' development possibilities, including their international trade position, international development assistance and the transfer of technology; (3) the sovereign rights of each country should be fully respected; (4) any action plan and action proposals should promote programmes designed to assist developing countries, including the provision of additional technical assistance and financial resources.[162]

In June 1972, at the request of the United Nations General Assembly, representatives from 113 countries convened in Stockholm for the United Nations Conference on the Human Environment. The Conference parties

---

156 See also IUCN/WWF/UNEP, Caring for the Earth (1991), p. 28.

157 Res 37/7, 1982, World Charter for Nature.

158 The Stockholm Declaration on the Human Environment was a Declaration (6–26 June 1972) containing 26 principles and 109 recommendations. It was not a legally binding agreement.

159 Hendricks, B., 'Postmodern Possibility and the Convention on Biological Diversity', NYU Envtl LJ, Vol 5 (1996), pp. 1–32.

160 GA Res 228, UN GAOR, 44th Sess, pt 1, Press Release GA/7977, pp. 300–1, UN Doc a/44/746/Add7 (1990).

161 This is a fundamental objective of the Convention on Biological Diversity itself.

162 GA Res 2849, UN GAOR, 26th Sess, Supp No 29, p. 70–1, UN Doc A/8429 (1972).

had a broad mandate to 'serve, protect and improve the human environment ... by means of international cooperation, bearing in mind the particular importance of enabling developing countries to forestall the occurrence of such problems'. Finally, in December of the same year, the General Assembly adopted a resolution expressing the fundamental idea that 'environmental policies should be considered in the context of economic and social development, taking into account the special needs of development in developing countries'.[163]

Under the ambit of these fundamental principles, the Stockholm Conference adopted a Declaration of 26 Principles and an 'Action Plan for the Human Environment' containing 109 recommendations. Principles 9, 11 and 12 propose financial and technical assistance to developing countries while Principle 20 encourages the transfer of 'environmental technologies ... to developing countries on terms, which would encourage their wide dissemination'. The principles of the Stockholm Conference Declaration have constituted the basis of a number of fundamental provisions of the CBD's final text.[164]

2.4.1.2 World Charter for Nature

Ten years after the Stockholm Declaration, the UN adopted the World Charter for Nature as a further environmental legal instrument.[165] Keeping to the same line as the Stockholm Declaration, the World Charter for Nature is no more than a declaration of principles under which the world's nations should perform their affairs. It contains a series of provisions regarding genetic resources, species and ecosystem protection and the sustainable use of natural resources, and finally a list of activities that might have an adverse impact on nature.[166]

The introduction of considerations on economic development was initially addressed in Principle 17 of the Declaration, stating that 'funds, programmes and administrative structures necessary to achieve the objective of the conservation of nature shall be provided'.[167]

---

[163] GA Res 2657, UN GAOR, 25th Sess, Supp No 28, p. 51, UN Doc A/2567 (1972).

[164] See for instance Articles 3, 7, 12 and 16 of the CBD.

[165] World Charter for Nature, UN GA RES 37/7.

[166] World Charter for Nature, pp. 17–18.

[167] When the negotiations were almost finalised, the US sought a delay in the voting in order to clarify the text and the enforceability of the document. However, the postponement was not granted and the US had the only dissenting vote as to the adoption of the World Charter for Nature.

2.4.1.3 The United Nations Conference on Environment and Development

No fewer than 18 years after the Stockholm Declaration, delegates called for a second UN Conference on the Human Environment and the General Assembly gave authorisation for the United Nations Conference on Environment and Development (UNCED), planned to coincide with World Environment Day in 1992.[168] A consensus on the final Resolution proved to be hard to achieve. Developed countries opted for a focus on environmental issues, while the developing world expressed the concern that environmental 'focus' might misplace issues of development and economic growth that were of interest for the developing world.[169]

The UNCED PrepCom managed to finally achieve consensus with regard to three documents: Agenda 21, the Rio Declaration and the Statement of Forest Principles.[170]

- Agenda 21 is an action programme aimed at altering human activities in order to minimise environmental damage and ensure sustainable development. Agenda 21 encompasses 115 programme areas, including access, transfer of biotechnology and measures that would assure the maintenance and extension of biological diversity.
- The Rio Declaration proposes the establishment of a new and equitable global partnership.[171] It reaffirms principles set out by the Stockholm Declaration, such as the sovereign right of states to exploit their own resources, as well as the principle that sustainable development and environmental protection is linked. Finally, its Principle 9 reiterates the need for exchange of scientific and technological knowledge as well as 'new and innovative technologies'.[172]
- The Statement of Forest Principles recognises the importance of forests to the biosphere and the sovereign right of countries to 'utilise, manage, and develop their forests in accordance with their development needs and level of socio-economic development'.[173] Its Principle 1 confirms that the international community should

---

168 NCED Resolution.

169 The major points of conflict were the location of the Secretariat for the conference, the extent of NGO participation, and the contents of the agenda.

170 Documents from the daily coverage of the UNCED PREP COM, http://www.iisd.ca/linkages/vol01/.

171 Rio Declaration, Report of the United Nations Conference on the Human Environment, Stockholm, 5–16 June 1972.

172 Rio Declaration, Principle 9.

173 Statement of Forest Principles, A/CONF.151/26 (Vol III).

share 'the agreed full incremental cost of achieving benefits associated with forest conservation and forest development'.

2.4.1.4 The IUCN Draft Commission

In 1988, the International Union for the Conservation of Nature (IUCN) prepared the first draft of what came to be known as the 'Species Convention'.[174] The IUCN's draft Convention mainly related to environmental concerns, with a limited list of provisions related to economic or developmental issues. In general, the IUCN draft was considerably intrusive into states' 'sovereign right' to exploit their natural resources and included the following major points:

(1) *The inclusion of a World List*: The IUCN draft provided for a 'World List of Areas of Outstanding Importance for the Conservation of Biological Diversity'.[175] Inclusion or removal from the list was dependent on the majority vote of the Conference of the Parties, recommended by an Advisory Committee.[176] Recommendations could also be made with regard to 'any measure to maintain, develop or support the maintenance of biological diversity'.[177]
(2) *An International Fund*: Another important aspect of the IUCN draft was the establishment of an International Fund for the Conservation of Biological Diversity.[178] This provision was an extension of the 'polluter pays' principle,[179] and according to it, the International Fund would receive its income from a 'tax' of all those wishing to access and use genetic resources. Another source of revenue would be licence fees and royalties originating from IPRs granted on genetic resources. In order to clarify the financing of the International Fund, the Worldwide Fund for Nature initiated a study of mechanisms of alternative financing resources. The report proposed

---

[174] World Conservation Union, Draft Articles Prepared by IUCN for Inclusion in a Proposed Convention on the Conservation of Biological Diversity and for the Establishment of a Fund for that Purpose – Draft 6, Final explanatory notes (June 1989), hereinafter IUCN draft articles.

[175] The criteria for inclusion on the World List included such factors as 'the importance of an area as one displaying high biological diversity, the existence in the area of wild relatives of cultivated plants or domesticated animals'.

[176] IUCN draft articles 20–1.

[177] IUCN draft article 18.

[178] IUCN draft article 21.

[179] The polluter pays principle is a principle of international environmental law providing that the party that pollutes will be the one to pay for the damage done to the natural environment.

the creation of a company under the name LIFETECH, with the objective of exploiting novel products and possible IPRs on biodiversity.

(3) *Access to genetic resources*: Article 15 of the IUCN draft provided that access to genetic resources should be guaranteed for research and conservation purposes but not for commercial uses. Further commercialisation of biodiversity-based products would be guaranteed by means of bilateral contracts between the private companies interested in accessing genetic resources and the country of origin of the genetic resources in question.[180]

The IUCN draft laid the ground for an international convention on biological diversity. Nevertheless, the provisions included were contentious both for developed and developing countries. A major objection concerned the fact that the international organisation vested powers over genetic resources that would traditionally fall under state sovereignty. Other debated provisions were the mandatory 'tax' paid by users of genetic resources and the 'intrusion' into the IPRs awarded on these resources. Finally, developing countries strongly opposed the International Fund proposal that was solely concerned with conservation issues while totally omitting issues on economic development.

The IUCN draft was reviewed by a group of scientists at the request of UNEP's executive director. In view of the meeting of the Ad Hoc Expert Group, the review group concluded that an international convention would be a positive development. The negotiations lasted for more than 18 months and the final negotiation session, in May 1992, was marked by difficulty achieving consensus among delegates on a number of provisions of the proposed convention. To remedy the unfortunate negotiation dead-end, the chairman and executive director introduced a draft Biodiversity Convention that incorporated a number of amendments inserted after informal consultations with all delegations. The chairman clarified that the new text represents an overall compromise and should thus be considered a 'package deal'. The International Negotiating Committee adopted this partly contentious text on the last day of the final negotiating session and proclaimed that the Convention on Biological Diversity would be open for signature at the Earth Summit in Rio de Janeiro in June 1992.

Already during the initial discussions for a 'Species Convention' in 1987, the states had expressed their concerns on the matter, as well as

[180] IUCN draft articles 15, 16, 17 and 18.

their belief in the importance of a financial arrangement that would have the active backing of the community of nations.[181] According to the Brundtland Report,[182] the establishment of a trust fund was deemed necessary, to which 'all nations would contribute, with those benefiting more from the use of these resources contributing an appropriate share'.

It nevertheless deserves to be noted that the role to be played by this funding mechanism has varied in the series of negotiations. The Stockholm Declaration regarded the financial mechanism as a support to developing countries for the conservation of their genetic resources, and not as compensation for the commercial exploitation of their resources. The Brundtland Report was in line with the Stockholm Declaration, but extended its scope to include those countries of origin sharing equitably in the benefits and earnings derived from use and commercialisation of those resources. This extensionist tendency has been based upon growing awareness that genetic resources can represent commercial interests and give rise to profits that countries of origin would be entitled to share.

The CBD adopts the Brundtland Report by including provisions on financial support, transfer of technology and sharing biotechnology knowledge derived from genetic resources. Nevertheless, the first proposal, with its specific legal principles regarding states' obligations to maintain ecosystems and 'maximum biological diversity', originates with the World Commission on Environment and Development.[183] This proposal, in combination with a report from the executive director on the rationalisation of international conventions on biological diversity, led UNEP's governing council to initiate the process of drafting a convention in 1989. An expert working group was established, soon to be converted to an intergovernmental negotiating committee with 70 participating states.

In 1990, UNEP's executive director underlined the imperative to respect states' sovereignty over their resources and provide for incentives for the conservation of biological diversity without creating barriers to growth or sustainable development. Early consensus was reached regarding the fact that those parties that will enjoy the economic benefits of biodiversity (the developed countries) should contribute equitably to the cost of conservation and sustainable management, ensuring that the

---

[181] Our Common Future, Report of the World Commission on Environment and Development, World Commission on Environment and Development, 1987. Published as Annex to General Assembly Document A/42/427, Development and International Co-operation: Environment (2 August 1987).

[182] The Brundtland Commission Report, 'Our Common Future', was published by Oxford University Press in 1987.

[183] Boyle (1996).

genetic resources will be accessible to all and that technology and information on their use should be transferable to all.

The goal of the negotiations was to provide for some form of cooperation between the biodiversity-rich developing countries and the technology-rich developed countries. Under pressure from developing countries who wanted something more than a conservation convention, UNEP's governing council had to further define the objectives of the negotiations in 1991 by stating that 'both the conservation of biological diversity and the rational use of biological resources shall be integral and inseparable elements of the Convention'.

According to the position of a group of 77 developing states taking part in the negotiations, the Convention was to be seen under the wider perspective of restructuring global economic relations to obtain the required resources, technology and access to markets. The objectives they presented could be summed up as follows:

- the need for establishment of special systems of IPRs and appropriate mechanisms for compensating developing countries for the biological resources provided by them;
- the need for mechanisms giving the developing countries access to biotechnological know-how that is applied to the genetic resources it provides;
- additional funding to facilitate implementation of the convention and access to technology.

Developed countries adopted a somewhat differentiated approach. In particular, the United States opposed the Convention's provisions on technology transfer, financial aid and regulation of access to genetic resources. According to President George H.W. Bush, the CBD 'threatened to retard biotechnology and undermine the protection of ideas'. Furthermore, the Convention's various weaknesses, its lack of a clear legal relationship with other treaties and its lack of adequate environmental impact assessments were pinpointed. However, although it was stated that the preparation of the Convention was 'hasty and disjointed' and that the text did not reflect the treaty-making process, President Clinton's newly appointed administration then signed the Convention – albeit without ever ratifying it.[184] The EU, on the other hand, expressed disappointment at the Convention's weaknesses but did not oppose the

[184] Nairobi Final Act of the Conference for the Adoption of the Agreed Text of the Convention on Biological Diversity, available at http://www.biodiv.org/doc/handbook/cbd-hb-09-en.pdf.

provisions concerning technology transfer and access to biotechnology; it therefore signed and ratified the Convention.[185]

2.4.2 The CBD and Its Objectives

According to Article 1 of the CBD, the Convention has two main objectives:[186]

(1) the conservation of biodiversity and the sustainable use of its components;
(2) the fair and equitable sharing of the benefits arising out of the utilisation of genetic resources.

The first objective of the Convention is a clear illustration of UNEP policy, according to which there is a certain interdependency between the conservation and the rational use of genetic resources. Although in the Preamble of the Convention, the 'intrinsic value' of biodiversity (from an ecological, cultural and aesthetic perspective) is stressed, the CBD is not a preservationist convention. It promotes human intervention and human use of genetic resources as important factors in the conservation of biodiversity.[187]

In the second part of Article 1, the Convention refers to 'appropriate' access to genetic resources, as well as to the 'appropriate' transfer of relevant technologies. The beneficiaries and thus the recipients of the transfer of technology are the source countries. They are committed to the conservation of genetic resources in which they are rich, and they should therefore be entitled to the benefits arising from their exploitation.

---

185 EC, 'Proposal for a Council Decision Concerning the Conclusion of the Convention on Biological Diversity', COM(92)509 final, Brussels (21 December 1992).

186 For an analysis of the CBD objectives, Smagadi, A., 'Analysis of the Objectives of the Convention on Biological Diversity: Their Interrelation and Implementation Guidance for Access and Benefit Sharing', Colum J Envtl L, Vol. 16 (2006), pp. 243–84.

187 Tinker, C., 'A New Breed of a Treaty. The United Nations Convention on Biological Diversity', in the 'Rio' Environmental Treaties Colloquium, Pace Env L Rev (Fall 1995), pp. 1–14.

2.4.3 Major Provisions

2.4.3.1 State sovereignty and rights of indigenous communities

Biodiversity is located within the territory of individual states, thus being subject to state sovereignty. States' permanent sovereignty over their natural resources had already been recognised in previous resolutions of the General Assembly, such as the World Charter for Nature.[188]

The Preamble of the CBD clarifies that the protection of biodiversity is 'the common concern of mankind', thus abandoning the 'common heritage of mankind' status of genetic resources. Article 15 of the CBD reaffirms states' sovereignty over their own biological resources.[189] However, states should 'endeavour to create conditions to facilitate access to genetic resources' to other parties. Access should be facilitated subject to terms and conditions stipulated in national legislation and providing for the fundamental principles of 'mutually agreed terms' as well as 'prior informed consent'.[190] According to Article 15(7), states shall provide for the fair and equitable sharing of the benefits arising from the commercialisation or other utilisation of TKGR.

2.4.3.2 Rights of indigenous and local communities

Article 8(j) provides for the protection of knowledge and innovations and practices of indigenous and local communities. In this respect, the subject matter of protection is further defined as that which embodies traditional lifestyles relevant for the conservation and sustainable use of biological diversity. In accordance with the said provision, states are faced with three major obligations.

States shall 'respect, preserve and maintain' such knowledge, innovations and practices, which also indirectly covers the obligation to respect indigenous communities as such. Furthermore, states should contribute to the 'wider application with the approval and involvement of the holders of such knowledge, innovations and practices'. This provision is a further illustration of the link between conservation, access and exploitation of TKGR that characterises the objectives of CBD. Exploitation of TKGR will result in benefits that incentivise indigenous and local communities

---

188 World Charter for Nature A/RES/37/7, Article 14.

189 Article 15(1) CBD. States' sovereignty over their TKGR is also subject to Articles 6–9 of the CBD.

190 According to one interpretation of Article 15, these two provisions allude to the introduction of a property right. See Hassemer, M., 'Genetic Resources', in von Lewinski, S. (ed), *Indigenous Heritage and Intellectual Property*, The Hague: Kluwer International (2004), pp. 151–217.

to preserve traditional lifestyles and further enhance TKGR. It should be highlighted that Article 8(j) introduces the requirement of indigenous communities' 'approval and involvement', while at the same time awarding them rightholder status. The choice of terminology alludes to the implicit introduction of a new entitlement covering TKGR granted to indigenous and local communities – an entitlement that is not based on existing rights provided by means of national *sui generis* or IP legislation.[191] The article continues with encouragement of the 'equitable sharing of the benefits arising from the utilisation of such knowledge, innovations and practices', presupposing a legal entitlement and contractual agreements providing for the transfer of TKGR.

2.4.3.3 IPRs

Provisions related directly or indirectly to IPRs were obviously considered to be very contentious both for developed and developing countries.[192] Although IP-related provisions had been discussed during the First Negotiating Session in November 1990, most countries did not include an IP expert in their delegations. The importance and relevance of IPRs became obvious, however, especially with respect to the negotiation of technology transfer provisions. More specifically, during discussions on the technology transfer provisions under the Second Session, delegations reiterated that IPRs, and in particular patents, should also be considered.

IPRs were further discussed during plenary sessions and working group negotiations during the Third Session, where it was underlined that IPR's recent inclusion in the General Agreement on Tariffs and Trade (GATT) negotiations might give rise to complications that the Committee should look into.

During the Fourth Negotiating Session, Norway proposed a provision that directly addressed IPR-related concerns:

> The Contracting Parties, recognising that patents and IPRs exist and are regulated by national legislation and international agreements, also recognising that such rights have an influence on the implementation of the present Convention, shall cooperate in this regard in accordance with national legislation and existing international law in order to ensure that these legal arrangements are supportive of and do not run counter to the objectives of this Convention.

---

[191] At the time of the entry into force of the CBD.

[192] See also Walden, J., 'Intellectual Property Rights and Biodiversity' in Bowman, M., Redgwell, C. (eds), *International Law and the Conservation of Biological Diversity*, London: Kluwer Law International (1996), pp. 182–9.

This provision was included in the provisional formulation of Article 16 at the Fifth Negotiating Session, and general agreement on this wording was achieved at the Sixth Negotiating Session.[193]

2.4.3.4 Technology transfer

The CBD is an international treaty with deep environmental roots, but is also closely connected to concerns of economic development. The Brundtland Report took the first step in this direction by presenting the link between environmental conservation and economic development. At the dawn of the CBD, developing countries changed their negotiation strategies and linked environmental concerns to benefits and technology transfer. According to the Brundtland Report, a prerequisite for any exchange of benefits is that the sustainability of ecosystems is guaranteed and that both parties to the exchange of natural resources need to agree that the basis of exchange is equitable.[194] The CBD, on the other hand, gives developing countries the possibility to await transfer of technology and other means of economic assistance when sharing their resources.

In the Convention's technology transfer provisions, no difference is considered between the technology owned by the government and that found under private proprietary regimes. According to Article 16, developed countries should take all appropriate measures in order to ensure

---

[193] The IPR-related provisions of the CBD and the interface between the CBD and IPR have been the major reasons behind US refusal to ratify the Convention. The most problematic provisions of the Convention, according to the Bush Administration, were Articles 16(3) and 19(2). See in this respect 'Biodiversity Treaty Risks Interfering with Patent Protection, Official Says', Int'L Trade Rep (BNA) No 25 (June 15, 1992), pp. 1071–2. See also Hardy, C., 'Patent Protection and Raw Materials: The Convention on Biological Diversity and Its Implications for US Policy on the Development and Commercialization of Biotechnology', US Pat J Int Bus L, Vol 15 (1994–5), pp. 299–326; Berke, R., 'Clinton Declares New U.S. Policies for Environment', *NY Times* (22 April 1993), stating that President Clinton expressed concerns similar to those of President Bush regarding certain provisions of the CBD. Clinton however signed the CBD, without ratifying it. See also the interpretative statement that accompanied the CBD when it was sent to the Senate for its ratification, Convention on Biological Diversity, S Doc No 20, 103d Cong 1st Sess 12 (1993), stating that 'the Administration will therefore strongly resist any actions taken by Parties to the Convention that lead to inadequate levels of protection of (patent) rights, and will continue to pursue a vigorous policy with respect to ... adequate and effective ... patent protection'.

[194] Brundtland Report at 67.

that technology transfer is made possible. The CBD requires that access to and transfer of technology is facilitated under fair and most favourable terms.

2.4.3.5 Supervision of the Convention's implementation and dispute settlement

The Conference of the Parties (COP) is responsible for supervising the Convention's implementation. Parties are required to adopt amendments, annexes and protocols and to consider information concerning projects of relevance to the objectives of the CBD. While the Convention provides for the participation of NGOs and UN agencies, there is no clear provision securing openness and publicity of information, and no independent monitoring or inspection is possible. Finally, the Convention lacks noncompliance mechanisms, even if the COP seems to fulfil such a role.

According to Article 27 of the CBD, conflicts between contracting parties concerning the 'interpretation and application' of the Convention can provide for disputes, of which the only method of settlement is negotiation. According to the same article, the parties may also resort to the International Court of Justice or to arbitration.

2.4.3.6 Disbursement of funds

The financial support provisions of the Stockholm Declaration and the Brundtland Report reflected a financial obligation on the part of all countries, while the CBD targets developed countries as the ones to bear the costs of biodiversity. The COP is vested with extensive powers to determine which parties are under the obligation to provide financial support; at the same time, voluntary contributions are welcomed.[195]

The CBD goes a step further, as it requires that developed countries disburse funds required for the effective implementation of the Convention. More specifically, these funds are to be used to 'meet the agreed full incremental costs to the obligations of this Convention and to benefit from its provisions'.[196] The determination of implementation costs will be a matter for negotiation between the country requiring economic support and the institution that administers the funds in accordance with the requirements set out by the COP. In the case of disagreement between

---

[195] Article 20 CBD. Obviously, developed countries were uneasy with the fact that the COP, where developing countries were the majority, would be able to reach such decisions.

[196] Article 20 CBD.

the two, the country applying for economic support may present its case at the COP.

2.4.3.7 Competent financial institution

The choice of the financial institution to administer and manage the biodiversity funds was as controversial as the financial support provision itself. Most developed countries proposed the Global Environment Facility (GEF),[197] while developing countries lobbied for the establishment of a new institution. Developing countries found support in the Stockholm Declaration and the Brundtland Report, both of which reiterated the importance of a new Biodiversity Fund. According to developing countries, the GEF was ultimately controlled by developed countries. The GEF itself attempted to defend its case at the Seventh Negotiating Session in May 1992, claiming that membership would be universal and that governance of the institution would be transparent, with a new voting system and decisions reached on a consensus basis.[198]

The compromise reached in the final text of the CBD designated the GEF as an interim financing mechanism from the entry into force of the Convention until the first COP or until the COP selects another institution.

2.4.4 The Implementation Process

Monitoring CBD implementation is a task conferred upon the Convention decision bodies, the COP and the Scientific Body (STSTBA), the Working Group on Article 8(j) and the Working Group on Article 15 of the Convention. These bodies, along with the Convention's Secretariat, have responsibility for controlling the implementation and interpretation of the Convention's provisions.

A considerable part of the ongoing work is concerned with environmental issues, a subject falling outside the scope and purpose of this book. However, of great interest are the negotiations of the abovementioned bodies that relate to ABS, technology transfer and transfer of the protection of indigenous knowledge, as expressed in Article 8(j) of the CBD. With regard to ABS, the COP has attempted an indepth analysis of the Convention's Article 15. Apart from the review of existing legislation relevant to ABS,[199] another matter of major importance is the

---

[197] Global Environmental Facility (UN Dev Prog New York, NY) (December 1991).

[198] Seventh Session at 7.

[199] See UNEP/CBD/COP/2/13.

collection of national reports referring to national experiences on IPR and transfer of technology.[200]

The COP's major achievement is, without a doubt, the adoption of the Bonn Guidelines. The Guidelines were recognised as a useful first step in an evolutionary process in the implementation of relevant provisions of the Convention related to access to genetic resources and benefit sharing. The Guidelines are seen as a major means to assist parties, governments and other stakeholders in developing an overall access and benefit-sharing strategy, and in identifying the steps involved in the process of obtaining access to genetic resources and benefit sharing.[201] The COP is constantly building upon the successful use and implementation of the Bonn Guidelines by defining key terms and reviewing the Guidelines' feasibility, their costs and the need for continuing capacity building on the part of the stakeholders involved. An important ingredient is the review of national experiences arising from the use of the Guidelines.[202] Another important contribution is the compilation of a database including case studies concerning ABS,[203] as well as national legislation regulating access to and sharing of benefits arising out of the use of genetic resources.

The CBD has been criticised for being vague and ambiguous and for omitting to dictate direct obligations and rights. Interpretation of the CBD provisions and debated terms has been ongoing since its entry into force, and continues in the work of the COP and in national and regional implementation initiatives.[204]

2.4.4.1 The first (1992–1998) and second (1999–2002) implementation periods

One major priority in the implementation process of the CBD was the establishment of the necessary administrative structures both at the

---

200 See UNEP/CBD/COP/2/17.

201 See COP Decision VI/24.

202 For this purpose, the COP decided in its decision VI/24 to refer to the Ad Hoc Open-Ended Group on Access and Benefit Sharing.

203 Case studies conducted in various parts of the world between 1996 and 2001 provide for a comprehensive overview of national and regional experience of ABS systems.

204 Columbia University School of International Public Affairs presented a paper that identifies the major issues that influence and characterise the level of efficiency of the CBD implementing legislation: 'Access to Genetic Resources: An Evaluation of the Development and Implementation of Recent Regulation and Access Agreements', Columbia University, School of International and Public Affairs (1999).

international and national levels. Further discussion on the substantive issues of CBD implementation focused mainly on the 'environmental' concerns of the Convention, biodiversity conservation, biological safety and ecosystem conservation.

As far as the ABS provisions of the CBD were concerned, this first implementation period was dedicated to the collection of information. While developing countries provided examples from national and regional implementation, developed countries initiated discussion forums in the industrial sector and in research communities such as universities.

The fourth COP, held in 1998, set up a panel of experts on ABS. Representatives of the private and public sectors and of indigenous and local communities were called to participate. The panel's task was to develop 'a common understanding of basic concepts and to explore all options for access and benefit-sharing on mutually agreed terms including principles, access and benefit-sharing arrangements'.[205] This development made the issue of ABS the focus of the COP negotiation and, for the first time, the active involvement of nonstate actors was permitted.[206] The second phase of the implementation process consisted of a review of the four years of consultations and negotiations that preceded the adoption of the Bonn Guidelines. The expert panel focused on issues of prior informed consent and mutually agreed terms, while IPRs were discussed with regard to measures that would need to be adopted by recipient countries.

2.4.4.2 The Bonn Guidelines; the third implementation period (2002)

The Bonn Guidelines were prepared by the Ad Hoc Working Group at the Bonn meeting in 2001, and adopted one year later at the sixth meeting of the COP in The Hague, in April 2002.[207] Negotiations

---

[205] SCBD 2003, 487. See also Siebenhuner, B., Suplie, J., 'Implementing the Access and Benefit Sharing Provisions of The CBD: A Case for Institutional Learning', 53 Ecological Economics (2005), pp. 507–22.

[206] It should be noted that the composition of the expert panel was criticised since all representatives were government-appointed.

[207] Convention on Biological Diversity (CBD) Conference of the Parties (COP), Decision VI/24 A (2002). See also Report of the Sixth Meeting of the COP to the CBD, UN Doc UNEP/CBD/COP/6/20, 2002, Annex 2, The Hague Ministerial Declaration, para 14. The COP-5 established an Ad-Hoc Open-Ended Working Group on Access and Benefit Sharing composed of government-nominated representatives and open to the participation of indigenous communities, NGOs, industry, scientific and academic institutions and intergovernmental organisations. Its mandate was to develop guidelines and other approaches and their respective

preceding the adoption of the Guidelines were characterised by the participation of a multiplicity of actors, including governments, intergovernmental organisations, indigenous communities, farmers, NGOs and scientists.[208]

A provision of the CBD which largely concerns the Guidelines is Article 15.7 and the requirement of 'mutually agreed terms'. The Guidelines recommend the development of standard form agreements and procedures for efficient negotiation. One major objective in relation to the specific article is the minimisation of transaction costs by developing 'framework agreements' under which repeated access to genetic material could be achieved, as well as 'standardised material transfer agreements and benefit-sharing arrangements for similar resources and similar uses'.

Clause 2 of the Bonn Guidelines clarifies that the Guidelines are not to alter the rights and obligations of the parties. This was specified by means of the CBD and will not affect the states' sovereignty over their national resources. The role of the Guidelines is to provide practical guidance to users and providers of TKGR in order to reduce the transaction costs in bioprospecting agreements.[209] According to the Guidelines, and although bioprospecting agreements need to be negotiated on a case-by-case basis, each country needs to develop an overall national strategy with regard to conservation of TKGR, access and benefit sharing.[210]

---

elements to serve as inputs for drafting legislative, administrative and policy measures.

[208] For an interesting overview of the negotiating history and content of the Bonn Guidelines, see Tully, S., 'The Bonn Guidelines on Access to Genetic Resources and Benefit Sharing', Reciel, Vol 12 (2003), pp. 84–98. The initial proposal for the text of the Guidelines was handed in by the Swiss government in cooperation with companies, universities and NGOs submitted to the Panel of Experts during 2001: CBD, 'Building a New Partnership: Draft Guidelines on Access and Benefit Sharing Regarding the Utilization of Genetic Resources', submission by Switzerland, UN Doc UNEP/CBD/WG-ABS/1/INF/5, 2001; see also Study of Complementary Options to Address Access and Benefit Sharing in the Framework of the CBD, UN Doc UNEP/CBD/EP-ABS/2/INF/1, 2001; CBD, 'Regulating Access and Benefit-Sharing: Basic Issues, Legal Instruments and Policy Proposals', Submission by Germany, UN Doc UNEP/CBD/WG-ABS/1/INF/4, 2001.

[209] Countries with no bioprospecting legislation/regulations in place at the time the Bonn Guidelines made their appearance benefited from a valuable checklist in the process of drafting their bioprospecting policies.

[210] Clauses 19 to 22 of the Bonn Guidelines.

A central requirement set forth by Article 15.5 of the CBD is that access to TKGR should be subject to prior informed consent. The Bonn Guidelines provide for the principal elements of a prior informed consent (PIC) system, including the procedures and processes that could be followed. The basic principles of a PIC system are: (1) legal certainty and clarity; (2) access to genetic resources facilitated at minimum cost; (3) restrictions of access to genetic resources should be transparent, based on legal grounds and not contrary to the CBD; (4) consent of the competent national authority in the country of origin. The consent of indigenous communities and other relevant stakeholders should also be acquired.

One of the most important components in the CBD's implementation process is in fact the establishment of competent authorities with the mandate to grant PIC. Establishing such an authority is a rather difficult issue, taking into consideration the lack of necessary infrastructure in the access country, its legal relation to the indigenous communities and the overlapping jurisdiction of a number of different governmental authorities. The reduction of transaction costs, a prerequisite for effective and broad use of bioprospecting agreements, is largely dependent on the establishment of one centralised, well-informed, competent authority, as well as on the drafting of a complete and overarching access and benefit-sharing strategy.[211]

An indicative list of potential benefits in bioprospecting agreements is included in Appendix II to the Bonn Guidelines. Benefits include capacity building, participation in product development, collaboration, access to *ex situ* facilities and databases, technology transfer, institutional capacity building, access to scientific information, social recognition and joint ownership of relevant IPR. Bioprospecting agreements should include a realistic timeframe with regards to the attribution of benefits and make sure that all parties contributing to the management of genetic resources are part of the benefit-sharing scheme.

2.4.4.3 The fourth implementation period (2002–2012)

At the COP meeting in 2002, the parties decided to establish an international regime on equitable ABS as well as on the implementation of Article 8(j).

In terms of the international regime on ABS, the Draft Decision includes a number of provisions of interest.[212] A major point has been the

---

211 See Clause 13 of the Bonn Guidelines.

212 UNEP/CBD/COP/9/ICG/-ABS/CRP1/Rev1, 28 May 2008.

legal status of the forthcoming international regime as a set of legally binding, and nonbinding, principles and norms. An important aspect that the Draft Decision attempts to tackle is its scope. The different options for a definition of the scope vary from conclusive formulations to detailed lists. The main differences between the alternative options relate to the inclusion or otherwise of genetic resources acquired prior to the entry into force of the CBD in 1993; the plant genetic resources subject to the FAO ITPGRFA, in particular those falling under the Multilateral System; and genetic resources found outside national jurisdictions.[213]

The Draft Decision includes a long list of components to be incorporated into the international regime: benefit-sharing mechanisms and benefit forms; access to and transfer of technology; awareness-raising initiatives; monitoring systems and enforcement. Part D concerns traditional knowledge and its protection under the framework of bioprospecting agreements. It expresses an increased interest in issues such as enforcement and compliance, with special regard to alternative dispute settlement and resolution mechanisms as well as recognition and enforcement of judgments across jurisdictions. Other considerations prioritised for the first time here are the calculation of transaction costs in bioprospecting contracts and the valuation of genetic resources. On the other hand, any reference to the relationship between ABS and IPRs is absent. Finally, there is no reference to any IPR-related means of protection for genetic resources and associated traditional knowledge.

In terms of the protection of traditional knowledge, the ad hoc group working on the implementation of Article 8(j) presented its proposal for an international agreement on such protection. The proposal includes issues such as documentation, preservation of traditional knowledge, the development of participatory mechanisms for indigenous and local communities and the general principles for a *sui generis* regime. The *sui generis* regime for the protection of traditional knowledge should take into consideration even customary rules. The development of such a regime should have the cooperation of indigenous and local communities, while at the same time linking the protection of traditional knowledge with successful bioprospecting practices.[214]

---

213 Important categories in this respect are marine genetic resources beyond national jurisdiction and genetic resources found in the Antarctic Treaty area.

214 At the Twenty-First Session of the WIPO Intergovernmental Committee on Intellectual Property and Genetic Resources, Traditional Knowledge and Folklore (the IGC), which took place in Geneva on 16–20 April 2012, the IGC discussed all the working and information documents prepared for that session, in particular documents WIPO/GRTKF/IC/21/4, WIPO/GRTKF/IC/21/5, WIPO/

The Code of Ethical Conduct reiterates principles such as transparency of negotiations with indigenous peoples, the requirement to obtain the prior informed consent of TKGR holders and the fair and equitable sharing of benefits. Other considerations included in the Code of Ethical Conduct concern the recognition and respect of sacred sites and indigenous lands, access to traditional resources and recognition of customary law, as well as the social structure of indigenous peoples. Thus, the Code of Ethics includes a number of principles and objectives that have been reiterated in post-CBD negotiations – without, however, pinpointing the ways/means to achieve these.[215]

2.4.4.4 The Nagoya Protocol

The Bonn Guidelines provided certain assistance to TKGR stakeholders in the drafting of contractual agreements, thus allowing for an *inter partes* accommodation of TKGR rights. Contractual guidelines and model clauses, while helpful, could not provide the necessary protection and left unanswered questions of central importance, such as the enforcement of rights originating from contractual agreements or legislation in the country of origin.

In order to promote the implementation of the CBD's third objective, 'fair and equitable sharing of the benefits arising from the utilisation of genetic resources', the World Summit on Sustainable Development in Johannesburg in 2002 called for the negotiation of an international regime, within the framework of the Convention, to promote and safeguard the fair and equitable sharing of benefits arising from the utilisation of genetic resources. The Convention's COP in 2004 mandated its Ad Hoc Open-Ended Working Group on Access and Benefit-Sharing to elaborate and negotiate an international regime on access to genetic resources and benefit sharing in order to effectively implement Article 15 and Article 8 of the Convention.

GRTKF/IC/21/INF/4 and WIPO/GRTKF/IC/21/INF/8. On the basis of these documents and comments made in plenary, it developed the text 'The Protection of Traditional Knowledge: Draft Articles' in accordance with the General Assembly mandate contained in document WO/GA/40/7. The IGC decided that, as at the close of the session on 20 April 2012, the text would be transmitted to the WIPO General Assembly for consideration by the General Assembly in accordance with the Committee's mandate contained in document WO/GA/40/7.

[215] COP 10 Decision X/42. The Tkarihwaié:ri Code of Ethical Conduct to Ensure Respect for the Cultural and Intellectual Heritage of Indigenous and Local Communities.

The Nagoya Protocol on Access to Genetic Resources and the Fair and Equitable Sharing of Benefits Arising from their Utilisation is the result of six years of intensive, and not always frictionless, negotiations.[216] The Protocol creates a link between the contracting states of the CBD by imposing the obligation to provide for an 'extraterritorial' enforcement of access and benefit-sharing regulations of source countries. Member states shall thus take all appropriate measures to provide that TKGR utilised inside their respective jurisdiction has been accessed in accordance with prior informed consent regulations.[217] In order to be able to monitor the utilisation of TKGR, the parties shall designate checkpoints,[218] while at the same time providing an international prior informed consent certificate for lawfully accessed TKGR.[219] In an attempt to address one of the most centrally debated weaknesses of ABS agreements – the difficulties of enforcement and dispute settlement – parties shall now include dispute resolution clauses in bioprospecting agreements, and also ensure that the countries of origin have the possibility to seek recourse under the national legal systems of the countries of commercialisation.[220]

---

[216] Nagoya Protocol on Access to Genetic Resources and Fair and Equitable Sharing of Benefits Arising from their Utilization to the Convention on Biological Diversity, 29 October 2010, Tenth Conference of the Parties to the Convention on Biological Diversity, Montreal, Canada: CBD, 2011, available at http://www.cbd.int/abs/doc/protocol/nagoya-protocol-en.pdf. On the Nagoya Protocol's compatibility with other means of genetic resources management see Halewood, M. et al., 'National Level of Implementation of the Multilateral System of Access and Benefit Sharing: Notes on Progress and Points of Intersection with the Convention on Biological Diversity', Discussion paper presented to the workshop on the Interface between the International Treaty and the Nagoya Protocol on ABS, ABS Capacity Development Initiative, Rome (January 2013). See also Halewood, M., López Noriega, I., Louafi, S., 'The Global Crop Commons and Access and Benefit-Sharing Laws – Examining the Limits of International Policy Support for the Collective Pooling and Management of Plant Genetic Resources', in Halewood, M., López Noriega, I., Louafi, S. (eds), *Crop Genetic Resources as a Global Commons Challenges in International Law and Governance*, New York: Routledge (2013), pp. 1–36.

[217] See Articles 15 and 16 of the Protocol. For an overview of the Nagoya Protocol see Greiber et al., 'An Explanatory Guide to the Nagoya Protocol on Access to Genetic Resources and Traditional Knowledge', IUCN, Environmental Law and Policy Paper No 83, Bonn, 2012.

[218] Article 17.1 of the Protocol.

[219] Article 17.4 of the Protocol.

[220] Article 18 of the Protocol.

The scope of the Protocol remains, naturally, the same as that of the CBD: genetic resources and traditional knowledge accessed after its entry into force.[221] Article 4.1 provides that the Protocol shall not affect the rights and obligations related to other international agreements. However, the exercise of those rights should not cause serious damage or threat to biological diversity. In the same provision, it is clarified that the Protocol does not create a hierarchy between the Protocol and other international instruments making all potential arguments as to the interpretation of the Vienna Convention inoperable. Article 4.2 leaves space for bilateral or international agreements regulating access and benefit sharing under the precondition that these are CBD and Protocol compliant, thus opening the way for further international developments in the field.

The Protocol provides for the 'fair and equitable sharing' with the source country of the benefits arising from the use of genetic resources,[222] as well as of the benefits arising out of the use of genetic resources held by indigenous communities.[223] This 'fair and equitable sharing' shall be based on mutually agreed terms.[224] Contracting states shall take 'all legislative, administrative and policy measures to implement Article 5.1 but also guarantee the sharing of the benefits with indigenous communities'.[225] Access procedures and prior informed consent are left to national legislation. Nevertheless, the Protocol provides for the framework and major principles ruling the access procedure. Article 6.3 contains a checklist of the important elements that should be included in 'mutually agreed' prior informed consent, but also a set of priorities and objectives. Thus, along with a list of provisions such as a dispute settlement clause and third-party use, there are also the priorities of transparency, legal certainty and clarity and information flow.[226]

221 Excluding though human resources.

222 Article 5.1 of the Protocol.

223 Article 5.2 of the Protocol.

224 Article 5.1 and 5.2 of the Protocol.

225 Article 5.3 and 5.5 of the Protocol.

226 Oldham, P., 'Defusing Disclosure in Patent Applications: A Positive Strategy to Strengthen Legal Certainty in the Nagoya Protocol on Access to Genetic Resources and the Fair and Equitable Sharing of Benefits Arising from their Utilization to the Convention on Biological Diversity and support WIPO's Intergovernmental Committee on Intellectual Property and Genetic Resources, Traditional Knowledge and Folklore', available at http://ssrn.com/abstract=1694899, p. 56.

The Protocol continues by regulating access to traditional knowledge and the requirement of involvement and prior informed consent of indigenous communities in Article 5.2 and Article 7.[227] Article 12 refers in detail to the treatment and protection awarded to traditional knowledge associated with genetic resources. Customary laws and community protocols are to be taken into consideration in the access procedure,[228] while contracting parties are under the obligation to inform TKGR users of the customary laws applicable and to assist indigenous communities in creating internal access policies and minimum requirements and model clauses for benefit-sharing agreements.[229] A new perspective introduced by means of Article 8 is that of national or international emergencies that would require expedient access and benefit-sharing procedures. This provision is a clear reminder of Article 31 of the TRIPS Agreement, giving the opportunity to circumvent 'classic' licensing procedures in favour of compulsory licences in case of national emergencies.[230]

Considering that genetic resources and traditional knowledge are very often shared by a number of different countries and communities, Article 10 of the Protocol offers the possibility of a global multilateral benefit-sharing mechanism, thus providing for a similar approach to that of the ITPGRFA Multilateral System.[231]

Another major contribution of the Protocol is the establishment of national authorities responsible for the access and benefit-sharing procedures. Contracting parties are required to designate a 'national focal point' for access and benefit sharing that will provide all necessary information on the specific national access regulation as well as customary and indigenous laws of relevance for the access to TKGR. That focal point shall be responsible for official liaison to the CBD Secretariat,[232] while

[227] The protection of traditional knowledge and the safeguarding of the rights of indigenous communities are also referred to in other articles of the Protocol. See for instance Article 11 and Article 16 of the Protocol.

[228] See Article 12.1. This provision is particularly interesting taking into consideration that contracting states have not always been on 'peaceful' terms with the indigenous communities found in the countries.

[229] Article 12.3 of the Protocol. Article 12.4 provides that indigenous communities shall be allowed to continue with customary exchange of TKGR in writing and between communities and should not be hindered by national access and benefit-sharing legislation.

[230] Article 7 also provides for the importance of taking food security issues into consideration.

[231] See Articles 10–13 of the ITPGRFA.

[232] The establishment of a national focal point is provided in Article 13 of the Protocol.

the authority might be the same as the 'Access and Benefit-Sharing Clearing-House and Information-Sharing' provided for in Article 14. The Clearing-House will receive and preserve information on the legislative and other measures relating to access and benefit-sharing, and on the national competent authority, prior informed consent, indigenous communities' representatives and model contractual clauses.[233]

2.4.4.5 From Nagoya to Brussels

On 4 April 2012, the EU Commission presented the text of the Regulation of the European Parliament and the Council on Access to Genetic Resources and the Fair and Equitable Sharing of Benefits Arising from their Utilization in the Union.[234] In the Explanatory Memorandum, it was confirmed that the text of the CBD does not provide concrete guidance as to the implementation of its provisions. The objectives of the Regulation are to facilitate access to TKGR and assist European researchers in access and benefit-sharing negotiations. The Regulation becomes an implementing instrument of the Nagoya Protocol, in its turn an implementing Protocol of the CBD. The Regulation emphasises the importance of exchange of information and discussion on ameliorated forms of access, and provides valuable input relating to the implementation of the Regulation and its impacts on different groups of users, incorporating in its text a self-evaluation process both a year after the submission of national reports and ten years after.[235]

The starting point of the Regulation is that TKGR is used by multiple actors in the EU, providing important leads in the processing of the discovery of genetic properties in genetic resources. While it is important to guarantee the continued use of TKGR, it is at the same time vital to limit, to the greatest degree possible, illegal access to TKGR, and to ensure legal certainty and enforcement.

Users of TKGR are under the obligation to carry out due diligence investigation on the origin and legal status of the TKGR they are using. The exercise of due diligence should be documented and saved for a period of time related to the life span of the possible (eventual) innovation. In particular, the user is to document and submit the results of due diligence when applying for a state grant or during a marketing

---

[233] Article 14.2 and 14.3 of the Protocol.

[234] Regulation of the European Parliament and of the Council on Access to Genetic Resources and the Fair and Equitable Sharing of Benefits Arising from their Utilization in the Union Brussels, 4.10.2012 COM(2012) 576 final 2012/0278 (COD).

[235] See Articles 12–16 of the Regulation.

authorisation procedure. Information on the origin, initial rightholders, date of access, rights and obligations related to transferred TKGR and access decisions and mutually agreed terms is to be equally documented and transferred to all subsequent users.[236]

Recital 20 of the Regulation's Preamble provides that in the majority of cases, the collection of genetic resources in the wild is undertaken for non-commercial purposes by university-based researchers and collectors. The Regulation furthermore underlines the role of intermediaries and agents in particular with regard to recently collected genetic resources.

The scope of the Regulation is limited to genetic resources accessed after the entry into force of the Nagoya Protocol. Moreover, the Regulation will not be applicable to genetic resources for which access and benefit sharing are governed by a specialised international instrument.[237] The Regulation clarifies that the user should not be content with reporting the available information, as is the case in some national disclosure requirements, but in cases where the information is not satisfactory should proceed to further investigation and evidence, going as far as to guarantee the legal status of the TKGR and renegotiate contracts of access if that is needed.[238]

The Regulation places under the responsibility of the EU Commission the establishment and maintenance of a Union register of trusted collections.[239] Trusted collections will be included in a special register after a member state's proposal and shall fulfil a number of preconditions related to the procedures for exchanging samples of genetic resources, supply to third parties, etc. Member states are responsible for ensuring that the set requirements are met on a regular basis.[240]

The proposed EU system is completed by the specification of designated national competent authorities and of a Union focal point that will provide information to those wishing to access TKGR in the Union. This will also constitute the necessary liaison to the Secretariat of the Convention on Biological Diversity.[241]

---

236 Article 4 of the Regulation.

237 Such as the ITPGRFA.

238 Article 4(b) and 4(c) of the Regulation.

239 Article 5 of the Regulation.

240 Collections that fail to fulfil the requirements will be removed from the Union register, Article 5.5 of the Regulation.

241 Article 6 of the Regulation.

Article 7 of the Regulation describes in detail the applicable monitoring mechanisms where users are bound to due diligence procedures. The results of these control mechanisms shall be transferred by the member states to the Commission every two years.[242] Furthermore, the Commission will request that competent authorities perform checks to verify compliance, to be performed either on the basis of information raising concerns regarding noncompliance or on the basis of concerns provided by a third party. These checks will be made in relation to either measures related to the due diligence procedure, records and documentation of performed due diligence, field audits or examination in instances as those provided for under Article 7.[243] Shortcomings in such checks will be documented and the competent authority will propose a list of remedial actions and, where necessary, even interim measures, including seizure of illegally acquired genetic resources and suspension of uses.

Penalties connected to the provisions in Article 4 and 7 of the Regulation shall be determined in detail by member states; however, the Commission provides an exemplification list. Penalties could include fines, immediate suspension of specific use activities and confiscation of illegally acquired genetic resources.[244]

The Regulation is certainly an important step forward in the implementation of the CBD at the EU level. It contains a number of noteworthy provisions relating to the due diligence obligation of users, shifting the focus from the time of access (very often in a non-EU country) to the time of use (often in the EU market). In that way, users bear the burden of proof of compliance with access regulations and benefit-sharing agreements. Ignorance of the origin of TKGR is no longer a viable excuse, as is the case in some national legislation providing for non-mandatory disclosure of origin in patent applications.[245] Should the users of TKGR be uncertain of the origin of TKGR, they should seize

---

[242] See Article 7. According to Article 7, the results shall be forwarded to the Access and Benefit Sharing Clearing House. Article 8 provides that the Commission will also handle applications of associations of users, related to best practice procedures. Best practice procedures will be published in an internet-based register, and will also be connected to the best practices list provided for in Article 20(2) of the Nagoya Protocol.

[243] See Article 9 of the Regulation.

[244] See Article 11 of the Regulation.

[245] This is the case even in Switzerland, sanctioning the nonrespect of the disclosure requirement.

commercialisation or research on the resources in question. Users should be able to present the results and documentation of due diligence in relation to various steps and activities, such as public funding, marketing authorisation or simple commercialisation. The control mechanisms and penalties system provided for under the proposed Regulation are also a positive factor for the efficiency of the new system.

Nevertheless, what strikes the reader of the proposed Regulation is the fact that, just as in the text of the Protocol, no reference is made to the role IPRs play with regard to either benefit sharing or monitoring activities. In the references in Articles 7.1 and 7.2 to acts that trigger the control of due diligence performed by a TKGR user, patent applications and applications of other IPRs are totally omitted. This seems a bit peculiar considering the fact that even mere commercialisation of a product based on TKGR requires proof of due diligence on access compliance. Although a patent application is a non-negligible contribution in the development of new technological products, patenting is not a mentioned activity that requires any form of proof of compliance. While there could be both an understandable and a justifiable objective to keep IPRs out of this new system in order to avoid controversial debates on the role of IPRs in an access compliance system, the fact that the Regulation does not address this important question raises further concerns.

2.4.4.6 The post-Nagoya implementation

The Nagoya Protocol, and as a consequence the implementing EU Regulation, are without doubt important developments in the post-CBD negotiations. The content of the Regulation deviates from previous attempts to address the protection of TKGR, and chooses not to opt for alternatives previously discussed in international fora. Although the perspective adopted is an interesting and realistic one – namely, placing the responsibility of the enforcement of ABS in context, and connecting it for instance to market authorisation procedures or research fund applications – no mention is made of IPRs and how the ABS system is to coexist or be mutually supportive with the IP system. In fact, both Nagoya and its implementing Regulation choose to ignore the important role the IPR system plays in the industries employing TKGR, namely the biotech and pharmaceutical industries. Although several provisions in the Protocol and Regulation concern the TKGR user's obligation to provide evidence of extensive due diligence in the different possible steps of the commercialisation process, no reference is made to the application or registration of IPRs. Patent offices are not included in the list of 'checkpoints', and patent applications are not among the activities referred to explicitly as processes in which ABS compliance will be controlled.[246]

This is of course a rather interesting choice, taking into consideration the vivid international debates on the link between the patent system and the protection of TKGR that preceded the adoption of the Nagoya Protocol. The parallel, and hopefully harmonised, implementation of the provisions of the CBD and those of the TRIPS Agreement has preoccupied the international community since its entry into force. After all, proceeding with a patent application reveals the commercial interest and potential of the invention, since the patent applicant has chosen to bear the costs involved with the patenting procedure, awaiting the reward and benefits of a legal monopoly. An efficient ABS monitoring system would be expected to include the patent application process, as one of the major enforcement mechanisms. It would be rather natural for a patent application to include reference to such due diligence in relation to the description of the invention. Patent offices have experience in the examination of documents, and, by examining the patent application, will be able to control the use of TKGR in the invention. They also have very well-organised databases and archives in which the documentation of due diligence could be archived and made public, if necessary. Article 11 of the Regulation provides for concrete sanction and enforcement mechanisms. Among those, it is stated that, should the user of TKGR be found to act in violation of the Regulation, immediate suspension of the activities is to be ordered. Naturally, the suspension of a patent application would be a very efficient measure for the enforcement of ABS.

Obviously, the noninclusion of patent offices in the list of checkpoints is not an omission. Taking into consideration the difficulties involved in concluding the negotiations preceding the Nagoya Protocol, it becomes obvious that the objective was to remove what was considered to be a politically sensitive issue.[247]

It is a fact that IPRs, and, more specifically, the patent system, are not expressly mentioned with regard to checkpoints and due diligence control, nor with regard to applicable sanctions of noncompliance; however, a question remains as to whether that means that this is excluded. There is nothing in the Nagoya Protocol or in the EU Regulation that prohibits a member state from including a patent office as a checkpoint or providing sanctions that are related to the patent system,

---

[246] See Institute for European Environmental Policy, 'Study to Analyse Legal and Economic Aspects of Implementing the Nagoya Protocol on ABS in the European Union', Final Report (10 August 2012).

[247] Institute for European Environmental Policy (2012).

such as, for instance, the invalidation or rejection of a patent application. Naturally, that would require that EU member states proceed to individual approaches and make maximum use of the EU Regulation's flexibilities. Though this possibility seems to be open, it will not be the first best option for the majority of member states – if for no other reason, due to fear of breaching other international obligations such as those originating in the TRIPS Agreement.[248]

While the implementation of the CBD has previously led to an intense national law-making process in access countries, user countries did not show similar interest in introducing ABS legislation. The Nagoya Protocol requires the introduction of ABS legislation even in developed countries, thus guaranteeing two-tier ABS enforcement possibilities. The EU Regulation slightly modifies this obligation and provides that EU member states are to introduce ABS monitoring legislation, but not necessarily ABS legislation if this is not needed.

ABS monitoring will to a large extent be left to national authorities, such as research grant authorities and market authorisation authorities, that will have to control access that has taken place in accordance with the national ABS legislation of the countries of access. One may of course wonder whether these authorities, already burdened with their normal tasks, will be able to take up the responsibility of enforcing and monitoring the requirements of the EU Regulation, determining whether the due diligence obligation of TKGR users was satisfactory and also evaluating whether ABS legislation in the country of origin was followed. These are without doubt very demanding tasks. What is more, these national authorities will have to make complicated distinctions as to whether the TKGR in question falls under the scope of the Nagoya Protocol (or EU Regulation) by controlling the date of access of the TKGR, or whether these specific TKGRs are instead subject matter covered by the ITPGRFA Multilateral System.[249]

The EU Regulation implementing the Nagoya Protocol has the very interesting effect of providing for extraterritorial enforcement of rights provided by national legislation in the countries of origin. It thus has the beneficial effect of international enforceability of national rules, remedying one of the most difficult aspects of the protection of TKGR – the fact

---

248 Commission Staff Working Document, Impact Assessment SWD (2012) 292 final. This would also entail a potential violation of the TRIPS Agreement.

249 See also Survey of Model Contractual Clauses, Codes of Conduct, Guidelines, Best Practices and Standards UNEP/CVD/ICNP/3/INF/2, 19 November 2013, covering the difficulties in the interface between different systems of access and the implications of the ITPGRFA multilateral system.

that legislation protecting TKGR and regulating access is introduced in the country of origin, while the use of TKGR, commercialisation, and thus the question of enforcement of rights becomes relevant in a completely different jurisdiction. It thus accomplishes the objective that could otherwise be achieved by means of an International Convention. Almost 25 years of negotiation in the post-CBD era have convinced even the most optimistic of those involved of the difficulties in acquiring consensus for an international convention for the protection of TKGR or an international ABS convention accompanied by sanctions.

The Nagoya Protocol, and thus the EU Regulation, solve this difficult issue in a rather simple and direct way, circumventing further negotiations and avoiding the need to deal with issues such as the definition of traditional knowledge – a subject matter of divergence even for the countries of origin. Furthermore, it does not have to provide for a 'one size fits all' system for all TKGR, allowing separate consideration to be made on the basis of the particularities of the country of origin and the structure of stakeholders. With this scheme, countries of origin can preserve their autonomy and the possibility to choose both the form of protection that is the most appropriate for their TKGR and the most applicable ABS system taking into consideration their infrastructure, cultural values and customary law.

Nevertheless, complicated and diverging ABS contractual schemes and the complex national structures of TKGR protection, provided for in some cases in several legislative acts and regulations, will not make things easier for checkpoints. In order for this new system to be viable, ABS legislation has to live up to certain standards. National ABS legislation and legislation providing for the protection of TKGR has to be as transparent and as simple and straightforward as possible. Access countries should make maximum use of this new opportunity to make their national systems of TKGR protection enforceable in the countries where use and commercialisation of their TKGR takes place. It would, however, be unrealistic to expect that governmental authorities in countries where use takes place (checkpoints) will be able to monitor and enforce ABS and TKGR legislation should these prove to be very complicated, involving several layers of rightholders, competing governmental authorities, unclear provisions and applicable provisions found in different legislative acts.

Post-CBD negotiations focused on remedying two considerable weaknesses of the CBD, namely the lack of a specific legal entitlement for TKGR and the lack of clarity on the relation between the protection of TKGR and the IP system as a whole. The Nagoya Protocol has definitely not brought any clarity to those central questions. The protection of

TKGR remains an issue for national or regional legislative acts to accommodate, and as such remains fragmented; the relation of TKGR to the IP system as a whole is still rather unclear. The extraterritorial enforcement of ABS contracts and access legislation by means of the Nagoya Protocol is without a doubt a step in the right direction: the question is, will this step lead to a stumble and fall within the almighty international IP system.

2.4.4.7 The WIPO Draft Treaties for the Protection of Traditional Knowledge and Traditional Cultural Expressions

After 13 years of negotiation, the World Intellectual Property Organization (WIPO) Intergovernmental Committee on Intellectual Property, Genetic Resources, Traditional Knowledge and Folklore has completed the drafting of two international treaties regulating the protection of TK and traditional cultural expressions (TCEs), respectively.[250]

The rights granted by means of the treaties are similar, namely the right to use, the right to prior informed consent, the right to attribution and, finally, the right to compensation. The treaties cover different subject matter: the draft TK Treaty protects 'know-how, skills, innovations, practices, teachings and learnings', while the draft TCE Treaty covers 'any form of artistic and literary, creative and other spiritual expression'.[251]

Source communities have the right to maintain control over and develop their traditions, and to prevent their use by others. When the right to use is granted, third parties are expected to proceed in a manner that respects the culture and traditions of the source community. The right to use is granted solely after the prior informed consent of the initial rightholders is given. The protection against misappropriation provided by means of the draft treaties is similar to that available under trade secrets protection.[252] Both treaties require that users attribute TK and TCE to the correct source communities. Users are expected to provide proper compensation to the source communities. The draft treaties'

---

[250] World Intellectual Property Organization, The Protection of Traditional Cultural Expressions: Draft Articles, 28th Sess, WIPO/GRTK/IC/28/6 (2 June 2014) (TCE Treaty). World Intellectual Property Organization, The Protection of Traditional Knowledge: Draft Articles, 28th Sess, WIPO/GRTKFGRTK/IC/28/5 (2 June 2014) (TK Treaty).

[251] Pager, S., 'Traditional Knowledge Rights and Wrongs', Virginia J Law & Tech, Vol 20 pp. 82–200.

[252] TCE Treaty, arts. 3.1(a)(iii), 3.2(d); TK Treaty, arts. 3.1(a)(ii), 3.2(d).

ambition is to provide a much needed international system of protection, for an indefinite period of time.

What both draft treaties fail to do is specify the status of beneficiaries, thus leaving unsolved a number of important questions, such as how to draw the line when it comes to recognising groups of beneficiaries, how to prioritise within conflicting claims on the same TK or TCE by different communities and the control that the state may exercise over the rights of communities. In fact, state intervention in and control over TK and TCE protection may entail a set of complications, taking into consideration the fact that the state very often has tense relations with indigenous communities. This dichotomy between the rights of indigenous communities and the sovereignty of the states has been one of the characteristic weaknesses of the CBD, and thus the draft treaties would be a good chance to provide for an internal hierarchy of rights. Unfortunately this has not been prioritised, or has been considered too sensitive to handle.

Both draft treaties opt for a rather broad scope of application. The definitions of the subject matter covered and of the list of beneficiaries allow for a broad application. At the same time, the rights granted are comprehensive.

Although negotiated in another forum – this time one more appropriate than the CBD – and after more than 20 years of national and regional implementation of the CBD, it seems that the draft treaties include one of the major weaknesses of the CBD, that is, its broad scope. Including, in principle, anything relating to tradition under its scope of application entails, unfortunately, rather vague and weak protection.

2.5 TKGR IN INVENTIONS AND PLANT VARIETIES: COMMODIFICATION THE IP WAY

The commodification of TKGR could in fact also be seen as a side effect of the commodification of biotechnological inventions and plant varieties. The international commodification of these two subject matters has been secured by means of the entry into force of the TRIPS Agreement, changing the international scenery of trade of intangibles, and thus also of TKGR trade. Other international instruments of interest in the commodification process are the UPOV Convention and the EC Directive on the Protection of Biotechnological Inventions 98/44 (Biotech Directive).

2.5.1 The TRIPS Agreement

The TRIPS Agreement provided for a drastic change in the field of international IPRs, including enforcement provisions while at the same time placing IP-related disputes under the auspices of the World Trade Organization (WTO) Dispute Settlement Resolution.[253] The patent-related provisions of the TRIPS Agreement are without a doubt those that received the most reaction and that are responsible for the general mistrust in the Agreement as a whole, especially on the part of developing countries.[254] Implementation of the TRIPS Agreement imposes the grant of patent rights on subject matter that was previously excluded and introduces a longer term of protection. TRIPS obviously has a considerable impact on the process of TKGR commoditisation since it provides for the patentability of biotechnological inventions but also for the protection of plant varieties, through patents or other *sui generis* rights.[255]

2.5.1.1 The patentability of biotechnological inventions

Article 27.1 TRIPS provides that 'patents shall be available for all fields of technology'. It is therefore not possible for national legislation to exclude from patentability pharmaceuticals or biotechnological inventions that fulfil the three patentability requirements of novelty, inventive step and industrial applicability.[256]

According to Article 27.3(b), 'members may exclude from patentability plants and animals other than micro-organisms, and essentially

---

[253] For a thorough presentation and analysis of the drafting history of the TRIPS Agreement and comments on its articles see Gervais, D, *The TRIPS Agreement. Drafting History and Analysis*, London: Sweet & Maxwell (1998).

[254] Regarding the globalisation of IPRs and their impact on the global economy see Maskus, K.E., *Intellectual Property Rights in the Global Economy*, Washington: Institute for International Economics (2000), pp. 171–97.

[255] See also Dutfield, G., 'TRIPS-Related Aspects of Traditional Knowledge', Case W Res J Intl L, Vol 33 (2001), pp. 233–49; Correa, C.M., *Intellectual Property Rights, the WTO and Developing Countries: The TRIPS Agreement and Policy Options*, London, New York and Penang: Zed Books and the Third World Network (2000). For an interesting overview of the impact of the dispute settlement and resolution system on the implementation of the Agreement, see Geuze, M., Wager, H., 'The WTO Dispute Settlement Practice Relating to the TRIPS Agreement', J Int Economic Law, Vol 2 (1999), pp. 347–84.

[256] However, since Article 27.1 does not provide any definition of the term 'invention', this allows Member States to exclude subject matter such as computer programs, schemes, methods for performing business, etc. (see Article 52.2 European Patent Convention (EPC)). Patentability requirements are not harmonised and differences in their applications are noted in different jurisdictions.

biological processes for the production of plants or animals other than non-biological and micro-biological processes'. Article 27.3(b) was negotiated during a period of great change in the development of biotechnology. At the same time, the discrepancies between developed and developing countries concerning the protection of biotechnological inventions were so major that consensus on a specific formulation was very difficult to achieve.[257]

At the time of the pre-TRIPS Agreement negotiations, most developed countries already provided for patent protection for living organisms, in the form of microorganisms, cells and DNA sequences. On the other hand, a few countries had adhered to the UPOV Convention.[258] The United States, Japan, Nordic countries and Switzerland were advocating a broad provision covering the patent protection of animals and plants,[259] while developing countries were opposing any form of protection for living organisms.[260] The non-negligible discrepancies between developed and developing countries explain the fact that Article 27.3(b) was the only TRIPS provision subject to early review.

Article 27.3(b) provides that members may exclude plants and animals from patentability. The special terminology employed in the text of the provision – 'plant varieties', 'animal varieties', 'microorganisms', 'essentially biological processes' – was employed in the patent legislation of all major jurisdictions even before the entry into force of the TRIPS Agreement.

2.5.1.1.1 Plant and animal varieties In Europe, 'animal varieties' and 'plant varieties' have traditionally been excluded from patentability.[261] However, the definition of these not-so-unproblematic terms has been

---

[257] On the possibilities to protect biological material by patent rights, see Llewelyn, M., 'Perspectives on Patenting Biological Material' in Heath, C., Kamperman Sanders, A. (eds), *Industrial Property in the Bio-Medical Age: Challenges for Asia*, The Hague: Kluwer Law International (2003), pp. 73–104.

[258] The UPOV protection system has 55 member states. The UPOV 1978 has 29 member states, the UPOV 1991, 24 member states, and the UPOV 1972, 2 member states.

[259] At the time, the EC opposed the patentability of plant and animal varieties.

[260] Stewart, T., *The GATT Uruguay Round, A Negotiating History (1986–1992)*, The Hague: Kluwer Law International (1993), p. 2294. See also Correa, C.M., 'The GATT Agreement on Trade-Related Aspects of Intellectual Property Rights: New Standards for Patent Protection', Eur Intell Prop Rev, Vol 16 (1994), pp. 27–35.

[261] Following Article 53(b) of the European Patent Convention.

dealt with in a number of important decisions of the Boards of Appeal of the European Patent Office (EPO). The term 'animal variety', which is defined as a species or a subunit of a species, is not to be interpreted in such a way as to encompass animals in general.[262] Article 4(2) of the Biotech Directive provided a certain clarification in this regard, stating that inventions that concern animals shall be patentable if the technical feasibility of the invention is not confined to a particular animal variety.[263] It is thus clear that an invention relating to an animal may be patentable as long as the technical aspect of the invention does not reside in a particular animal variety.

The interpretation of 'plant varieties' has followed the same track as that of 'animal varieties'. In the Ciba–Geigy case,[264] the Technical Board of Appeals stated that claims for plant propagating materials that had been chemically treated so as to make the material resistant to other agricultural chemicals were not claims to a 'plant variety'.

In the Plant Genetics Systems case, the Technical Board of Appeals stated that a plant variety 'is characterised by at least one single transmissible characteristic distinguishing it from other plant groupings and which is sufficiently homogenous and stable in its relevant characteristics'.[265] The Board of Appeals concluded that 'while claims relating to plant cells might be patentable, claims which encompass or are based on a plant variety are not'. Such reasoning could entail the exclusion of all genetically modified plants from patentability, and thus the Plant Genetic Systems decision has been harshly criticised.[266]

Plant Genetic Systems is no longer the source of interpretation for the 'plant variety' exception, due to the Biotech Directive and the Novartis case.[267] Article 4(2) of the Biotech Directive states that 'inventions which concern plants ... shall be patentable if the technical feasibility of the invention is not confined to a particular plant ... variety'.

---

262 Harvard/Onco-mouse (1990) EPOR 4; (1989) OJEPO 451 (Exam).

263 Introduced in the EPC by means of EPC Rule 23c(b) (now Rule 27(b)); Implementing Regulations to the EPC (introduced by 1999 OJ EPO 437).

264 Ciba-Geigy/Propagating material application, T49/83 (1979–83) C EPOR 758.

265 Plant Genetic Systems/Glutamine syntease inhibitors (1995), OJ EPO 545.

266 Barton H., 'The Impact of Contemporary Patent Law on Plant Biotechnology Research', in S.A. Eberhart et al (eds), *Global Genetic Resources: Access and Property Rights*. Madison: Crop Science Society of America (1998), pp. 85–97.

267 NOVARTIS/Transgenic plant (G01/98), [2000] EPOR 303, available at http://legal.european-patent-office.org/dg3/pdf/t961054eu1.pdf.

The Enlarged Board of Appeals adopted a similar approach in the Novartis case,[268] providing that a claim wherein specific plant varieties are not individually claimed is not excluded from patentability under Article 53(b) even though it may embrace plant varieties. Consequently, claims that encompass more than one variety are not excluded under Article 53(b). The exclusion is only applicable when the claims cover a plant variety per se.

2.5.1.1.2 Essentially biological processes Article 27.3(b) provides that members may exclude from patentability essentially biological processes for the production of plants or animals. Thus, processes that lead to the production of plants or animals and that are essentially biological may not be patentable.[269] These are processes that 'consist entirely of natural phenomena such as crossing or breeding'.[270] The interpretation of the said exception seems to have evolved around the issue of the degree of human intervention needed in order for a process to fall outside the scope of the category of 'essentially biological' processes. According to the EPO Board of Appeals, the question arose as to whether a claim for an essentially biological process had to be judged on the basis of the *essence of the invention*, taking into account the totality of human intervention and its impact on the result achieved.[271,272] The scope of this exception has been tested recently in G1/08 and G1/07, where the Enlarged Board of Appeal ruled that any process for the production of plants which contains or consists of the steps of sexually crossing whole genomes of plants is in principle excluded from patentability for being 'essentially biological' within the meaning of Article 53(b) EPC.[273]

Closely related to the definition of the term 'biological processes' is that of 'micro-biological processes'. In the Plant Genetic Systems case,[274] the Board of Appeals stated that a microbiological process is a process in which microorganisms or their parts are used to make or modify products.

---

268 NOVARTIS/Transgenic plant.

269 And not the products or offspring of these processes.

270 Biotech Directive, Article 2(2).

271 Lubrizol/Hybrid plant T320/87 (1990) OJEPO 71.

272 The EPO Board of Appeal said in the Novartis case that the view adopted by the Biotech Directive is even more flexible, stating in Article 2(2) that in order for a process to be essentially biological, it should consist entirely of natural phenomena.

273 G1/08 Tomato, G2/07 Broccoli.

274 T 0356/93 (Plant cells) of 21.2.1995.

2.5.1.2 The review of Article 27.3(b)

Article 27.3 (b) contains an inbuilt review provision, with the review to be completed four years after the entry into force of the Agreement. When the revision process was initiated in the 1999 TRIPS Council, developed countries were unwilling to drastically revise the Article's language and were more interested in gathering information on implementation experiences. On the other hand, developing countries proposed a complete alteration of the scope and content of the said article, a change that would reflect other relevant international commitments in the field of biotechnology, such as those provided for in the text of the CBD. The revision of Article 27.3(b) has been approached from diverging angles by different member states. Approaches have included:

- rewriting the Article (suggesting that instead of requiring patenting of microorganisms, it should exclude patents for any organisms or genetic material);
- defining, in detail, what an effective plant variety protection system is;
- extending protection to traditional or indigenous knowledge;
- making explicit linkages with obligations for conservation and use of biodiversity, including mandatory disclosure of the source of genetic materials used in deriving a patented invention, and creating obligations to record arrangements for access to genetic resources as evidence of prior informed consent.

In order for the revision of Article 27.3(b) to proceed in accordance with the rules of Article 71.1, it should take into account the implementation and application experiences of member states. This has been rather problematic, since developing countries have been granted transition periods for the implementation of the TRIPS Agreement and as a result have had no implementation experience to relate to. Accordingly, they would not have had the opportunity to experience the effects of the Article's applicability on their respective economies, in traditional farming practices and in general regarding the interrelationship between users and owners of IPR.[275]

[275] This concern has been highlighted in South African Development Community's Communications, 1 October 1999, WT/L/317. Communication from Norway IP/C/W/167 stated that the revision of Article 27.3(b) should not have an impact on the patentability of biotechnological inventions. On the other hand, the parties should take into consideration the provisions of the CBD, and in particular those regarding the benefit-sharing requirements by means of the

At this stage, India proposed the inclusion of a clause providing for a 'disclosure of origin of genetic resources' requirement in Article 27.3(b).[276] The European Community Member States (EC/MS) have traditionally been proponents of the patentability of living organisms.[277] Patents on genetic resources would be the only means by which to make it possible for source countries and indigenous communities to receive some kind of remuneration. However, introducing a new requirement for patent applicants to provide an official certificate for the origin of genetic resources and the prior informed consent of the source country would only complicate the grant of a patent and thus would not be desirable. Furthermore, the EC/MS were supportive of an international instrument for the protection of traditional knowledge.[278]

The United States has naturally been of the opinion that the text of the TRIPS Agreement should remain intact.[279]

---

revision process. In this respect, compatibility between CBD and TRIPS should be ensured.

276 In the case of the patent *Steptomyces Vioaceus*, a micro-organism accessed from the soil in Hyderabad, India, Patent No 4992376 granted by the USPTO in 1991 to Bristol-Myer Squibb would not be a valid patent. The US delegation, in their Communication dated 20 September 2000 (IP/C/W/209), answered that the said patented invention is a pure culture of *stremtomyces violaceus* which is capable of producing the antibiotic BU-3839T in a recoverable quantity upon cultivation in a culture medium containing assimilable sources of carbon and nitrogen under submerged aerobic conditions. The comparison between the said subject matter and prior art is proof that all three patentability criteria are fulfilled. This artificial distinction between biological and microbiological processes and material was also pinpointed by the African Group in its Communication (WT/GC/W/302).

277 EC/MS Communication, IP/C/W/254.

278 This could partly be achieved through patentability, while geographical indication could be a potential system of protection.

279 Communication from the United States, IP/C/W/162 presented a different approach to the issue of patentability of life forms. According to this approach, the exception to patentability authorised by Article 27.3(b) is not mandatory and biopiracy can be stopped by other means. The US persisted in its initial position regarding the mutual supportiveness of the TRIPS Agreement and the CBD. According to the US Communication of March 2006, effective protection of TKGR is to be found in national access and benefit-sharing legislation, independent of the patent system. A disclosure requirement would not contribute to the protection of TKGR; in support of this argument, the US actually referred to the patents listed in IP/C/W/459, where the patent applicants disclosed the origin of the genetic resources and were still granted patents on TK.

In the 1 October 1999 Communication,[280] a group of developing countries highlighted the need to 'operationalise' Articles 7 and 8 TRIPS by providing effective transfer of technology on fair and equitable advantageous terms.[281] Moreover, Article 27.3(b), should, according to the said Communication, be revised in light of the provisions of the CBD and of the IU (FAO). The latter, according to the Communication, is a very good example, since it has managed to take into account conservation and the sustainable use of biological diversity, protection of the rights and knowledge of indigenous and local communities, and promotion of Farmers' Rights. According to the same Communication, the implementation of Article 27.3(b) should not in any way restrict traditional farming practices such as the right to exchange and save seeds. Anticompetitive practices that could threaten the food sovereignty of people in developing countries should be prevented by measures such as those provided for in Article 31 TRIPS. Paragraph 19 of the Doha Declaration instructed the TRIPS Council to continue the review of Article 27.3(b) TRIPS and to examine the relationship between that and the CBD. In this regard, Articles 7 and 8 of the TRIPS Agreement would be taken into consideration. The Doha Declaration broadened the mandate of negotiations for the Article 27.3(b) revision, while establishing a clear link between the text of the provision and development issues.

In the aftermath of Doha, the EC/MS considered that there was no reason to proceed to an amendment of Article 27.3(b); the negotiations should rather be oriented towards the technical issues of its implementation.[282] In addition, the disclosure requirement should only cover the geographical origin of the genetic resources,[283] and it should not become an additional formal or substantial patentability requirement.[284] In relation to its earlier communication, Switzerland proposed an amendment to the regulations of the Patent Cooperation Treaty (PCT) that would enable

---

280 WT/GC/W/355.

281 The countries were Cuba, Dominican Republic, Egypt, El Salvador, Honduras, India, Indonesia, Malaysia, Nigeria, Pakistan, Sri Lanka and Uganda.

282 EC/MS Communication of 16 September 2002, IP/C/W/383.

283 If the disclosure were to cover more than that, there would be a risk that the system would not be able to function in practice, since a great number of source countries still lack access and benefit-sharing regulations.

284 Civil law remedies, for instance. See also in this respect recital 27 of the Preamble of the EC Directive 98/44 stating that 'patent applications should, where appropriate, include information on the geographical origin of biological material of plant or animal origin, if known … that is without prejudice to the processing of patent applications or the validity of rights arising from granted patents'.

the contracting parties to require patent applicants to disclose the geographical origin of genetic resources.[285] According to the Swiss proposal, such a provision should be added to the Patent Law Treaty (PLT). In cases where the patent applicant fails to provide accurate information upon the origin of genetic resources and on the grounds of fraudulent intention, the validity of the patent should be affected.[286]

Brazil claimed that the absence of a disclosure requirement in the patent system would have as a consequence that the source countries would have to initiate costly and time-consuming procedures to challenge the validity of patents that have already been awarded. The requirement to disclose prior informed consent and the fair and equitable sharing of benefits would not, however, be a burden for the patent authorities, since a patent applicant that has complied with national access legislation would be ready to supply such information. Leaving the sanctions of noncompliance outside the scope of patent law would render it ineffective.[287] Contracts,[288] or national legislation,[289] could not be sufficient to regulate international phenomena such as biopiracy.

On the other hand, developed countries proposed that developing countries' concerns be accommodated by making use of the TRIPS Agreement's flexibilities at the national level. The EC/MS stated that a strict definition of the novelty requirement would in fact exclude all naturally occurring genetic resources from patentability.[290] In this regard, Switzerland presented the most elaborate proposal for a disclosure requirement. In the Communication of November 2004, Switzerland submitted an analysis of alternative forms of such a requirement. A disclosure requirement could, according to the proposal, be formal, informal, optional or mandatory.[291] The disclosure requirement was further elaborated in the Communication of Bolivia, Brazil, Colombia, Cuba, Dominican Republic, Ecuador, India, Peru and Thailand submitting their proposal for a new patentability requirement. According to the

---

285 Communication from Switzerland, dated 21 May 2003, IP/C/W/400.

286 On the other hand, verifying the prior informed consent and the fair and equitable sharing of the benefits would be an extreme burden for the patent authorities and would make the system inoperable.

287 See in this respect Communication from India IP/C/M/39, para 232.

288 Parties are of vastly unequal bargaining strength.

289 National legislation might have no impact upon the rights granted in another jurisdiction.

290 Communication for the European Communities and their Member States to the Council of TRIPS of 17 October 2002, IP/C/W/383. This view was once more presented in the March 2004 Meeting of the TRIPS Council.

291 IP/C/W/433, 25 November 2004.

said Communication, patent applicants would be required to disclose evidence of fair and equitable sharing of benefits with the TKGR rightholders. Failure to comply with the requirement could entail the revocation of the patent, transfer of rights and civil and penal sanctions.[292] A TRIPS Agreement amendment in order to provide for a mandatory disclosure requirement was also supported by Norway. Introducing such a requirement would induce patent applicants to consider CBD compliance. However, under Norway's proposal, the disclosure requirement would not entail patent-related sanctions.[293]

Developed countries' reactions to the TRIPS amendment did not leave room for surprises. The United States, Japan, Australia, New Zealand, Canada and Korea stated that while they were opposed to biopiracy, they were not convinced that the disclosure requirement would be an effective way of addressing the problem.[294] The EU provided that it was willing to negotiate a disclosure requirement, without, however, including any prior informed consent or benefit-sharing requirement.[295] Although the negotiations for the revision of Article 27.3(b) continued, it seems that a major shift occurred between the multinational negotiations and those of the bilateral Free Trade Agreements.[296]

2.5.1.3 TRIPS-plus: bilateral Free Trade Agreements

Bilateral Free Trade Agreements (FTAs) were employed by the US as early as the 1980s in order to increase the level of IP protection in developing countries.[297] Since the entry into force of the TRIPS Agreement, FTAs have been used as an indirect mechanism for sharpening

---

[292] IP/C/W/442, 18 March 2005.

[293] WT/GC/W/566, TN/C/W/42, IP/C/W/, 16 June 2006.

[294] See, IP/C/W/434, IP/C/W/449, IP/C/W/469, IP/C/W/472 and IP/C/W/504.

[295] IP/C/W/383.

[296] See Note from the WTO Secretariat 'The Relationship between the TRIPS Agreement and the Convention on Biological Diversity: Summary of Issues Raised and Points Made', IP/C/W/368/Rev.1 (8 February 2006). The latest WTO document relating to the issue of the compatibility of the TRIPS Agreement with the CBD and the potential revision of Article 27.3(b) was the report of the Director General, 'Issues Related to the Protection of Geographical Indications Provided for in Article 23 of the TRIPS Agreement to Products other than Wines and Spirits and Those Related to the Relation between TRIPS Agreement and the Convention on Biological Diversity', WT/GC/W/633 TN/C/W/61, 21 April 2011.

[297] For a thorough investigation of the FTAs and the impact they might have, see Heath, C. Kamperman Sanders, A. (eds), *Intellectual Property and Free Trade Agreements*, Oxford: Hart Publishing (2007) pp. 3–282.

developing countries' IP legislation to TRIPS-plus level.[298] TRIPS-plus FTAs have traditionally addressed the expansion of patentable subject matter, the redefinition of certain patentability criteria and the facilitation of patents relating to living organisms.[299] During the past 20 years, FTAs have even reflected the relationship between IPRs, trade and biodiversity. They thus provide valuable experience as to how these distinct issues can be bridged and referred to in one binding document.

While any reference to biotechnology – and thus to biodiversity – in FTAs was previously concerned with the strengthening of the IP level of protection, the US FTAs with Peru and Colombia signalled a certain change in the approach adopted. These agreements incorporate 'an understanding regarding biodiversity and traditional knowledge'.[300] In fact, parties to the agreements have recognised the importance of prior informed consent and fair and equitable sharing – principles that also reflect the objectives of the CBD.[301] In some cases, bilateral trade negotiations have been combined with environmental cooperation agreements.[302]

Even the EU, which has generally been reluctant in supporting the protection of TKGR when that would entail a limitation of IPRs, has – in

---

[298] The US continued the aggressive bilateral strategy by using Special Section 301 to suspend trade benefits of countries identified as not adequately protecting IPRs. At the same time, the provisions on IPRs in post-TRIPS trade negotiations have been promoted as being of vital importance in exchange for access to US markets.

[299] The TRIPS Agreement does not refer to the Budapest Treaty on the International Recognition of the Deposit of Microorganisms signed in 1977; however, the majority of FTAs refer to the obligations stipulated in the stated Treaty. The US FTA with Korea and Morocco allows only for exceptions to patentability related to 'public order' or linked to diagnostic, therapeutic and surgical procedures, in that way establishing an obligation to provide for patent protection for plants and animals.

[300] Understanding on Biodiversity and Traditional Knowledge on 12 April 2006, Annex to the Free Trade Agreement between the United States and Peru, available at http://www.ustr.gov/trade-agreements/free-trade-agreeements/peru-tpa/final-text.

[301] It is also stated that the parties shall promote the quality of patent examination to ensure that the conditions of patentability are satisfied.

[302] Canada is a very good example of a country that has used FTAs to strengthen the bilateral protection of TKGR. In the latest FTAs, Canada established provisions regarding the importance of the CBD, putting in place an information system that would prevent illegal access to TKGR.

its agreement with the Forum of Caribbean States (CARIFORUM)[303] – referred to the relationship between IPRs and TKGR with a special focus on traditional knowledge.[304] The CARIFORUM agreement contains a clause regarding the establishment of *sui generis* rights for traditional knowledge and the mutually supportive implementation of the CBD and the patent provisions of the agreement. Finally, the agreement provides for a disclosure requirement reminiscent of the text of Recital 27 of the Biotech Directive.[305] An interesting new aspect related to the CARIFORUM agreement is the identification of products that could benefit from the protection of geographical indications (GIs).[306]

In the EU–Colombia/Peru FTAs, the negotiations proved more dramatic, with proposals being exchanged and the text being adjusted a number of times. The rights and obligations stipulated under the CBD are included in the IP chapter of the agreement – a choice with a certain bearing with regard to potential interpretation of the text. Similar to the CARIFORUM text, the EU–Columbia/Peru FTAs contain provisions on the fair and equitable sharing of the benefits arising out of the use of TKGR, as well as a disclosure requirement.[307] The disclosure requirement is linked to transparency regarding the use of genetic resources and associated traditional knowledge. The sanctioning of such a requirement is, however, left to national legislation. The part of the FTA referring to GIs provides for the extension to other products of the higher levels of protection given to wines and spirits. It includes a mutual protection scheme and a fast-track procedure to protect listed GIs according to agreed levels of protection.[308]

---

303 EU-CARIFORUM EPA. See also Santa Cruz, M., 'Intellectual Property Provisions in European Union Trade Agreements' (June 2007), ICTSD Programme on IPRs and Sustainable Development, Issue Paper No 20.

304 Article 150, entitled 'Genetic Resources, Traditional Knowledge and Folklore'.

305 Although the CARIFORUM uses the term 'source' and not 'origin', which could be considered to include a broader scope.

306 The EU committed to look into the issue of TKGR protection by means of GIs.

307 Available at http://trade.ec.europa.eu/doclib/press/index.cfm?id=691.

308 See also Santa Cruz, M., 'Intellectual Property Provisions in the European Union Trade Agreements and Implications for Developing Countries' (June 2007), available at http:/www.iprsonline.org/resources/docs/santa-cruz%20blue 20.pdf.

The EFTA–Colombia agreement presents the most recent FTA negotiating experience.[309] Its IP chapter contains a section called 'Measures Related to Biodiversity'. The insertion of this section was requested by Colombia and Peru and accepted by Switzerland and Norway. The disclosure requirement in this agreement determines that the parties 'shall' require that the patent applications contain a declaration of origin or source of a genetic resource. Thus for the first time the disclosure requirement becomes an obligation instead of a facultative possibility.[310] Furthermore, this is the first time that a bilateral trade agreement provides for the sanctioning of the disclosure requirement.

The inclusion of protection of TKGR and other biodiversity issues in the text of the FTAs presents considerable challenges for future interpretation and implementation. In this way, for the first time, TKGR protection becomes an integral part of a binding – though bilateral – trade agreement. Consequently, disputes related to the interpretation or application of TKGR protection-related clauses will be an integral part of the agreement and will be subject to the dispute settlement mechanism.

2.5.2 The UPOV Convention

The first UPOV Convention was drafted in 1961.[311] Member states of the Convention were developed countries wishing to enact a form of protection for breeders and the upcoming agricultural industry. This original document was revised in 1972, 1978 and 1991,[312] and the number of acceding member states has increased considerably, with a list of developing countries participating in the system.

The 1978 UPOV Act set out a detailed protection system with regard to the subject matter of protection, eligibility requirements, exclusive rights, terms of protection and exceptions and limitations to exclusive rights.

The 1978 version of the Convention limits the grounds on which plant variety certificates may be annulled and cancelled. The only way to

---

309 The EFTA–Colombia agreement was initially negotiated parallel to the EFTA–Peru one; however, eventually the EFTA–Colombia agreement was finalised separately.

310 The EFTA–Colombia agreement provides also for a PIC requirement 'as far as provided for in their national legislation'.

311 The International Convention for the Protection of New Varieties of Plant from December 1961, last revised March 1991, provided for a *sui generis* regime for the protection of plant varieties.

312 The UPOV 1991 entered into force on 24 April 1998.

circumvent breeders' rights is for reasons of 'public interest', while the right to remuneration should always be guaranteed. Breeders are awarded provisional rights for the period between the filing date and the date on which protection is granted. UPOV 1978 does not impose protection for all plant varieties. According to Article 4,[313] member states shall extend protection to an increasing number of genera or species, starting with five on the date the treaty entered into force, and ending with 24 within an eight-year period. At the same time, member states can exclude certain genera or varieties from protection. Genera, species or varieties that are protected under the plant variety system cannot be protected by patent protection.[314] The subject matter of protection under UPOV 1978 is also extended to discovered plant varieties that have resulted from a natural source of initial variation.[315]

Plant varieties falling under the scope of UPOV 1978 have to be new,[316] distinct from existing or commonly known varieties,[317] homogenous or uniform,[318] and stable.[319] Protection is extended to the plant variety's reproductive or vegetative propagating material. Protection is awarded for a minimum period of 15 years, with the exception of vines, forest trees, fruit trees and ornamental trees, which are protected for at least 18 years.

In the 1978 version of the Convention, the farmers' exception was more of an implicit provision. Article 5 of the Convention, enumerating breeders' rights, did not include any mention of acts of third parties without a commercial purpose. Both saving seeds for use during the next

---

[313] Article 4 of the UPOV Act 1978.

[314] Article 2(1) of the UPOV Act 1978.

[315] Inferred from Article 6.1(a) of the UPOV Act 1978.

[316] A plant variety is considered to be new when it has not been sold on the market for more than a specified number of years prior to the date of the application.

[317] In order to be protected, a variety should be clearly distinguishable in one or more important characteristics from any other variety whose existence is a matter of common knowledge at the time protection is applied for. The UPOV 1978 does not provide for any further definition of the term 'distinguish'.

[318] A plant variety is homogenous with regard to the particular features of its sexual reproduction or vegetative propagation. This requirement is one of the elements of the UPOV protection system criticised as an incitement to diminish variability of agricultural practices.

[319] Article 6 of the UPOV Act 1978. The breeder has to show that the essential characteristics of its variety are homogenous or uniform over time, even after repeated reproduction or propagation.

season and informal seed exchange between farmers were thus classified as acts exempted from infringement.

Under the 1991 Revision, Breeders' Rights experienced a considerable broadening in terms of the scope and strength of the rights granted. UPOV 1991 requires acceding members to protect a minimum of 15 plant varieties and to extend protection to all plant varieties within a period of ten years.[320] Contrary to the 1978 version, the 1991 Revision provided a definition of the term 'plant variety',[321] restricting the flexibility of member states in this sense. Furthermore, the prohibition of dual protection stipulated under UPOV 1978 was removed, and thus the same plant variety can be protected both by plant variety and patent protection.[322] Discovered varieties are protected in the same way as developed varieties, under an explicit provision.[323]

Breeders are protected by any acts of production or reproduction regardless of their purpose or commercial nature.[324] What is more, the scope of breeders' rights extends to harvested material that is obtained by means of the unauthorised use of propagating material of the protected variety.[325]

Obviously, the 1991 version limits the scope of the exception and the excepted use is strictly regulated. It is confined within reasonable limits and acceptable only providing that the legitimate interests of the breeder are preserved. Farmers are not allowed to exchange saved seeds with other farmers for propagating purposes.[326] Parties to the Convention can further specify the conditions and terms for the exempted uses by, for

---

[320] Article 3(2) of UPOV 1991.

[321] According to Article 1(vi) of UPOV 1991, a plant variety is a plant grouping within a single botanical taxon of the lowest known rank which can be defined by the expression of the characteristics resulting from a given genotype or combination of genotypes; distinguished from any other plant grouping by the expression of at least one of the said characteristics; and considered as a unit with regard to its suitability for being propagated unchanged.

[322] When the jurisdiction in question allows for the patentability of plant varieties.

[323] Article 1(iv) of UPOV 1991.

[324] Article 14(1)(i) of UPOV 1991.

[325] Article 14(2) and 14(3) of UPOV 1991. Article 15(2) states: 'Each Contracting Party may … restrict the breeder's right in relation to any variety in order to permit farmers to use for propagating purposes, on their own holdings, the product of the harvest which they have obtained by planting on their own holdings, the protected variety or a variety covered by Article 14(5)(i) or (ii).'

[326] For an interesting review of Farmers' Rights, see Blekeney, M., 'Protection of Plant Varieties and Farmers' Rights', 9 Eur Intell Prop Rev, Vol 9 (2002), p. 24.

instance, determining the seed quantity that could be saved, or the number of pieces of land that are involved.[327]

2.5.3 The EC Biotech Directive

The EC Commission's interest in a Directive concerning the protection of biotechnological inventions dates back to the 1980s. The aim of the Directive was to increase the protection of biotechnological inventions, while at the same time clarifying what patentable subject matter in fact was. The first proposal was rejected by the European Parliament on March 1995. The main reason was the fact that the proposed Directive seemed to remove many restrictions on the patenting of living subject matter. In December 1995, the Commission presented an amended proposal, which took into consideration the ethical dimension of the patentability of biotechnological inventions and the concerns previously expressed by member states.[328]

According to Article 1 of the Directive, member states are required to protect biotechnological inventions under national patent law. Inventions which are new and involve an inventive step and which are susceptible to industrial application shall be patentable even if they include biological material, or a process by means of which a biological material is produced, processed or used.

'Biological material' is defined as any material containing genetic information and capable of reproducing itself or being reproduced in a biological system.[329] Biological material that is isolated from its natural environment or produced by means of a technical process may be the subject of an invention.[330] In the Recitals of the Directive, it is underlined that a DNA sequence without indication of a function does not contain any technical information and is therefore not a patentable invention.[331] Nevertheless, when the sequence is used to produce a protein or part of a

---

327 See for instance Council Regulation (EC) No 2100/94 of 27 July 1994 on Community Plant Variety Rights.

328 The European Parliament posted 66 amendments to the December 1995 text. All 66 amendments were accepted by the Commission. The latter presented a new proposal in August 1997, put before the Council in November 1997, which approved the proposal by a qualified majority. On 16 June 1998 the Council of Ministers passed the Directive.

329 Article 2(1)(a).

330 Even if it occurred previously in nature. See Article 3(2).

331 Recital 23.

protein, or where the specific function of the sequence is disclosed, the DNA sequence could qualify as an invention.[332]

The Biotech Directive contains one provision with direct relevance to the protection of TKGR, namely Recital 27, which states:

> Whereas if an invention is based on biological material of plant or animal origin or if it uses such material, the patent application should, where appropriate, include information on the geographical origin of such material, if known; whereas this is without prejudice to the processing of patent applications or the validity of rights arising from granted patents.

Disclosure of the origin of the biological material is thus encouraged, albeit not sanctioned in the text of the Biotech Directive. The disclosure requirement is, however, not elevated to a mandatory or patentability-related requirement.

2.6 TRADITIONAL KNOWLEDGE IN OTHER INSTRUMENTS OF INTERNATIONAL LAW

The protection of traditional knowledge has been an issue regulated by a number of different international fora, often such that we do not directly relate it to TKGR. In fact, WIPO, in cooperation with the United Nations Educational, Social and Cultural Organization (UNESCO), has organised a number of workshops relating to traditional knowledge and folklore. As early as 1982, the expert committee meeting adopted the Model Provisions for National Laws on the Protection of Expressions of Folklore against Illicit Exploitation and Other Prejudicial Actions.[333] In order to provide for the protection of intangible cultural heritage, UNESCO adopted the Convention on the Safeguarding of Intangible Cultural Heritage, which was subsequently followed by the Convention on the Protection and Promotion of the Diversity of Cultural Expressions.[334]

---

[332] The Directive makes extensive reference to biotechnological inventions relating to the human body.

[333] WIPO, Model Provisions for National Laws on the Protection of Expressions of Folklore against Illicit Exploitation and Other Prejudicial Actions, reprinted in 16 Copyright Bulletin 62 (1982).

[334] See UNESCO, Convention for the Safeguarding of the Intangible Cultural Heritage, 17 October 2003, MISC/2003/CLT/CH/14, entered into force 20 April 2006; UNESCO, Convention on the Protection and Promotion of the Diversity of Cultural Expressions; UN Doc CLT-2005/CONVENTION DIVERSITE-CULT REV (October 20, 2005).

In the field of environmental regulation, the role and protection of traditional knowledge was referred to in the UN Convention to Combat Desertification (UNCCD).[335] The Convention requires that member states provide mechanisms for the 'appropriate return from the benefits derived from traditional knowledge on equitable and mutually agreed terms, to the local populations concerned'.[336] The UNCCD Secretariat has continued working in the field of TK protection and has produced a compilation of the most important applications of TK.[337] The work of the COP has focused on the protection of TK in several sessions, and the work of the Secretariat focuses on views as to how traditional knowledge can contribute to fulfilling the objectives of the Convention.

Another international organisation that has actively worked with the issue of the protection of traditional knowledge is the International Labour Organization (ILO). Convention No 169 is a binding international convention concerning the rights of indigenous and tribal peoples.[338] The predecessor of ILO 169 was a convention from 1957, the Indigenous and Tribal Populations Convention.[339] Its objective was to ameliorate the standard of living of indigenous communities as well as providing the necessary assistance in order for them to adjust to 'modern methods of production and marketing'. Contrary to ILO 107, ILO 169 provides for the inclusion and participation of indigenous communities in projects that affect them and their lands. Although ILO 169 is a positive development compared to its predecessor, it has not met the expectations of indigenous communities. It does not include explicit provisions for the protection of TK and has received little attention among states. This also means that it has a very limited impact on the negotiations for the protection of TKGR as well as for national legislation or for other international law instruments.[340]

---

335 United Nations Convention to Combat Desertification in Those Countries Experiencing Serious Drought and/or Dessertification, 17 June 1994, 33 ILM 1328.

336 UNCCD Article 17.

337 UNCCD Secretariat, *Revitalising Traditional Knowledge: A Compilation of Documents and Reports from 1997–2003*, Bonn: UNCCD (2005).

338 ILO Convention 169, International Labour Organisation Convention No 169 Concerning Indigenous and Tribal Peoples in Independent Countries, 27 June 1989, 28 ILM 1382 (1989) entered into force, 5 September 1991.

339 ILO Convention 107, International Labour Organisation Convention (No 107) Concerning the Protection and Integration of Indigenous and Other Tribal and Semi-Tribal Population in Independent Countries, 26 June 1957, 328 UNTS 247, 2 June 1959.

340 The Convention has been ratified by only 20 states.

The protection of TK has been regulated in a number of human rights instruments. The UN General Assembly adopted the Declaration on the Rights of Indigenous Peoples providing for the right of indigenous communities to maintain, control, protect and develop TK.

The World Health Organization (WHO) has considered the value of TK for global public health and refers to it as 'traditional medicine'. The WHO Global Traditional Medicine Strategy in fact encourages states to integrate traditional and modern scientific medicine.[341]

The protection of TK has been an issue in the work of other UN organisations, such as the United Nations Conference on Trade and Development (UNCTAD)[342] and the United Nations Development Programme (UNDP). Both of these organisations have included TK in their agenda and provided for declarations and policy documents, without, however, going as far as to provide for a binding legal instrument.[343]

2.7 TKGR PROTECTION: A MOSAIC OF INTERNATIONAL AGREEMENTS

2.7.1 Where Commodification Meets the 'Heritage of Mankind'

The goal of the ITPGRFA is to harmonise the provisions of the IU with the CBD. It recognises the sovereignty of the parties over their genetic resources, while at the same time pinpointing the importance of exchanging PGRFA between parties to an agreement. The ITPGRFA reduces transaction costs that could arise from bilateral exchange of plant genetic resources in accordance with Article 15 of the CBD. To this end, it proposes a multilateral system of exchange that would facilitate access to plant genetic resources while at the same time providing for a benefit-sharing mechanism.

The ITPGRFA is an agreement at the crossroads of access and management of genetic resources and the IP system. Thus, the relation of the ITPGRFA to the TRIPS Agreement must, inevitably, be considered. Two of the provisions that have been extensively discussed in this respect are those of Article 12.3(d) and (f), concerning access to PGRFA.

341 WHO Traditional Medicine Strategy 2002–2005 (2002).

342 UNCTAD Sao Paulo Consensus, 25 June 2004, 4TD/410 (Eleventh Session, Sao Paulo, 13–18 June 2004) at para 68.

343 Dagne, T., 'The Protection of Traditional Knowledge in the Knowledge Economy: Cross-Cutting Challenges in International Intellectual Property Law', Intl Comm L Rev, Vol 14 (2012), pp. 137–78.

According to Article 12.3(d) of the ITPGRFA, 'recipients shall not claim any intellectual property or other rights that limit the facilitated access to the plant genetic resources for food and agriculture, or their generic parts or components, in the form received from the Multilateral System'. Obviously, this provision does not limit the patentability of plant genetic resources in general, but only with regard to subject matter that is found in the form received from the Multilateral System. Article 12.3(f) provides that 'access to plant genetic resources for food and agriculture protected by IPRs shall be consistent with relevant international agreements and with relevant national laws'. It could thus be concluded that the ITPGRFA provisions are not to be interpreted contrary to the provisions of the TRIPS Agreement.

The overlapping scope of the CBD and FAO regulations with regard to certain plant genetic resources, but also cases in which genetic resources are solely regulated by one or the other system, have been major factors leading to the adoption of the ITPGRFA.

Article 15.3 of the CBD sets out the scope of the Convention: 'For the purposes of this Treaty, the genetic resources being provided by a Contracting Party ... are only those that are provided by Contracting Parties that are countries of origin of such resources or by the Parties that acquired the genetic resources in accordance with the Treaty.' This article applies from the date of entry into force of the CBD, 29 December 1993. It covers the removal of genetic resources from the country of origin subsequent to this date. However, access to genetic resources from countries that are not countries of origin, as well as countries that, at the time of the removal, were not parties to the CBD, are left outside the scope of the Convention.

Consequently, genetic resources held in *ex situ* collections, in seed banks or even in botanical gardens do not fall under the scope of the CBD. In this respect, the gap is somewhat filled by means of FAO instruments (previously the IU and now the ITPGRFA) that contained no such temporal limitation. Besides this temporal limitation, the scope of the CBD is broader than that of the ITPGRFA, since the former contains all forms of genetic resources, while the latter solely contains plant genetic resources for food and agriculture.

While FAO instruments traditionally opted for a multilateral system of access and a strengthened role of international institutional mechanisms, the CBD expresses a clear preference for bilateral access agreements. This is more than obvious in Article 15 of the CBD, where it is stated that 'each Contracting Party' will reach 'mutually agreed terms' based on 'prior informed consent'. Article 15 requires the 'sharing in a fair and equitable way of the results of research and development and the benefits arising from the commercial and other utilization of genetic resources'.

The CBD, contrary to the ITPGRFA, does not require that benefits should be 'reinvested' in the conservation of genetic resources. The country of origin is thus free to decide where and when to use the benefits in question. The CBD does not make any direct reference to Farmers' Rights but contains a relevant provision regarding the rights of indigenous communities.

The wording of Article 8(j) is rather vague, allowing for considerable discretion in the implementation of the provision. These obligations are accompanied by phrases such as 'as far as possible and appropriate' and subject to national legislation'. In other words, while the CBD proclaims the need and importance to guarantee the fair and equitable sharing of benefits, it fails to include a binding provision to this end. In addition, further interpretation is needed as to whether it is the state or the indigenous communities that are entitled to the benefits and, in the case that both of them are the beneficiaries, how such 'sharing' would be possible.

The IU, on the other hand (and the ITPGRFA later on), presents an alternative model of multilateral benefit-sharing mechanism concretised in the form of a fund. The role of the fund is not to reward traditional knowledge, but rather to invest in capacity building for improved PGRFA management and conservation.

The FAO/CBD interface, and more specifically the interface between the bilateral bioprospecting approach of the CBD also advocated by the Nagoya Protocol and the Multilateral System created by means of the ITPGRFA, is a troubling issue for member states, which have to implement systems of access and benefit sharing and at the same time take into consideration international IP standards.

One important issue to consider is the scope of the Multilateral System – that is, the plant genetic resources that are to be included under the Multilateral System. In fact, the Multilateral System was not created with the intention of being limited to the 64 crops and forges mentioned in Annex 1 of the ITPGRFA. The ambition is that the Multilateral System will continue to expand and cover new plant diversity. This expansion is not to take place solely on the basis of such resources falling automatically under the scope of the Multilateral System (for instance, crops in the public domain), but mainly on the basis of voluntary inclusion. This voluntary inclusion might in fact entail the transfer of certain genetic resources from one regulatory framework (that of the CBD and the Nagoya Protocol) to another (that of the Multilateral System). However, such a switch may not be carried out without taking into consideration the interests of all potential rightholders. It is thus important that rightholders are informed of the change, and that their rights are safeguarded by means of the SMTAs.

Furthermore, under the ITPGRFA, parties are to provide facilitated access to plant genetic resources under the Multilateral System for uses 'solely for the purpose of utilisation and conservation for research, breeding and training for food and agriculture, provided that such purpose does not include chemical, pharmaceutical and other non-food/ feed industrial uses'. The question that arises is what happens when a request for access to a plant genetic resource covered by the Multilateral System aims at one of the uses expressly excluded from the scope of the Multilateral System. What are the responsibilities of the holder of these resources (for instance of a gene bank), which SMTAs are to be used and how does the holder control whether the alleged uses are actually the real ones?

Another aspect that might create complications in the CBD/ Multilateral System interface is the fact that CBD implementation has been a time-consuming and very often cumbersome procedure for several member states, and thus when legislation regulating access is finally introduced it acquires a central place in the field of access to plant genetic resources. While this is a positive development for the regulation of access of such resources falling under the scope of the CBD, it might create hindrances for the introduction of an alternative access regulation, such as for PGRFA included under the Multilateral System. In cases where different governmental agencies are responsible for the respective systems, the situation may become even more complicated. A factor that further contributes to this end is the fact that the CBD enjoys a higher level of recognition and awareness, and at the same time a higher status, than the ITPGRFA. The difference in the way these two different systems are handled, in some cases justified partly by the fact that the CBD is 11 years older than the ITPGRFA, is also obvious when considering which governmental authorities have the responsibility to implement the respective regulatory instruments. While CBD is handled by governmental authorities of the highest rank, the Multilateral System is very often the responsibility of agricultural research organisations and departments of genetic resource conservation, which often have a low profile even within their own ministries.

The European Genebank Integrated System (AEGIS) and some European countries have employed the Multilateral System's SMTAs for non-Annex 1 PGRFA. Although this policy choice has been made in order to facilitate the work of governmental agencies and provide for a coherent legal framework of access, it also contributes to the creation of categories of PGRFA with a grey legal status.[344] A concluding remark here is that the CBD provides for a broader scope than that of the FAO Agreements, even though it does not cover genetic resources collected prior to the entry into force of the Convention. While, according to the CBD, access to genetic resources should be followed by benefit sharing, all on the basis of bilateral contractual agreements, the Convention does not offer any international standards for such agreements.[345] It should also be noted that while conflicting interests might exist between the CBD and the TRIPS Agreement, the same does not seem to be the case between the ITPGRFA and the TRIPS Agreement.[346]

2.7.2 The TRIPS Agreement and the UPOV Agreements

States that are members of the WTO, and thus of the TRIPS Agreement, are not required to adhere to the UPOV Convention. Article 27.3(b) TRIPS requires member states to provide an effective form of *sui generis* protection for plant varieties.[347] Consequently, member states may adopt UPOV 1991 or UPOV 1978 in order to comply with the requirements of Article 27.3(b).[348] States that are already members of the UPOV protection system need to extend protection to all plant varieties and provide for effective enforcement mechanisms.[349]

---

344 Halewood, M. et al., 'Implementing "Mutually Supportive" Access and Benefit Sharing Mechanisms under the Plant Treaty, Convention on Biological Diversity, and Nagoya Protocol', Law, Env & Development J, Vol 9 (2013), pp. 68–96.

345 For the transfer from the 'commons' to the era of commodification see Thompson, C. 'International Law of the Sea/Seed: Public Domain versus Private Commodity', Nat Resources J, Vol 44 (2004), pp. 841–66.

346 Final Report IPDEV Work Package 5, 'The International Treaty on Plant Genetic Resources for Food and Agriculture – Implications for Developing Countries and Interdependence with International Biodiversity and Intellectual Property Law' (2006).

347 An interesting analysis of the relationship between TRIPS and UPOV can be found in Dbar, B., 'Sui Generis Systems for Plant Variety Protection', Options under TRIPS (April 2002) QUNO.

348 By the end of 2004, 24 states were members of both the WTO and UPOV 1978, while 27 were members of UPOV 1991 and the WTO.

349 With regard to the relation between PVP and TKGR protection see Heath, C., 'Plant Varieties, Biodiversity and Access Rights' in Heath, C., Kamperman Sanders, A. (eds), *Industrial Property in the Bio-Medical Age: Challenges for Asia*, The Hague: Kluwer Law International (2003), pp. 3–32. See also Donavanik, J., 'Plant Varieties and Access Rights in Asia and the South', in Heath, C.,

2.7.3 The CBD–TRIPS Interface

It is obvious that there are some points of 'collision' between the two treaties, taking into account the differences in their starting points as well as their respective underlying principles.[350]

The overarching objectives of the CBD are the conservation of genetic resources and the sustainable use of its components. In particular, the CBD prioritises *in situ* conservation. The task of *in situ* conservation lies with developing countries, which are granted the rights over genetic resources and the right to enjoy a share of the benefits arising out of their use.[351] The TRIPS Agreement, on the other hand, is concerned with exclusive rights on products or processes, with no concern as to their origin or to starting materials.[352]

Indeed, the parallel implementation of the two Agreements' provisions can prove problematic. Members implementing the CBD are under the obligation to cooperate and ensure that IPRs are 'supportive of and do not run counter to the [CBD] objectives'. According to Article 22 of the CBD, the provisions of the Convention will not affect countries' obligations to 'any existing international agreement except where the exercise of these rights and obligations would cause a serious damage or threat to biological diversity'. Guidance as to the issue of parallel implementation of two colliding international treaties can be found in the principle of *lex posterior derogat lex anterior*,[353] which entails that the convention that

Kamperman Sanders, A. (eds), *Industrial Property in the Bio-Medical Age: Challenges for Asia*, The Hague: Kluwer Law International (2003), pp. 49–72.

350 On the potential conflicts between the TRIPS Agreement and the CBD, see Zerbe N. 'Biodiversity, Ownership, and Indigenous Knowledge: Exploring Legal Frameworks for Community, Farmers and Intellectual Property Rights in Africa', Ecological Economics, Vol 53 (2005), pp. 493–506.

351 Curci, J., 'The New Challenges to the International Patentability of Biotechnology: Legal Relations between the WTO Treaty on Trade-Related Aspects of Intellectual Property Rights and the Convention on Biological Diversity', Intl L & Mgmt Rev, Vol 2 (2005–6), pp. 1–42, Helfer, L.R., 'Regime Shifting: The TRIPS Agreement and the New Dynamics of International Intellectual Property Lawmaking', Yale J Int Law, Vol 29 (2004), pp. 2–81.

352 For the implications of the TRIPS Agreement on TKGR protection and the CBD, see Gervais, D., 'Intellectual Property, Trade & Development: The State of Play', Fordham L Rev, Vol 74 (2005–6), pp. 505–34.

353 See Article 30 of the Vienna Law of the Treaties.

has been signed last is the one to prevail. The application of this principle of treaty interpretation would entail the prevalence of the TRIPS Agreement.[354]

2.7.3.1 The precautionary principle in the CBD and in the TRIPS Agreement

According to the precautionary principle, measures for the protection of the environment are to be taken into consideration where a serious threat exists. The precautionary principle was codified in Principle 15 of the Rio Declaration, providing that 'When there are threats of serious or irreversible damage, lack of full scientific certainty shall not be used as a reason for postponing cost-effective measures to prevent environmental degradation'. The same principle is found in international treaties, national legislation and domestic court decisions.[355] In the Preamble of the CBD it is stated that 'where there is a threat of significant reduction or loss of biological diversity, lack of full scientific certainty should not be used as a reason for postponing measures to avoid or minimize such threat'.[356]

The 'precautionary principle' or precautionary approach has been incorporated into several international environmental agreements, and is now recognised as a general principle of international environmental law. In the WTO framework, the precautionary principle applies only in cases where there is scientific evidence that would justify a trade restriction.[357] Where there is a lack of scientific evidence, trade-restrictive measures may only be adopted on provisional terms. According to Article 27.2

---

354 Although this could also be debatable since the two agreements do not have the exact same scope.

355 See UN Agreement for the Implementation of the Provisions of the UN Convention of the Law of the Sea of 10 December 1982 Relating to the Conservation and Management of Straddling Fish Stocks and Highly Migratory Fish Stocks, opened for signature 4 December 1995 (entered into force 11 December 2001); UN Convention on Biological Diversity (1992); The Environmental Code Act of 1998 (Sweden); *Director-General of National Parks and Wildlife Services v. Shoalthaven City Council* (1993, NSWLEC 191).

356 The European Commission has provided for an interpretation of precautionary principle stating that 'recourse to the Precautionary Principle presupposes that potentially dangerous effects deriving from a phenomenon, product or process have been identified and that scientific dangerous effects does not allow the risk to be determined with sufficient certainty': Communication from the European Commission on the Precautionary Principle, WTO document WT/CTE/W/47, of 27 June 2000, paragraph 4.

357 See SPS Agreement, Article 5.7.

TRIPS, members may exclude inventions from patentability in order to avoid serious prejudice to the environment, but only under the precondition that the exclusion from patentability is necessary to prevent its commercial exploitation.

Thus, although the precautionary principle is found both in the text of the CBD and in that of the TRIPS Agreement, the contribution it might make with regard to the harmonious implementation of the two agreements is rather questionable.

2.7.3.2 Article 8(j) of the CBD and the TRIPS Agreement

Article 8(j) calls for the respect, preservation and maintenance of traditional knowledge that is associated with biodiversity at the national level, provided such protection is deemed possible and appropriate by each contracting party. Article 8(j) does not require the legal protection of traditional knowledge in the sense of establishing exclusive, enforceable proprietary rights.

The TRIPS Agreement, on the other hand, does not seem to set any limits as to the nature of the invention, provided that it fulfils the patentability requirements. There are actually cases in which TKGR inventions have been granted patent protection.[358] Furthermore, the TRIPS Agreement clearly covers the subject matter of the product of traditional knowledge techniques, namely GIs. Taking into consideration the protection of GIs as well as the fact that TKGR is a trade-related matter, it seems that TKGR protection could fit under the TRIPS umbrella. In any case, the protection of TKGR under existing IPR, where the requirements for acquiring the protection are met, is not per se contrary to the TRIPS Agreement.

2.7.3.3 Article 15 CBD and Articles 27 and 28 of the TRIPS Agreement

According to Article 15.7 CBD, each contracting party:

> shall take legislative, administrative or policy measures, as appropriate, and in accordance with Articles 16 and 19 and … with the aim of sharing in a fair and equitable way the results of research and development and the benefits arising from the commercial and other utilization of the genetic resources with the Contracting Party providing such resources.

---

[358] See WIPO document WIPO/GRKTF/IC/ of April 2003, Information on National Experiences with the Intellectual Property Protection of Traditional Knowledge, where there are examples of patents granted on TKGR-based inventions in Russia and Vietnam.

Article 15.7 stipulates that a bioprospector making use of TKGR is under the obligation to share benefits and associated knowledge arising out of such use with the initial holders of the material. In principle, this obligation is irrespective of any subsequent IPRs that arise, though Article 15.7 makes reference to Article 16.[359]

Thus, in accordance with Article 15.7, any commercial and other utilisation of TKGR should give rise to benefit-sharing mechanisms. Obviously, when such utilisation is performed under the realm of an intellectual property right, monitoring and enforcement of a benefit-sharing mechanism will be easier to achieve. Taking into consideration the fact that TKGR utilisation usually takes place in jurisdictions distant from the one where the resources originated, registration of IPRs could function as an effective way of monitoring and controlling such uses.

The TRIPS Agreement and the IP system in general do not encompass a benefit-sharing mechanism, and no reference is made to the fact that starting material contributes to the development of an invention when this contribution is neither novelty nor inventive step-destroying. Starting materials or the use of sequential innovation do not have an impact on the determination of inventorship, and in the absence of shared inventorship there is no possibility to acquire a share of the benefits originating from the patented invention.

2.7.3.4 Technology transfer under Article 16 CBD and the TRIPS Agreement

According to Article 16 of the CBD, both access to and transfer of technology among contracting parties are essential elements for the attainment of the Convention's objectives. Under this provision, states are to provide for and facilitate the transfer of technology relevant to the conservation and sustainable use of biological diversity. Taking into consideration that patents and other IPRs may have an influence on the implementation of the CBD, parties shall cooperate, subject to national legislation and international law, in order to ensure that such rights are supportive of, and do not run counter to, its objectives.[360]

Article 16.5 leaves a number of fundamental questions unanswered, with its vague formulation. More specifically, the wording 'subject to' and 'ensure that such rights do not run counter of its objectives' does not give an answer to the question: which system would prevail in the case

[359] See also Tejera, V. 'Tripping over Property Rights: Is It Possible to Reconcile the Convention on Biological Diversity with Article 27 of the TRIPS Agreement?', New Eng L Rev, Vol 33 (1998–9), pp. 967–88.

[360] Article 16.5 of the CBD.

that a conflict arises? Would it be possible to circumvent a TRIPS provision that is considered to run counter to the objectives of the CBD? Would patented technology, necessary for the attainment of the CBD objectives, be made accessible contrary to the prescriptions of national legislation and international IP agreements?

Technology transfer is in fact an objective under the framework of the TRIPS Agreement. According to Article 8, member states can provide 'measures necessary to protect public health and nutrition and to promote the public interest in sectors of vital importance to their socio-economic and development'. Article 66.2 includes a technology transfer provision according to which developed countries are under the obligation to provide for incentives for the promotion and the encouragement of technology transfer to least developed countries. Technology transfers can be conducted either by informal or formal means.

Furthermore, the TRIPS Agreement provides in its objectives and principles (Articles 7 and 8) that IPRs protection should contribute to the promotion of technological innovation and the transfer and dissemination of technology, to the mutual advantage of producers and users of technological knowledge and in a manner conducive to social and economic welfare, with a balance of rights and obligations. However, the abovementioned articles have proven to have limited impact on the ways in which other provisions of the TRIPS Agreement are implemented and enforced.

Taking into consideration the vagueness of the international agreements, regional and national implementation initiatives are of considerable interest for any attempt to assess and evaluate entitlements granted on TKGR.

3. TKGR protection: major implementation lines

3.1 CBD IMPLEMENTATION: A WORK IN PROGRESS

Genetic resources are not only the basic components of biodiversity, and thus important from an environmentalist perspective; they are also of growing economic value for humanity, since they constitute building blocks for a range of new products and technological applications in biotechnology, agriculture and medicine.

The drafters of the Convention of Biological Diversity (CBD) left a major part of the traditional knowledge and associated genetic resources (TKGR) protection system to be clarified and settled by means of regional and national implementation. As expected, the implementation process was initiated in developing countries, the major TKGR *demandeurs*. Implementing the provisions of the CBD and thus giving principles such as 'facilitated access', 'prior informed consent' and 'fair and equitable sharing of benefits' concrete form while at the same time developing the necessary institutional basis and administrative routines to guarantee attainment of the objectives has been a challenge. Countries that lacked the necessary institutional capacities and experience in the field faced the challenge of introducing legislation at the national level while at the same time monitoring and participating in relevant international negotiations.

An interesting aspect of the implementation process was its timing. In 1993, when the CBD entered into force, the negotiations leading to the adoption of the World Trade Organization (WTO) package deal – including the TRIPS Agreement – had just been finalised. Countries that previously lacked intellectual property (IP) legislation – or, at least, had excluded the disputed subject matter, biotechnological inventions, from the scope of protection – were faced with the obligation to take their TKGR regulations into consideration and ensure compatibility with the provisions of the TRIPS Agreement.[1]

[1] WTO members that have not yet implemented the TRIPS Agreement need to take into account the requirements of the TRIPS Agreement. Otherwise, they risk ending up in the WTO dispute settlement procedure.

Several states are still in the process of this double implementation. There are also some regional and national implementation initiatives that provide valuable experience and insight into the nature of the proposed legal entitlements, the structure of the institutional framework necessary to put the entitlements in practice and the general form of the protection system provided.

The lack of specific rights and obligations under the CBD and a great deal of unclear interplay between the CBD and other relevant international conventions are major challenges in implementation. In fact, the CBD is an international agreement containing a number of soft law provisions, mainly in the form of general principles to be applied. Therefore, national implementation is required to make main features of the Convention operational, such as 'fair and equitable sharing', 'protection of traditional knowledge' and 'state sovereignty'.[2]

In order to assist in the process of national implementation, regional organisations have developed model laws, guidelines and a coordinated platform for international negotiations. There are three major regional implementation initiatives in the field: the Organization of African Union Model Legislation;[3] the Andean Council Decision;[4] and the ASEAN Framework Agreement.[5] These implementing regulations have the common objective of assisting member states in the drafting of national

---

[2] See section 2.4.3.

[3] On 9 September 1999, the Heads of State and Government of the Organization of African Unity issued a Declaration (the Sirte Declaration) calling for the establishment of an African Union, with a view, inter alia, to accelerating the process of integration in the continent to enable it to play its rightful role in the global economy while addressing multifaceted social, economic and political problems, compounded as they are by certain negative aspects of globalisation.

[4] The original Andean Pact was founded in 1969 by Bolivia, Chile, Colombia, Ecuador and Peru. In 1973, the Pact gained its sixth member, Venezuela. In 1976, however, its membership was again reduced to five when Chile withdrew. Venezuela announced its withdrawal in 2006, reducing the Andean Community to four member states. Recently, with the new cooperation agreement with Mercosur, the Andean Community gained four new associate members: Argentina, Brazil, Paraguay and Uruguay. These four Mercosur members were granted associate membership by the Andean Council of Foreign Ministers meeting in an enlarged session with the Commission (of the Andean Community) on July 7, 2005.

[5] The Association of Southeast Asian Nations includes all ten countries of Southeastern Asia. ASEAN was established on 8 August 1967 in Bangkok, Thailand, with the signing of the ASEAN Declaration (Bangkok Declaration) by the Founding Fathers of ASEAN, namely Indonesia, Malaysia, Philippines, Singapore and Thailand. In 2000, ASEAN adopted the Framework Agreement on

legislation, pinpointing problematic intersections between the CBD and other international agreements and proposing concrete model provisions. Concretising the link between TKGR protection and the IP system has been another central task.

3.1.1 Regional Implementation Initiatives

3.1.1.1 OAU Model Law

The member states of the Organization of African Unity (OAU) have been under considerable pressure to implement the TRIPS Agreement and the CBD in parallel.[6] In order to facilitate this process, the OAU developed model legislation structuring the grant of exclusive *sui generis* rights, compatible with both the TRIPS requirements on IP protection and the 'fair and equitable' sharing of benefits requirement stipulated in the CBD.[7]

The Model Law was the result of a coordination initiative on the part of 25 African countries,[8] and was drafted in direct reference to Article 27.3(b) of the TRIPS Agreement.[9] The primary goal of the model legislation was 'to ensure the conservation, evaluation and sustainable use of biological resources, including agricultural genetic resources and

---

Access to Biological and Genetic Resources concerning the implementation of the CBD and the interplay between its objectives and IPRs.

[6] Concerned with the growing phenomenon of biopiracy, the OAU's Scientific, Technical and Research Commission organised a meeting of experts and the Symposium of Traditional African Medicine and Medicinal Plants in Kampala, Uganda in 1996. Although rather limited in its scope, this meeting represented the first official recognition of the problem of ownership, access and sharing of benefits. The meeting was a forum for the expression of African policymakers' concerns.

[7] For a detailed review of the OAU model legislation see Ekpere, J.A., 'TRIPs, Biodiversity and Traditional Knowledge: OAU Model Law on Community Rights and Access to Genetic Resources', unpublished paper presented at the ICTSD Multi-Stakeholder Dialogue on Trade, Environment and Sustainable Development, Libreville Gabon (2000), available online at http://www.ictsd.org.

[8] For a review of the background and the objectives of the OAU Model Law, see also Ekpere, J.A., '*Sui Generis* Systems: The Case of the OAU Model Law on the Protection of the Rights of Local Communities, Farmers and Breeders and for the Regulation of Access to Biological Resources', paper presented at the International Seminar on Systems for the Protection of Traditional Knowledge', New Delhi, India (3–5 April 2002).

[9] One of the main goals of the Model Law was to assist African countries in the implementation of Article 27.3(b).

knowledge and technologies in order to maintain and improve their diversity as a means of sustaining all life support systems'.[10]

The OAU Model Law opted for a broader scope than the CBD, covering not only *in situ* genetic resources but also those held in *ex situ* conditions.[11] Furthermore, its scope also covers derivatives from biological resources, community knowledge, innovations, technologies and practices, local and indigenous communities and plant breeders.[12] The Model Law defines the scope of access to biological resources,[13] as well as the nature and scope of community rights and plant breeders' rights,[14] and presents necessary institutional arrangements and enabling provisions.[15] It includes detailed provisions concerning the process of applying for access to biological resources and community knowledge,[16] the registration of the application,[17] the grant of access,[18] the contents of the access agreement,[19] and benefit-sharing arrangements,[20] as well as restrictions to the grant of access and revocation of access permits.[21] The importance and necessity of indigenous communities' prior informed consent and prior consultation is underlined in several provisions.[22]

Article 26.1 of the OAU Model Law provides that the rights of farmers will include:[23]

---

10 Article 1 of the OAU Model Law.

11 In that way also covering the genetic resources that fall outside the scope of the CBD but under the ambit of the ITPGRFA.

12 Article 2.1.

13 Articles 3–15.

14 Nature and scope of community rights, Articles 16–24; plant breeders' rights, Articles 28–56.

15 Institutional arrangements, Articles 57–66; enabling provisions, Articles 67–8.

16 Article 4.

17 Article 6.

18 Article 7.

19 Article 8.

20 Article 12. Article 21 specifies that at least 50 per cent of the benefits received under Article 12 will be awarded to the indigenous communities.

21 Article 13 and 14.

22 See Articles 5, 18 and 19.

23 Despite the fact that there have been strong reactions to the scope and nature of rights stipulated in the African Model Legislation, they are quite close to the text of UPOV 1978. According to the 1978 text of the UPOV Convention, farmers were allowed to save seed produced on-farm even when the saved variety was protected under a plant breeders' certificate.

the protection of their traditional knowledge relevant to plant and animal genetic resources;

the equitable sharing of benefits arising from the use of such resources;

participation in decision making at the local and national levels on matters related to the conservation and sustainable use of plant and animal genetic resources;

the right to save, use, exchange and sell farm-saved seed/propagating material of farmers' varieties;

the use of a breeders' variety protected under this law to develop farmers' varieties;

the right to collectively save, use, multiply and process saved seed of protected varieties.

One of the CBD's major starting points is the prevalence of the property rights paradigm. By means of property rights to biodiversity and traditional knowledge, the CBD works in favour of a contractual bilateral market structure that will gradually achieve efficiency and equity in the management of biodiversity. The legal framework introduced by the CBD is introduced as a prelude to the introduction of bilateral market-like contracts between biological resources' holders,[24] on one hand, and their users,[25] on the other.

The OAU, on the other hand, leans towards a communitarian perspective. It focuses on the concept of communal rights, a property structure closely related to the historical centrality and importance of communities in African history and tradition. Part IV of the Model Law is dedicated to community rights, with detailed and explicit provisions regulating the collective rights of indigenous communities. Articles 16 to 23 provide for the recognition of the status of customary law with regard to access to TKGR, but also with regard to 'community intellectual rights'.

An interesting and very much disputed provision of the OAU Model Law is that of Article 9, where it is stated that 'patents over life forms and biological processes are not recognised and cannot be applied for'. This provision could be interpreted as a violation of Article 27.3(b) and has been subject to harsh critique.[26]

---

[24] States, public organisations or indigenous communities.

[25] Biotech and the pharmaceutical industry as well as research centres.

[26] A very narrow interpretation of the provision would avoid it being considered contrary to the TRIPS Agreement, where the subject matter in question would be identical to that received. See also Article 21 of the ITPGRFA.

Although the elaboration of the OAU Model Law has been the result of the active participation of a considerable number of African states, there are only a limited number of national legislation measures developed that have in fact employed its provisions.[27]

3.1.1.2 The Andean Community Decisions

Andean Community Decision 391 establishes a regulatory framework for access to TKGR,[28] and could also be employed in the form of implementation guidelines for the members of the Andean Community wishing to implement the provisions of the CBD.[29] It should be noted that all decisions of the Andean Community are subject to direct applicability.

Decision 391 includes the protection of TKGR of populations that have a different historical, traditional and geographical background than the 'endemic' indigenous communities, such as the Afro-American communities.[30] An important definition provided in Decision 391 is that of the country of origin. For the purposes of the Decision, this is the country that possesses genetic resources in *in situ* conditions, including those which, having been in *in situ* conditions, are now found in *ex situ* conditions. The Decision enjoys a broad scope, specified in Article 3. It covers genetic resources for which member states are countries of origin,[31] their byproducts and their intangible components, as well as genetic resources 'of the migratory species that for natural reasons are found in the territories of the Member Countries'.[32]

Article 3 provides for two explicit exclusions from the scope of the Decision: one relates to a specific subject matter, namely human genetic

---

[27] Countries that have moved towards the elaboration of legislation adopting the OAU Model legislation are Ethiopia, Gambia and Zambia.

[28] The Andean Community is an organisation with four members: Columbia, Bolivia, Peru and Ecuador. This cooperation originates in the Cartagena Agreement signed in 1969 (with Chile as an additional member). Decisión 391 Régimen Común sobre acceso a los recursos genéticos (1996).

[29] Article 5.1 of the Andean Pact affirms member states' sovereignty over their genetic resources. Furthermore, in Article 5.2 it is stated that member states' legislation should comply with the CBD as well as with the provisions of the Andean Pact.

[30] Afro-American communities are separately mentioned but awarded the same status as indigenous communities and local communities. See Preamble point 5 and 6.

[31] The term 'country of origin' enjoys a broad interpretation. See Article 1 of the Decision.

[32] Obviously, this broadens the scope of the term 'country of origin' even more.

resources,[33] and the other to specific forms of exchange of TKGR. The Decision explicitly excludes the exchange of biological resources and the associated intangible knowledge used among native, Afro-American and local communities of the member countries for their own consumption. The Decision proclaims the national sovereignty of the member states, while at the same time stating that genetic resources and their byproducts are the member states' heritage.[34] The Decision's objectives coincide with those of the CBD, with the additional aim of strengthening the negotiating and coordination power of member states in subsequent relevant negotiations.[35] Article 11 includes the national treatment principle, according to which member states will grant each other national and nondiscriminatory treatment in matters relating to access to genetic resources. National treatment may be extended even to third countries that offer equal treatment.[36]

Articles 16–46 provide for detailed rules and procedures relating to the grant of access to TKGR. The procedure followed with regard to access applications is described in detail, while a number of deadlines are included in order to provide for transparent and time-effective procedures. The Decision creates a notification platform between member states regarding applications for access, access authorisations and the suspension and termination of such contracts, in order to coordinate sanctions for noncompliance and exchange information on bad practices.[37]

Decision 391 has taken into consideration the role of IPRs related to technology transfer. In accordance with Article 16 of the CBD, technology transfer shall take place in harmony with the intellectual property laws of the member states. Second, the Decision stipulates in its third complementary provision that no rights over biotechnological inventions based on TKGR will be recognised if access to those has not complied with the provisions of the Decision. Member states may even request nullification or bring opposition to proceedings in other jurisdictions where IPRs are granted.

The third complementary provision provides for a disclosure requirement. As a prerequisite for grant of IP rights, IP authorities shall require the applicant to give the registration number of the access contract and supply a copy of it. To this end, the competent national authorities will

---

[33] This is the dominant interpretation of the scope of the CBD, also confirmed in the Bonn Guidelines.

[34] Article 5.1 of the Decision.

[35] Article 2 of the Decision.

[36] Article 12 of the Decision.

[37] Article 48 of the Decision.

cooperate with the IP National Offices and exchange information on the status of access applications/authorisations and patent applications, respectively.

Decision 391 is much more than a model law: it is the founding platform for the future cooperation of the Andean member states in the field. However, Decision 391 is not the only Andean Decision of relevance to TKGR protection.

Decision 523 on the Regional Biodiversity Strategy for Tropical Andean Countries was a further development in the cooperation between members of the Andean Community.[38] The objectives of the Biodiversity Strategy are the creation of viable, sustainable, regional development alternatives based on the subregion's natural resources and the co-ordination of joint positions at the various international negotiation forums.

The Andean Community makes direct reference to the protection of TKGR in yet another Decision: Decision 486 on the Common Intellectual Property Regime.[39] In Article 3 of this Decision, the Andean Community states that the granting of IPRs will be subject to respect for TKGR protection and conformity with access and benefit-sharing regulations.[40] Furthermore, Article 3.2 of the Decision states that the provisions of the Decision will be interpreted and applied in conformity with the stipulations of Decision 391.

While Article 16 of the CBD makes the application and interpretation of the Convention's provisions subject to member states' intellectual property obligations, Article 3.2 of Decision 486 makes the application and interpretation of the Common Intellectual Property Regime provisions subject to the obligations of the member states originating in Decision 391 regarding access to TKGR and benefit-sharing regulations.

According to Article 26 of Decision 486, patent applications covering genetic resources originating in one of the member states must include a copy of the access contract certifying the access procedures' conformity with the requirement set out in Decision 391. The same requirement

[38] Decision 523 of the Andean Community Council of Foreign Affairs Ministers, adopted on 7 July 2002.

[39] Decision 486. Régimen Común sobre Propiedad Industrial, Lima, Perú, a los catorce días del mes setiembre del año dos mil.

[40] Article 3.2 reaffirms the recognition of the rights and authority of indigenous, African American and local communities in respect of their collective knowledge.

applies with regard to patent applications employing traditional knowledge.[41] Failure to submit a copy of the access contract results in the patent's invalidation.[42]

3.1.1.3 The ASEAN Agreement

The ASEAN Agreement reiterates the importance of the principles stipulated in the CBD; the sovereign rights of member states over their genetic resources; the recognition, respect and conservation of traditional knowledge; the fair and equitable sharing of the benefits arising from the utilisation of TKGR; and finally, the conservation and sustainable utilisation of TKGR.[43]

Article 1(e) provides that member states shall regard biological and genetic resources as sacred heritage of mankind and reject the application of the patent system thereto. Formulation of the rejection of the patent system on TKGR also raises some concerns, especially with regard to the compatibility of the said principle with Article 27.3(b) of the TRIPS Agreement. The rejection of IPRs to TKGR is further reiterated in Article 4.3, where it is stated that member states shall not allow the patenting of plants, animals and microorganisms or traditional knowledge.[44]

The scope of the ASEAN Agreement covers not only the subject matter of protection of the CBD, but also matters excluded from the scope of the CBD, such as TKGR held in *ex situ* conditions prior to the adoption of the CBD.[45]

This Agreement includes three major provisions. Article 10 provides in detail for the application and grant of prior informed consent.[46] Article 11 refers to the fair and equitable sharing of the benefits arising out of the utilisation of TKGR, while Article 12 establishes a Common Fund for Biodiversity Conservation. The Fund will receive a share of the revenues acquired from the commercialisation of TKGR, access application fees and further benefit-sharing arrangements.

---

41 Article 26(i) of Decision 486.

42 See Article 75(g) and (h).

43 Articles 1(a)–1(d) of the ASEAN Framework Agreement.

44 Article 4.3 provides that member states shall not allow for IP protection for human genetic resources.

45 Article 4.2 of the ASEAN Framework Agreement. The ASEAN Framework Agreement shall not apply to the traditional uses of TKGR by indigenous and local communities.

46 The procedure shall be conducted in the language understandable by the indigenous communities. See Article 10.2.

3.1.1.4 National implementation

Regional model laws and harmonisation decisions are valuable support mechanisms in the implementation of the CBD, bringing its vague principles and objectives closer to practice.

However, the operability of TKGR protection depends on national legislation. A number of countries have developed interesting implementing legislation presenting a multitude of different protection schemes, allowing us to draw conclusions with regard to alternative forms of entitlements and the effects these have on the efficient and fair protection of TKGR. This also provides important experience with regard to the flexibilities of the international framework.

3.1.1.5 Peru

Peru was one of the first countries to implement the CBD.[47] In Peruvian legislation, TKGR rightholders are divided into three distinct groups:[48] native communities;[49] Campesino communities;[50] and indigenous communities.[51] Access to TKGR for the development of environmentally sound technologies and for the sustainable use and conservation of genetic resources is a priority.[52] In this respect, national needs are to be taken into consideration.[53] When genetic resources are transferred to an *ex situ* collection and further commercialised or covered by some form of IP protection, a royalty of 2.5 per cent is to be paid to the Peruvian state.[54]

While the Peruvian state is the major provider of genetic resources,[55] indigenous populations can restrict access to 'intangible components' associated with genetic resources.[56] In fact, Peruvian legislation provides

---

[47] Bill to Regulate Access to Genetic Resources (January 1995, modified March 1999).

[48] Article 1 of the Bill.

[49] Native communities have origins in tribal groups of the forest. They share the same idiom or dialect, cultural and social life and have a common and permanent tenancy on their grounds.

[50] Campesino communities are public interest organisations with legal existence and juridical identity, integrated by families that live on and control determined territories, with ancestral, social, economic and cultural ties.

[51] Indigenous communities are defined in the same way as in the ILO Convention 169.

[52] Article 3 of the Bill.

[53] Article 3.2 of the Bill.

[54] Article 4.2 of the Bill.

[55] Article 1.7 of the Bill.

[56] Article 6.1 of the Bill.

for a distinct framework for both the tangible and intangible aspects of TKGR. Genetic resources are subject to national sovereignty, while traditional knowledge is an asset of indigenous populations whose authorisation is required in order to be accessed. It should be noted that indigenous populations' authorisation is required even in cases where access activities are to be performed on their respective territories.[57]

Article 11 of the Bill enumerates the contents of the access application that should be handed in to the competent national authority.[58] A summary of the application papers should be published in the Official Journal of Peru, making it possible for third parties to present their objections to the competent national authority within a period of 15 days.[59] Following the access grant, parties are to proceed to the necessary contractual arrangements.[60] The access procedure has to fulfil a number of requirements, including the participation of national professionals in the collection of material and the gathering of data;[61] compensation for access to material through access to scientific and technical knowledge resulting from the activities;[62] restrictions on the possibility of transferring material to third parties;[63] and relevant clauses regulating future intellectual property protection over the material transferred.[64] Finally, the requester has to deposit duplicate samples of the accessed material.[65]

In the Bill, it is stipulated that the competent national authority will receive 5 per cent of the value of the transaction and 2.5 per cent of the gross margin of profits resulting from the commercial or industrial use of

---

[57] Article 6.3 of the Bill.

[58] For the purposes of this Bill, the competent national authority is the National Commission of Genetic Resources (CONARGE). See Article 29 of the Bill. The access application has to include the name of the requester and the providers of the genetic resources and the intangible knowledge, where that is the case. Furthermore, it has to disclose the identities of the national support institution, the responsible technical person in the project of access, the parties involved in the access project and the geographic area in which access is sought, as well as the terms of collection; finally, it must submit a copy of the complete and detailed access project in which the precise activities of access are established.

[59] Article 12 of the Bill.

[60] Article 13 of the Bill.

[61] Article 21(a) of the Bill.

[62] Article 21(b) of the Bill.

[63] Article 21(e) of the Bill.

[64] Article 21(f) of the Bill.

[65] Article 21(l) of the Bill.

the material in question.[66] The benefits are to be collected in the Fund for the Conservation and Development of Genetic Resources.[67] The Fund is also the institution that collects the monetary fines imposed on parties that have violated access requirements set out in this Bill.[68]

Interestingly enough, the abovementioned royalties do not cover access to the intangible components. This access would be subject to further compensation schemes and agreements.[69] Should access requirements set out in this Bill not be respected, the National Competent Authority can impose a series of sanctions, ranging from cancellation of the access agreement to fines.[70]

Nevertheless, the central provisions of the Peruvian Bill are in fact to be found in its Complementary Provisions. In the First Complementary Provision, it is stated that when the 'requester' applies for a patent or a plant variety certificate on material based upon accessed genetic resources, he or she would have to submit in the patent application a copy of the authorisation of access. Failing to do so could result in denial of a grant or nullification of the patent.[71] In other words, access legislation is directly linked to patent legislation. Noncompliance with the access procedures stipulated in the Bill affects the validity of the patent.

The Bill makes an attempt to regulate the status of *ex situ* collection of genetic resources. By means of its First Transitory Provision, it requires that those involved with *ex situ* collection of genetic resources hand in a report about their technical and legal situation. Failure to do so would result in prohibition from transferring or acquiring any type of genetic resources.[72]

Peru adopted a law on the conservation and sustainable use of biological diversity.[73] The Legislative Act is more of an overriding framework of principles, where general objectives such as the conservation of biological diversity, sustainable use and the just and equitable sharing of benefits arising from the use of biological diversity are

---

66 Article 23.1 and 23.2 of the Bill.

67 Article 23.4 of the Bill.

68 Article 37(c) of the Bill.

69 Article 23.3 of the Bill.

70 For cancellation see Article 28(c) of the Bill. For a fine up to 1000 Unidades Impositivas Tributarias see Article 28(e) of the Bill.

71 First Complementary Provision of the Bill.

72 First Transitory Provision.

73 Law on the conservation and sustainable use of the biological diversity, Law No 26839, June 1997.

provided. Among a majority of regulations of an environmental nature,[74] there are some general provisions of interest such as the affirmation of national sovereignty with regard to conservation and sustainable use of biological diversity.[75] Article 5 underlines the value of traditional knowledge and its role in the conservation and sustainable use of biological diversity. 'Local, native and farmer communities' are to decide upon the access and use of biological diversity, and shall be guaranteed a just and equitable distribution of benefits.[76]

3.1.1.6 Brazil

Brazil implemented the CBD by means of its Federal Bill of Law No 306/95.[77] The Bill's scope of application covers genetic resources,[78] genetic material both *in situ* and *ex situ* and the associated traditional knowledge.[79] Article 2 affirms that genetic resources and derived products are the public property of the Brazilian nation and thus should be transferred only under the preconditions stipulated in the Bill. It expressly excludes human genetic material from its scope of application.[80]

Article 4 includes a long and rather detailed list of definitions of key terms. Local communities and indigenous populations are defined as human groups differentiated by their social, cultural and economic conditions, organised in total or in part by their customs or traditions or by special legislation. Another interesting definition included in the same article is that of 'derived product',[81] which is defined as the isolated natural product of biological origin, or as being structurally based on it, or having been created by the utilisation of a traditional knowledge associated with it.

---

[74] See for instance, Article 5 of Law No 26839, June 1997.

[75] Article 4 of Law No 26839, June 1997. Peru introduced Law No 27811 (published in the official journal, *El Perouano*, on 10 August 2002).

[76] Article 24 of Law No 26839, June 1997.

[77] It deserves to be noted that there are states that have enacted their own legislation. An example is the state of Amapa with its Law No 0388/97. At the same time as Law 306/1995 was enacted, a number of ABS Bills were elaborated in the Senate. Since the adoption of the CBD, Brazil has enacted various national legislation in its attempt to regulate TKGR trade.

[78] According to Article 7, the scope of the Act covers inland, coastal, marine and island genetic resources and their derived products existing in Brazilian territory, or having Brazil as the country of origin.

[79] Article 1 of Bill of Law No 306/95.

[80] Article 3 of Law 306/95.

[81] According to Article 1 this falls under the scope of the Law.

The growing awareness of access and benefit sharing (ABS) and the rising number of ABS agreements in Brazil activated the legislative process, and the federal government decided to issue Provisional Act 2052/2000, the first real ABS law in Brazil. Its implementation was initiated in April 2002 with the establishment of the Department of Genetic Heritage (DGP), a division of the Ministry of Environment, as well as the first meeting of the Genetic Heritage Management Council (CGEN), in which 19 ministries and federal institutions are participating. The DGP is responsible for the administrative procedure of receiving and processing access requests. Access authorisations, on the other hand, are issued by the CGEN.

A fundamental requirement for access is the signature of a contract for use of genetic heritage and benefit sharing, which will ensure that all contracting parties, private or public landowners, indigenous communities and the state will share the benefits of access. Since 2009, the CGEN has approved and registered 22 contracts, most of them relating to bioprospecting at the initial stage of product development. Only one of these contracts concerned a foreign party.

One of the major weaknesses of the system is the fact that where the landowner cannot be specified, the contract cannot be signed. Therefore, there is a forthcoming proposal providing that a contract with CGEN will solely be required where the TKGR will be transferred to a foreign party. In all other cases a contract will not have to be negotiated, and bioprospectors will be required to contribute to a public fund of benefit sharing based on a fixed percentage rate of benefits from commercial sales or licensed patents.

General principles affirmed in the Act include national sovereignty,[82] as well as the requirement of the indigenous populations' prior informed consent for access to genetic resources located in the lands these populations inhabit and for access to their traditional knowledge.[83] Access to genetic resources should be conducted under a petition scheme very similar to the one stipulated in the Peruvian Bill.[84] In the contract of

---

[82] Article 5.II of Law 306/95.

[83] The Act is not applicable to transfer of genetic resources and traditional knowledge from one community to the other.

[84] Article 15 of Law 306/95. The requirements set out are comparable to the ones set out in the Peruvian Bill: identification of the petitioner; identification of the rightholder of natural resources but also of traditional knowledge; the name of the public institution in collaboration with which the project is to be performed. According to Article 16 of Law 306/95, the requester is to proceed to the publication of an abstract of the petition in the Federal Official Gazette.

access, the state, the petitioner and the agency of access are designated as the contracting parties.[85] Where an access agreement involves the transfer and use of traditional knowledge, a separate agreement needs to be annexed where the indigenous population, the rightholder, the petitioner and the access agency will be the contracting parties.[86] In this annex agreement, the terms of fair and equitable sharing of the benefits arising from the utilisation of the traditional knowledge are to be stipulated.[87]

Brazilian legislation makes extensive reference to the issue of confidentiality that covers petition documents and other relevant data. The petitioner is allowed to select nonconfidential information to be included in the published document.[88] The Brazilian Bill regulates a range of different contractual relationships. Parties are given the opportunity to enter into 'provisional bioprospecting contracts'[89] which do not have to comply with the strict requirements of Article 15 of the Bill, but are of limited scope and duration.[90] Additional contracts of access are agreements necessary for the implementation of the framework agreement.[91] These would have to be compatible with the Act but also with the contract of access, to which they owe their existence.[92]

The Brazilian state is on the list of beneficiaries of fair and equitable sharing provisions included in access contracts.[93] Benefits shall be collected in a Fund that will invest in the conservation but also the further research of genetic resources. In the same way as the Peruvian legislation, the Brazilian Bill establishes a clear link between access regulation and patent rights. Patents or other IP certificates on inventions that have violated the provisions of the Act shall be invalidated.[94] Patent

---

[85] Article 19 of the Law. The petitioner has to deposit samples of the material accessed. See Article 39, sole paragraph.

[86] Article 20 of the Law; see Article 39 of the Law.

[87] The field of use of the traditional knowledge needs to be determined.

[88] The selection of nonconfidential information is not possible where issues of public interest, environmental security or protection of the rights of indigenous communities are at stake. See Article 24. See also Article 24, §§1–3.

[89] Article 27.

[90] For scope see Article 27(III). Provisional contracts can be in force only for one year after the date of signing, without the possibility of renewal. See Article 27(I).

[91] Articles 28–32.

[92] Additional contracts become effective when contracts of access are initiated. A nullification of the contract of access leads to the nullification of the additional contract. See Article 32.

[93] Article 35.

[94] Article 41.

applicants should include a copy of the access contract in the application documents.[95]

The scope of application of the Act is broad, covering access to genetic resources held *ex situ* both when these collections are located in Brazil and when the material in question originates from Brazil.[96] This would entail an obligation for a party requiring access to genetic resources held in *ex situ* conditions in another country, but originating from Brazil, to request authorisation of access from the Brazilian competent authority under the prerequisites set out by the Act.

The Act dedicates a separate title to issues that concern the protection of TKGR.[97] In order to facilitate the determination of the rightholder with regard to specific elements of TKGR, the competent national authority is under the obligation to initiate and maintain a traditional knowledge register whereby local communities and indigenous populations can document their traditional knowledge.[98,99] Noninclusion in the list does not have any impact on the rights recognised under the Act. TKGR rightholders are the ones to decide upon the grant of access to traditional knowledge.[100] Access agreements that entail the use of TKGR need to submit the written authorisation of TKGR rightholders.[101] Indigenous populations' right to self-determination with regard to the use of their lands is also recognised; they should therefore be consulted, as well as compensated,[102] when genetic resources are to be accessed on their lands. The populations retain the right to refuse such endeavours that threaten their natural or cultural patrimony.[103] Transfer of technologies of relevance to the conservation and sustainable use of biological diversity is to be prioritised and furthered,[104] without, however, violating IPRs that potentially cover the technology in question.[105]

[95] Article 41, sole paragraph.

[96] Article 42 of the Law.

[97] Title IV, The Protection of Traditional Knowledge Associated with Genetic Resources.

[98] Foreign traditional knowledge can also be included in the TK register. See Article 44 §3.

[99] Article 44 §2.

[100] Article 45.

[101] Article 45, sole paragraph.

[102] Article 46.

[103] Article 46, sole paragraph.

[104] Article 50.

[105] Article 51.

Violations of the Brazilian Bill are subject to sanctions ranging from civil to criminal and administrative.[106]

3.1.1.7 The Philippines

The Philippine Law on Access to Bio-Resources No 247 makes a distinction between two major types of access agreements: the commercial research agreement and the academic research agreement.[107] The legislation regulates the 'minimum' terms to be included in an access contract of commercial nature.[108] Section 5(a)–(c) is concerned with the use of specimens and samples and the obligation to submit samples of all extracted specimens and to disclose all relevant data to the Philippine state. Furthermore, any subsequent commercialisation of products derived from the accessed material or traditional knowledge should be disclosed to the Philippine government.[109]

The Law provides a technology transfer obligation by requiring the participation of Philippine scientists in the related project,[110] as well as by providing for the 'encouragement' of the 'commercial collector' to use the services of Philippine universities.[111,112] Academic research agreements are subject to blurry but comparatively more flexible terms.[113,114]

Administrative Order No 96-20 provides for more detailed regulation of access to TKGR. Section 2 includes an extensive list of definition of key terms. It is worth remarking that the list of definitions provides for a further distinction between lands of different legal status wherefrom the genetic resources are to be accessed, such as ancestral lands and

---

[106] Articles 52–7.

[107] Sections 3.2 and 3.3. The academic research agreement is only applicable in cases where the petitioner is a Philippine university or academic institution, or governmental or intergovernmental entity.

[108] Section 5(a)–(l). Such a contract will be valid for a maximum of three years, with the possibility to request renewal. See Section 5(k).

[109] Section 5(d). The agreement should also include a provision concerning payment of royalties to the Philippine state but also to indigenous communities. Provisions covering other forms of compensation are also possible. See Section 5(e).

[110] Section 5(h).

[111] Section 5(i).

[112] In the Administrative Order, Section 8.2(3) it is stated that the collector of the material will have to donate part of the equipment used in the conduct of the research to the Philippines.

[113] See Section 5(m).

[114] An academic research agreement is valid for a maximum of five years, with the possibility of renewing it.

protected areas.[115] Similarly, the Administrative Order has been more detailed with regard to the classification of the material in question. It clarifies the distinctions between biological diversity,[116] biological resources,[117] genetic material,[118] genetic resources,[119] derivatives and byproducts.[120] Rather innovative here are, firstly, the separate classification of biological resources,[121] and secondly, the distinction between byproducts and derivatives, which in other legislation is treated as a tautology.[122]

The sovereignty of the state over its biological and genetic resources is reaffirmed in Section 16 of the Order. The Order regulates the application procedure in detail and refers extensively to all respective steps and to the documents that need to be submitted.[123] The part of the application procedure that enjoys extensive reference in the text of the Order is that referring to prior informed consent.[124] Rightholders, and other parties that could have an interest in the access agreement, are 'informed' by means of mass media advertisements in which the whole application document is published.[125] Publicity endeavours are combined with other 'information-related' activities such as a call for community assemblies where the project is discussed with regard to its details and relevant documents are made available.[126] The competent national authority in the Philippines is the Inter-Agency Committee on Biological and Genetic

---

[115] Ancestral lands are the lands occupied by members of indigenous populations. See Section 2(d). Protected areas are areas that are designated or regulated and managed in a way to achieve specific conservation objectives. See Section 2.1(x).

[116] Section 2(f).

[117] Section 2(g).

[118] Section 2(o).

[119] Section 2(p).

[120] For derivatives, Section 2(m). For byproducts, Section 2(j).

[121] Biological resources include genetic resources, organisms or parts thereof, populations or any other biotic components of ecosystems with actual or potential use or value for humanity such as plants, seeds, tissues and other propagation materials, animals, micro-organisms, live or preserved, whether in whole or part thereof.

[122] Byproducts are biological and genetic resources such as feathers, furs, internal organs, roots, including compounds indirectly produced in a biochemical process or cycle. On the other hand, derivatives are blood, genes, resins, seeds. It is obvious that the distinction between the two is rather unclear.

[123] Section 6 of the Order.

[124] Section 7 of the Order.

[125] Section 7.1.1 of the Order.

[126] Section 7.1.2 of the Order.

Resources,[127] whose composition, duties and functions are regulated in detail through Section 10 and Section 11 of the Administrative Order.

3.2 PROTECTION OF TKGR WITHIN THE PATENT SYSTEM

Taking into account that the implementation of the CBD needs to evolve under the limitations and rules set by the IPRs, and in particular the patent system, it is important to investigate the possibility of achieving protection of TKGR and at the same time implementation of the principles and objectives within it. One central approach related to the protection of TKGR under the framework of the patent system has been its recognition as 'prior art', a defensive form of TKGR protection. Closely related to the defensive form of protection is the introduction of a disclosure requirement as a formal or substantive patentability requirement, in order to facilitate both the prior art search and the monitoring and enforcement of prior informed consent (PIC) and bioprospecting agreements.

3.2.1 TKGR as Prior Art

The impact of proclaiming the prior art status of TKGR, both on rightholders and on 'users' of TKGR and potential inventors of TKGR-based products, has often been discussed. A non-negligible hindrance in this respect is the fact that prior art does not enjoy an internationally harmonised definition.[128]

Investigating whether TKGR is part of the 'public domain' presupposes defining it. Definition of the public domain has been attempted through two major lines of thought: the positive definition,[129] and the

---

[127] Representatives of various governmental authorities such as the Department of Agriculture, the Department of Science and Technology, the Department of Health, the Department of Environment of Natural Resources and the National Museum of the Philippines, as well as nongovernmental organisations and representatives of indigenous communities, participate in the Inter-Agency Committee on Biological and Genetic Resources.

[128] See Tvedt, M.W., 'How Will a Substantive Patent Law Treaty Affect the Public Domain for Genetic Resources and Biological Material?', J Int Property Law, Vol 8 (2004), pp. 311–42.

[129] The positive definition, developed mainly by Marienhoff, refers to the public domain in terms of a set of public property rights that are inalienable and cannot be limited or expropriated into a private exclusive right. See Tvedt (2004).

negative one.[130] An example of the application of the positive definition of public domain is that adopted by Costa Rica, using its sovereign right to declare genetic resources to be *dominio público* for the benefits of Costa Rican people.[131] Another attempt to proclaim 'public domain' status – this time on an international level – is the Multilateral System of the ITPGRFA, which in principle creates a catalogue of genetic resources that will be kept free and open.[132] However, such instruments are of limited scope, since they refer to limited categories of plant genetic resources.

The defensive protection of traditional knowledge and its recognition as prior art has been one of the central issues in the 'biopiracy' debate. Patents granted on TKGR, such as those covering neem,[133] turmeric[134] and ayahuasca,[135] were considered by some as proof of defective application and examination of the novelty and inventive step requirements.

3.2.1.1 Prior art: its role and definition

The two fundamental patentability requirements are novelty and inventive step.[136] An invention should be 'new' in relation to everything that has been made available to the public. An invention disclosed or 'anticipated' in the prior art will not be granted a patent, or, if it has been granted, the patent could be revoked.[137] The examination of both the novelty and inventive step requirements builds upon and starts with the definition of 'prior art'. According to the general definition of the term, 'prior art' is the entire body of knowledge available to the public before the filing date or, if priority is claimed,[138] before the priority date of the patent application.[139]

---

130 In the negative definition of the public domain, the limits of the public domain will be decided on the basis of what is left outside the scope of IPRs. See Tvedt (2004), p. 318.

131 See Ley de Biodiversidad, No 7788 of April 1998, Article 6.

132 The codes of conducts of CGIAR Centres could in fact be considered precedents of the Multilateral System.

133 US Patent No 4946681 and US Patent No 5124349.

134 US Patent 5401504, granted in 1995 (Turmeric).

135 US Plant Patent 5751, granted in 1986 (Ayahuasca).

136 Article 52(1) of the EPC.

137 Article 138(1) of the EPC.

138 Cf Article 4 of the Paris Convention.

139 With regard to the patentability of TKGR see also Cullet, P., Germann, C., Muller, A.N., Pasadilla. G., 'Intellectual Property Rights, Plant Genetic Resources and Traditional Knowledge', in Biber-Klemm, S. and Cottier, T. (eds),

In Europe, under Article 54(2) of the European Patent Convention (EPC) 2000,[140] prior art is broadly defined as including everything made available to the public by means of a written or oral description, by use or in any other way, before the date of filing of the European patent application.[141]

In Japan, Section 29(1) of the Patent Law provides a definition of 'absolute novelty' in line with that of the European Patent Convention:

> Any person who has made an invention which is industrially applicable may obtain a patent therefore, except in the case of the following inventions:
>
> (i) inventions which were publicly known in Japan or elsewhere prior to the filing of the patent application;
> (ii) inventions which were publicly worked in Japan or elsewhere prior to the filing of the patent application;
> (iii) inventions which have been described in a distributed publication or inventions which became available to the general public through telecommunication lines in Japan or elsewhere prior to the filing of the patent application.[142]

In the Japanese Patent Office's guidelines,[143] it is stated that 'available to the general public' means the information is in a state by which it can be seen by unspecified persons, and does not necessarily imply that it has actually been accessed.[144] Consequently, when traditional knowledge is published on the internet, the date of its publication will be the date of posting on the internet.[145] In the case that traditional knowledge holders wish to invoke an earlier date, they will have to prove the 'earlier' availability to the public.

Rights in Genetic Resources and Traditional Knowledge, Basic Issues and Perspectives, Wallingford: CABI (2005), pp. 112–54.

[140] Convention on the Grant of European Patents (European Patent Convention) of 5 October 1973, as revised by the Act revising Article 63 EPC of 17 December 1991 and the Act revising the EPC of 29 November 2000.

[141] Product process, information, etc. See Guidelines for Examination in the European Patent Office, Part C, Chapter IV, paragraph 5.1.

[142] Note that prior art, under Japanese law, includes prior art worldwide. This is a relatively recent change to Japanese patent law. Prior to amendments that became effective as of 1 January 2000, prior art was limited to what had been disclosed in Japan.

[143] Operational Guidelines on Treatment of Technical Information Disclosed on the Internet as Prior Art (December 1999).

[144] Article 2(3) of the Operational Guidelines.

[145] In this regard, electronic technical information shall be handed in.

The United States adopts a much more limited approach to novelty-destructive prior art. According to 35 United States Code Section 102(a), (b):

> A person shall be entitled to a patent unless—
>
> the invention was known or used by others in this country, or patented or described in a printed publication in this or a foreign country, before the invention thereof by the applicant for the patent, or
>
> the invention was patented or described in a printed publication in this or a foreign country or in public use of on sale in this country, more than one year prior to the date of the application for patent in the United States.

Consequently, in order to constitute prior art, foreign activity has to be described in printed form.[146] Obviously, the approach adopted in the United States causes the most complications with respect to the recognition of traditional knowledge as prior art. Traditional knowledge, usually found outside the US borders, is orally transmitted. Application of Section 102(a) would entail the exclusion of a considerable part of TKGR from the scope of relevant prior art.

In an attempt to remedy the situation, the US Patent and Trademark Office (USPTO) has underlined the need to create more accessible nonpatent-literature databases that will codify TKGR. In this way, TKGR can be documented and placed in classification systems that can be easily searched and retrieved. Traditional knowledge databases would be integrated in the patent information retrieval systems and thus easily accessible for patent examination purposes.[147]

Section 1.104 of Chapter 37 of the US Code of Federal Regulation provides that national applications shall be subject to an international search in order to discover:

> everything that has been made available to the public anywhere in the world by means of written disclosure (including drawings and other illustrations) and which is capable of being of assistance in determining that the claimed invention is not new and that it does not involve an inventive step (i.e. that it

---

[146] In this respect, the Code of Federal Regulations provides that, on taking up an application for examination, the examiner shall make 'a thorough investigation of the available prior art relating to the subject-matter of the claimed invention'. See 37 CFR §1, 104(a)(1).

[147] Letter by Robert W. Saifer, Director General, International Liaison Staff, USPTO, addressed to Dr R.A. Mashelkar, Director General, Council of Scientific and Industrial Research (CSIR), Government of India, dated 27 August 1999.

is not obvious), provided that the making available to the public occurred prior to the international filing date.[148]

There have been a number of attempts to harmonise the definition of prior art, especially in the framework of the long ongoing negotiations regarding a substantive patent law treaty (SPLT) in the World Intellectual Property Organization (WIPO).[149] At the tenth session of the Standing Committee on the Law of Patents (SCP), the United States, Japan and the European Patent Office (EPO) submitted a joint proposal according to which the agenda's major priority should be harmonisation of the definitions of 'prior art', 'grace period', 'novelty' and 'inventive step'.[150] The proposal provided that, once an international agreement was reached on prior art-related issues, discussions in the SCP could focus on other issues. The same proposal, in essence, was submitted to the WIPO General Assembly in September 2004 by the United States and Japan – without, however, ever reaching consensus.[151] Another issue that remains unsolved is that of the compatibility of other international treaties – such as the ITPGRFA, for instance – with direct impacts on the definition of 'public domain'.[152]

3.2.1.2 TKGR and prior art

The codification and publication of TKGR in online databases has been presented both as a remedy with regard to the deficiencies of jurisdictions such as the United States that adopt a narrow definition of prior art, and a means for facilitating its accessibility. The process of publication and classification was one of the major points of interest in the work of the Intergovernmental Committee on Intellectual Property and Genetic Resources, Traditional Knowledge and Folklore (IGC) during the first years of negotiation.[153] To this end, the WIPO prepared a number of documents and provided for practical assistance to TKGR rightholders that wished to document and disclose TKGR.[154]

---

[148] Rule 33.1(a), Regulations under the PCT.

[149] WIPO, Draft Substantive Patent Law Treaty, Standing Committee on the Law of Patents, Tenth Session, SCP/10/4 (September 2003).

[150] SCP/10/9.

[151] WO/GA/31/10.

[152] For an analysis of the impact of the SPLT on public domain and prior art see Tvedt (2004), pp. 315–40.

[153] Classification is necessary in order to integrate TKGR databases in prior art searches. During the first years of negotiations, documentation of TKGR was considered a priority in the work of WIPO.

[154] See WIPO/GRTKF/IC/2/6.

With regard to TKGR accessibility for prior-art search purposes, the IGC proposed integrating TKGR under the patent classification system as a short-term measure in order to later proceed to the development of detailed classification tools for TKGR.[155] Furthermore, TKGR-related periodicals could be included under the so-called minimum documentation rule of Article 15(4) of the Patent Cooperation Treaty (PCT).[156] Indeed, publication of TKGR in online databases has been considered the most appropriate measure for increasing the accessibility of TKGR for patent examiners, and numerous proposals have been made in this respect. The elaboration of a TKGR international database has also been discussed in other international negotiations,[157] which have set out five main parameters: (1) a TKGR database should be an international database available to national, regional and international patent authorities as well as national courts; (2) taking into consideration the high costs of developing such an international database, it would be preferable to link existing regional, national and local databases; (3) this international database would be administered by WIPO,[158] in cooperation with other relevant international bodies; (4) documentation of TKGR should be proceeded on a voluntary basis;[159] (5) the holders of TKGR may decide that part of the traditional knowledge published remains confidential, that is, only available to patent examiners.

The documentation and registration of TKGR in databases may be a solution to the practical problem of accessibility and thus inclusion in the prior art searches of the patent offices, but at the same time it could give rise to a new set of concerns, including risks that such documentation processes entail TKGR disclosure to the public and destroy both trade secret protection and possible patent protection. The disclosure of TKGR to the public would hinder not only third parties' acquisition of IPR, but even that of the indigenous communities (the initial rightholders) themselves. It could also have a negative impact on the potential value of the TKGR itself: no one wants to pay for something that is available to the

[155] See WIPO/GRTKF/IC/2/6, p. 23.

[156] According to Article 15(4) of the PCT, 'the International Search Authority shall endeavour to discover as much of the relevant prior art as its facilities permit, and shall, in any case, consult the documentation contained in the Regulations'.

[157] See Communication to the TRIPS Council, SCIT/4/8, para 41.

[158] WIPO was considered to have the necessary expertise and technical capacity.

[159] Documentation of TKGR should be made with the consent of the rightholders and should have no impact on the possible rights regarding TKGR.

public. The same concerns apply for *sui generis* protection systems that have some kind of a novelty requirement.

The process of documentation/registration of TKGR reached its peak in the late 1990s and was promoted as the primal strategy for the protection of TKGR. WIPO organised a series of regional workshops and prepared relevant documents promoting documentation initiatives with enthusiasm.[160]

3.2.1.3 Disclosure of origin and prior informed consent

The introduction of a disclosure and PIC requirement has been one of the most debated ways of providing a compromise between objectives of the CBD, the current IP system and the implementation of the TRIPS Agreement,[161] with quite an impact on international negotiations concerning the future harmonisation of the patent system, such as the work of the Standing Committee on the Law of Patents (SCP).[162] Obviously, the introduction of a supplementary disclosure requirement in the patent system quickly gained the broad support of developing countries.[163] Its role has been considered so important that it has been directly linked to

---

160 See WIPO/GRTKF/IC/5/5 Report on the Toolkit for Managing Intellectual Property when Documenting Traditional Knowledge and Genetic Resources; WIPO/GRTKF/IC/5/6 Practical Mechanisms for the Defensive Protection of Traditional Knowledge and Genetic Resources within the Patent System; WIPO/GRTKF/IC/4/5 Draft Outline of an Intellectual Property Management Toolkit for Documentation of Traditional Knowledge; WIPO/GRTKF/IC/3/5 Inventory of Traditional Knowledge-Related Periodicals; WIPO/GRTKF/IC/3/6 Inventory of Existing Online Databases Containing Traditional Knowledge Documentation Data.

161 The requirement to disclose information as to the 'origin' of the invention is not a new concept. According to 35 USC §202, contractors are bound by the obligation to inform about government funding in their patent application. Under the said provisions, contractors have a double disclosure obligation: they must disclose the existence of the subject inventions to the funding agency and they must inform that the government may request title to the invention. Such an acquisition, however, is not automatic: 'the agency may request title within 60 days of learning the failure to disclose within the specified times'.

162 Proposal by the USA and Japan for Establishing a New Work Plan for the Standing Committee on the Law of the Patents, WIPO Doc WO/GA/31/10 (27 August 2004).

163 The supplementary disclosure requirement is hereinafter referred to as 'the requirement'. De Carvalho, N.P., 'Requiring Disclosure of the Origin of Genetic Resources and PIC in Patent Applications Without Infringing the TRIPS Agreement: The Problem and the Solution', 2 Wash U J Law & Policy (2003), pp. 371–401.

issues such as developing countries' right to economic development under the UNHCR.[164] A number of developed countries, however, considered its introduction as incompatible with the TRIPS Agreement, and, as a development, hazardous to the patent system as a whole.[165]

Proponents of the requirement have stated that its major objective would be to allow developing countries (and in general holders of TKGR) to monitor use of their resources, respect for benefit-sharing provisions of bioprospecting agreements and general compliance with the national legislation implementing the provisions of the CBD. The group of developing countries lobbying for the inclusion of the disclosure requirement has also argued that the role of such a requirement is important with regard to the credibility of the IP system through reducing bad patents (patents that should not have been granted), enabling the patent office to efficiently examine the inventive step requirement, improving compliance with national laws and PIC provisions and allowing TKGR holders to trace the filing of bad patents and challenge them in the relevant jurisdictions.[166]

Noncompliance with the requirement could lead to various actions, from the imposition of administrative sanctions to the failure to grant or the revocation of a granted patent. Developing countries have asserted that without such a mandatory requirement with direct effect on patentability, possibilities of monitoring inventions that have used TKGR are limited to nonexistent. In a few cases, the contribution of TKGR is the predominant 'inventive' characteristic in a patent. However, while a disclosure requirement accompanied by effective sanctions is presented as the key to obtain compensation for the access and use of TKGR, its compatibility with the current patent system is debatable.[167] In the

---

[164] Proposal by Argentina and Brazil for the Establishment of a Development Agenda for WIPO (with the support of delegations from South Africa).

[165] Working Group on Reform of the Patent Cooperation Treaty, WIPO Doc PCT/R/WG/6/12 (7 May 2004).

[166] The Relationship between the TRIPS Agreement, the Convention on Biological Diversity and the Protection of Traditional Knowledge, WTO Doc IP/C/W/403 (24 June 2003). In IP/C/368/Rev.1 of 8 February 2006, the WTO Secretariat undertakes extensive investigation of the different opinions presented in WTO negotiations regarding the pros and cons of the introduction of a disclosure requirement.

[167] For a discussion on the disclosure requirement and its compatibility to the patent system see Correa, C.M., 'The Politics and Practicalities of a Disclosure of Origin Obligation', Occasional Paper 16, Quaker United Nations Office Geneva (2005); Dutfield, G., 'Thinking Aloud on Disclosure of Origin', Occasional Paper 18, Quaker United Nations Office Geneva (2005); Dutfield, G.

majority of cases, it is TKGR that leads researchers to a new and inventive biotechnological invention, and determining its contribution to the final invention becomes a difficult task.

Creating synergies between different legal regimes – such as, in this case, IPRs and ABS regulations – raises important political, legal and economic considerations that have been debated both on a national and international level.

Proposals regarding the amendment of patent application requirements have also addressed the requirement to disclose compliance with PIC and equitable benefit sharing.[168] Disclosure of compliance with PIC would involve either certification by the competent national authorities or a certified contract between the patent applicant and the national authorities.[169] Extension of the scope of the disclosure requirement to cover even bioprospecting agreements is based on the fact that disclosing the origin of genetic resources does not provide for any monitoring of compliance with access legislation. The additional certification requirement would lift the burden of proof from the patent applicant and presuppose the applicant's compliance with ABS legislation.

A system requiring evidence of PIC would allow a host country to bring a lawsuit alleging false or misleading certification of compliance, or failure to certify compliance. Such a requirement entails a number of difficulties that need to be overcome in order for the system to be functional. Patent offices will have to examine and control compliance with foreign law. On the other hand, the country of origin could reach decisions that would be applicable as 'acts of state' and could not be reviewable by the administrative body granting the patent.

Imposing a disclosure of PIC would obviously raise awareness of the CBD-originating objectives. Patent offices could avoid grant of patents as the end result of CBD violations. It should, however, be noted that there is very limited experience regarding the regional and national regulations

---

'Disclosure of Origin: Time for a Reality Check?', paper presented at the ICTSD/CIEL/IDDRI/IUCN/QUNO Dialogue on Disclosure Requirements: Incorporating the CBD Principles in the TRIPS Agreement on the Road to Hong Kong, WTO Public Symposium, Geneva (21 April 2005); Queen Mary, Intellectual Property Research Institute, 'Disclosure of Origin in Patent Applications', Report to the European Commission (2004).

168 See Submissions from Bolivia, Brazil, Cuba, Ecuador, India, Pakistan, Peru, Thailand and Venezuela, IP/C/W/438.

169 See Abbott, F., 'Preservation and Use of Genetic Resource Assets and the International Patent System', A study for the Ministry of Foreign Affairs of Norway, Draft of 31 March, rev 1.2, Hong Kong Ministerial Revision (2005).

of PIC and the institutions responsible for PIC grants and monitoring are still not in place in the majority of national jurisdictions, making compliance with such a requirement even more burdensome.

3.2.1.4 Compatibility of a disclosure and PIC requirement with relevant international agreements

The introduction of a disclosure and/or PIC and ABS requirement in the current patent system has been a subject of great debate over the past ten years. This is particularly true when taking into consideration compatibility with international agreements, and above all with the TRIPS Agreement.[170]

3.2.1.4.1 The disclosure requirement and the TRIPS Agreement There are three provisions in the TRIPS Agreement that are of decisive importance when considering whether to include a disclosure requirement in the national patent legislation, namely Articles 29.1, 32 and 66.1.

Article 29.1 provides for the duty of the patent applicant to disclose the invention. Article 32 allows the revocation of patents due to insufficient disclosure of the invention, and this could be yet another venue for including a disclosure of origin requirement. Finally, Article 62.1 provides that 'members may require, as a condition of the acquisition or maintenance of the IPRs provided for under Section 2 through 6 of Part II, compliance with reasonable procedures and formalities. Such procedures and formalities shall be consistent with the provisions of this Agreement'.

In order to introduce a formal requirement not explicitly mentioned in Article 29.1, it has to be reasonable and consistent with the rest of the TRIPS Agreement's provisions. A reasonable formal requirement could be one that allows patent offices to assess whether the three substantive requirements are met. Another formal requirement that could be considered to pass the 'reasonable' test would be the introduction of formal conditions that allow the patent offices to identify the inventor or his/her legal successors. Such formal requirements that facilitate the identification of the applicant are included both in the PCT and the Draft SPLT.[171] The compatibility of formal requirements concerns the identification of the owner but also that of other actors who may have

---

170 For an elaboration on the disclosure requirement's compatibility with major international agreements see Safrin, S., 'Hyperownership in a Time of Biotechnological Promise: The International Conflict to Control the Building Blocks of Life', Am J Int L, Vol 98 (2004), pp. 641–85.

171 Article 4.1(iii) PCT; Article 4 SPLT.

proprietary interests in the invention.[172] The same applies to requirements of procurement or maintenance fees.

Under Article 27.1 TRIPS, the introduction of such a complementary requirement solely in the field of biotechnological inventions would arguably constitute discrimination against one field of technology (cf Article 20). On the other hand, any provision requiring disclosure of origin or PIC would be considered as TRIPS consistent if, besides being considered 'reasonable' in the meaning of Article 62, it also applies to all fields of technology. Article 27.2 provides that no exceptions are acceptable other than those explicitly stipulated, and the implementation of CBD is not one of those.[173] Therefore it must be concluded that a disclosure and PIC requirement would only be TRIPS consistent if it is not a precondition for acquiring a patent or a cause for revocation of a patent.

The introduction of a disclosure requirement in the TRIPS Agreement was discussed extensively during the TRIPS Council negotiations for the revision of Article 27.3(b).[174] Discussions concentrated on the amendment of the TRIPS Agreement to include the disclosure requirement as an additional formal condition of patentability. In the Doha Ministerial Declaration, explicit reference was made to the relationship between the TRIPS Agreement and the CBD.[175] However, after the Doha Declaration, no substantive progress was made on the matter. A number of delegations have submitted proposals as to possible amendments of the TRIPS Agreement,[176] while others have shed light on alternative ways of incorporating the disclosure requirement into the IP regulatory framework.[177]

---

172 An interesting example of such a requirement that has been considered as TRIPS-consistent is that imposed by means of 35 USC § 202, where contractors under government funding are required to mention in the patent application the fact that the invention was made under federal financial funding.

173 As not all members of the WTO are members of the CBD, it would be unreasonable to impose obligations on them to which they have not committed.

174 WT/GC/W/590, TN/C/W/49. Furthermore, the disclosure requirement would also ensure that the prior informed consent of indigenous and local communities would be obtained before such resources or knowledge is used.

175 Doha Ministerial Declaration §19 WTO Doc WT/MIN/(01)/DEC/1 (20 November 2001).

176 The African Group submitted a paper related to the incorporation of the disclosure requirement in the TRIPS Agreement. See Taking Forward the Review of Article 27.3(b) of the TRIPS Agreement, WTO Doc IP/C/W/404 (26 June 2003).

177 Switzerland informed the PCT of its proposal. See Article 27.3(b), Regarding the Relationship between the TRIPS Agreement and the Convention of Biological Diversity and the Protection of Traditional Knowledge, WTO Doc IP/C/W/400/Rev.1 (18 June 2003).

A number of countries expressed the view that the disclosure requirement should not be a substantive or formal patentability requirement that could lead to the revocation of the patent in case of nonrespect as a whole; others, such as the United States, discarded the disclosure requirement as a nonappropriate means of remedying the problems regarding patents granted on TKGR.[178]

3.2.1.4.2 Disclosure requirement and the UPOV Both UPOV 1978 and 1991 provide that the grounds for revocation of a plant variety certificate are lack of novelty, distinctness or stability, including in the case that the breeder failed to provide the authority with the information, documents or materials deemed necessary for the maintenance of the variety (stability), in the case that the breeder failed to pay maintenance fees or in the case that the breeder did not propose a suitable denomination previously submitted and cancelled after the grant of the right.[179] According to Articles 21–22 UPOV 1991, members are not allowed to expand the grounds for revocation of plant variety certificates. Consequently, a breeder that has acquired the plant variety without the PIC, and without disclosing in his application the origin of the variety in question, could not be sanctioned by revocation of the plant variety certificate.

This interpretation is in line with the view of the UPOV Secretariat. According to a communication of the Secretariat addressed to the TRIPS Council, 'if a country decides, in the frame of its overall policy, to introduce a mechanism for the disclosure of countries of origin or geographical origin of genetic resources, such a mechanism should not be introduced in a narrow sense, as a condition for plant variety protection'.[180] Thus, on the whole, UPOV member states may introduce a

---

[178] See Article 27.3(b), Relationship between the TRIPS Agreement and the CBD, and the Protection of Traditional Knowledge and Folklore, WTO Doc IP/C/W/434 (26 November 2004). In its paper, the United States restated its opinion that the disclosure requirement is not an appropriate measure. According to this paper, the disclosure requirement will have a negative effect on patents, making the patent procedure an extremely cumbersome one, while a more appropriate measure would be that of prior art databases.

[179] Article 21–2 UPOV 1991.

[180] Review of the Provisions of Article 27.3(b), Relationship between the TRIPS Agreement and the Convention on Biological Diversity and Protection of Traditional Knowledge and Folklore, Information from Intergovernmental Organisation, Addendum, International Union for the Protection of New Varieties of Plants (UPOV), WTO Doc IP/C/W/347/Add3 (11 June 2002).

disclosure requirement in their national legislation insofar as the requirement is not a condition for obtaining or conserving the right.

3.2.1.4.3 Disclosure requirement and the PCT The compatibility of the disclosure requirement and the Patent Cooperation Treaty (PCT) is indirectly addressed in Article 27.1 of the PCT. According to this provision, 'no national law shall require compliance with requirements relating to the form or contents of the international application different from or additional to those which are provided for in the Treaty and the Regulations'.[181]

Article 27.5 of the PCT provides that no formal requirements other than those expressly stipulated can be demanded for international applications.[182] Article 27.8 contains a number of exceptions to the general rule of Article 27.5. Neither the disclosure of origin nor the PIC requirement seems to fall under this provision.[183] But obviously, nothing prevents PCT members from including such a requirement once the application enters the national phase.[184] Switzerland proposed that Rule 4 should include both mandatory and optional information that may be obtained in a PCT application. The optional information may address matters likely to be required by patent offices at the national stage.[185] That change would enable the national legislator to require patent

---

181 According to the footnote to the final text of Article 27.1 of the PCT, the requirements relating to form and contents are principally provided for in Articles 3 (International Application), 4 (Request), 5 (Description), 6 (Claims), 7 (Drawings) and 8 (Claiming Priority), and the Rules pertaining to these Articles (mainly Rules 3–13). The words 'form or contents' are used to emphasise something that could go without saying, namely that requirements of substantive patent law (criteria of patentability) are not included.

182 Article 27.5 PCT provides that 'nothing in this Treaty and Regulations is intended to be construed as limiting the freedom of any Contracting State to prescribe such substantive conditions of patentability as it desires'.

183 Article 27.8 states: 'nothing in this Treaty and the Regulations is intended to be construed as limiting the freedom of any Contracting State to apply measures deemed necessary for the preservation of its national security or to limit, for the protection of the general economic interests of that State, the right of its own residents or nationals to file international applications.' A case in which Article 27.8 has been applicable is that of the United States imposing a limitation with regard to the filing of patent applications in other countries.

184 In the United States, patent applicants are required to submit an additional document containing an oath or declaration of an inventor complying with the requirements of section 115. See 35 USC §371(c)(4) (2000).

185 See also Rule 4.17. Communication from Switzerland IP/C/W/400/Rev1, 18 June 2003, at pp. 19–20. Rule 51 bis.1 is intended to give effect to Article 27

applicants to declare the source of genetic resources and traditional knowledge in patent applications if an invention is directly based on such resources or knowledge. The Swiss proposal would entail that patent applicants are given the opportunity to satisfy the requirement either at the time of filing an international patent application or later, during the international phase.

An alternative proposal is to include the disclosure requirement in the Budapest Treaty on the International Recognition of the Deposit of Microorganisms for the Purposes of Patent Procedure. According to this approach, the deposit of microorganisms and biological material would be completed with the disclosure of geographical origin or legal provenance.[186]

Article 6.1 of the Patent Law Treaty (PLT) provides that the proposed amendment of the PCT Regulations would also apply to the PLT once the PLT enters into force, and would thus be relevant to national patent applications.

3.2.1.4.4 The disclosure requirement and the Patent Law Treaty The mandatory disclosure and/or PIC requirement does not seem to fit so easily with the PLT.[187] According to Article 10(1) of the PLT:

> Non-compliance with one or more of the formal requirements referred to in Articles 6(1), (2), (4), and (5) and 8(1) to (4) with respect to an application may not be a ground for revocation or invalidation of a patent, either totally or in part, except where the non-compliance with the formal requirement occurred as a result of a fraudulent intention.

Furthermore, Article 6(1) states that 'except where otherwise provided for, no Contracting Party shall require compliance with any requirement relating to the form or contents of an application different from or additional to the requirements relating to form or contents which are

---

of the PCT and provides a number of additional requirements that could be relevant in the national phase, depending on national legislation.

[186] Muller, M.R., 'Disclosure of Origin and Legal Provenance: The Experience and Implementation Process in South America', Policy Brief Number 7 (June 2010).

[187] The Patent Law Treaty, adopted on 1 June 2000, will enter into force once ten states have deposited their instrument of ratification or accession (see Article 21(1) PLT). For the requirement see Girsberger, M., 'Transparency Measures under Patent law regarding Genetic Resources and Traditional Knowledge. Disclosure of Source and Evidence of Prior Informed Consent and Benefit-Sharing', J World Int Property, Vol 7 (2004), pp. 451–89.

provided for in respect of international applications under the Patent Cooperation Treaty'. In other words, requirements such as the disclosure and/or PIC requirement that are not explicitly stated either in the PLT or in the PCT are not PLT-compliant.[188]

3.2.1.5 Disclosure of origin/PIC or benefit sharing: regional and national initiatives

3.2.1.5.1 Regional attempts at a disclosure requirement The OAU Model Law and Andean Decision 391 provide regional examples of a disclosure requirement.

According to the third complementary provision of the Andean Decision 391, IP authorities shall require the applicant to give the registration number of the access contract and supply a copy of it as a prerequisite to grant the respective rights. To this end, the competent national authorities will cooperate with the IP National Offices and exchange information on the status of access applications/authorisations and patent applications, respectively.

The Andean Community makes direct reference to the protection of TKGR in yet another Decision:[189] Decision 486 on the Common Intellectual Property Regime.[190] In Article 3 of Decision 486, the Andean Community makes the grant of IPRs subject to respect for TKGR protection and conformity with access and benefit-sharing regulations.[191] Furthermore, Article 3.2 of the Decision states that the provisions of the Decision will be interpreted and applied in conformity with the stipulations of Decision 391. While Article 16 of the CBD subjects the application and interpretation of the Convention's provisions to the

---

[188] WIPO Doc WIPO/GR/00/4 (14 April 2000). See also 'Matters Concerning Intellectual Property and Genetic Resources, Traditional Knowledge and Folklore', WIPO Doc WO/GA/26/6 (7 August 2000).

[189] The Andean Community is Bolivia, Colombia, Ecuador and Peru. For the implementation of a disclosure requirement in South America, see Ruiz Muller, M., 'Disclosure of Origin and Legal Provenance: The Experience and Implementation Process in South America' in Werth, A. and Reyes-Knoche, S. (eds), *Triggering the Synergies between Intellectual Property Rights and Biodiversity*, Eschborn: gtz Project Sector (2011), pp. 258–70.

[190] Decision 486. Régimen Común sobre Propiedad Industrial, Lima, Perú, a los catorce días del med setiembre del año dos mil. Full text available at http://www.comunidadandina.org.

[191] Article 3.2 reaffirms the recognition of the rights and authority of indigenous, African American and local communities in respect of their collective knowledge.

parties' intellectual property obligations, Article 3.2 of the 486 Decision subjects the application and interpretation of the Common Intellectual Property Regime provisions to the obligations of the member states originating in Decision 391 regarding access to TKGR and benefit-sharing regulations.[192]

According to Article 26 of Decision 486, patent applications covering genetic resources originating in one of the member states are required to include a copy of the certificate of conformity with the requirement set out in Decision 391. The same requirement applies with regard to patent applications employing traditional knowledge.[193] Failure to submit a copy of the access contract results in the patent's invalidation.[194]

Finally, European countries were invited to legislate on this issue through the 1998 European Commission Biotechnology Directive. Under this Directive, disclosure by patent applicants is encouraged but not mandatory.

It was Denmark that, at the time of negotiations, proposed the inclusion of a reference to disclosure requirements in the Directive. This became a subject of debate between the member states,[195] and, due to the objections of some countries, the requirement was finally placed in the Preamble and not in the main text.

3.2.1.5.2 Disclosure requirement on the national level The First Complementary Provision of the Peruvian Bill states that when the 'requester' applies for a patent or a plant variety certificate for material based upon accessed genetic resources,[196] he or she must submit a copy of the authorisation of access in the patent application. Failure to do so could

---

[192] On the introduction and implementation of a disclosure requirement in South America, see Ruiz Muller (2011).

[193] Article 26(i) of Decision 486.

[194] See Article 75(g) and (h).

[195] See 'Policies, Measures and Experiences Regarding Intellectual Property and Genetic Resources: Submission by the E European Union and its Member States', IGC Sixteenth Session, Geneva (3–7 May 2010), WIPO/GRTKF/IC/16/INF/15. Another interesting review of national attempts to introduce a disclosure requirement and its relation to the disclosure requirement can be found in Hoare, A., Tarasofsky, R., 'Asking and Telling: Can Disclosure of Origin Requirements in Patent Applications Make a Difference?', J World Int Property, Vol 10 (2007), pp. 149–69. See also WIPO/GRTKIF/IC/16/INF/14, Policies, Measures and Experiences Regarding Intellectual Property and Genetic Resources: Submission by Switzerland (19 February 2010). For a summary of the proposals presented by Switzerland see WIPO/GRTKF/IC/11/10.

[196] Legislative Decree No 823, which entered into force on 24 May 1996.

result in denial of the grant or nullification of the patent.[197] In other words, access legislation is directly linked to the patent legislation. Noncompliance with the access procedures stipulated in the Bill affects the validity of the patent.[198]

In Brazil, subsequent to the implementation of Article 31 of the Provisional Act in 2006 and Resolution 23 of the CGEN, the Brazilian National Institute of Industrial Property (INPI) issued Resolution No 134, with adjustments to the form and internal procedures for processing patent applications. According to this, each patent applicant will have to declare whether he/she has obtained genetic resources or traditional knowledge and whether this proceeded in compliance with national legislation, and must also provide the number of the relevant authorisation. Due to practical difficulties caused by the new provisions, Resolutions No 34 of the CGEN and No 207 of INPI were issued in 2009, allowing for a broader time interval between the patent application and the submission of the access authorisation. Now, information related to access is to be submitted at the technical examination stage, thus after the formal preliminary examination and the publication of the patent application. On the other hand, should the patent examiner consider that the said invention made use of genetic resources or traditional knowledge, the INPI has the right to request that the patent applicant submits the form of access. In the case that the patent applicant fails to do so within a period of 60 days, the patent application is suspended. Nevertheless, the patent applicant has the right to appeal at any time and submit the requested form.

Costa Rica patent applications must be accompanied by a certificate of origin and PIC.[199] In Andean Community member countries, disclosure is mandatory. Where noncompliance occurs, the patent application shall not be processed, or where the patent is granted, it would be declared void. On the other hand, the disclosure requirement is limited in scope; it only concerns TKGR within their own territory. In fact, Brazil and Costa Rica only require disclosure in relation to their national resources, while Peru and the other members of the Andean Community require disclosure for resources from the whole area.

---

197 First Complementary Provision of the Bill.

198 First Complementary Provision of the Bill.

199 See Medaglia, C., 'The Disclosure of Origin Requirement in Central America. Legal Texts, Practical Experiences and Implementation Challenges', ICTSD (June 2010). See also Costa Rica's Biodiversity Law (BL) of 27 May 1998.

The Swiss legislation uses a slightly different terminology and requires the declaration of the 'source' rather than 'origin'. The term 'source' was used in order to cover situations where the origin is unknown, and is defined as the entity that is competent to grant access to GRs or to participate in sharing the benefits arising from their utilisation. Applicants are required to declare the 'primary source', which may be the country or community providing GRs; or, if this is unknown, to disclose the 'secondary source', for example a gene bank or botanic garden; or even to disclose sources such as scientific journals or databases.[200] Failure to comply results in rejection of the patent application,[201] while wrongful declaration is prosecuted *ex officio* and the applicant is liable to a fine of up to 100,000 Swiss francs.[202] The judge may also order publication of the ruling.[203] In order for the disclosure requirement to become applicable, the inventor should have had access to the genetic resource or the related traditional knowledge in a means that allows identification of their specific properties relevant to the invention. Another situation that could trigger the application of the disclosure requirement is when the invention is directly based on the genetic resource or traditional knowledge; that is, where the invention makes immediate use of and depends on the identified specific properties. The disclosure requirement becomes applicable also with regard to international patent applications that designate Switzerland.[204]

Norway opted for an even broader scope of the disclosure requirement. For inventions concerning or using biological material, the applicant is required to disclose the country providing this material, or the country of origin if this is different. The applicant has to demonstrate that PIC has been sought if this is a requirement in the providing country or country

---

[200] See Article 49a of the Swiss PatA.

[201] According to Article 59 para 2 and Article 59a para 3 subpara b, the Swiss Federal Institute of Intellectual Property requires that the patent applicant corrects the defect in the patent application within 30 months of the filing date or the priority date. If this period expires without correction, the Institute shall reject the application.

[202] See Article 81a PatA.

[203] Article 81a PatA.

[204] See Article 138 subpara b PatA. For an analysis of the Swiss proposals see also Addor, F. 'Switzerland's Proposals for Disclosure of the Source of Genetic Resources and Traditional Knowledge in Patent Applications' in Chouchena-Rojas, M., Ruiz Muller, M., Vivas, D. and Winkler, S. (eds), *Disclosure Requirements: Ensuring Mutual Supportiveness between the WTO TRIPS Agreement and the CBD*, Geneva: ICTSD (2005), p. 40.

of origin. In cases where the country of origin is not known, this should be stated.[205]

None of the European national legislations require proof of fair and equitable sharing of benefits. One of the fundamental objections to this was that 'fair and equitable' contains a certain level of subjectivity. Furthermore, it is almost impossible for the patent applicant to describe the commercial value of the invention at the time of the patent application. Nor do these laws refer to the use of traditional knowledge, as a result of concerns about the difficulties of defining this concept.

Another area in which member states vary in their approaches concerns sanctions to the disclosure requirement. A substantive law sanction has not been adopted by any of the EU countries, mainly due to industry concerns but also for fear of violating the TRIPS Agreement. Thus, noncompliance affects neither the examination of the patent application nor the validity of the patent. However, penalties could be imposed under the penal code on the basis of the general obligation to provide correct information to a public authority. While Denmark and Norway have opted for criminal sanctions,[206] the Swedish legislation does not enable prosecution in the case of a false declaration within a patent application. Consequently, the Swedish disclosure requirement is voluntary, left without any sanctions for noncompliance.[207]

In Belgium, noncompliance with the disclosure requirement was initially presented as an act contrary to public order and morality, since the invention in question was developed contrary to the CBD. However, in the end Belgium simply introduced a formal requirement. Noncompliance results in a patent application not being processed. It deserves to be noted that the Belgian Patent Office is not a searching authority and lacks research facilities, thus possible noncompliance is not checked. In theory, though, if a Belgian patent is granted, and is found to

---

[205] Extending the disclosure requirement to cover PIC was also considered in Sweden, Denmark and Switzerland. Due to the considerable objections to the feasibility of this measure, it was found that the disclosure of PIC is not necessary; disclosure of origin is sufficient to achieve the objectives of the measure.

[206] The Danish requirement is provided in section 2(4) of chapter 2 of the Danish Order on Patents and Supplementary Protection Certificates, Order No 93 of 29 January 2009.

[207] Swedish Patent Decree Sect 5a (SFS 2004:162).

violate the above stated provisions, then criminal sanctions could be sought for wrongful disclosure.[208]

It could be added that in China the patent law was revised on 1 October 2009 to provide, inter alia, in Article 5 that 'no patent rights shall be granted for any invention-creation which is completed on the basis of genetic resources of which the acquisition or use breaches the stipulations of related laws and regulations'.[209] This is supported by requirements in Article 26 stating that, for an invention that relies on such genetic resources, an applicant must disclose in the patent application the direct and original source of such genetic resources, and if the applicant cannot identify these, he or she must specify reasons for the failure to do so. Failure to comply with such disclosure requirements could result in the denial or invalidation of a patent.

There is a long list of alternative national initiatives for the introduction and implementation of a disclosure requirement. A patent applicant wishing to pursue a patent application in different jurisdictions would thus have to comply with a number of different requirements. The legal uncertainty that is related to limitless variations and to the fragility of the national systems provides for an antidisclosure requirement argument. The variations in the scope and impact of these national systems reveal the need for international harmonisation.[210]

3.2.1.6 Equity and efficiency evaluation of disclosure requirement

The efficiency of a possible disclosure requirement is a concern both for the patent applicants and for the institutions that should administer the system. Evaluation of the disclosure requirement is rather complicated, since it has had a limited impact in countries that have introduced relevant legislation. Its limited impact is due to the fact that the relevant

---

[208] Article 15, §1, 6 BPL (28 March 1984). Loi modifiant la loi du 28 mars 1984 sur les brevets d'invention, en ce qui concerne la brevetabilité des inventions biotechnologiques No 2005/11224.

[209] Article 5, §2.

[210] For a table illustrating a number of national disclosure requirement alternatives see Henninger, T., 'Disclosure Requirements in Patent Law and Related Measures; A Comparative Overview of Existing National and Regional Legislation on Intellectual Property and Biodiversity' in Werth, A. and Reyes-Knoche, S. (eds), *Triggering the Synergies between Intellectual Property Rights and Biodiversity*, Eschborn: gtz Project Sector (2011), pp. 293–327. See also IPDEV, Work Programme 8, Final Report, 'Disclosure of Origin in IPR Applications: Options and Perspectives of Users and Providers of Genetic Resources', Chatham House (May 2006).

legislation was enacted during the past few years,[211] but also the fact that disclosure requirements concern solely national applications, and thus only a limited number of patent applications are affected.[212] In Europe, only the Norwegian Patent Office holds data on the number of patent applications in which disclosure is made. Other patent offices estimate that these applications are very limited in number, if indeed any exist. In some cases, such as in Brazil and Peru, although the legislation provides for a disclosure requirement, the implementing regulations with regard to the practicalities have not yet been established. Both Brazil and Peru have expressed frustration regarding the malfunctions of the system.[213] It becomes obvious that legislation entailing a disclosure requirement should be carefully designed if it is to be efficient and serve its cause without creating unnecessary hindrances for applicants and for the patent office.

As already indicated, patent applicants have difficulty complying with the requirement. In some cases they are unable to determine the geographic origin of a resource they have used, and yet another problem occurs when the patent legislation provides for a PIC requirement while the genetic resources in question were accessed in a country lacking ABS legislation. It is often difficult to establish the link between a resource and the invention.

To conclude, disclosure requirements limited to national applications can only have a very limited impact. Naturally, the best and most effective way forward would be harmonisation on the international level, and for that reason proposals have also been submitted, as mentioned, during both WTO and WIPO negotiations.[214] The international regulation of the disclosure requirement would set common standards with regard to its scope and its legal effects, while at the same time facilitating the task of patent examiners.

---

211 The Andean Community Decisions 391 and 486 entered into force in 1996 and 2000 respectively. Costa Rica's legislation passed in 1998 and Brazil's in 2001. Denmark introduced a disclosure requirement in 2000, Sweden in 2004 and Belgium in 2005.

212 The Norwegian Patent Office states that 20 per cent of all patent applications that it receives are national. The Swedish Patent Office has stated that only 25 per cent of all biotechnology-related applications are national applications.

213 See IPDEV Final Report (2006) p. 8.

214 WIPO Technical Study on Patent Disclosure Requirements Related to Traditional Knowledge and Genetic Resources (Geneva, 2004).

In the neem tree case, a disclosure or PIC requirement would have been of importance, since it would have facilitated monitoring the application. In the case of enola beans, the patent applicant, Proctor, disclosed the origin of the beans he used. In the same way, Eli Lilly's rosy periwinkle researchers disclosed that their source of know-how on the specific plant was TKGR originating in the Philippines. In fact, Eli Lilly initially relied on rosy periwinkle found in Madagascar for supply, and later established its own cultivations in Texas. Researchers from the University of Ontario received relevant TKGR on rosy periwinkle from Jamaica and disclosed that they were inspired by TKGR. In the majority of national legislation, this information would be enough to fulfil the disclosure requirement.

In the hoodia cactus case, the patent specification disclosed the name of the plant without, however, disclosing the origin or the related traditional knowledge. Obviously, disclosing relevant prior art is necessary in the patent application, irrespective of whether knowledge is traditional or not. In this case, information on the possible applications of the specific plant was found in published literature.[215]

The international instruments requiring a disclosure requirement provide for a number of different authorities that could be burdened with the task of providing access authorisation.[216] In the CBD and the Bonn Guidelines, it is required that the contracting party providing the resources give its prior informed consent in order for access to genetic resources to be CBD-compliant. Furthermore, paragraph 31 of the Bonn Guidelines requires that indigenous communities give prior informed consent in accordance with traditional practices and national access policies, and subject to domestic laws.[217] Article 32 of the Guidelines requires that prior informed consent 'should be obtained from the competent national authority and/or body governing the ex situ collection concerned as appropriate'.

In the ITPGRFA system, on the other hand, a number of entities are involved in access to plant genetic resources for food and agriculture (PGRFA) – not only the contracting parties, but also natural and legal persons who have chosen to include their PGRFA in the Multilateral System (Article 11.3), developers of PGRFA (Article 12.3), the holders of IPRs to PGRFA (Article 12.3(f)) and the recipients of PGRFA and any entity having control over or ownership of PGRFA found in *in situ*

[215] See also Dutfield, G., 'Thinking Aloud on Disclosure of Origin', QUNO Occasional Paper 18 (October 2005).

[216] See also Girsberger (2004), pp. 451–89.

[217] Bonn Guidelines (2002).

conditions (Article 12.3(h)). In the Multilateral System established by means of the ITPGRFA, there are no 'individual accessions'. An equally important issue to clarify with respect to the practical application of the disclosure requirement is what triggers the application of the requirement. Patent applicants have required such a clarification.[218] In its proposal for a new Rule 51bis 1(g)(i) of the PCT Regulations, Switzerland has attempted to clarify the situation by requiring that the invention be 'directly based' on a 'specific genetic resource to which the inventor has had access'.

The EU has proposed that the disclosure requirement should be applicable when biological resources and traditional knowledge are 'used in the invention'.[219] In the proposal of the African Group, it is sufficient that biological resources and traditional knowledge are 'used or involved in the invention'. Taking into consideration the fact that genetic resources and traditional knowledge are of such a diverse nature and the circumstances under which these are involved or employed vary, it is rather difficult to come up with general guidelines. Regardless of the practical difficulties, specifying what triggers the application of the disclosure requirement is of considerable importance for legal certainty. Patent applicants have to know when their patent application is subject to a disclosure requirement, and patent offices should be able to consider whether or not a specific patent application must disclose the origin of genetic resources and traditional knowledge.

It is equally important to consider the scenario in which the source of the genetic resources is unknown to the patent applicant. One possible solution would be to allow the patent applicant to state that the source of

---

218 The Norwegian Patent Office in response to an interview with IPDEV, Final Report (May 2006).

219 Brazil et al, 'The Relationship between the TRIPS Agreement and the Convention on Biological Diversity and the Protection of Traditional Knowledge', Submission by Bolivia, Brazil, Cuba, the Dominican Republic, Ecuador, India, Peru, Thailand and Venezuela, WTO Doc IP/C/W403 (24 June 2003). See also 'The Relationship between the TRIPS Agreement and the Convention on Biological Diversity and the Protection of Traditional Knowledge: A Checklist of Issues', Submission by Brazil, Cuba, Ecuador, India, Peru, Thailand and Venezuela, WTO Doc IP/C/420 (2 March 2004); EC and Member States 2002, 'Review of Article 27.3(b) of the TRIPS Agreement and the Relationship Between the TRIPS Agreement and the Convention on Biological Diversity (CBD) and the Protection of Traditional Knowledge and Folklore. A Concept Paper', Communication from the European Communities and their Member States, WTO Doc IP/C/W/383 (17 October 2002).

relevant material is unknown.[220] This scenario would be conceivable in cases where the genetic resources are accessed from a gene bank and for which no further information is available. In such cases, patent applicants should be able to declare that they do not have the necessary information and thus are unable to fulfil the disclosure requirement. This is, of course, of interest in jurisdictions where the disclosure requirement is sanctioned.[221]

In order for the disclosure requirement to be fair and efficient, there are a number of other issues that need to be clarified. The requirement may only fulfil its objectives by providing 'source countries' with an overview of patent applications that refer to these countries in the source disclosure.

An interesting proposal is that of the establishment of a list of governmental agencies competent to receive information on the disclosure of origin. According to this proposal, when a patent office receives a patent application containing a disclosure of source, it would inform the listed governmental authority that the country in question has been disclosed as the country of source and also provide information on the patent applicant and the invention in question. The list of competent governmental authorities would be available on both the WIPO website and the Clearing House Mechanism of the CBD website. The proposal could be broadened to cover even nongovernmental entities that are relevant to the access and benefit-sharing regulations, such as indigenous communities, organisations and other NGOs. Such a supplementary measure would increase the efficiency of the measure and assist in linking it with effective sanctioning of access and benefit-sharing violations.[222]

The industry is obviously interested in clarifying the meaning and role of a potential disclosure requirement. The Biotechnology Industry Organization (BIO) and the International Federation of Pharmaceutical Manufacturers and Associations (IFPMA) have expressed doubts as to whether such a requirement would achieve the goals of the CBD, as well as their

---

220 See Switzerland's proposal; also Brazil et al (2003).

221 Correa, C., 'Establishing a Disclosure of Origin Obligation in the TRIPS Agreement', Occasional Paper 12, Quaker United Nations Office (August 2003), available at http://www.geneva.quno.info/pdf/Disclosure%20OP%2012.pdf. See also Chouchena-Rojas, M., Muller, R., Vivas, D. and Winkler, S. 'Disclosure Requirement: Ensuring Mutual Supportiveness between the WTO TRIPS Agreement and the CBD', IUCN Gland, Switzerland and Cambridge, UK; ICTSD Geneva Switzerland (2005).

222 Switzerland (2002).

certainty that such a requirement would unduly burden patent applicants.[223] Both provided an interesting review of their members' experiences with regard to ABS Agreements in national jurisdictions,[224] referring to an evaluation of the paper submitted by Peru regarding potential cases of biopiracy.[225] Resources that could constitute the subject matter of biopiracy in Peru were, according to BIO and IFPMA, available in Peru at the time with no restrictions and on common commercial terms. Even if Peru introduced legislation regulating access, it could not apply retroactively. A disclosure requirement could introduce uncertainty into the system that would not be justified by the effects it might have with regard to CBD objectives.[226]

In order to guarantee the efficiency and also the fairness of the system, it is important to clarify a number of different elements:[227]

- What is the scope of the information that should be disclosed?
- What is the meaning of origin/source?
- What kind of information/documentation should be submitted? Is mere reference to the origin enough, or should the authorisation of the competent national authority in the country of access be annexed?
- When will the requirement be examined and by whom?
- Which IPRs will be subject to the disclosure requirement? Will it be limited solely to patents?

Since one of the major arguments against the introduction of a disclosure requirement in the current system of IPRs is the difficulty sometimes entailed in the examination process, it is of interest to consider how patent examination was influenced by a similar disclosure requirement regulation. The US Bayh–Dole Act contains a requirement for the

---

223 WIPO/GRTKF/IC/16/INF/16/6 Prov.

224 WIPO/GRTKF/IC/16/INF/21. An interesting conclusion of the report was that the main field of patent applications was not biotechnology or pharmaceuticals, but herbal remedies and human nutrition. Furthermore, only a very limited percentage of these patents – 4 per cent – concerned an isolated chemical compound.

225 WIPO/GRTKF/IC/8/12.

226 See also Henninger (2011). WIPO/GRTKF/IC/16/INF/2,1 p. 7.

227 See Madaglia, C.J., 'The Disclosure of Origin Requirement in Central America: Legal Texts, Practical Experience and Implementation Challenges' in Werth, A. and Reyes-Knoche, S. (eds), *Triggering the Synergies between Intellectual Property Rights and Biodiversity*, Eschborn: gtz Project Sector (2011), pp. 270–93.

disclosure of federal funding for inventions covered by patent applications in the United States.[228] According to the Bayh–Dole Act, patent applicants are required to include clauses in patent applications stating the governmental interest and informing the federal agency of the pursuit of patent rights. The major question was thus whether or not this disclosure requirement was to be considered as an additional patentability requirement. The answer was given in *University of Rochester v. Searle et al.* In this case, Rochester argued that Searle had infringed the patent on a COX2 inhibitor. Searle appealed and claimed that Rochester had not met the written description requirement. The Court clarified that there is no connection between the Bayh–Dole Act and the patentability requirement: 'The Bayh-Dole Act was intended to enable universities to profit from their federally-funded research. It was not intended to relax the statutory requirements of patentability.'[229] One could in fact draw parallels between the disclosure requirement provided for under the Bayh–Dole Act and the disclosure requirement introduced in order to provide for the indirect protection of TKGR. The difficulties in connecting the disclosure requirement to the patentability of an invention are similar in nature.

3.2.2 *Sui Generis* System of Protection

The necessary adaptations of the international patent system to accommodate the objectives of the CBD and provide for the protection of TKGR are subject to the set of complexities described above. The introduction of a *sui generis* system designed on the basis of the particularities and special characteristics of the TKGR could be a less complicated step forward. However, in this regard, the absence of an international agreement introducing a *sui generis* system for TKGR is a major weakness. In this respect, regional and national *sui generis* systems of protection provide valuable experiences. The variations among the selected regional and national implementation initiatives are proof of the vagueness and flexibility of the CBD provisions. They adopt different perspectives in the protection system and a very differentiated scope regarding the subject matter that is protected. Two forms of protection

---

228 35 USC 200–12, Chapter 18 – Patent Rights in Inventions Made with Federal Assistance. On the Bayh–Dole Act see also Rai, K.A. and Eisenberg, R., 'Bayh-Dole Reform and the Progress of Biomedicine', Law & Contemporary Problems, Vol 66 (2004), pp. 289–314.

229 Case 03-1304, *University of Rochester v. G.D. Searle & Co, Inc. Monsanto Company, Pharmacia Corporation, and Pfizer Inc.* (2004).

schemes have been tested: firstly, the regulation of access to TKGR; secondly, the grant of exclusive rights on TKGR.

3.2.2.1 Alternative *sui generis* systems on a national and regional basis

The OAU Model provides for a *sui generis* right of a communitarian nature.[230] It focuses on the concept of communal rights, a property structure relevant to the historical centrality and importance of communities in African history and tradition.[231] Part IV of the Model Law is dedicated to community rights, with detailed and explicit provisions regulating the collective rights of indigenous communities. Articles 16 to 23 provide for recognition of the status of customary law with regard to access to TKGR, but also with regard to 'community intellectual rights'.[232]

While not falling directly under the framework of CBD implementation, Directive 2004/24/EC concerning traditional herbal medicinal products refers to the promotion and facilitation of TKGR products.[233] The said Directive provides for an exception to the provisions of Directive 2001/83/EC on the requirements for applications for authorisation to place a medicinal product on the market. In order to qualify as a traditional herbal medicine, it has to be shown that the medicinal product in question has been in medicinal use for a period of at least 30 years preceding the date of the application, including at least 15 years within the Community.[234]

---

[230] African Model Legislation for the Protection of the Rights of Local Communities, Farmers and Breeders, and for the Regulation of Access to Biological Resources (1998), accessed at http:/afjn.cua.edu.

[231] See also the report of Professor Ekpere (former Executive Secretary of the OAU Scientific, Technical and Research Commission) on 'Sui Generis Systems and the Case of the OAU Model Law on the Protection of Rights of Local Communities, Farmers and Breeders and For the Regulation of Access to Biological Resources', presented at the International Seminar on Systems for the Protection of Traditional Knowledge, New Delhi, India (3–5 April 2002).

[232] Community intellectual rights encompass the rights of traditional professional groups and community innovation that will be protected under the principles of customary law of the community in question.

[233] Directive 2004/24/EC of the European Parliament and of the Council of 31 March 2004 amends, with regard to traditional herbal medicinal products, Directive 2001/83/EC on the Community code relating to medicinal products for human use.

[234] Article 16.1(c) of Directive 2004/24/EC.

A similar approach is that of Council Regulation 509/2006,[235] providing for the protection of the traditional speciality of agricultural products or foodstuffs by means of a registration system. In order to enjoy protection under the Regulation, the agricultural product or foodstuff shall either be produced using traditional raw materials or be characterised by a traditional composition or a mode of production.[236] The Regulation provides for collective rights,[237] and includes specification of the product and description of the method employed.[238] The protection granted covers both the product and its name.[239] Both the Directive and the Regulation aim to facilitate the trade of TKGR products; the Regulation also seeks to safeguard them from attempts at misappropriation.

The Act on Protection and Promotion of Traditional Thai Medicinal Intelligence offers a very illustrative and detailed example of national legislation establishing a *sui generis* protection for TKGR. The subject matter of protection is 'traditional Thai medicine intelligence', defined as the basic knowledge and capability concerned with traditional Thai medicine.[240] The Act establishes a Committee for the Protection and Promotion of Thai Medicinal Intelligence, with the mandate to advise the minister on issues related to traditional medicine, promote cooperation between relevant governmental authorities and approve the withdrawal of registrations on IPRs to traditional Thai medicine. Furthermore, the Committee will consider appeals on registrations and licensing decisions, and lay down rules concerning appeal procedures and the registration of IPRs to traditional Thai medicine.[241]

---

235 Council Regulation (EC) No 509/2006 on Agricultural Products and Foodstuffs as Traditional Specialties Guaranteed.

236 Article 4 of the Regulation.

237 Article 7 of the Regulation.

238 Article 6 of the Regulation.

239 According to Article 5, the Regulation shall apply without prejudice to Community rules or those of the member states governing intellectual property, geographical indications and trademarks.

240 Section 3 of the Act.

241 Traditional Thai medicine is defined as 'the medicinal procedures concerned with examination, diagnosis, therapy, treatment or prevention of, or promotion and rehabilitation of the health of humans or animals, traditional Thai massage, and also includes the production of traditional Thai drugs and the invention of medical devices, on the basis of knowledge or text that has been passed on from generation to generation'. For the Indian approach, see Collet, P., 'Property Rights over Biological Resources: India's Proposed Legislative Framework', J World Int Property, Vol 4 (2001), pp. 219–22.

Section 14 of the Act states that the IPRs for traditional Thai medicine cover the protection of the formula and the text on traditional medicine. Section 15 continues by referring to the three different levels of the traditional Thai IPR: national formula/national text, general formula/general text and personal formula/personal text. A formula/text of traditional Thai medicine that is of benefit or that has special medicinal or public health value is classified as a national formula/text by the minister.[242] Formulas/texts of traditional medicine that have been widely used or whose protection has expired are classified as general formulas.[243] Finally, a formula/text of traditional medicine that may be eligible for IP protection counts as a personal formula/text.[244]

Registration can be applied for by an inventor, improver or inheritor of the formula for traditional Thai drugs. Registration of a personal formula/text shall be denied in three situations:[245] when the formula/text is a national formula/text or a general formula/text, or when the formula has been developed on a nonmedical basis, or finally when it was produced through a transformation that is not considered a rough transformation.[246]

Where more than one registration application is handed in for the same formula/text, the first to be handed in is the one that will be awarded the right.[247] Third parties that claim ownership of the right in question may object to granted registrations within a period of 60 days from the day the registration was published.[248] The duration of the right is 50 years post mortem of the rightholder.[249] After the expiration of the term of protection, the formula/text will be classified as a general formula/text. The rightholder is granted the exclusive right to the production of the drug and research, distribution and development of the formula. The exceptions to the rights of the rightholder are stipulated in Section 34, and include any act that is of benefit to studies or research, preparation of drugs according to prescription and production of drugs for household use or by state hospitals or government and state agencies.

---

242 Section 17 of the Act.

243 Section 18 of the Act.

244 Section 20 of the Act.

245 Section 22 of the Act.

246 According to Section 3 of the Act a rough transformation is defined as the mixture, blend or transformation of herbs or the quality of herbs in order to obtain substances as a whole by original procedures and newly developed procedures without differentiating the pure ingredients of different substances.

247 Section 26 of the Act.

248 Section 29 of Act.

249 Section 33.3 of the Act.

The *sui generis* right to traditional Thai medicine is nonassignable.[250] Upon the death of the rightholder, the successor may acquire the intellectual property right after application for registration. Where there are no successors, or in cases where the successor fails to apply within two years of the rightholder's death, the formula/text is classified as a general formula/text and thus considered as part of the public domain.[251] Where the rightholder exercises his/her right against the public order or morals, or when the exercise of the right leads to serious damage of intellectual property rights to traditional Thai medicine, the right shall be revoked.[252]

Section 43 of the Act contains a reciprocity clause providing that the nationals of other countries that will grant Thai nationals intellectual property protection for traditional Thai medicine inventions in their jurisdictions will be granted IP protection for their traditional medicine in Thailand.

Chapter 3 of the Act introduces yet another subject matter of protection: herbs. The said chapter covers all herbs that are of study or research value, have important economic value or may become extinct. If a herb falls into this protection category, the minister, with the advice of the Committee, shall have the power to issue a notification in the Government Gazette, where the kind, characteristic, type and name of the herb in question will be published.[253] The notification shall also refer to procedures and conditions for the possession, use, conservation and transportation of the controlled herbs.[254] These regulations will also specify the rules, procedures and conditions concerning the export of controlled herbs for commercial and noncommercial purposes and their distribution or transformation.[255] In order for a third party to research, export, sell or transform a protected herb, a licence must be acquired by the competent authority.[256] The licence term is three years.[257] Finally, Chapter 6 provides for the setting up of the Fund on Traditional Thai Medicine Intelligence, which will finance expenses related to work on the conservation and promotion of intelligence on traditional Thai

---

250 Section 35 of the Act.
251 Section 35 of the Act.
252 Section 41 of the Act.
253 Section 44 of the Act.
254 Section 45.1–45.6 of the Act.
255 Section 45.5 of the Act.
256 Section 46.1 of the Act.
257 Section 46.2 of the Act. According to Section 49, the licensee has the opportunity to apply for renewal of the licence.

medicine and will be financed in turn by subsidies from the state, private funds, interest and benefits from those funds and other earnings obtained from the functioning of the Fund.

Portugal's Decree No 118/2002 introduced a mechanism for the legal registration of the aforementioned types of material,[258] which will also form the basis for the fair allocation of the benefits generated by the use of this material among the parties involved.[259] The scope of the Decree covers local plant varieties and other 'spontaneously occurring autochthonous material of plant species'.[260] Plant material shall be registered in the Register of Plant Genetic Resources (RGGV). The registration is valid for a period of ten years and will be renewed for subsequent periods of the same duration, provided that the required conditions are maintained.[261] The scope of the Decree covers traditional knowledge, which is defined as all the intangible elements associated with commercial or industrial utilisation of these plant genetic resources.[262] In order for traditional knowledge to qualify for protection, it should be identified, described and registered in the RGGV.[263] The description should be clear enough to allow third parties to apply the traditional knowledge in question and acquire identical results to those claimed in the registration.[264]

With regard to traditional knowledge that has not yet been used in commercial or industrial activities, the local community will have the right to object to its direct or indirect reproduction, imitation and/or use by unauthorised third parties for commercial purposes; assign, transfer or license rights on traditional knowledge, including transfer by succession; and exclude from protection any traditional knowledge that may be covered by specific industrial property registrations.[265] The registration of traditional knowledge shall be effective for a period of 50 years from the date of the application and renewable for an identical period.[266] The Decree links the protection of plant genetic resources and traditional knowledge to the protection of goods with an appellation of origin or geographical indication. According to Article 6 of the Decree, the plant

258 Decree No 118/2002, 20 April 2002.
259 See Preamble of the Decree.
260 Article 2.1 of the Decree.
261 Article 4 of the Decree.
262 Article 3.1 of the Decree.
263 Article 3.2 of the Decree.
264 Article 3.2(b) of the Decree.
265 Article 3.4 of the Decree.
266 Article 5 of the Decree.

material used in making goods with a protected appellation of origin or geographical indication must be registered in accordance with the provisions of the Decree.

Access to plant genetic resources and traditional knowledge is to be granted by the competent authority, the Technical Council of the Ministry of Agriculture, Rural Development and Fisheries on Agrarian Genetic Resources, Fisheries and Agriculture (CoTeRGAPA), after having heard the owner of the registration.[267] According to Article 7.4 of the Decree, a prerequisite for access is the fair allocation of benefits resulting from such use and prior agreement with the owner of the registration. The owner of the registration could be a private or public entity or an individual that represents the interests of the geographical area in which the local variety is most widely found or where the spontaneously occurring autochthonous material displays the greatest genetic variability.[268] The owner shall be responsible for the conservation *in situ* of the plant genetic resources in question.[269] Article 13 lists a number of economic sanctions for potential abuses of the system. Article 14 continues, with other sanctions such as loss of access authorisation, liability for misuse of the system and of property, prohibition from exercising a profession and removal of the right to market. Finally, the owner of the registration reserves his or her right to claim civil liability, and the right to compensation and a share of benefits.

Brazil recognises and to a certain degree protects the rights of indigenous peoples and traditional communities over their knowledge.[270] The Provisional Act dictates that informed consent of the communities involved is a requirement in order to obtain access authorisation. One of the weak points of the system is the representation of the traditional knowledge holders. In the Provisional Act, this is resolved by declaring respect for the preexisting social organisations and political representations of indigenous communities. Also, information on the research project and the access activities is to be made available to the holders of traditional knowledge in a language and in means that offer them access. In fact, Brazilian legislation provides one of the most demanding traditional knowledge (TK) protection schemes, with the procedure for obtaining PIC involving a 'mini' anthropological report mapping the social and political organisations of indigenous communities and assessing the level of awareness of the TK value. Brazilian legislation creates a

---

267 Article 7.1 and 7.2 of the Decree.
268 Article 9.1(a) of the Decree.
269 Article 10.3 of the Decree.
270 Provisional Act No 2186-16/01.

'de facto' *sui generis* protection of TK, but without formally declaring the creation of a new exclusive right.[271] The scope of national regulation is differentiated in a number of ways. Some national protection systems define their scope of application on the basis of the use of TKGR (i.e. medicinal or agricultural), while others provide for different sets of provisions: one for each of the prespecified sectors and some with general application, in some cases. The scope of regulation has been defined on the basis of the association of traditional knowledge to tangible resources, traditional knowledge on biodiversity, traditional knowledge on eco-systems and traditional knowledge on genetic resources. Finally, it has been defined on the basis of the specified rightholders, indigenous peoples, 'Indian tribes' and farming communities.

The African Model Legislation leaves the task of defining the protection requirements to the National Competent Authority.[272] And while the vagueness of the African Model Legislation can be justified taking into consideration its Model Law function,[273] the lack of any reference to protection requirements in the Philippine legislation is less understandable. Thailand makes an indirect reference to the requirements TKGR is to fulfil in order to be protected.[274] Peruvian legislation, on the other hand, includes a long list of requirements, with specific definitions related to the nature of the knowledge and the group of rightholders.[275]

Portugal provides for a two-level form of protection with two different sets of requirements. The first protection level requires that TKGR shall

---

[271] Vélez, E., 'Brazil's Practical Experience with Access and Benefit Sharing and the Protection of Traditional Knowledge', ICTSD, Policy Brief No 8, June 2010.

[272] See Article 58(iv) of the African Model Legislation.

[273] The African Model Legislation was introduced as a guideline, assisting the implementation of the relevant international agreements in the African countries.

[274] Section 3 provides that traditional Thai medicine contains the qualification that the medicinal procedures, massage, production of traditional drugs or the invention of medical devices have to rest 'on the basis of knowledge or text that has passed on from generation to generation'.

[275] Knowledge that is collective, related to biological diversity, developed by indigenous peoples and is not part of the public domain. See Articles 2(a) to 2(e). The meaning of knowledge in the public domain is further defined. For the purposes of Peruvian legislation, knowledge in the public domain is such knowledge that has been made accessible to persons other than the indigenous peoples by mass communication media such as publication, or when the uses or characteristics of a biological resource are concerned where it has become extensively known outside the community. See Article 13. Similar requirements are found in the Brazilian legislation.

be identified, registered,[276] and described in such a way as to enable third parties to reproduce or utilise the knowledge.[277] The additional protection is awarded when one of the following conditions is fulfilled: either the TKGR has not been used in industrial activities or it is not known outside the local community where it originated.[278]

The nature of the legal entitlements introduced is both contradictory and confusing. Aside from the specific right to refuse access to their TKGR,[279] the OAU offers more of a list of principles of rights, without specifying their structure and nature.[280] A mere statement of principles is also found in the Philippines Act.[281] The Brazilian regulation, on the other hand, provides for an ambitious mixture of trade secret protection, copyright-like moral right and a patent-like exclusive right,[282] which does not, however, include any experimental use exception.[283] A patent-like regime for the protection of TKGR is introduced in the traditional Thai Medicines Act,[284] recognising the 'sole right ownership on the production of the drug and the sole right over the research, distribution, improvement or development of formulas on traditional Thai medicine'.[285]

The duration of the legal entitlement granted to TKGR also varies considerably from jurisdiction to jurisdiction. Peru, Brazil and the Philippines include no provision concerning the duration of rights granted. On the other hand, the OAU Model Law states in Article 23 that 'Community Intellectual Rights of the local communities, including traditional professional groups, particularly traditional practitioners, shall at all times remain inalienable'. Thailand provides that the IP right to

---

276 In the register of Plant Genetic Resources.

277 See Article 3.2 of the Decree.

278 See Article 3.4 of the Decree.

279 Where such access will be detrimental to the integrity of their natural or cultural heritage. See Article 19.

280 It provides, for instance, that the Model Law recognises the rights of communities over their knowledge and technologies without, however, stating what these rights will be. See Article 16.

281 See Sections 32 and 34.

282 Unauthorised third parties are not allowed to use the invention and derive economic profit from the economic exploitation of TKGR, while TK holders are allowed to license their TKGR. See Article 9.

283 According to Article 9(a), unauthorised third parties are not allowed to proceed to tests, research or investigation relating to TKGR.

284 Although the Thai Medicines Act provides for a private use exception and for the exception of uses that are in the benefit of studies and tests.

285 Comparable to that of the patent application procedure. Sections 22–6 of the Thai Medicines Act.

traditional Thai medicine shall be valid during the lifetime of the rightholder of the registration and shall extend for another 50 years after his death, with an obvious source of inspiration in copyright law.[286] Finally, Portugal provides for 50 years of protection with regard to traditional knowledge,[287] while plant genetic material registration is valid for ten years.[288]

Sanctions and enforcement mechanisms may provide some guidance for the nature of the proposed entitlement. The OAU Model Law classifies the provided sanctions under the ambit of the access regulations, including cancellation/revocation of the access permission, banning access to community knowledge and publication of the violation on the competent authority's database.[289] The Brazilian Provisional Measure provides for the right to indemnification based on the gross income from marketing the product or from licensing the product or process.[290]

According to Peruvian legislation, indigenous peoples have the right to bring an infringement action, laying the burden of proof of the violation on the defendant. This action will shift the ownership of the TKGR in question and lead to the indemnification of the rightholders.[291] However, no clear definition is provided regarding the nature of the right, nor is a reference to confiscation or cessation of production included. The Thai Medicines Act is even more confusing with regard to sanctions, referring mostly to sanctions imposed on the holders of IP on traditional Thai medicines when the exercise of their rights is contrary to public order.[292] The Philippines' regulation stipulates the competence of the Council of Elders in the settlement of disputes and in the administrative procedures that go before any court proceeding, but does not clarify the nature of the sanctions imposed in cases of breach of the exclusive rights granted.

---

[286] Section 23 of the Thai Medicines Act. According to Section 34, in the case of joint ownership the right extends for 50 years from the date the last owner died.

[287] Article 3(6).

[288] Article 5. Protection is renewable for both subject matters.

[289] Article 23 of the OAU Model Law.

[290] Articles 26–30 of the Brazilian Provisional Measure.

[291] Article 45 of the Peruvian Law.

[292] Actions contrary to public order or good morals or contrary to the conditions specified in the Ministerial Regulation. See Section 36.2 of the Act.

3.2.2.2 *Sui generis* protection: experiences from the past

During the past decades the international IP scene has experienced a wave of novel subject matter and small-scale innovations suffering from market failure phenomena and seeking protection by means of a legal entitlement. The protection of computer programs, integrated circuit designs, biotechnological inventions, plant varieties and databases has extended IP structures or induced the introduction of novel protection frameworks.

All of this emerging subject matter bears the risk of extensive free-riding duplicators that deprive innovators of their natural lead time in the market. The typical response to this risk has been the introduction of *sui generis* regimes of exclusive rights, as variations/adaptations of traditional IPRs. In order to remedy such market failure, policymakers have turned to the property rights paradigm and elaborated a new combination of patent law and copyright law principles, thus introducing a number of mini-monopolies.

This cyclical pattern reveals the economical and doctrinal contradictions associated with the grant of exclusive rights protection on what would otherwise constitute small-scale innovations. According to Lewis and Reichman, these *sui generis* regimes suffer from one major structural defect: that of choosing to solve the puzzle of the protection of small-scale innovation by means of a property rule.[293]

A dominant belief with regard to those *sui generis* regimes of protection seems to be that they fail to successfully provide the protection they were planned for. The approach adopted by policymakers is in some cases a strong hybrid regime of exclusive rights and in others one of weaker protection schemes, with no general evaluation ever made of the needs and special characteristics of the particular subject matter and the market in question.

The historical examples of *sui generis* rights illustrate their lack of systematic capacity to promote the needs of the market players involved. Granting exclusive rights for routine applications of technological know-how may lead to unnecessary and harmful limitation of the public domain. Transactions will only be possible via contractual arrangements entailing the emergence of new and, in some cases, uncalculated transaction costs, as well as entrance barriers.

---

[293] Lewis, T., Reichman, J., 'Using Liability Rules to Stimulate Local Innovation in Developing Countries: Application to Traditional Knowledge' in Maskus, K.E., Reichman, J. (eds), *International Public Goods and Transfer of Technology Under a Globalized Intellectual Property Regime*, Cambridge: Cambridge University Press (2005), pp. 337–66.

3.2.3 Equity and Efficiency in *Sui Generis* Protection

With the exception of GIs, both plant variety protection and database protection have been criticised, and their respective results questioned.

Examples of the application of these *sui generis* rights reveal the potential defects of such alternative methods of protection. While they enjoy considerable flexibility, taking into account that they are in fact creating an entitlement to protect a specific subject matter in order for it to operate in a specific market, they still seem to fall short of initial expectations. They very often underprotect or overprotect the subject matter in question. In some cases they are accused of imposing unnecessary obstacles on the market; in others they offer rights that are easy to circumvent. Uncertainty as to whether the rights introduced are the appropriate means for remedying underlying market failures is obvious in the field of plant variety protection in the United States, where the system has shifted a number of times from trademark protection to utility patents. Another interesting conclusion drawn from the *sui generis* right on databases is the fact that some objectives may be achieved by alternative means, such as the US approach of a contractual substitute.

The GI experience is valuable since its efficiency builds upon international recognition, as in the case of TKGR. The lengthy negotiations related to GIs and the difficulties that have appeared in terms of countries being divided into two main groups – potential rightholders and 'users' – should provide valuable lessons for TKGR negotiations. Considering that international consensus is a *sine qua non* for efficient and fair TKGR protection, it is important to carefully document needs and expectations and weigh the pros and cons of alternative ways of protection, since changes and adaptations will be almost impossible.

There are unfortunately, no easy solutions in this respect. The *sui generis* rights introduced by national or regional regulations provide us with an initial illustration of the potential pitfalls that might be presented by a *sui generis* right on TKGR. Different layers of rightholders, unspecified subject matter and unclear structure and content of the rights provided are examples of the concerns expressed regarding the national *sui generis* rights proposed. The complexity of the subject matter, and its international character, requires a careful and thorough analysis of the preconditions as well as the potential side effects of such a system. A 'copy-paste' of other rights or a bad copy of an existing regime cannot be a solution.

4. Contractual accommodation of rights to TKGR

4.1 A BIOPROSPECTING BOOM

Given the lack of an international regime for the protection of TKGR and the uncertainties related to the different national regulations on TKGR trade, it has been natural to resort to the contractual accommodation of rights and obligations on TKGR trade.

The starting point of bioprospecting agreements has been the promise and expectation that TKGR may find a new form of protection through commercialisation. Due to the character of TKGR and the difficulties encountered in introducing or adapting already existing protection systems to cover TKGR, bioprospecting agreements have been considered the most immediate and direct form of protection.[1] Bioprospecting agreements were first seen in the pre-Convention on Biological Diversity (CBD) period. Obviously, after the CBD entered into force, expectations related to benefit sharing were higher, while at the same time no real changes in the legal status of TKGR were introduced.[2]

Plants have increasingly regained popularity in pharmaceutical research. The sophistication of biotechnology, chemistry and genomics has broadened the range of subject matter used for the development of medicines and agricultural products.[3] The methods employed are automated and the time needed to complete screening and research is considerably reduced compared to previous practices.[4]

---

[1] See Richerzhagen, C., Holm-Mueller, K. 'The Effectiveness of Access and Benefit Sharing in Costa Rica: Implications for National and International Regimes', Ecological Economics, Vol 53 (2005), pp. 445–60.

[2] See Contractual Practices and Clauses Relating to Intellectual Property, Access to Genetic Resources and Benefit-Sharing, WIPO/GRTKF/IC/5/9.

[3] Mulligan, S., Stoett, P., 'A Global Bio-Prospecting Regime: Partnership or Piracy', Intl J, Vol 2 (1999–2000), pp. 224–46.

[4] Polski, M., 'The Institutional Economics of Biodiversity, Biological Materials, and Bioprospecting', Ecological Economics, Vol 53 (2005), pp. 543–57.

Plant genetic resources are valuable subject matter mainly because they are so diverse and numerous. Thus, the problems faced with regard to screening or the poor solubility and instability of plant genetic resource samples are outweighed to the extent that one of the major challenges faced by research and development in the pharmaceutical industry nowadays concerns ameliorated access to and identification of useful plant resources for commodification.[5]

Bioprospectors usually employ phytogenetic information to collect samples of the same taxon as those that have already shown positive results in laboratory tests. Botanists never walk into the forest blindfolded, but have as their starting point essential components of traditional pharmacopoeia. Another bioprospecting technique is based on the observation of interactions between plants and insects, and between plants and other plants where chemicals are produced to deter predators. This method is rarely used in modern bioprospecting, since it is time-consuming and thus expensive.

Modern techniques and the advent of robotics have facilitated the screening of plant samples, allowing for a high-compound screening of 100,000 compounds a day. Another technological advancement of importance for bioprospecting is the advent of bioinformatics; that, along with combinatorial chemistry, has contributed to the development of databases containing collections of compounds produced in research institutions and accessed by researchers to find compounds similar to the ones they are searching for. Finally, modern bioassay methods have considerably reduced the cost of screening plants. Currently, 200–500 grams is sufficient for the entire screening process, compared to the 1–10 kilograms required for the initial research phase with the old techniques. Bioactive compounds can be synthesised, making it unnecessary to reaccess *in situ* material. Moreover, secondary metabolites can be produced on an industrial level.

4.1.1 Regulations and Guidelines

Due to the vague formulations of the CBD provisions and the historical lack of an institutional and legal framework for the protection of TKGR, international attention has turned to bioprospecting agreements and thus to the protection that these could give TKGR. The regulation of access to

[5] Also on the specific approach of creating value from exploiting TKGR see Liebig, K., Alker, D., *Governing Biodiversity: Access to Genetic Resources and Approaches to Obtaining Benefits from Their Use: The Case of Philippines*, Bonn: German Development Institute (2002), p. 87.

TKGR and benefit-sharing mechanisms was left for contractual arrangements developed in some cases as framework agreements, or in others as multilateral or even bilateral contractual structures.[6]

The CBD provides for the fundamental principles and procedures to be followed during bioprospecting processes, including mutually agreed terms, facilitated access, fair and equitable sharing of the benefits and prior informed consent. Furthermore, the Bonn Guidelines were developed in order to assist parties to the CBD when developing and drafting legislative, administrative and policy measures on access and benefit sharing, and also when developing contracts and other arrangements under mutually agreed terms for access and benefit sharing.

In its Decision VI/24, the Conference of the Parties (COP) encouraged the World Intellectual Property Organization (WIPO) to 'make rapid progress in the development of model intellectual property clauses which may be considered for inclusion in contractual agreements when mutually agreed terms are under negotiation'.[7]

The Intergovernmental Committee on Intellectual Property and Genetic Resources, Traditional Knowledge and Folklore (IGC) has been working with questions related to bioprospecting agreements since its first sessions in 2001.[8] One of the tasks stipulated at its first meeting was the development of guidelines on intellectual property (IP) aspects of contractual agreements for access to genetic resources and benefit sharing. The IGC elaborated a set of principles as well as a set of guidelines based on the already existing bioprospecting experiences.[9] A Guide of Contractual Practices was developed, aiming at playing a capacity-building and informative role without however having any impact on the sovereign rights of the states, which should regulate access and benefit sharing (ABS) mechanisms inside their territories.[10]

---

[6] Warner, J., 'Reframing the Bioprospecting Debate', Ind J Global Legal Stud, Vol 13 (2006), pp. 647–58.

[7] Decision COP VI/24C, para 9.

[8] For the evolution of the IGC work on the specific issue, see IPO/GRTKF/IC/7/9.

[9] WIPO/GRTKF/IF/6/5.

[10] The guidelines would assist in capacity building, awareness raising and also with respect to the information dissemination. The Guidelines prepared solely concerned the IP-related clauses, since all other matters fall outside the scope of the WIPO mandate.

4.1.2 Bioprospecting Agreements: The Experiences

Bioprospecting agreements are characterised by a plurality of parties and considerable geographical diversification, with different forms and structures; in some cases these take into consideration the particularities of the political and regulatory environment of the source countries, as well as of the parties involved. Most of the bioprospecting agreements include sample and collection fees, representing the most secure and direct form of compensation.[11] With the exception of the bioprospecting contracts signed by Biotics, the majority of bioprospecting contracts include some form of advance payment. Merck provides for advance sample fees, while Shaman finances locally recommended projects, investing in the local infrastructure for the supply of raw plant material – which is also a form of upfront payment. International Cooperative Biodiversity Groups (ICBG) invests in the establishment of biodiversity inventories and Shaman apprentice programmes. Iwokrama's first contractual framework includes advance payments that will be used to set up the institutional framework needed to shift to the second regime.

All of the contractual schemes involve payment of royalties. The royalty rate paid by Merck is estimated to reach up to 5 per cent, while Biotics provides for a share of royalties with the source country at the rate of 50 per cent. ICBG and Shaman provide for the payment of royalties as a reward for the contribution of traditional knowledge in the development of a product. Finally, Iwokrama takes royalty compensation a step further by providing that TKGR will be documented and thus royalties will be paid on the basis of IPRs to TKGR, as in any other licensing agreement.

Bioprospecting contracts usually include nonmonetary benefits such as technology transfer, capacity building and institutional support. In some cases technology transfer provisions concern the development of other biodiversity projects, or conservation activities, but quite often they are meant to facilitate and ameliorate the conditions of the specific bioprospecting agreement. The INBio/Merck contract provides that part of the upfront payment is to be used for the training of scientists, office supplies and computers to be used in the project. Both the ICBG

---

[11] See Blakeney, M., 'Bioprospecting and the Protection of Traditional Medicinal Knowledge of Indigenous Peoples: An Australian Perspective', Eur Intell Prop Rev, Vol 17 (1997), pp. 298–303. Blakeney, M., 'Ethnobotanological Knowledge and Intellectual Property of Rights of Indigenous Peoples in Australia', in Blakeney, M., et al (eds), *Intellectual Property Aspects of Ethno-Biology*, London: Sweet & Maxwell (1999), pp. 15–157.

framework and Shaman contractual relationships provide for the training of scientists from the source country and cooperation in capacity building. Finally, part of the benefits of the bioprospecting agreements are earmarked for conservation activities. Both Shaman and ICBG agreements identify the benefits distributed for conservation purposes with the benefits granted to indigenous communities.

Corporate parties' interest in bioprospecting processes has not been solely limited to their role as 'users' of TKGR. There are companies that have actually built their commercial activities on bioprospecting, while others limit their services to that of a 'bioprospecting' intermediary. Apart from 'isolated' contracts, there has even been an attempt to institutionalise the bioprospecting process, mainly by means of the ICBG programme that provided the financial and regulatory framework for a number of subsequent agreements.[12]

4.1.2.1 Bioprospecting agreements in the pre-CBD era

It might be surprising that bioprospecting agreements made their debut long before the entry into force of the CBD. The agreements were concluded at a time when there was a total lack of an institutional framework, as well as of any international recognition of a legal entitlement on TKGR. The major pre-CBD agreements were employed by Shaman Pharmaceuticals, but there is another notable example in the INBio–Merck research agreement.

4.1.2.1.1 Shaman Pharmaceuticals Shaman Pharmaceuticals was one of the first companies to present and make use of a bioprospecting strategy, as early as 1989. The company cooperated with more than 30 indigenous communities in Africa, Latin America and Southeast Asia, and used indigenous knowledge in order to cut down the rate of screened samples. Shaman Pharmaceuticals claimed that by employing traditional knowledge, one marketable pharmaceutical would be found out of every two plants screened. Traditional knowledge has thus been employed as a central element of the Shaman Pharmaceuticals R&D process.

---

[12] See Costanza, R., D'Arge, R., de Groot, R- Farber, S., Grasso, M., Hannon, B., Lindburg, K., Naem, S., O'Neil, R.V., Paruelo, J., Raskin, R.G., Sutton, P., van den Belt, M., 'The Value of the World's Ecosystem Services and Natural Capital', Nature, Vol 387 (1997), pp. 253–60. See also Dávalos, L.M., Sears, R.R., Raygorodetsky, G., Simmons, G., Cross, H., Grant, T., Putzel, L., Porzecanski, A.L., 'Regulating Access to Genetic Resources under the Convention on Biological Diversity: An Analysis of Selected Case Studies', Biodiversity and Conservation, Vol 12 (2003), pp. 1511–24.

The company developed an official benefit-sharing mechanism for the turnover of any product developed in cooperation with indigenous communities, but this did not evade criticism.[13] The benefit sharing was to be provided by means of the Healing Forest Conservancy, a nonprofit organisation created by Shaman. This organisation was in charge of contacting communities, investigating their needs and channelling compensation accordingly. Under its principles, benefits are shared by all communities cooperating with Shaman, independent of origin.[14]

The most important research result for Shaman Pharmaceuticals was the medicinal properties of *Sangre de Drago*. Indigenous communities in the Amazonian basin used *Sangre de Drago* for its properties in wound healing, anti-inflammatory treatments, haemorrhoids and skin problems. The multitude of traditional medicinal uses of *Sangre de Drago* motivated Shaman to proceed to further research that finally led to the isolation of a specific alkaloid with healing capacity. The use of the alkaloid – the final marketed product – for which Shaman applied for patent protection was in fact for the treatment of herpes.[15]

In February 1999, Shaman Pharmaceuticals changed its name and profile, after considerable economic pressure. The new company, with 24 employees (compared to Shaman Pharmaceuticals' 90), was renamed Shaman Botanicals and concentrated on the development of herbal remedies instead of drugs. The problems that forced the company's reorientation were due to lengthy and costly procedures on the part of the Food and Drug Administration (FDA).[16]

---

[13] The company's cooperation with the indigenous community of Jatun Molino, in eastern Ecuador, focused on the researchers' contact with the traditional healer. In effect, it has been claimed that the benefits provided were meant to cover the expenses and needs of the company's expedition team. See Reyes, V., 'The Value of Sangre de Drago' (1996), https://www.grain.org/article/entries/313-the-value-of-sangre-de-drago. See also King, S.R., Carlson, T.J., 'Biocultural Diversity, Biomedicine and Ethnobotany: The Experience of Shaman Pharmaceuticals', Interciencia, Vol 20 (1995), pp. 134–9.

[14] Conte, L. 'Shaman Pharmaceuticals' Approach to Drug Development', in Balick, M. et al (eds), *Medicinal Resources of the Tropical Forest: Biodiversity and Its Importance to Human Health*, New York: Columbia University Press (1996), pp. 94–100.

[15] See http://www.natura.lt/documents/mokslas/10_SangreHS.pdf.

[16] A week before the press release announcing the changes to occur in the company, an FDA committee published its objections to tests the company had used to prove that its proposed Provir drug alleviated the symptoms of AIDS diarrhoea. See also MutlexInvestor, 'Shaman Pharmaceuticals Inc – Business Description' (2002).

4.1.2.1.2 INBio–MERCK research agreement INBio is a private, nonprofit institution with ties to the Costa Rican government's Ministry of Environment and Energy (MINAE),[17] which ministry created and administered a system of conservation areas, containing about 25 per cent of Costa Rica's land area, as protected wildlands. One of the priorities of MINAE was to create an inventory of Costa Rica's biodiversity, and in this process it has collaborated with the indigenous communities of the area. INBio entered into a bioprospecting agreement with the pharmaceutical company Merck on 1 November 1991, which was subsequently renewed in July 1994 and August 1996.

The economic substance of INBio does not depend on benefits arising out of bioprospecting agreements. Only 15 per cent of INBio's budget is derived from such agreements; the other 85 per cent is obtained through project grants from diverse sources. Although INBio has the status of a nongovernmental organisation (NGO), it is in close cooperation with MINAE, and this was also formalised in a cooperation agreement signed in October 2004. The relationship between INBio and MINAE is specified in detail in 13 clauses. Clause 1 states that INBio and MINAE will work together on the national biodiversity inventory, which expressly resulted in severance of the agreement and application of the Wildlife Conservation Law.[18] Clause 8 states that MINAE allows INBio to collect biological samples for the purpose of bioprospecting. Another very important provision is Clause 12, which provides that 50 per cent of any economic and material benefits INBio receives through bioprospecting are to be transferred to MINAE, and that these resources will be exclusively invested in management and conservation of wild lands administered by MINAE.

---

[17] A detailed discussion of the bioprospecting agreement can be found in Columbia University School of International and Public Affairs, 'Access to Genetic Resources: an evaluation of the Development and Implementation of Recent Regulation and Access Agreements', Environmental Policy Studies, Working Paper 4, prepared for the Biodiversity Action Network (June 1999). See also Gàmez, R., 'The Link between Biodiversity and Sustainable Development: Lessons from INBio's Bioprospecting Program in Costa Rica' (2003), pp. 1–15, https://www.cbd.int/financial/bensharing/costarica-absinbio.pdf. Another interesting report on the program is Gámez, R., Piva, A., Sittenfeld, A., Leon, E., Jimenez, J., Mirabelli, G., 'Biodiversity Prospecting: Using Genetic Resources for Sustainable Development', Costa Rica Conservation Program and National Biodiversity Institute (INBio), World Resources Institute, Washington (1993), pp. 53–68.

[18] Law on Wildlife Conservation, No 7317 of 30 October 1992.

According to the provisions of the agreement entered into with Merck, INBio will supply samples for pharmaceutical screening during a two-year period in return for US$1 million, as well as additional benefits at a later stage of the agreement that would contribute to the development of local sample preparation and screening. The agreement provides for a share of potential royalties.[19] INBio, on the other hand, is under the obligation to extract and collect samples from a number of plants, animals, insects and microorganisms processed in Merck's labs in Spain.

The agreement includes a confidentiality clause,[20] according to which parties are prevented from disclosing any 'confidential information' to third parties for a period of seven years from the expiration of the agreement.

Another important provision in this agreement is Clause 7, according to which INBio is prevented from supplying other organisations interested in human and animal health or agriculture with the samples it provided Merck for a two-year initial evaluation period. After this period has expired, Merck may extend the exclusive evaluation period indefinitely for up to 1 per cent of the samples provided to it. INBio is free to offer all other samples to third parties and thus can enter into other bioprospecting agreements for the same material.

An important issue to be resolved in the specific agreement was the ownership of genetic resources. According to Article 6 of Costa Rican Law 7788, biochemical and genetic resources of wildlife and domesticated breeds belong to the public domain, while the state is granted the right to grant authorisation regarding its exploitation, investigation, bioprospecting, use and exploitation. On the other hand, Article 76 stipulates that the private owner providing for elements to be accessed is entitled to compensation. According to the bioprospecting agreement, the samples of genetic resources will be collected from 'the Conservation Areas of Costa Rica and other areas of the private domain'.[21] In conclusion, taking into consideration the fact that Costa Rican legislation remains silent with regard to the issue of ownership while at the same time the INBio–Merck agreement regulates ownership under a vague and

---

[19] See Calibrera, M.J., 'Bioprospecting Partnerships in Practice: A Decade of Experiences at INBio in Costa Rica', IP Strategy Today, Vol 11 (2004), pp. 27–40.

[20] Clause 9 of the Agreement.

[21] The regime applicable to conservation areas is specified in Article 28 of Law 7788. According to the said provision, this falls under the general supervision of MINAE and includes wildlife areas, areas with a high degree of fragility and private areas with commercial exploitation.

unclear provision, it could be claimed that the ownership of genetic resources is transferred to Merck.

With regard to IPR, both the INBio agreement and the Costa Rican legislation are very explicit. The agreement grants both parties the authority to submit, follow up and maintain patents, under the precondition that they consult with the other party.

Merck's monetary obligations remain unclear. Merck provided US$1 million during the first two years for the purchase of laboratory equipment and materials that would contribute to the operation of INBio's processing laboratory. According to the agreement, INBio would provide MINAE with US$100,000 for reinvestment in conservation.[22] There is no information on the financial arrangements included in the extension agreements, and there is no report of royalties being paid on the basis of this agreement.[23]

The INBio–Merck agreement contains detailed provisions concerning conflict resolution. The agreement underlines the importance of frequent communication between the parties.[24] In case of a conflict, the agreement provides for a three-level dispute settlement resolution procedure.[25] Parties should attempt to resolve the issue through discussion in good faith. Should they fail to reach agreement after a period of two months, the dispute is to be discussed in a group containing a single high-ranking official from each party. If no agreement is reached after a period of four months, the issue is to be handed over to an arbitrator.[26] Lacking in the provisions of the specific bioprospecting agreement, however, is any reference to the rights of indigenous communities and thus any guarantee as to their participation in the benefit-sharing arrangements.

It is not possible to make an overall assessment of the agreement. The confidentiality agreement signed by the parties does not allow the disclosure of a number of major provisions, such as that regulating the royalty rate and other financial provisions. Nor has any commercial

---

[22] The agreement provided that INBio would contribute to conservation with 10 per cent of the available budget.

[23] Sittenfeld, A., Gámez, R., *Biodiversity by INBio. Biodiversity Prospecting: Using Genetic Resources for Sustainable Development*, Washington, DC: World Resources Initiative (1993), pp. 69–98.

[24] Article 9 provides that project directors should realise informal consultations in person and by telephone regarding the management of the agreement and must regularly exchange the results of research and technical knowledge.

[25] Article 10(j) of the agreement.

[26] The parties have the right to initiate a judicial process.

exploitation of the accessed genetic resources been possible to date, which further limits the scope of assessment of the agreement's efficiency.[27]

The INBio agreement and the example of Costa Rica are often described and presented as a raw model of a bioprospecting agreement. Although the results are not measurable, the agreement is very often employed as evidence of the positive effects of bioprospecting endeavours. The difficulties of benefit appreciation are often reiterated in the works of a plurality of authors; however, there are very few direct critiques.[28]

4.1.2.2 Bioprospecting agreements in the post-CBD era

Bioprospecting agreements have gradually become more or less standard procedure. A major characteristic of this era is the introduction of major framework agreements, such as that of the ICBG programme, as well as of other agreements of limited scope and of pure commercial nature, such as those signed by Biotics.

4.1.2.2.1 Biotics Biotics is a private company that functions as an intermediary between source countries and pharmaceutical companies. Biotics is a collector with contacts in a vast range of source countries. Pharmaceutical companies prefer to contact collectors than to enter into bioprospecting agreements directly with the source country. Biotics' bioprospecting agreements provide for a payment of £25 per sample and 50 per cent of any royalties obtained by Biotics. The contracts also provide that a share of the royalties paid to the collector will finance biodiversity development projects in the source country.[29]

4.1.2.2.2 ICBG agreements The ICBG programme has been one of the central policy schemes in a major bioprospecting programme established by US agencies, the National Institutes of Health, the National Science Foundation and the US Agency for International Development,[30]

---

[27] Richerzhagen, Holm-Mueller (2005), pp. 452–5.

[28] For one author who has greatly criticised the immense attention given to the INBio agreement over the years see Castree, N., 'Bioprospecting: From Theory to Practice (and Back Again)', Transactions of the Institute of British Geographers, New Series, Vol 28 (2003), pp. 35–55.

[29] For information about the company see http://www.bioticsresearch.com.

[30] For information about the program see http://www.icbg.org. See also http://www.fic.nih.gov/programs/pages/biodiversity.aspx. Some of the ICBG projects have also set up their own homepages: see for instance http://lingington.chemistry.ucsc.edu//ICBG/index.html.

with the goal of building and promoting partnerships between the industry and scientists in the United States and the source countries.[31]

The philosophy behind drafting the ICBG programme was that natural product research and development can bring both short- and long-term benefits to the countries and communities that are the stewards of TKGR. Benefit-sharing opportunities would function as an incitement for conservation and sustainable use. Therefore, the ICBG was designed to provide models for the sustainable use of biodiversity, as well as to investigate whether bioprospecting could contribute to: (1) improving human health through the discovery of natural products with medicinal properties; (2) conserving biodiversity through training and infrastructure building to aid in management; and finally (3) promoting communities' sustainable economic activity.

Each of the groups is run by an academic principal investigator, responsible for research in natural products chemistry, drug development or ethnobotany, which at the same time coordinates the activities of several associated programmes. The associated programmes include other academic research institutions and local and international NGOs active in host countries. An ICBG programme presupposes the active participation of host country individuals and organisations, multidisciplinary research into diseases of both local and international significance, local training and infrastructure development in both drug discovery and biodiversity management.

The contractual agreements, signed under the framework of an ICBG programme for the financed projects, adopted different structures in different jurisdictions. The basis of the ICBG projects is always a contract, a cooperative agreement between the US government and a principal investigator situated in an American university. The US government agrees to fund the group's work to carry out the project as described in the application. Each project will enter the other necessary subsequent agreements, which primarily take the form of access and benefit-sharing agreements.

The application procedure for the ICBG Awards opened in 1993 and continued until 1994. Of 34 applications, 5 projects were chosen. The

[31] Rosenthal, J., 'Equitable Sharing of Biodiversity Benefits: Agreements on Genetic Resources', National Institute of Health, paper presented at the International Conference on Incentive Measures for the Conservation and Sustainable Use of Biological Diversity, Cairns, Australia (25–28 March 1996). See also Swanson, T., Göschl, T., 'Property Rights Issued Involving Plant Genetic Resources: Implications of Ownership for Economic Efficiency', Ecological Economics, Vol 32 (2000), pp. 75–92.

selected projects were the following studies: (1) rainforest plants in Suriname; (2) insects and related organisms from the dry tropical forest in Costa Rica; (3) land plants in Argentina, Chile and Mexico; (4) medicinal plants (traditional medicine) in Peru; and (5) parasitic diseases from the rainforest plants of Cameroon and Nigeria. The Costa Rican ICBG programme adopted the 'one contract' model. Parties to this contract have included Cornell University, Cornell Research Foundation, INBio, and Bristol-Myers Squibb Pharmaceutical Research Institute. The adoption of the 'one contract' model was possible in this case because of the fact that INBio had both a broad mandate and sophisticated know-how in the field of bioprospecting. The ICBG Latin American programme, on the other hand, adopts a 'wheel of contracts' structure. The principal investigator in this case, Arizona University, entered into a number of bilateral agreements with eight different institutions in host countries. Finally, the Suriname ICBG presented a dual-contract structure separating the research and development contract and the benefit-sharing agreement. There was no major commercial partner in this specific ICBG project.

The parties to both types of contracts are host country institutions. This specific contractual model allows for a separation of the provisions regulating access to tangible and intangible resources, respectively; while at the same time allowing for different provisions depending on whether the agreement in question is a purely research one, or a commercial one. This structure also reflects commercial partners' reluctance to negotiate and enter into contracts with indigenous communities. It is highly probable that indigenous communities would benefit from direct negotiation of an agreement with their commercial partner since this would allow for a better valuation of the tangible and intangible resources accessed.[32]

The Suriname project was one of the ICBG-submitted proposals to receive financing. Parties to the project, led by the Virginia Polytechnic Institute and State University (VPISU), included Conservation International (CI), an international NGO; Bedrift Geneesmiddelen Voorziening Suriname (BGVS), a pharmaceutical company owned by the Surinamese government; Missouri Botanical Gardens (MBG), an American botanical research institution; and Bristol-Myers Squibb (BMS), an American pharmaceutical company. The programme's objectives were to

---

[32] For an interesting evaluation of the effects of the Costa Rican ICBG program see Richerzhagen, Holm-Mueller (2005), pp. 445–60. See also Swanson and Göschl (2000).

promote drug discovery and at the same time contribute to the conservation of biological and ethnobotanological knowledge.

Parties in the Suriname programme were linked by means of a series of oral and written agreements. The relationship between the Saramaka people and CI was regulated by means of a letter of intent,[33] which specified that CI be granted the authorisation to begin ethnobotanological research in cooperation with the Saramaka people. A basic prerequisite for the authorisation was that CI would represent the Saramaka people's interests in the evolution and development of the project. The authorisation was to be renewed on a periodical basis subsequent to negotiations with the tribe's representatives. CI made sure that the participating shamans' informed consent was obtained before the collection expedition began.

The first goal of the programme was to document medicinal traditional knowledge, developed over the past hundred years and stored solely in the minds of the shamans. Another important objective was the transfer of technology, capacity building and training so that in the long run, local scientists would be able to benefit from their countries' biological resources. The third goal of the Suriname ICBG was to develop commercial drugs from plant extracts in order to finally create a conservation-financing institution.

Even in the initial ICBG research agreement, detailed specification of the duties/obligations of each participant was provided. MBG was to be responsible for random botanical collections while CI would be responsible for ethnobotanical collections (the ICBG Suriname programme adopted both methods of collection in order to increase success rates). In effect, one aspect of the programme was to compare these two methods and investigate which of the two had the highest 'hit' rate. Both systems of collection employed local scientists and indigenous populations. The MBG employed Surinamese scientists, students of the University of Suriname and indigenous peoples whom they trained in the methodology of random botanical collection.

The CI employed Surinamese ethnobotanists and community members in their ethnobioprospecting expeditions. These collections took place in the shaman's medicinal 'garden' as well as in the forest surrounding the villages. During the collection process, the 'collecting team' filled in a form containing information about the area where the sample was found,

---

[33] The Saramaka people are represented by the Granman, the paramount chief representing more than 17,000 Maroons living in villages along the Suriname River.

the soil, the habitat, the visibility, the portions of the plant utilised and the local names of the plant. Finally, the information database was updated with information concerning the shaman and his use of the plant, which diseases the plant was used to treat, how the medicine was prepared and the dosage, method of application and side effects of its use.[34]

At this stage the corporate parties' participation in the programme was limited. In fact, a system for encoding the samples was developed in order to avoid the pharmaceutical companies seeking access to valuable samples in other source countries as well as in order to keep confidential the collection process adopted for the collection of a specific sample. All plant samples were tested for anticancer and anti-infective activity.[35] BMS could perform other tests on the precondition that VPISU and BGVS were informed by means of a confidential letter as to the list of therapeutic purposes for which the samples would be screened. BMS had the obligation to inform VPISU about the properties of the samples screened,[36] and had a predefined period of time to express interest in the sample. After the expiration of this deadline, BMS would lose the exclusive right and the sample would enter a pool of samples available to other interested corporate users.

It deserves to be noted that at this point the corporate partners in the programme had no information as to the location where the sample was extracted, or of its traditional uses.[37] Information on the plant name and its uses was released only subject to the prior informed consent of the shaman. Samples and extracts were not available to third parties without the authorisation of VPISU. In order for BGVS to provide extracts to third parties, VPISU needed to get confirmation from BMS and BGVS that they were not interested in the samples. The Suriname ICBG programme contained detailed provisions as to the benefit-sharing mechanisms employed. The plurality of the parties and the different interests they had in the programme dictated the conclusion of a number of agreements on the basis of which the sharing of benefits would be regulated.

---

[34] During the first stage of the programme, 500 grams of roots, barks, twigs and leaves of each plant were collected. At the second annual meeting of the programme, the quantity was limited to 100 grams per plant.

[35] The testing is to be performed by Bristol-Myers Squibb.

[36] VPISU thereafter sends the list to BVGS, CI and MBG.

[37] In cases where the corporate partners are interested in a specific sample, BGVS notifies CI, which in turn contacts the collection team and goes back to the shaman, and a new collection is made.

The ICBG research agreement regulated the distribution of benefits arising out of inventions and patents. Inventions were to be reported to designated officials of each party, which were to decide on the inventorship and ownership of the invention on the basis of the various parties' scientific contribution. The law applicable to these negotiations was US patent law. According to the ICBG contract, where the invention was the result of collaboration with the shaman, the patent application would be filed jointly.[38]

BMS had the right to opt for an exclusive licence for any invention developed under the framework of the Suriname ICBG programme. If BMS did not exercise its rights within a period of one year from the date the first patent application was handed in, or when the parties could not reach an agreement as to the terms and conditions of the licence agreement, then the owners of the patent were free to license their rights to third parties. Fees paid by BMS were reduced as the scientific differences between the active compound and the natural product increased.[39] Royalties are due during the lifetime of the patent, or, if no patent is granted, for a number of years after the first commercialisation of the product.

The Statement of Understanding, on the other hand, regulated the relationship between the Granman of the Saramaka people, CI and BGVS. It provided for two different schemes of benefit sharing, depending on whether the active compound was derived from ethnobotanological or random collection.[40]

In the framework of the Suriname ICBG agreement, a trust fund named the Forest People's Fund was established to ensure that benefits reached indigenous communities.[41] The Fund finances projects, research and training exchanges.[42] Similar to most other bioprospecting agreements, benefits arising from the Suriname ICBG programme have mostly taken the form of capacity building, technology transfer, upfront collection payments and employment possibilities. There is no report of any commercial product having been developed from samples accessed under the Suriname ICBG programme.

---

[38] Where BMS is a partner in the patent application procedure, it bears the costs of patenting and prosecuting subsequent patent violations.

[39] The rate of the royalties remains confidential.

[40] Obviously, the former gives rise to higher royalty rates.

[41] The fund was established in 1994. The financials of the fund depended to a large extent on donations from BMS.

[42] Programme activities have included projects concerning community development, biodiversity conservation and health care.

4.1.2.2.3 Iwokrama Iwokrama is a governmental authority established in 1996 by the Parliament of Guyana.[43] In the Iwokrama Operational Plan, it is stated that biodiversity will function as a source of 'large payments and substantial royalties'. Iwokrama values the ethnobotanical aspect of TKGR, and sets the documentation of ethnobotanical knowledge and the acknowledgement of the IPRs associated with that knowledge as one of its major goals.[44] Iwokrama initiated its Bioprospecting Programme in 2000, with the partnership of the Centre for Agriculture and Biodiversity International UK (CABI), the Royal Botanic Gardens Kew, the University of West Indies and the University of Guyana.[45]

The Iwokrama bioprospecting scheme includes two levels of agreement. On the first level, Iwokrama can sell licences for prospecting rights with an advance payment and a limited royalty rate. This form of cooperation will be applicable until Iwokrama puts in place the necessary institutional framework to allow for the application of the second contractual level. This second level provides that Iwokrama can sell samples with royalties on the commercial products. However, no report has been made on the agreements and provisions included, and thus there is no way of assessing the programme's deliverables.

4.1.2.2.4 Yellowstone–Diversa bioprospecting agreement Bioprospecting endeavours in Yellowstone Park date back to 1898. The interest in bioprospecting in this park came about with interest in the heat-resistant enzyme Taq polymerase, derived from the bacterium *Thermus aquaticus*, a bacterium that survives high temperatures. The qualities of *Thermus aquaticus* were discovered in 1966, and the Taq enzyme was patented and later sold to Hoffman-La Roche for US$300 million in 1991.

In 1997, Yellowstone Park signed a bioprospecting agreement with the Diversa Company – in fact, the first bioprospecting agreement signed in

---

[43] The institutional framework of the Iwokrama project was financed by United Nations Development program and other international development agencies.

[44] Iwokrama finances and manages a number of programmes related to sustainable use of biodiversity and the economic development of SMEs in the region. One example is the 'Forest Connect' project. The goal of the project is to link local SMEs with service providers in other countries.

[45] Reported achievements of the programme include the sampling of 22 different species, the preparation and screening of more than 3400 fungus and 60 plant extracts for biological activities in 23 different assays and fractionation of eight bioactive extracts. In the achievements we also find reference to the draft agreements for Iwokrama IPR policy document.

the United States.[46] This agreement was the first attempt to provide for the sharing of benefits arising from the development of a commercial product based on genetic resources found in public lands. The contractual agreement signed between Yellowstone and Diversa was drafted with the guidance of previously signed bioprospecting agreements in other parts of the world, while the parties investigated the compatibility of its clauses with the objectives of the CBD.

The fact that the genetic resources in question were found in a national park clarified the ownership status of the agreement, facilitating the agreement's conclusion. The collection permit granted did not have an impact on the ownership status of the specimen. This clarity with regard to the ownership of resources and the representation of the park's rights simplifies procedures, particularly with regard to the procedure regarding prior informed consent.

The commercial transfer of physical resources is prohibited under the agreement, while 'specimens and data derived from consumed specimens' must be 'available to the public and publications resulting from a research specimen collection permit shall be filed with the superintendent'. The benefit-sharing provisions of the agreement provided that Yellowstone Park would receive an annual payment of US$100,000 for five years for sample collecting and collaborative research activities. Furthermore, Diversa is under the obligation to provide 'in-kind services and resources valued at US$375,000'. The royalties provided in the agreement have not been disclosed to the public, but both parties have referred to royalties varying from 0.5 to 10 per cent of the income resulting from the commercial exploitation originating in the organisms accessed in the park. The park is bound to use all benefits for the conservation of the park's biodiversity and for research purposes.[47]

---

[46] The regulatory framework applicable in the Yellowstone–Diversa Agreement is that of the National Park Service Organic Act and the Federal Technology Transfer Act. The National Park Service Organic Act governs the collection of research specimens on national park land. Authorisation granted by the competent authority is dependent on a 'statement of work' in which the applicant describes in detail the objectives and methods of collection activities. The Research Specimen Collection Permit does not grant exclusive or proprietary rights to the researcher and does not constitute a sale of material or knowledge derived therefrom.

[47] The resolution of disputes arising between the parties would be resolved by the National Park Service (NPS).

4.1.2.2.5 Bioprospecting and the Xa21 gene Rice is a very sensitive crop, often destroyed by bacteria and fungi. Rice scientists have thus long searched for pest-resistant rice varieties. A major development in the field of research for more resistant rice species was the discovery of a wild rice, *Oryza longistaminata*.[48] The Bela people used the stem of *O. longistaminata* to fence off territories in which official ceremonies took place, while a person would be covered by *O. longistaminata* during traditional ceremonies.

This wild rice variety, considered a weed by scientists, was regarded as a major food crop in the past, and continues to be seen as such – particularly for the landless populations of Mali. Indigenous communities have developed detailed traditional knowledge on the uses, the taxonomy and the *in situ* conservation of this specific plant variety. At a time when Malian agricultural scientists were totally unaware of the beneficial characteristics of the specific plant variety, the traditional knowledge of the Bela community included ecological and ethnobotanical details about the characteristics of the specific plant variety, including its resistance to rice blight. *O. longistaminata* is in fact resistant to almost all known crop diseases.[49]

This wild rice variety was brought to the *ex situ* conservation of the International Rice Research Institute (IRRI) in Manila as early as 1978. Scientists at the Institute managed to introduce the resistance characteristic of the wild variety into cultivated rice varieties through traditional plant-breeding methods.[50]

The pathogen-resistant characteristic of the rice variety was traced to a gene called Xa21 whose sequence was mapped by Professor Pamela Ronald at Cornell University in 1990. The mapped Xa21 gene was expected to have broad commercial applications, with regard not only to rice varieties but also to other major crops, such as the wheat and barley varieties often infected by the *Xanthomonas* pathogen.

The Regents of the University of California filed a patent application, with 24 claims on the Xa21 gene, in 1995. According to the abstract of the patent application, the invention boiled down to providing 'nucleic acids encoding polypeptides which confer resistance to *Xanthomonas*

---

[48] This specific rice variety was discovered by an Indian scientist, Dr Devadath.

[49] There is even a bird, the chironi, which eats *O. longistaminata* and thus indicates the presence of the rice variety in the lands.

[50] Synthesis of Case Studies on Benefit Sharing, UNEP/CBD/COP/4/Inf.7, 4 May 1998.

spp. The nucleic acids can be used to produce transgenic plants resistant to the pathogen'. The Xa21 patent was granted in 1999.[51]

A benefit-sharing mechanism was set up in 1996 in the form of an independent institution, the Genetic Resources Recognition Fund (GRR Fund). The goals of the GRR Fund were: to provide for a mechanism of recognition of the developing countries' contribution in germplasm; to provide a means for scientists to patent their inventions while continuing their cooperation with scientists from developing countries; to encourage contact between the industry and the university for the commercialisation of genetically engineered products; to create a constructive solution that would be easy to implement; and, finally, to create economic incentives for the conservation and sharing of germplasm.

The initiators of the GRR Fund faced a major hindrance in defining the rights to TKGR on Xa21.[52] The ambition was that the GRR Fund would constitute a model benefit-sharing scheme adopted by the University of California, even in other cases of bioprospecting. Access to Xa21 would be available free of any economic commitment to publicly funded research programmes and noncommercial researchers under the limitation that they would not develop any commercial products on the basis of the genetic material in question. According to the MTA drafted by UC Davis, Xa21 could only be used in cooperative scientific research. The party accessing the genetic material would not have the right to provide 'these materials, their progeny or derivatives to any other party or use them for commercial purposes without the express written consent of The Regents of the University of California'. The rightholders declared their willingness to allow developing countries to use the patented gene freely and incorporate it in their plant varieties.[53]

It deserves to be noted that there were no economic contributions to the GRR Fund. The Fund was not favoured at UC Davis and its use never became common among scientists. Another flaw of the Xa21 benefit-sharing structure was the lack of contact and flow of information between the different actors involved. It was in fact shown that scientists in Mali working with agricultural research were not aware of the existence of the GRR Fund.

The case of Xa21 provides for a very interesting illustration of one of the major weaknesses of bioprospecting agreements in general, namely that of the different overlapping layers of claims on specific genetic

---

[51] USPT 5859339.

[52] Professor Ronald with the consultancy of Professor Barton.

[53] For the scientific contributions of the Xa21 invention see http://indica.ucdavis.edu/publication/reference/r0004.pdf.

resources that, in their turn, lead to a number of layers of property rights. Agricultural scientists in Mali were aware of the fact that the specific rice variety containing the Xa21 gene grew together with two other rice varieties, *Oryza barthii* and *Oryza glabberma*. They were also aware of the fact that this wild rice variety spreads so widely that in some cases fields have to be abandoned. In general, *O. longistaminata* was considered to be a weed to be controlled by any means.[54]

The Xa21 bioprospecting experience is proof of a number of significant hindrances associated with the bioprospecting process, and the GRR Fund illustrates the weaknesses of such benefit-sharing mechanisms. Firstly, the identification of TKGR rightholders has proved to be a very complicated task. In the specific case described, the Bela people were the only ones to have developed traditional knowledge on the uses, cultivation and characteristics of the plant variety. The identification of rightholders is not illustrated in the benefit-sharing plan of the GRR Fund. Nowhere in the goals or regulations of the Fund was there a provision with regard to the rights of the Bela people. At the same time, local farmers had no interest and had not been engaged in the conservation of the TKGR in question.

Secondly, bilateral plans are hardly recognised and are applied on a broad scale by universities in developed countries. The GRR Fund is an illustration of the difficulties in actually collecting funds, as well as in communicating their existence and goals to the relevant stakeholders, in this case the Malian scientists. Research on the Xa21 gene did not involve local scientists, nor is there documented participation of Malian research institutions in the research project.

4.1.2.2.6 Bioprospecting and Ancistrocladus korupensis *Ancistrocladus korupensis* (AK)[55] was first collected by botanists in the early years of the twentieth century in Nigeria. The second major collection phase was in 1987 in Korup National Park, under the initiative of MBG, the National Cancer Institute (NCI) and the University of Yaoundé.[56]

In 1990, the NCI discovered that a chemical substance/extract of AK, michellamine B, could inhibit the HIV virus' killing of human cells. After michellamine B was approved for pre-clinical development at the

---

[54] Scientists tried to control this 'weed', even using a well-known weed killer product, without success.

[55] A rainforest liana.

[56] For more details on the bioprospecting agreement see UNEP/CBD/COP/4/Inf 25 (20 April 1998).

NCI, the MBG, in collaboration with the University of Yaoundé and with the funding of the NCI, expanded its research programme in Cameroon in order to assess the density and distribution of the population of AK. Initially, research studies concentrated upon the distribution and taxonomy of AK, in order to proceed to an intensive cultivation programme in a second phase.[57]

In August 1992, under the auspices of their extended work for the NCI in Cameroon, MBG representatives met with representatives at the University Centre for Health Sciences of the University of Yaoundé to discuss the NCI letter of intent, finally signed in 1993. The government of Cameroon later revoked the initial letter of intent, since it considered the University of Yaoundé incapable of defending the country's interests.

The increased involvement of government agencies was in line with the entry into force of the Convention on Biological Diversity and the concerns relating to access and benefit sharing. While the initial letter of intent was revoked, no other official agreement regulating access to the biological resources in question was negotiated. That led to further confusion of the roles and responsibilities in the bioprospecting process. Between the University of Yaoundé, the NCI, the MBG and the several governmental agencies and ministries of Cameroon involved in the project, it was unclear who the primal rightholder was and who had the responsibility to initiate and conclude negotiations.

Finally, an Inter-Ministerial Committee was established and a meeting was held to address the issues raised by AK. The meeting resulted in the decisions to: (1) declare the genetic and biological material of AK a 'national treasure'; (2) prohibit the export of live plant material and seeds; (3) examine the possibility to proceed to a research cooperation agreement with NCI; (4) introduce the Production and Exploitation Committee and the Research Committee; and finally (5) set up a Legal Aspects Committee. Notwithstanding the fact that establishing these committees was an important step forward, there remains confusion as to the competence and responsibilities of the involved ministries, leading to a hold-out situation.[58]

By means of the bioprospecting agreement, the Korup Project and the University of Yaoundé gained, in terms of benefit-sharing, training in collection and agronomic techniques, provision of infrastructure in the

---

[57] Cultivation was deemed essential in order to secure a sustainable distribution of the biological resources in question, since AK was extremely localised in its occurrence and the leaves were difficult to reach in the forest canopy.

[58] NCI is no longer pursuing research on michellamine B because of its high level of toxicity.

form of equipment, research results and investments in potential income-generating and capacity-building schemes.

4.1.2.2.7 Prunus Africana *Prunus Africana* (pygeum) is a hardwood species native to mountain forests in Africa, with a range extending from Cameroon across mainland Africa to Kenya and Madagascar and as far south as the Cape. In Cameroon, pygeum appears in the forests of the north-west and south-west regions, and has been used by local populations for carving as well as for medical purposes. The qualities of this plant were discovered by phytomedical companies in Europe 20 years ago,[59] with the plant material sold as a treatment for benign prostatic hyperplasia and total sales estimated at around US$150 million per year. In the majority of cases, the exploitation was unsustainable, with trees being felled rather than harvested.[60]

In an effort to avoid the complete erosion of the plant in question, an agreement was signed between the main purchasing company, Plantecam Medicam,[61] and the village of Mapanja,[62] called the 'Agreement for Sustainable Management of the Species and Production of P. Africana at Mapanja Village'. The Ministry of Forests and Environment and the Mount Cameroon Project were also involved in the regulation of access and sharing of benefits arising out of the exploitation of pygeum.[63]

The first time Medicam gained access to pygeum, the legal framework regulating such initiatives permitted a two-year exploitation period.[64] Medicam contacted the government of Cameroon and, after substantial negotiations, the official exploitation of pygeum began in 1976.

Pygeum has been used by indigenous communities in carving, construction and medicine. However, it was only after the access contract with Medicam that massive collection started. Medicam arranged a

---

[59] Prunus Africana is sold as a component of herbal preparations, as a component of hair tonic sold in Japan and as sawn timber and furniture within Africa.

[60] Between 3200 and 4200 tons of material are extracted for export every year.

[61] A French-owned phytomedical company.

[62] The Bakweri villages of Mapanja and Bokwongo, located in the Mount region of Cameroon.

[63] The Mount Cameroon Project is a local conservation and sustainable development project which actually facilitated the signing of this agreement. *Prunus Africana* represents approximately 88 per cent of the medicinal plant material Plantecam Medicam. For more details on the bioprospecting agreement see UNEP/CBD/COP/4/Inf 25 (20 April 1998).

[64] Decree No 74/1357 of April 1974.

programme to train collectors in order to guarantee sustainable exploitation of the resources in question. In 1993, in order to increase income from the exploitation of pygeum, the government of Cameroon permitted access for three domestic companies that lacked the means to put in place any sustainability measures. By 1994, illegal exploitation of pygeum was massive.

Local communities did not show any interest in protecting the plant genetic resources and served as middlemen, providing interested buyers – one of those being Medicam – with pygeum bark. The close and direct collaboration between villagers and Medicam served as grounds for the drafting of a cooperative system for the sustainable, and this time legal, exploitation of pygeum. The terms of the agreement were negotiated by a team from Medicam, the Ministry of Environment and Forests and the Mount Cameroon Project. The first step was capacity building, with the villagers having meetings for general feedback and information.

According to these agreements, the Prunus Harvesters' Union would harvest the bark instead of Medicam's recruited workers,[65] at the same rate Medicam used to buy from middlemen.[66] Every villager was allowed to harvest a maximum of 30 kg a day; from this, 2 kg would be contributed to the Village Development Fund,[67] and 1 kg to the Union's Fund. In addition to the monetary benefits gained from the agreement, the villages that were parties in the agreement acquired benefits in the form of training, capacity and institution building and infrastructure and equipment.

The specific agreement has been considered a successful illustration of bioprospecting, which is said to depend considerably upon the special characteristics of the phytomedical industry, whose survival in the market depends upon secured access to key plant genetic resources. Undoubtedly, bioprospecting of *Prunus Africana* has been beneficial for all involved parties. Indigenous communities gained both short- and long-term profits; the government of Cameroon benefited from taxes originating from the commercialisation of the plant genetic resources, as well as from the establishment of a sustainable and well-functioning industry; and Medicam in this way guaranteed the supply of pygeum bark, essential for the production and commercialisation of high-quality products.

---

[65] The villagers of Mapanja and Bokwongo.

[66] Middlemen used to buy material from the villagers at a very low price and then sell at a higher price to Medicam. See UNEP/CBD/COP/4/Inf.25 20 April 1998, Benefit-sharing case studies Aristocladus korupensis and Prunus Africana.

[67] After a period of five years the Fund held a sum of about 1 million CFA. The villagers decided to use the money for a long-awaited water project.

4.2 AN OVERALL ASSESSMENT

4.2.1 Structure/Form

Access and benefit-sharing agreements can be structured in a number of ways. They can be based on a one-contract structure or a network of interconnected agreements.[68]

One of the most important components of bioprospecting agreements is the letter of intent that constitutes the preliminary agreement on the general framework of collaboration. Bioprospecting agreements usually also include confidentiality agreements. Material transfer agreements (MTAs) are very often used in commercial and academic research and cover the transfer of genetic material and germplasm. A common characteristic clause of MTAs is the limitation of uses of the material. Licensing agreements regulate the rights the provider is entitled to grant, such as the agreements to license the use of genetic resources as research tools or to license the use of associated traditional knowledge (TK) or other subsequent IP rights.[69] Finally, another contractual structure that frequently appears is that of research agreements or research and development agreements – framework agreements regulating the contribution to research and development, the financial contribution and the contribution in materials and equipment. Such agreements set out in detail the different tasks of the parties to the agreement, its monetary and nonmonetary benefits and the benefit-sharing arrangements.

4.2.2 Subject Matter

Taking into consideration the variability of industries making use of TKGR as research material, the subject matter in focus varies considerably. The pharmaceutical industry is mainly interested in plant genetic resources and microorganisms, while startup biotech companies usually

---

[68] Another interesting evaluation of how the bioprospecting agreements system works is Laird, A.S., ten Kate, K., 'Biodiversity Prospecting: The Commercial Use of Genetic Resources and the Best Practice in Benefit-Sharing', in Laird, A.S. (ed), *Biodiversity and Traditional Knowledge: Equitable Partnerships in Practice*, London: Earthscan Publications (2001), pp. 241–86.

[69] For the particular characteristics of bioprospecting, see Hedit, R., 'Maintaining Incentives for Bioprospecting: The Occasional Need for a Right to Lie', Berkeley Tech LJ (1998), pp. 667–720, discussing the rights of patients in further commercialisation of research results. One can also draw parallels with TKGR bioprospecting.

focus on specific species of plant genetic material or on compounds isolated from an organism.[70]

The seed and botanical industries seek novel plant genetic resources, and have a growing tendency to investigate the properties of marine organisms and fungi. The sophistication of biotechnology has allowed the 'transfer' of properties of animal genetic resources to plants.[71] The same tendency is noted in the cosmetics and personal care industry, where companies increasingly engage in marine prospecting programmes.

Bioprospecting presupposes access to genetic resources in the form of raw samples or even extracts. In some cases, genetic resources are accompanied by ethnobotanological know-how or traditional knowledge. Finally, at times, companies seek samples that have already undergone screening processes in which bioactive compounds have been identified.

The first classification can be based on the type of genetic material concerned. The nature of the genetic material can influence the spirit and the content of the agreements' intellectual property clauses. For an agreement that concerns the transfer of animal genetic resources, what would deserve to be underlined are the trade secrets, while as far as the transfer of microorganisms is concerned, what is important is the allocation of patents. An initial means of categorisation is the degree of human improvement and innovation that the material will be submitted to.

The sectorial distinctions (i.e. between sectorial types of genetic resources) are also important. The unique character of certain genetic resources, such as those that concern food and agriculture, call for different formats of contracts and for special intellectual property clauses that take into consideration these special characteristics.

Finally, another important factor to be taken into consideration is the legal status of genetic resources. TKGR enjoys a somewhat nuanced legal status depending on where the resource and the parties in the agreement are located. Consequently, when an agreement concerns the transfer of genetic material that has been provided from *ex situ* conservation, the applicability of the provisions of the CBD depends on whether it was acquired prior to or after the entry into force of the CBD. If the genetic material is held in trust under the FAO–CGIAR agreements, the intellectual property policy contained in the agreement should also be reflected in the bioprospecting agreements.

---

[70] Soejarto, D., 'Biodiversity Prospecting and Benefit-Sharing: Perspectives from the Field', J Ethnopharmacology, Vol 51 (1994), pp. 590–9.

[71] A very well-known example is that of fish genes coding for tolerance to low temperature.

4.2.3 Method of Selection

The selection of genetic resources and the method employed for that purpose are fundamental parts of the bioprospecting process. There are four major selection categories:[72]

- Random selection, where the company decides to select genetic resources from a specific geographical area in order to acquire a sample of local biodiversity.
- Biorational selection, where collections are based on the observation of ecological relationships between species, which might in turn lead to the production of secondary compounds.
- Chemotaxonomic selection, in which collections are based on knowledge of certain classes of compounds of value to research and screening.
- Ethnobotanical selection, according to which collections are based on traditional knowledge regarding the use and properties of the resources in question.

The method of selection chosen is of direct relevance to the determination of the benefits to be shared. It is also of interest with regard to the form of the benefit sharing. The more specific the selection, the more valuable the resources. The more active the holders of TKGR are required to be, for instance by participating in the selection process, the more immediate the compensation of at least part of the agreed benefits.

4.2.4 The Parties

Although industry is the principal actor in making use of bioprospecting practices, companies usually avoid negotiating and signing bioprospecting agreements. For this purpose, companies employ botanic gardens, gene banks, universities and research institutions or other small companies to function as intermediaries.[73]

Intermediaries/indirect parties to the agreement undertake contact with source countries, bear the responsibility for selection and collection of

---

[72] Laird, S., 'Natural Products and the Commercialisation of Traditional Knowledge' in Greaves, T. (ed), *IPR for Indigenous Peoples: A Sourcebook*, Oklahoma City: Society for Applied Anthropology (1994), p. 148.

[73] ten Kate, K., 'Biodiversity Prospecting Partnerships', Biotechnology and Development Monitor, Vol 25 (1998), p. 18.

genetic resources and agree upon the terms and conditions of benefit-sharing arrangements. Thus, a bioprospecting agreement can include the participation of a number of intermediaries, responsible for different parts of the process.

Stakeholders in bioprospecting agreements vary from individuals to community groups and organisations. Another tendency noted is that of partnerships and joint research programmes. Such initiatives, taking place in source countries and under the overall goal of capacity building of local scientists, provide for value-added resources.[74]

Government participation is increasingly becoming the rule in bioprospecting agreements since the majority of national legislation requires that competent governmental authorities process access requests and monitor compliance with benefit-sharing arrangements. The state agencies usually involved are the Ministry of Natural Resources or the Ministry of Science and Technology.

Source-country institutions that bear the responsibility for collection and sample processing are very often direct parties to the agreement. A national institution's participation in the bioprospecting agreement entails two categories of benefits. Direct benefits are gained by a party to the bioprospecting agreement in the form of upfront payments, and indirect benefits through advancing its level of scientific research. Where bioprospecting involves access to traditional knowledge, or where bioprospecting takes place in indigenous people's lands, an organisation or a council or representatives of the community in question participate in negotiations. Nevertheless, an indigenous community is very rarely a direct party to the agreement.[75] Usually, national legislation imposes the prior informed consent of the community by means of a supplementary agreement or annexed certificate.[76]

The list of stakeholders in a bioprospecting agreement may be broadened even after conclusion of the agreement. The identification of relevant stakeholders in a specific bioprospecting case, as well as their

---

[74] Brush, S., 'Whose Knowledge, Whose Genes, Whose Rights?', in Brush, S., Stabinsky, D. (eds), *Valuing Indigenous Knowledge: Indigenous People and IPR*, Washington, DC: Island Press (1996), p. 3; King. S., 'Establishing Reciprocity: Biodiversity, Conservation and New Models for Cooperation between Forest Dwelling Peoples and the Pharmaceuticals Industry' in Greaves, T. (ed.), *IPR for Indigenous Peoples: A Sourcebook*, Oklahoma City: Society for Applied Anthropology (1994), pp. 69–82.

[75] An exception to this is the Verata–USP Agreement in Fiji.

[76] The same requirement applies for bioprospecting taking place in private lands.

representation, is by far the most complicated aspect of the negotiation process. When identification is incomplete or when representation is not legitimate, bioprospecting agreements become a defective and time-consuming endeavour. Third parties may subsequently oppose a bioprospecting agreement and claim its nullity because they have not been consulted or represented in the negotiations.[77]

4.2.5 Rights Transferred

The rights transferred by means of a bioprospecting agreement vary and could be divided into three main categories.[78] The first category relates to the property of the lands, and the organisms found on the lands: plants, animals, microorganisms, etc. The second category includes genetic material, genetic information and, thus, the property rights related to the genes isolated from a specific genetic resource. The third category comprises knowledge: know-how related to the use of the genetic resource in question, and thus to the intangible property right covering it, if any. In order to circumvent the problematic aspects of the multiple layers of rights, most of the bioprospecting activities take place in publicly owned lands where the government is the owner of the lands as well as of the genetic material.[79]

The right to the lands in which genetic resources are found is in some cases attached to genetic resources property. In the Yellowstone–Diversa contract, the US government (owner of the park) was also automatically considered the owner of genetic resources extracted from it. Nevertheless, the majority of bioprospecting agreements detach the property rights on lands from the property rights on the genetic material.[80] In the INBio

---

[77] In the Yellowstone–Diversa case, third parties initiated a lawsuit attacking the benefit-sharing agreement and aiming at stopping the benefit-sharing activities in the park.

[78] Mulholland, D., Wilman, E., 'Bioprospecting and Biodiversity Contracts', Environment and Development Economics, Vol 8 (2003), pp. 417–35.

[79] There are even cases where an initially broad bioprospecting scheme is limited solely to publicly owned lands in order to avoid having to address different levels of ownership. A good example is the UNIP bioprospecting contract, where the company restricted its request only to access in the Intervales State Park.

[80] In the Philippines bioprospecting agreement, there are two groups of landowners: those with private land rights and indigenous people with rights on their ancestral lands. The agreement is clear in that in both cases, genetic resources extracted from these lands are to be considered the property of the government.

agreement, for instance, an explicit distinction was made between the genetic material belonging to the public domain and genetic resources found in land containing it that could belong to a private party.

4.2.6 Benefit Sharing

An important aspect of bioprospecting agreements, even for those signed before the entry into force of the CBD, is the sharing of benefits arising out of the commercialisation/other use of a product based on the resources accessed. There is an almost endless list of variations and combinations of benefits employed, which could be grouped into three major categories: economic, social and environmental. Benefit sharing varies considerably from industry to industry, with regard both to the form of the benefits and to the mechanism employed to distribute them.

Pharmaceutical companies offer a combination of monetary and non-monetary benefits, mainly in the field of capacity building. Monetary benefits consist of milestone payments and royalties at rates specified in detail in the agreement. Biotech companies are unfamiliar with benefit sharing and usually choose to acquire TKGR from *ex situ* collections, where the link between access and benefit sharing is considered to be broken.

The seed industry, on the other hand, operates in a market reminiscent of the times when research was principally financed by public funds. Genetic resources are usually accessed free of any monetary obligations. The process of seed bioprospecting involves a number of actors participating in the different stages, from access to breeding and commercialisation. In this specific industry, sophisticated access and licensing agreements appear in the later stages of development. For the horticulture industry, bioprospecting agreements are an almost unknown practice. Horticulture companies perform all research inhouse, and research and cooperation agreements are the exception rather than the rule.

The phytomedical industry has experienced considerable growth in recent years.[81] Estimates of market sales in the EU amount to US$6 billion, while sales in China alone accounted for US$5 billion. R&D in this industry is largely focused on well-established species, while at the same time limited by strict regulatory requirements. Finally, since the

---

[81] Growth of about 13.5–15 per cent per year. See UNEP/CBD/COP/4/Inf 25 (20 April 1998).

development and manufacture of products depends upon raw materials, consistency in quality is of great importance.[82]

Another important and rather problematic aspect of the benefit-sharing process is the determination of beneficiaries of the benefits distributed. There is a long list of potential beneficiaries, ranging from government, academic institutions, companies and communities to individuals. Obviously, the higher the geographical and administrative rank, the more direct the access to benefits distributed. Individuals and communities may become beneficiaries when governmental policy provides for it. Bioprospecting agreements may refer to a governmental authority as the beneficiary, while others may include reference to a number of different levels. In cases where the beneficiary stated in the main bioprospecting agreement is a research institution, there are usually a number of additional agreements with other stakeholders that regulate the further distribution of benefits.[83]

In order to avoid inserting detailed benefit-sharing provisions in view of benefits that may never come, a number of bioprospecting agreements transfer the benefit-sharing provisions to future negotiations.[84] Postponement of benefit-sharing negotiations has, in some cases, been motivated by problems posed by national regulations or the fact that national legislation was in the process of implementation in parallel with negotiation of the bioprospecting agreement.

Monetary benefits have been distributed solely in the form of upfront payments or other collection fees. To date there have been no reports of monetary benefits in the form of royalties or other benefits of commercialisation of products arising from genetic resources accessed by means of a bioprospecting agreement. The most effective and direct form of benefit-sharing mechanism concerns nonmonetary payments in the form of capacity building, training and technology transfer.[85]

---

82 The African ICBG Agreement refers to 'process' benefits, resulting from the research and development phase, and 'long term' benefits which arise from commercialisation.

83 Moran, K., King, S., Carlsson, T., 'Biodiversity Prospecting, Lessons and Practices', Annual Review of Anthropology, Vol 30 (2001), pp. 505–26.

84 The NCI/UNIP bioprospecting agreement as well as the NCI/University of Yaounde bioprospecting agreement.

85 See Bioresources International at http://www.miraculin.com.

4.3 PROTECTION OF TKGR BY MEANS OF BIOPROSPECTING AGREEMENTS: WEAKNESSES AND POSSIBILITIES

Bioprospecting agreements involve a broad spectrum of disciplines in which social, environmental and economic considerations are equally important. The evolution of a new legal framework to accommodate them, as well as the *sui generis* partnerships that these impose between private and public entities, NGOs, research institutes and commercial actors, raise new questions and challenges. It seems, however, that the efficient design of contracts remains an ambition in those special contractual structures that are both multipurpose and multilateral. Obviously, the current ABS system and the limited experience of bioprospecting agreements leave major questions unanswered. There is still uncertainty as to why and how to protect the future market value of TKGR when considering the difficulties of enforcing such agreements.

On the top of these major economic considerations, we also have the very general principles embodied in the CBD and the lack of effective implementation and clarification of ABS principles in the majority of national and regional initiatives. The Bonn Guidelines could be a means of bringing about a more stable and clear legal regime.[86]

The anticommons environment developed by the increasingly demanding ABS legislation allows limited opportunities for bioprospecting projects to flourish. Obviously, research institutes and commercial entities are not always willing to deal with the time-consuming hurdles set out by an ABS procedure, given the uncertainty of the outcome. Furthermore, in the short history of bioprospecting agreements, we find interesting stories in which ABS was not possible. For example, the ICBG invested two years and some hundreds of thousands of dollars in the process of acquiring ABS in Mexico, acquired prior informed consent (PIC) from 47 communities, but was in the end forced to abandon the project due to opposition from the confederation of local healers' organisations.[87]

---

[86] Siebenhuner, B., Dedeurwaerdere, T., Brousseau, E., 'Introduction and Overview to the Special Issue on Biodiversity Conservation, Access and Benefit-Sharing and Traditional Knowledge', Ecological Economics, Vol 53 (2005), pp. 439–616, pp. 439–44.

[87] For the process of the ICBG in Mexico and the reasons that led to a final failure of the project, see Safrin, S., 'Hyperownership in a Time of Biotechnological Promise: The International Conflict to Control the Building Blocks of Life', Am J Int Law, Vol 98 (2004), pp. 641–85.

4.3.1 The Value of TKGR

Valuation of TKGR is a necessary but complicated matter with a direct impact on the efficiency of bioprospecting agreements. TKGR does not in itself involve an end product that could be subject to direct valuation. Difficulties in valuation of the accessed subject matter lead to uncertainties in the determination of benefit sharing schemes.

Bioprospecting contracts usually employ a combination of two payment methods: collection fees and royalties. Collection fees are paid partly or in total in the form of services such as training, capacity building and technology transfer. Often, the corporate party in a bioprospecting agreement prefers royalty payments, since then no interest costs are due to the company if payments are made before the product is marketed.

It is important to underline that, in general, bioprospecting in pharmaceutical research requires at least 12 years of product development and US$230 million to bring a product to market, and only one successful product is developed for every 12,000 samples collected. In other words, companies undertake considerable risk in bioprospecting and will attempt to reduce the total cost of a bioprospecting agreement.[88]

Bioprospecting experts provide practical illustrations of the variations in a bioprospecting agreement's benefit sharing that may consequently have an impact on the value of TKGR.[89] The example given by Lesser and Krattiger shows clearly that a preference for increased upfront payment turns out to be a costly choice for the value of the bioprospecting agreement as a whole.[90] The value of genetic resources will obviously increase when the access country is able to provide the bioprospector with screened samples, as well as when genetic resources

---

[88] Yusuf, A. 'Technology and Genetic Resources: Is Mutually-Beneficial Access Still Possible?' in Sánchez, V. and Juma, C. (eds), *Biodiplomacy: Genetic Resources and International Relations*, Nairobi: African Centre for Technology Studies Press (1994), pp. 233–40.

[89] Lesser, W., Krattiger A., 'Valuation of Bioprospecting Samples: Approaches, Calculations and Implications for Policy-Makers', in Krattiger, A., Mahoney, R.T., Nelsen, L., et al (eds), *Intellectual Property Management in Health and Agricultural Innovation: A Handbook of Best Practices*, Oxford: MIHR and Davis: PIPRA (2007). Available at http://www.iphandbook.org. See also Rausser, G.C., Small, A.A., 'Valuing Research Leads: Bioprospecting and the Conservation of Genetic Resources', Journal of Political Economy, Vol 108 (2000) pp. 173–206.

[90] Although this change decreases the value of the contractual agreement as a whole.

are combined with traditional and ethnobotanological knowledge.[91] The increased value of the samples in these cases will be reflected in the upfront payments and royalty rates. An advantage of providing bioprospectors with screened samples or samples that involve specific traditional applications is that they are much easier to track, and thus it is easier to enforce a bioprospecting agreement and benefit-sharing clauses. When the subject matter of a bioprospecting agreement is thousands of raw samples it would seem almost impossible to be able to follow up on their future applications, equivalents and derivatives. In this respect, benefit sharing in terms of capacity building might be an appropriate long-term investment. Another aspect that might have an impact on the value of the collected samples is exclusivity. Exclusivity may be twofold. Subject matter that is country specific is more valuable, since TKGR holders are in a better negotiating position (bioprospectors have to negotiate with the specific source country to gain access to the genetic resources). On the other hand, exclusivity may also entail that the bioprospector is granted an exclusive right on the specific TKGR. The obligation of TKGR holders not to share the specific subject matter with third parties should have a direct impact on its value.

It is obviously difficult to carry out an empirical study of the value of TKGR and thus assess the value of bioprospecting agreements, since the benefit-sharing clauses very often remain confidential. Another factor blurring the economics of bioprospecting is the fact that there is currently no report available on the commercial exploitation of samples accessed by means of a bioprospecting agreement.[92] Both the NCI and ICBG programmes offered a rather obvious conclusion: commercialised research results from biodiversity agreements are a very rare phenomenon, or simply are long-term benefits.[93]

4.3.2 Unequal Partnerships

Parties to bioprospecting agreements are characterised by a considerable degree of disparity. On the side of TKGR providers, one finds developing

---

[91] The probability of finding a hit increases to 1/6000.

[92] See also Barbier, E.B. and Aylward, B.A., 'Capturing the Pharmaceutical Value of Biodiversity in a Developing Country', Environment and Resource Economics, Vol 8 (1996), pp. 157–81.

[93] Miller, J., 'Impact of the Convention on Biological Diversity: The Lessons of Ten Years of Experience with Models for Equitable Sharing of Benefits' (2002), available at http://www.ssrn.org.

countries' newly established research institutions, governmental committees and authorities, their universities and representatives of indigenous communities. On the 'user' side, we find developed countries' universities as well as pharmaceutical and biotech companies.[94] There is obviously a clear discrepancy in negotiating experience, but the same is also the case with regard to knowledge about the technology employed under the framework of the agreement, the potential uses of material accessed and the appropriateness of the monetary and nonmonetary benefits proposed.

Source countries are often dependent on developed countries and thus not in a position to negotiate independently. The 'users' of TKGR are a limited number of strong actors. Thus, the demand side of bioprospecting agreements is characterised by the presence of strong monopsonists, able to control the terms and conditions of agreements and decide, to a large extent, on the development of the market. Although monopsonistic behaviour could be punishable under national and regional regulations, there is no international competition law agreement regulating such abuses.

The elimination of tariffs, and the international trade agreements of the World Trade Organization (WTO), unleashed competition forces and facilitated the creation of a global marketplace for TKGR. At the same time, when geographical boundaries of markets expand and firms operate in several national markets, competition law remains strictly territorial.[95] Multinationals, operating in a global market without global rules, are offered a unique opportunity to employ anticompetitive practices that are probably inconceivable in their home jurisdiction. Although governmental trade barriers have, to a large extent, disappeared, private forces have been able to monopolise sectors of the world economy as a result of regional or international cartels, with mergers ultimately creating dominant firms and monopolies. A blatant example is the abuse of monopsonistic behaviour in agrocommodity markets, illustrating practices that could be equally applicable to TKGR.

---

[94] Tansey G. 'Trade, Intellectual Property, Food and Biodiversity', discussion paper commissioned by Quaker Peace & Service and Quaker United Nations Office London and Geneva (1994). For an interesting analysis of competition law from a global perspective, see Schovsbo, J. 'Fire and Water Make Steam: Redefining the Role of Competition Law in TRIPS' in Kur, A. and Levin, M. (eds), *Intellectual Property Rights in a Fair World Trade System*, Cheltenham: Edward Elgar (2011), pp. 308–59.

[95] With the exception of the EU.

4.3.3 Enforcement/Monitoring of the Agreements

The enforceability of bioprospecting agreements is a complicated matter. The main sources of complication are the nature of genetic resources, the number of actors involved in the access and use process, the unclear uses of the material in question at the time of the contract and the limited legal and institutional capacity of source countries.

The enforceability of individual bioprospecting agreements thus depends on the relationship of the contractual parties, the contractual environment and the availability of a legal system that would resolve disputes should these arise. Bioprospecting agreements usually include preventive mechanisms, such as consultations, frequent communications and exchange of information between parties to the agreement to avoid the appearance of disputes.

Some jurisdictions have included a supervising national institution in their national legislation. Noncompliance with the agreement might lead to fines, confiscation of equipment and samples and the revocation of permits. In other cases, national legislation requires that a performance bond is posted to ensure compliance with the terms and conditions of the agreement.

Apparently, apart from upfront and collection payments, all other benefits originating in bioprospecting agreements are long-term benefits. Unfortunately, even 18 years after the conclusion of one of the first bioprospecting agreements signed, there are still no visible results that could form the basis of an evaluation of that bioprospecting agreement and its compatibility with the objectives of the CBD. Bioprospecting agreements have gradually adopted as simplified a structure as possible, limiting the number of parties involved. Although this might be necessary in order to conclude negotiations on a time-effective basis, it may also jeopardise the validity of the agreement as a whole.

Bioprospecting agreements involve parties such as governmental authorities and ministries, and take place on public lands.[96] Benefits reach research institutions and governmental authorities, which in turn take up the responsibility to find a way to finance conservation projects.[97] Nevertheless, these conservation mechanisms, 'external' to the bioprospecting process, remind us of old practices and can hardly be considered a successful means of implementing the conservation strategies envisaged in the CBD. Indigenous communities are the primary

---

96 In particular the clauses specifying the royalty rates provided.

97 Usually by establishing conservation funds.

responsible actors for the conservation of TKGR, but usually figure as merely the indirect recipients of benefits of bioprospecting endeavours.[98]

Finally, the regional and national implementation of the CBD has created, in certain jurisdictions, a very tightly regulated negotiating environment for bioprospecting agreements. National regulations are often far from clear and concise, creating cumbersome procedures dependent on mechanisms implemented by newly established institutions and authorities that lack any experience of negotiating processes, and in some cases lack a specific mandate. Furthermore, the different layers of TKGR rights provided for under the provisions of the CBD, and consequently of regional and national regulation, lead to overregulation of the specific subject matter. Negotiations can become timely and costly, with a considerable level of risk inherent to the uncertainty in procedures and the specification of rightholders.[99]

In order to deal with the problems of cumbersome national regulations, a number of bioprospecting agreements are concluded with the help of intermediaries that include different layers of contractual arrangements, giving rise to a spiral of enforcement concerns. The recipient of TKGR enters into an agreement with the source-country organisation, thereafter leaving the subsequent arrangements for signed contracts to the source-country organisation and local authorities. Furthermore, some bioprospecting agreements postpone the negotiations of all crucial provisions – including the benefit-sharing provisions – to future deals.[100]

In conclusion, the protection awarded to TKGR by means of a bioprospecting agreement does not seem to go beyond collection fees and other costs of providing for the biological material. It would be far-fetched to claim that there is contractual protection of TKGR, recognising an 'informal' intellectual property right that is licensed and compensated by means of the agreement. Nevertheless, bioprospecting

---

[98] Hunter, C.J., 'Sustainable Bioprospecting: Using Private Contracts and International Legal Principles and Policies to Conserve Raw Medicinal Materials', 25 Boston Coll Environ Aff Law Rev (1998), pp. 129–75.

[99] Laird, S.A., 'Contracts for Biodiversity-Prospecting' in Reid, W.V, Laird, S.A., Meyer, C.A., Gamez, R. Sittenfield, A., Janzen, D., Gollin, M.A. and Juma, C. (eds), *Biodiversity Prospecting: Using Genetic Resources for Sustainable Development*, Washington, DC: World Resources Institute (1993), pp. 1–52.

[100] Moran, K., 'Mechanisms for Benefit-Sharing: Nigerian Case Study for the Convention on Biological Diversity', 4th Meeting COP, Bratislava, Slovakia (1998).

agreements will most certainly continue to play a crucial role in the TKGR market. An entitlement on TKGR would give these agreements a more solid legal basis and better chances of enforceability.

5. To protect or not to protect

That which is common to the greatest number has the least care bestowed on it.

Aristotle, fourth century BC

5.1 ENTITLEMENTS

While the introduction of an entitlement covering TKGR seems a necessity, how this will be structured and elaborated remains to be seen. National and regional implementation of the Convention on Biological Diversity (CBD) provides valuable experience with regard to flexibilities in states' international obligations as well as with regard to the alternative forms of entitlements that could be employed concerning TKGR protection. This book previously reviewed the limitations as well as the potentials for TKGR under the traditional intellectual property (IP) system. A conclusion of central importance is that, on the one hand, the almost automatic choice to place the discussion of TKGR protection under the property paradigm is not necessarily justified by the objectives and general legal framework of the protection, but on the other there is no consensus on what property rights entail or how these may be structured and managed.

In fact, in order to develop a legal entitlement for TKGR that lives up to the double objectives of fairness and efficiency, it is necessary to review major protection schemes that could be applicable while also analysing their respective legal content and theoretical foundations. Discussing the theoretical framework as well as the practical impact of different forms of entitlements allows a better evaluation of the alternative forms of protection for TKGR that have been tested in practice, or discussed in theory through the lens of efficiency and fairness.

5.1.1 The Source of Rights

Under a set of theoretical assumptions made by neoclassical economics, a perfectly competitive market will gradually reach the point of Pareto efficiency.[1] Where, however, there are externalities – where some of the costs or benefits of an activity are not borne by the decision maker engaging in that activity – the market will fail to produce an optimal result.[2] If the externality is negative – a cost not borne by the decision maker – the market will overproduce the product associated with it. If, on the other hand, the externality is positive, a benefit not enjoyed by the decision maker, the market will underproduce the product in question.[3]

During the past few decades, the TKGR market gradually turned into a typical market with obvious negative and positive externalities. Uncompensated access and use of TKGR in research and in the development of pharmaceutical and other biotech patents and cases of 'biopiracy' were both proof of positive externalities. On the other hand, environmental degradation, biodiversity loss and the extinction of an endless list of plant and animal species were indicators of a series of negative externalities. The traditional TKGR 'commons' regime did not provide for the internalisation of either positive or negative externalities. A property theorist would claim that TKGR is a textbook example of a market in need of a new legal entitlement.

As early as the work of Aristotle,[4] we find the fundamental position, to be reformulated later by Demsetz, Hardin and others – namely that, in the absence of private property rights to protect them, natural resources can be abused to the point of destruction. In his article 'The Tragedy of the Commons', Hardin states that since population and demand grow with time, there will come a day when depletion threatens the stock of commonly owned resources.[5] According to Hardin, as rational beings, each member of the community seeks to maximise his gain. In the quest to maximise their gains, individuals remove units of goods out of the common pool. In order to make an illustration of this practice, Hardin describes the practice of herdsmen in a pasture open to all. Herdsmen

---

1 Fudenberg, D. and Tirole, J., *Game Theory*, Cambridge: MIT Press (1983), pp. 59–63.

2 For a critique of welfare economics see Markovits, R., 'A Constructive Critique of the Traditional Definition and Use of the Concept of the Effect of a Choice of Allocative Economic Efficiency: Why the Kaldor-Hicks Test, the Coase Theorem, and Virtually All Law-and-Economics Welfare Arguments Are Wrong', U Ill L Rev [1993], pp. 485–500.

3 Hardin, G., 'The Tragedy of the Commons', Science, Vol 162 (1968) pp. 1243–8.

4 Mayhew, R., 'The Communism of Property: A Note on Aristotle', Politics, Vol 1263a (1995), pp. 8–15.

5 Hardin (1968), pp. 1243–8.

will have to balance the profit of adding an animal to their herd with the drawback of overgrazing.

However, although the profits gained will be on an individual basis, the costs will be shared by all herdsmen and all members of the community. The resulting scarcity, and thus depletion of the resources in question, is a cost to the community as a whole, while the benefits of intensive exploitation accrue to the individual. The same problematic situation, occurs with regard to environmental pollution, although in a reverse way: the 'rational' polluter finds that the damage occurring, because of the chemicals and other waste, will affect society as a whole while he will enjoy the benefits of purifying his wastes. Hardin sums up: 'the commons, if justifiable at all, is justifiable under low population density. As the human population has increased, the commons has had to be abandoned in one aspect or the other.'[6]

In order to remedy this 'tragic' situation, Hardin suggests that there should be a change in the individuals' values.[7] This change could occur by means of a system of private property; by a system of public ownership, with the government controlling use rights and allocating them by merit; on a 'first come first served' basis; or through auctions, taxation systems or other 'coercive laws'. Hardin concludes that none of these systems is satisfactory per se, but reasons of necessity that motivate the abandonment of 'commons' with regard to pollution of food and farmland shall also be applicable in the case of natural resources.[8] According to Hardin, 'freedom in a commons brings ruin to all'. Hardin proposed two alternative solutions to the 'tragedy'. The first was to sell the commons off as private property; the second was 'mutual coercion, mutually agreed upon', related to government regulation.[9]

---

[6] Hardin (1968), pp. 1243–8.

[7] Hardin has been criticised for assuming that rational private owners would never exploit their resources to destruction. Brunet presents a number of cases in which private owners have done the exact opposite of what is stated in Hardin's assumptions. See Brunet, E., 'Debunking Wholesale Enforcement of Environmental Rights', Harv J Law & Public Policy, Vol 15 (1992), pp. 311–24.

[8] Hardin has, in another publication, claimed that private property and socialism are the only viable solutions to the tragedy of the commons. See Hardin, G., 'Political Requirements for Preserving Our Common Heritage', in Brokaw, H.P. (ed), *Wildlife and America*, Washington, DC: Council on Environmental Quality (1978), pp. 310–17.

[9] Governmental regulation has been employed a number of times with regard to environmental commons problems and has adopted a variety of forms. In some cases, the government owns the resource in question, and can thus exclude some users/uses and charge fees to others for use. Resources might, on

Hardin's theory, though fundamental in the field, has been harshly criticised. One of the weaknesses is the very choice of terminology.[10] The term 'commons' has traditionally had a double meaning. It connotes both common ownership regimes and open access regimes. The former is a property rights system, in which group members jointly hold property rights on the resource in question. Members of the group may not exclude each other from the resource, but may exclude third parties. Open access, on the other hand, presupposes the lack of any property rights on the resources in question. Obviously, Hardin's analysis is based on open access regimes and the term 'tragedy of open access' would be a more appropriate description of his work.

In light of the extensive work undertaken by Elinor Ostrom on resources held under a common property structure, Hardin's theoretical framework seems incomplete.[11] Common property could in fact constitute a third alternative remedy to the 'tragedy of the commons'.[12]

Historically, common grazing areas such as those described by Hardin were not 'open to the public' but rather lands of limited access: only those who belonged to a closed group had the privilege to use resources. What is more, use by those with access was also heavily restricted.[13] In order to be able to clarify the legal content of the terminology employed, one has to resort to the history of land use in England, which was in fact divided into three major periods. During the first period there were private parcels, which later gave way to a system of mixed private and

---

the other hand, be privately owned, but the government may issue command-and-control regulations imposing specific conditions on use, taxes and fees for noncompliance.

[10] Smith, H., 'Semi Common Property Rights and Scattering in the Open Fields', J Legal Studies, Vol 29 (2000), pp. 131–69.

[11] Ostrom, E., *Governing the Commons: The Evolution of Institutions for Collective Action*, Cambridge: Cambridge University Press (1990); Ostrom, E., 'Self-Governance of Common-Pool Resources', in Newman, P. (ed), *The New Palgrave Dictionary of Economics and The Law*, Vol 3, New York: Macmillan (1998), pp. 424–32.

[12] Such regimes only work under a particularised set of cultural conditions that are not so often seen in today's global economy. The success of such regimes depends largely on the cultural environment under which they are applied, and despite their beneficial characteristics, they could not be considered a standard.

[13] Strict rules of governance were introduced in order to restrict the actions of those with access.

common use, the open fields. The final phase was that of privatisation, widely known as the enclosure movement.[14]

The first regime of land tenure was that of individual and/or family property, while at a later stage fragmentation and crop rotations became the prevailing property regime. This form of property did not provide for precisely marked boundaries, and family property was redistributed on a periodical basis in order to adjust shares.[15]

The property system that succeeded this regime was that of 'open fields', one of the two major property land regimes of medieval and early modern England. The 'commons' were in fact rights to graze animals and remove resources that belonged only to members of the community. In some cases, not all members of the community had rights of common. Under the 'open fields' regime, peasants had the right to grain crops they grew on scattered strips of land, and during specific periods of time, farmers would be required to open the strips for grazing. The group of strips would form one large grazing commons. However, even during this period the commons regime entailed limited access, since only those owning strips of land were allowed to graze animals on the commons land.

The 'open fields' were also strictly regulated. The regulations stipulated the number of animals that a peasant was allowed to graze,[16] the precise aspects of use, times for grazing and the use of and provision for common herdsmen.[17]

The shift from 'commons' to private property – the so-called enclosure movement – has been a complex legal phenomenon. The justification of this evolution differed from place to place, generally involving the consolidation of holdings, the abolition of common rights and the placing

---

[14] Merill, T., Smith, H., 'What Happened to Property in Law and Economics?', Yale LJ, Vol 111 (2001) pp. 357–98.

[15] Baker, A., Butlin, R.A., 'Conclusion: Problems and Perspectives in Studies of Field Systems in the British Isles' in Baker, A., Butlin, R.A. (eds) *Studies of Field Systems in the British Isles*, Cambridge: Cambridge University Press (1973), pp. 619, 624–7. The property system of the time was close to a system of usufructs, but became more durable in time with the increasing resource pressure.

[16] The number of animals (usually sheep) allowed to graze in the commons was determined on the units owned by the landowners for grain growing.

[17] These regulations were very strict but could be revoked in times of famine or pestilence. North, D., Thomas, R.P., *The Rise of the Western World: A New Economic History*, Cambridge: Cambridge University Press (1973).

of borders between neighbouring parcels.[18] Wealth distribution was a major factor in this development, and its timing was connected to the overall level of production: in that period, the value of wool was rising, while technology changed with the introduction of intensively grown sheep-fodder crops. It was no longer advantageous to operate as unspecialised farmers, and thus the benefits of the 'open-field' system were not worth their costs.

Another interesting theoretical framework that attempts to justify the emergence of property rights is that elaborated by Demsetz,[19] according to whom property rights appear as a result of the desires of market actors and are related to the cost–benefit interface.

Demsetz refocuses the evolution of rights justification. According to his 'theory of property rights', the main allocative function of property rights is the internalisation of beneficial and harmful effects, and consequently the emergence of property rights can be understood best by their association with the emergence of new or different beneficial and harmful effects. Changes that can trigger the emergence of new beneficial and harmful effects are mainly changes in knowledge and technology, and thus changes in market values. In this regard, property rights develop when the gains of internalisation become higher than its costs.

In order to support his views, Demsetz employed the results of ethnological research conducted on the Indians of the Labrador Peninsula, showing that these specific tribes had a long-established tradition of property in land. The link between the development of private rights on land and the commercial fur trade has been documented in the work of Leacock.[20] In fact, prior to the commercialisation of fur, hunting had the main purpose of providing food and clothing for the members of the tribe. The externality was already present at this stage, but still negligible. Hunting was thus performed freely and the need for private rights on land was absent.

Obviously, the fur trade brought significant changes in the land property regime. Furs became valuable for Indians, and as a result

---

[18] Both 'commons' and 'open fields' were subject to enclosure which took place between 1450 and 1849.

[19] Demsetz, H., 'Toward a Theory of Property Rights', 57 American Economic Review, Papers and Proceedings of the Seventy-Ninth Annual Meeting of the American Economic Association (May 1967), pp. 349–59.

[20] Leacock is an anthropologist who has carried out research on the subject of private land rights of Indians in relation to the development of fur trade. See Leacock, E. 'The Montagnes Hunting Territory and the Fur Trade', American Anthropologist, Vol 56, Part 2, Memoir No 78 (1992), 124–35.

interest in hunting rose rapidly. Consequently, externalities related to fur hunting increased, triggering a change in the property rights system. Commercial hunting was conducted in 'common' lands; hunters were not concerned by issues such as stock conservation, which in turn led to overintensive hunting phenomena. Gradually, the need to secure the conservation of stock and the husbanding of animals became urgent.

As the fur trade grew, the benefits of internalisation became higher than the costs. The first step in the internalisation process was a seasonal allotment system,[21] to be followed by the husbanding of fur-bearing animals. The same phenomenon was present in the case of Indians of the Northwest, where private family rights to lands were elaborated.[22] Even in this area, forest animals dominated and local tribes had close cooperation with fur traders.

Demsetz's beaver story describing how property rights evolved together with the evolution of the fur trade was once more confirmed in the work of Umbeck,[23] and in the Libecap study on the rights to gold and silver fields in California and Nevada.[24] The California gold rush signified a sharp increase in the value of lands and mines, initiating a change in their 'open access' status, while at the same time open access was the first regime, since no preexisting society existed in the same lands.

Although Demsetz's theory has had a broad range of applicability, there are many cases in which property rights did not emerge, even as asset values increased considerably. Rights to oil and gas developed over the course of more than a century.[25] At the same time, other resources, such as wild bison herds,[26] were not subject to a privatisation process, although their value increased dramatically with the advent of the bison

---

[21] The Indians would mark off the hunting ground they had selected by blazing the trees with their crests so that they would never encroach on each other. See Demsetz (1978), p. 351.

[22] These property regimes even included the right to inheritance.

[23] Umbeck, J. 'Might Makes Rights: A Theory of the Formation and Initial Distribution of Property Rights', Economic Inquiry, Vol 19, 38–59, reprinted in Pejovich, S., ed., *The Economic Foundation of Property Rights*, Cheltenham: Edward Elgar (1997), pp. 122–43.

[24] Libecap, G.D., *Contracting for Property Rights*, New York: Cambridge University Press (1989), pp. 1–28.

[25] Libecap, G.D., Smith, J., 'The Economic Evolution of Petroleum Property Rights in the United States', J Legal Studies, Vol 31 (2003), pp. 589–608.

[26] Lueck, D., 'The Extermination and Conservation of the American Bison', J Legal Studies, Vol 31 (2002), pp. 609–52.

hide market. Another example is that of the fisheries remaining under an open access regime.

Demsetz concluded that increases in the net benefits of enforcing rights would increase the level of rights enforcement. His work, however, did not concern the costs of a property regime, the mechanism of choosing rights or the form of property rights. Andersson and Hill extended Demsetz's model to include the costs and benefits of defining and enforcing property rights. In support of their thesis, they analysed the evolution of property rights in the Great Plains.[27] Their illustration is divided into three parts: the evolution of property rights in lands, in livestock and in water.

Land in the Plains presented a number of interesting characteristics: the lack of rainfall did not allow the use of land for farming purposes, the forage was mainly short grass, and finally, the lack of trees in most of the Plains did not allow for natural fencing. In the late nineteenth century, a number of laws and regulations restricting land use were passed. However, these did not stop livestock from crossing range boundaries. The sole means of achieving this would be physical barriers. In the Plains, where wood and rock were expensive subject matter, the cost of fencing was not at all negligible. The situation changed in the 1870s, with the introduction of barbed wire that provided for a 'cheap' way of enclosing land.

Livestock, in its turn, presented its own set of difficulties. The Western livestock producer had to run his or her livestock over a large acreage, while at the same time pasturing them in lands that he or she did not own. One of the most common methods employed for the identification of private property rights was initially assured by branding, granting the branding practice the status of legal proof of ownership. As herds increased, branding was considered an insufficient means of defining and enforcing property rights. The use of barbed wire had an impact on livestock rights and, as in the case of lands, became the primal means of property rights enforcement.

Finally, property on water has been even more problematic, both because of the subject matter's nature and because of its scarcity in the specific area. Access to water was probably the most important consideration for settlers, and property on water was closely connected to the property of the stream's bank. Along with increasing settlement pressure came the pressure to provide for a change in the property regime on

---

27 More specifically Montana and Wyoming.

water rights due to the obvious changes in the benefits and costs of defining and enforcing property rights.

Property theorists have challenged Demsetz's fundamental thesis. According to Field, an increase in the value of a resource will lead not only to increased benefits of exclusion but also to an increase in the costs of exclusion. As a resource becomes more valuable and scarce, the number of parties wanting to access it will increase. Consequently, the increased value of a specific subject matter might not be a sufficient incentive for the emergence of property rights.

5.1.2 History Repeated

The problems encountered with regard to the recognition of an entitlement – be it property rights or others – on traditional knowledge are very similar to the debate that took place centuries ago concerning indigenous peoples' rights to their lands under the pressure of extensive colonialism.

In this respect, the TRIPS Agreement shares common features with the Las Casas–Sepulveda (1550) case, which considered the question of whether or not the peoples of the New World would be treated as owning their land. The lands discovered in the 'Age of Exploration' were 'unfortunately' inhabited. Thus, the question that naturally emerged was whether the lands discovered were owned by the native inhabitants or the colonisers.

Much of the Discovery Doctrine depended on the hypothesis that indigenous peoples did not own their lands, an argument used to justify the recognition of 'Western world-like' property rights.[28] Parallels could be drawn here with indigenous agricultural knowledge or traditional medicinal knowledge, developed and used in ways not envisioned in the 'Western world legislation' and thus a *de facto* part of the public domain. Interestingly enough, the same reasoning employed to demonstrate why Aboriginals could not claim rights on their lands is employed to justify why traditional knowledge and land races are not covered by IPRs while hybrids and salient traits are.

The contours of the property right institution are very much obscure; the criteria for what will be deemed property and the components of

---

[28] At the time, the property question focused on the question of whether the kinds of uses to which the 'native peoples' put their land amounted to ownership or to a property right. Obviously, in the majority of the cases the answer was 'no'. In *Johnson v. M'Intosh* 21 US (8 Wheat) 543 (1823), the US Supreme Court claimed that the Painkashaw Indians were not more than simply inhabitants of the lands.

property rights institution still remain unsettled. In colonial times, the legal system rejected claims of nonwhites, non-Europeans and non-Christians. Nowadays, claims of the same populations remain devalued, but this time on more neutral terms. Although the theoretical justifications of past colonial practices have been rejected as sophistry, they seem to be making their way back into the international law arena.

International and regional negotiations on the protection of TKGR, as well as national implementation experience, all seem to point towards a property rights regime. On the other hand, those invoking the 'public domain' status of the specific subject matter base all their arguments on experiences stemming from the property rights paradigm itself and the difficulties related to the introduction of yet another property right. It deserves to be noted that although all the proposed entitlements for the protection of TKGR are placed under the property rights paradigm, they present a mosaic of different characteristics and structures.[29] They employ various protection schemes, with requirements and sanctions. The variety of entitlements, as well as their vagueness, raises doubts as to their nature and status.[30]

Do all these created entitlements fall under the ambit of the property rights paradigm? What are in fact the main characteristics of the property rights paradigm, and what distinguishes it from other forms of entitlements? Is the choice of property rights equivalent to a choice of private property rights? Is it natural to resort to property rights, or are there other, alternative forms of protection?[31]

Answering these questions is of utmost importance in order to provide a fine-tuned *sui generis* right for TKGR or to adjust the traditional IP system to accommodate the needs of TKGR as a subject matter. In order to do that, one has to consider the theoretical framework of the different forms of entitlement that may be applicable in the field of TKGR, namely property rights, liability and reward systems. It is worthy of note here that the review of available theoretical frameworks will concern not only the legal content of the different forms a TKGR entitlement might adopt, but also the management models whose consideration could be relevant. Although the legal content of each alternative entitlement is of

---

[29] In regional regulation and national legislation.

[30] Coombe, R., 'The Recognition of Indigenous Peoples and Community Traditional Knowledge in International Law', St Thomas L Rev, Vol 14 (2001), pp. 275–85.

[31] The protection of subpatentable innovations has been an oft-debated issue. See Nordell, P.J., 'Skyddet för funktionellt betingande utstyrslar', NIR, Vol 5 (2005), pp. 433–63.

course a very important starting point, the way these are managed is equally crucial.

5.1.3 TKGR as a Commodity: In Need of a New Entitlement

Both the CBD and the TRIPS Agreement recognise the predominant role of property rights in the progression of technological development and transfer of technology. The fundamental difference in the perspectives adopted by the two agreements is, to a large extent, due to the CBD focus on indigenous communities' contribution to the preservation of the genetic resources and the accompanying traditional knowledge on the one hand, and to the adoption of the *terra nullius* status of this starting material adopted by the TRIPS Agreement on the other.[32]

The CBD adopts the view that environmental degradation and the loss of genetic resources are a result of the absence of entitlements on TKGR. Reiterating a version of Hardin's 'tragedy of the commons' that has already been applied in other environmental agreements,[33] the legal framework introduced by the CBD builds upon the enclosure of TKGR. In order to achieve TKGR conservation, the CBD removes it from the 'commons', where it was initially placed, to the framework of different kinds of entitlements and market transactions. Market exploitation is in fact considered to be a prerequisite to the sustainable use of TKGR. The CBD thus mandates the commodification of traditional knowledge and genetic resources, similarly to the TRIPS Agreement, by means of the patentability of biotech inventions; the former also introduced a mandatory benefit-sharing scheme.[34]

Although much of the post-CBD discussion has been placed under the scope of the property rights paradigm, and more specifically under IPRs, nothing in the provisions of the CBD mandates the resort to property rights. When exploring the flexibilities available under the international legal framework and considering alternative forms of entitlement, it is important to look into their respective theoretical justifications as well as

---

[32] For the predominance of TRIPS and the practices of biopiracy as well as different proposals for providing for a remedy, see Ho, C., 'Biopiracy and Beyond: A Consideration of Socio-Cultural Conflicts with Global Patent Policies', U Mich JL Reform (2005–6), pp. 433–542.

[33] Hardin (1968).

[34] Carvalho de, N., 'From the Shaman's Hut to the Patent Office: How Long and Winding is the Road?' Teil 1: Revista da ABPI, Vol 40 (1999), p. 3.

to clarify their legal content.[35] A theoretical analysis will be employed in order to evaluate whether the proposed and implemented *sui generis* regimes in fact connote a property rights regime or whether other, alternative methods of protection, namely liability rights or reward systems, are more appropriate.[36]

5.1.4 Alternative Entitlements

The debate with regard to the structure and nature of new entitlements has, to a large extent, focused on the dilemma between property rights and liability rules. This has also been one of the major preoccupations of legal scholars.[37] Choosing between the two is a challenge, since their legal content is still rather unclear. In particular, the theoretical framework concerning justification for the introduction of property rules or what their legal content includes is both extensive and considerably divergent.

In an attempt to simplify the dichotomy between the two central forms of entitlements, one could say that property rules are in principle protected by remedies that deter all 'takings' of the entitlement they cover without the owner's consent. Thus, a nonconsensual taking of an entitlement normally becomes less attractive than bargaining a price with the owner. On the other hand, liability rules allow third parties to make use of the entitlement that is protected as long as these are compensated at a rate determined by the court (or other competent authority).

The first resort, and the most direct remedy to market failure situations such as the one experienced in the case of TKGR, has historically been the introduction of new *sui generis* property rights or the extension of the scope of existing ones. Such is also the case for the entitlement protecting TKGR, where negotiations and discussions have proceeded on the basis of a property-based framework. The vague provisions of the CBD have been interpreted to allude to the 'birth' of a new property right

---

[35] Bebchuk, L.A., 'Property Rights and Liability Rules: The Ex Ante View of the Cathedral', Michigan L Rev, Vol 100 (2001), pp. 601–39.

[36] Of course, the 'standard' dichotomy between property rights and liability rules has been nuanced even further: see Westerman, W.S., 'Strong versus Standard Property Entitlements: Toward a New Theory of Legal Entitlements' (23 October 2007), available at SSRN: http://ssrn.com/abstract=102408, discussing the various nuances from 'strong' property rights to liability rules.

[37] Calabresi, G., Melamed, D., 'Property Rules, Liability Rules, and Inalienability: One View of the Cathedral', Harvard L Rev, Vol 85 (1972), pp. 1089–128.

and national legislation is slowly but steadily opting for the property right paradigm.[38]

Negotiations taking place in the aftermath of the CBD's entry into force have focused on the property right paradigm without examining other alternatives. This study adopts the position that the first and most important step in the schematisation and introduction of a new legal entitlement is the choice of the party entitled to prevail, the party beneficiary of the entitlement. In the field of TKGR, the international community has made a choice, by means of the CBD, to award TKGR entitlement to indigenous communities and the countries of origin – the providers.

The TRIPS Agreement, on the other hand, adopts the contrary approach. The entitlement is awarded to the users of TKGR, those incorporating it in inventions and protected by patent rights. Due to its precision and structural severity, the TRIPS Agreement has gone a step further and determined the form of the entitlement: that of private intellectual property rights (IPRs).

In the work of Calabresi and Melamed, there are three major considerations of importance for the choice between different groups of beneficiaries, but also between different forms of entitlements, when introducing a new entitlement: economic efficiency, distributional preferences and other justice considerations. Economic efficiency is usually set as an equivalent to administrative efficiency and limited enforcement costs. It is claimed, though, that administrative efficiency is taken into consideration only when there are no other differences between the entitlements in question.

Another approach to the question of economic efficiency could dictate the allocation of resources that would contribute to reaching Pareto optimality.[39] In a Coasean world with no transaction costs, the initial allocation of entitlements would not hinder the allocation of resources to the party that can make the most of it, and would thus be done in the most value-effective way. Calabresi and Melamed concluded that basing entitlement choices upon economic efficiency would be equivalent to allowing the actors to perform knowledgeable choices between social

---

[38] For the evolution of property rights on environmental goods see Cole, D., 'New Forms of Private Property: Property Rights in Environmental Goods', in Bouckaert, B., Degeest G. (eds), *Encyclopedia of Law and Economics*, Vol 2, Cheltenham: Edward Elgar (2000), pp. 274–311.

[39] For the origins of the concept see Eisermann G., 'Pareto, Vilfredo (1848–1923)' in Smelser, N.J., Baltes, P.B. (eds), *International Encyclopedia of the Social & Behavioral Sciences*, Berlin: Elsevier (2001), pp. 11048–51.

benefits, the social costs of obtaining them and the social benefits and social costs of avoiding them.[40] In order for this to be possible, costs need to be left to the party able to perform a cost–benefit analysis, and thus to the party that may most efficiently avoid them.[41] Calabresi and Melamed add that where it is unclear who that party is, the entitlement should be awarded to the party that can provide a re-allocation of the entitlement in question for the lowest possible social costs.

Apart from economic efficiency considerations, the choice of the nature and allocation of entitlements depends on wealth distribution considerations. Holders of TKGR could benefit by means of an entitlement either because they constitute a group which society has chosen to prioritise or because of the fact that, by benefiting this group, society will in its turn benefit by means of conservation of TKGR and its sustainable use. Wealth distribution principles are rather hard to discern and analyse, and certainly much more unclear than economic efficiency considerations. Calabresi and Melamed refer to a third category of considerations that have an impact on the entitlements choice: that of justice.[42]

5.1.4.1 Developing the theory of property rights

Property is one of these concepts that no one is able to define, though everyone knows a lot about it. According to Demsetz,[43] property is a social institution that creates incentives to efficiently use assets and to maintain and invest in them. The law is not the only way of enforcing property rights: they may be enforced by customs and norms as well as through repeated transactions.[44]

Although the definition of property has been the subject of lengthy and thorough academic endeavours, its precise meaning and scope remains blurry. Two leading methodological approaches to property analysis have

---

40 Calabresi, Melamed (1972).

41 Bebchuk, L.A., 'Property Rights and Liability Rules: The Ex Ante View of the Cathedral', Michigan L Rev, Vol 100 (2011), pp. 601–39; Harvard Law and Economics Discussion Paper No 347, available at SSRN: http://ssrn.com/abstract=301283 or DOI: 10.2139/ssrn.301283. Burk, D.L., 'Property Rules, Liability Rules, and Molecular Futures: Bargaining in the Shadow of the Cathedral' in Van Overwalle, Geertrui (ed), *Gene Patents and Clearing Models: From Concepts to Cases*, Cambridge: Cambridge University Press (2009); UC Irvine School of Law Research Paper No 2009-12.

42 This is also the conclusion of Calabresi and Melamed.

43 Demsetz (1967).

44 Ellickson, R., *Order Without Law: How Neighbors Settle Disputes*, Cambridge, MA: Harvard University Press (1991).

dominated the debate: instrumentalism (represented by law and economics) and formalism/conceptualism.[45]

Filling the gap in the theoretical framework and definition of these two approaches has been considered so important that representatives of one approach have often accused representatives of the other of being ignorant of the true meaning of property law.[46] Law and economics avoided investigating the meaning of property, perceived for the purposes of the analysis as a bundle of rights. In this academic environment, the discussion on property has been based upon the Coasean approach, in which property rights are background rights, created in order to later be reallocated by means of contracts. The theory of property rights evolved in a number of different historical periods, representative of the views of major theorists of the time but also of the specific societal, economic and political environments. The starting point for this theoretical review and the focus of the property paradigm differed considerably, and with it differed the overall view of the importance and role of property rights.[47]

5.1.4.1.1 Natural rights justification One of the major lines of property (and thus even intellectual property) justification is found in what are called the 'natural rights' theorists.

Aristotle marked his disagreement with Plato's preference for common property and elaborated on the merits of private property. He claimed that the right to property is a right inherent to moral order, an incitement for individuals to attend their own affairs. Aristotle placed the right to exclude at the centre of his property theory. The right to exclude allows the property owner to waive the right and share the benefits of property ownership with others.[48]

Aristotle's preference for private property was further developed in the work of Hegel and in his personality theory. He claimed that property is the appropriate mechanism for self-actualisation, for personal expression and for dignity and recognition of the individual. The three basic pillars of Hegel's philosophy are the concepts of human will, personality and

---

45 Formalism, otherwise called conceptualist scholarship.

46 Merill T. and Smith H., 'What Happened to Property in Law and Economics?', Yale LJ, Vol 111 (2001), pp. 357–98.

47 A very interesting publication on the different theories that evolved with regard to intellectual property is Menell, P., 'Intellectual Property: General Theories', in Bouckaert, B. and de Geest, G. (eds), *Encyclopedia of Law & Economics*, Vol 2, Cheltenham: Edward Elgar (2000), pp. 129–88.

48 Mayhew, R., 'Aristotle on Property', Rev Metaphysics, Vol 46 (1993), pp. 803–31.

freedom. Personality is identified as the will's struggle to actualise itself. According to Hegel, the self is a kind of property. The difference between external property and the self (internal property) is that the former can be alienated. Human will, which is of central importance to Hegelian philosophy, is a person's main point of interaction with the external world. The will seeks to dominate this interaction and conquer the external world mainly by means of property rights. Hegel thus concludes that property rights are not introduced in order to satisfy physical needs. Property plays another much more important role in a person's self-actualisation,[49] and in their recognition.[50] Property is an expression of the will, a part of the personality, creating the basis for further free action. The societal framework guaranteeing the respect of property rights provides the will with the means to proceed to further abstraction and objectification.[51] Where society acknowledges and approves the individual property claims upon objects, possession is transformed into property and the expression of the individual's human will coincides with societal will.

It is thus clear that property becomes linked to work. The individual has, by means of his labour, altered the object so as to reflect his personality. At the same time, the altered object gives the individual an opportunity to externalise his personality and, by changing the external world, even to change himself.[52] In order to preserve property rights upon an object, the individual needs to express his will regarding it continuously. When the will is no longer manifested upon the object, the object is to be considered as abandoned. The individual could even proceed to an express withdrawal of his will from the object by means of alienation.

The individual will can be expressed in different ways, one of the most important being labour. According to Hegel, an individual can occupy an object without using it. In an attempt to specify the occupation preconditions, Hegel provides a list of three different ways to occupy an object: (1) seize it, (2) impose a form upon it, and (3) mark it.

---

49 The first step in self-actualisation is the person's acting upon things.

50 Recognition plays a central role in Hegel in connection to the relation of individuals with each other and to society as a whole.

51 See Knowles, D. in 'Hegel on Property and Personality', Georgetown LJ, Vol 287 (1988), pp. 330–50.

52 The change in the individual occurs because he has to take responsibility for the object in question, and shape his will and intentions to fit this new relationship. See Waldron, J., *The Right to Private Property*, Oxford: Oxford University Press (1988). See also Hegel, G.W.F., *The Philosophy of Right* (trans. T.M.), Cambridge: Cambridge University Press (1967 [1821]), pp. 189–95.

Radin further develops Hegel's personality theory and allows for excessive forms of self-actualisation.[53] Property can be found to have adverse effects upon the holistic self-actualisation of the person.[54] With regard to inequality in the distribution of property rights, Hegel stated that what is important is that all individuals are given the same possibility to obtain property. A dominant interpretation of this statement is that property could be denied to one individual A if that would lead to individual B not being offered the possibility to acquire property rights. Hegel refers to private rights in his theory – rights that express the will of the individual. Even if the ultimate goal of the individual is to participate in an ethical community, the point of reference remains the individual. In Hegel's work, intellectual property serves the purpose of materialising intangible ideas and bestowing 'personal traits' upon material objects that can be possessed, owned, used and alienated. Without IPRs, the alienation of personal traits would be impossible in the Hegelian philosophical framework.

In order to establish property rights, there are three elements that are essential: possession, enjoyment and alienation. Possession is the identification of a specific object belonging to a specific individual. In other words, possession is the stage where the possessor is distinguished from the nonpossessor, where the possessor excludes all others from the object in question. Possession of intellectual property, though, seems rather problematic. Intellectual property can be shared by an indefinite number of parties without depriving the 'creator' and original owner of it. In order to overcome this impediment, some commentators have replaced the concept of 'possession' with that of 'acquisition'.[55]

A Hegelian view of possession of intellectual property is that the creator constructs intersubjective recognisable means by which he or she is expressed. The majority of IP legislation requires that the owner apply for a form of registration or the publication of the subject matter. In this sense, the 'creator' proceeds to marking the subject matter and thus can be considered 'in possession' of it.[56]

---

[53] Radin, M., 'Property and Personhood', Stanford L Rev, Vol 34 (1982), pp. 957–1015, available at http://cyber.law.harvard.edu/ipcoop/82radi.html.

[54] One could draw a parallel between this part of the Hegelian philosophy on property and Locke's 'enough and as good' precondition.

[55] See for instance Mossof, A., 'What Is Property? Putting the Pieces Back Together', Arizona L Rev, Vol 45 (2003), pp. 371–445.

[56] Even trade secrets fall under this 'possession' requirement. A trade secret is only protected when measures are taken to keep it secret.

An important issue that arises in relation to the protection of intellectual property is that of alienation. How could one justify the fact that the intellectual creator, while ceding his work, preserves the right to produce further copies? Hegel has an interesting explanation regarding the alienation of intellectual works. An artist embodies his will in the works of his mind. When someone else copies the original work, the copy is the expression of the will of the copyist and not a work infringing the original creator's property. Here, the importance of intellectual commons becomes obvious. The fact, thus, that the original creator sells a copy of his work allows the buyer to incorporate the mental process of the creator into his self, but does not provide the right to produce further copies. This is reserved to the creator, since it is one of the methods he/she can use to express himself via the intellectual product in question.

It is obvious that a philosophical framework basing the grant of property rights on intellectual works on the latter's relation to the creator's personality does not provide a satisfactory answer. Under Hegel's theoretical framework, intellectual property protection depends on the link between the work and the personality of its creator. However, when this link is established one cannot fail to note that different forms of intellectual works require different levels of personality expression. A strict interpretation of Hegel's theory would most probably lead to dynamic frameworks of protection that abide by the level of personality embodied. Naturally, literary works are a much clearer expression of the creator's personality than a mechanical invention could be.

Alienation of IPRs could be total, including the sale of rights, or a conditional transfer of rights, such as, for instance, patent licences. The total alienation of an intellectual property right is an act that, by definition, denies the personality link that initially justifies property rights. The alienation of IPRs is another hindrance to the application of personality theory.

Another major natural rights theorist is Locke, who presented his 'labour-centric' justification of property rights in an era where the dominant theory in the field was that of divine rights.[57] His starting point is a state of nature in which goods are held in common through a grant from God.[58] However, the goods cannot be enjoyed in this 'state of nature', which means that individuals have to convert them to private

---

[57] Locke, J., *Two Treatises of Government*, New York: Cambridge University Press ([1690] 1988), p. 464.

[58] Chapter V of the Second Treaty, p. 29.

property by means of their labour.[59] Individuals have the opportunity to extract goods that are commonly held and convert common property to private property by means of their labour.[60] Locke expressed the view that 'every man has a property in his own person'[61] and that as a result, property rights extend to objects by means of the 'works of his hands'.[62] When a person mixes a natural resource with his labour, he 'makes it his property'. Before that mixing occurred, resources belonged to the 'children of men in common'.[63] A second Lockean justification of property rights is based on the value added to the good held in common by means of the applied labour. The effort of labouring and the result of added value distinguish a labour justification from a 'first occupancy' justification. Labour may also create social value, and that value deserves reward. A third Lockean perspective to the justification of property rights is that of created incentives. If an individual exercised labour upon an object without being certain of its subsequent appropriation, which in its turn would be subordinate to the consensus of all mankind, there would be little incentive to undertake such an effort.[64]

A very important part of Locke's labour theory is based upon two fundamental prerequisites: the 'enough and as good' condition and the 'waste condition'.[65] The 'enough and as good' position limits an individual's appropriation of goods to an extent that does not deprive other individuals of the opportunity to acquire 'as good and enough' goods. On the other hand, the individual should not acquire more than he is able to use. Building upon the 'waste' limitation, Locke states that even when individuals have left the state of nature, there could still be 'enough and as good' property for all.

---

59 Hughes, J., 'The Philosophy of Intellectual Property', Georgetown LJ, Vol 77 (1988–9), p. 297.

60 The choice to proceed to the exercise of the labour must depend upon the fact that expected benefits of this private property exceed the costs of labour applied.

61 This phrase has caused theoretical debates among Locke's commentators. Epstein considers what Locke considered first possession to be the first basis for the establishment of property rights, while Hughes criticises this thesis and states that Locke has never used possession as part of his labour theory. See Epstein, R.A., 'Possession as the Root of Title', GA LJ, Vol 14 (1979), pp. 1221–7.

62 It is important to note that, according to Locke, people's property includes their 'lives, liberties and estates'. He thus refers to a much broader concept than our limited 'private property'.

63 Locke (1988), Section 39.

64 The transaction costs of such a global consensus would be prohibitive.

65 According to Hughes, Locke considers there to be no good reasons for not granting property rights where these two preconditions are met.

Locke's theory is, of course, not flawless. The fact that an individual mixes his labour with an object does not necessarily mean that society will recognise his property rights upon the object in question. Even if one accepts the special relationship that develops between the individual and the object, there is no logical explanation as to why this would lead to the establishment of a property right imposed on other individuals.[66] According to Becker,[67] labour sometimes leads to property rights, and sometimes the mere application of labour is thus no guarantee for the creation of property rights. Naturally, accepting such a reconstruction of Locke's theory would mean depriving the labour justification of property rights of all its legitimacy.

In his attempt to apply Lockean theory to intellectual property, Hughes explains that ideas are part of some form of intellectual commons;[68] when these are mixed with labour, they materialise and become subject matter apt for privatisation. Hughes draws the parallel between intellectual property creators and other labourers and concludes that the former and the latter should have the same opportunities to appropriate the 'fruit' of their labour. According to Hughes, labour theory is more appropriately applied to IPRs than to physical property, since the privatisation of a tangible expression of an idea does not limit others from sharing the same idea. Thus, the 'as good and enough' prerequisite is always fulfilled.

As has already been stated, the justification of property rights within the Lockean framework does not necessarily have to build upon labour per se. The 'value-added' labour theory seems to be even more applicable to intellectual works. The social value produced by intellectual works, and its reward by means of rights, has been one of the traditional arguments in defence of intellectual property.[69] The appropriateness of this perspective in the field of IPRs emanates from the fact that people usually go to court for things that are valuable. It is very hard to imagine a company litigating for a trade secret that has absolutely no value.[70]

[66] Haddad, B. 'Property Rights, Ecosystem Management, and John Locke's Labor Theory of Ownership', Ecological Economics, Vol 46 (2003), pp. 19–31.

[67] Becker, D., *Property Rights: Philosophic Foundations*, Boston: Routledge and Kegan Paul (2003).

[68] Hughes (1988–9).

[69] In his article, Hughes refers to various IPR case law in which the Court has reasoned on the basis of such a value-added perspective.

[70] The 'inventive step' requirement in patent law is an example of the application of the 'value-added' theory.

5.1.4.1.2 Positivism Positivism has traditionally been a very important theoretical school of resource commodification. Positivists go beyond the mere justification and origin of property rights and proceed to elaboration on the legal content of property, namely which rights have to be included in order for a certain entitlement to be considered a property right, or, on the other hand, how divergent the legal content of property rights may be. The contribution of this approach is vital, since it can determine whether a *sui generis* right is in fact a property right or not.

One of the proponents of the positivist theory, Adam Smith, relied heavily on the distinction between *in rem* rights and *in personam* rights in his work on rights and their protection. Smith elevated IPRs to the status of all other property rights, stating that 'the property that one has in a book he has written or a machine he has invented' is the paradigmatic example of real rights, because such rights can be vindicated against anyone in the world. According to Smith, property is the foundation for exchange and a vindication of the owner's legitimate expectations.[71]

Ownership/property includes a number of components listed by Honoré as the 'right to possess, the right to use, the right to manage, the right to income of the thing, the right to the capital, the right to security, the rights or incidents of transmissibility, and absence of term, the prohibition of harmful use, liability to execution and the incident of residuarity'. Honoré has further elaborated the 'bundle of rights' approach and characterised the 'unified' approach to property as a 'distortion' of the past, built on a concentration of absolute rights of use, exclusion and transfer.[72]

Schlager and Ostrom,[73] meanwhile, identified five different layers of rights, all components of the property rights regime: the right to access the subject matter of protection, the right to withdrawal, the right to management, the right to impose exclusions and the right of alienation. Schlager and Ostrom reject the approach to property as a one-package deal and elaborate on the existence of different property rightholders owning one or more of the above stated layers of rights, but not necessarily all five of them. The different categories of property holders are: authorised entrants (having the right to access), authorised users

---

[71] Smith, A., *The Theory of Moral Sentiments*, eds Raphael, D.D., MacFie, A.L., Oxford: Clarendon Press (1976), p. 412.

[72] Honoré, A.M. 'Ownership' in Guest, A.G. (ed), *Oxford Essays in Jurisprudence*, Oxford: Oxford University Press (1961), p. 107, pp. 112–24.

[73] Schlager, E., Ostrom, E. 'Property Rights Regimes and Natural Resources', Land Economics, Vol 68 (1993), pp. 249–62.

(having the right to access and the withdrawal right), claimants (that also have the right to participate in management), proprietors (who can also determine who will or will not have access to the 'resources') and owners, who, in addition to all the above, also have the right to alienate.

The dominance of the 'bundle of rights' approach has been considered by some as a factor leading to the decline of property law. According to Thomas Grey, 'the substitution of a bundle-of-rights conception of property has the ultimate consequence that property ceases to be an important category in legal and political theory'.[74] In his analysis, Grey concluded that this approach had 'disintegrated' the concept of property, and what was left was a collection of distinct rights referred to by courts and academics as a 'bundle'.

5.1.4.1.3 The role of the in rem *character of property rights* Both civil law and common law jurisdictions recognise that certain legal rights are enforceable 'against the world', while others apply only against certain persons.

Hohfeld defined a primary right *in personam* as a 'unique right residing in a person and availing against a single person'. On the other hand, a primary right *in rem* is defined as one of a large class of fundamentally similar yet separate rights, actual and potential, residing in a single person but availing respectively against persons constituting a very large and indefinite class of people. He explained that rights *in rem* are not in fact rights 'against one thing', but as with all other 'jural relations' they too apply to persons. *In rem* rights exist not only for tangible objects but also for intangibles, such as intellectual property. These rights can coexist with a variety of other privileges, powers and immunities.[75]

Hohfeld considered that *in rem* rights could be broken down into an indefinite number of potential *in personam* rights. In other words, *in rem* rights are, in practice, qualitatively indistinguishable from *in personam* rights. His views did not, however, remain uncontested. In particular, Penner managed to show that *in personam* rights attach directly to persons while *in rem* rights attach to persons only because of their relationship to a particular thing. According to Penner, *in rem* rights

---

[74] Grey, T., 'The Disintegration of Property', in Epstein, R.A. (ed), *Liberty, Property and the Law*, Quebec City: SLS Publications (2000), pp. 223–8.

[75] See Jaffrey, P., 'Hohfeld's Power–Liability/Right–Duty Distinction in the Law of Restitution', Canadian J Law & Jurisprudence, Vol 17 (2004), pp. 295–313.

'allow strangers to interact with each other in a rule-governed way, though their dealings are not personal in any significant respect'.[76]

In a series of publications investigating the nature and definition of property, Thomas Merill and Henry Smith attempt to reintroduce coherence to property rights, building on two central parameters: the *in rem* nature of property rights and the *numerus clausus* principle, under which property rights 'must track a limited number of standard forms'.[77]

Merill and Smith argued that the *numerus clausus* principle (the theory according to which an entitlement has to include a number of parameters in order to constitute a property right) is justifiable from an economic perspective. By permitting various different forms of property while at the same time not allowing the courts to recognise new ones, the *numerus clausus* principle strikes the necessary balance between the proliferation of property forms and excessive rigidity. According to Merill and Smith, allowing for free customisation of property rights would considerably increase the external information costs of third parties, in the form of high measurement costs. The *numerus clausus* principle channels all changes in the legal content of property to the legislature.

In order to create an *in rem* right, it is necessary to specify particular resources and to identify a specific person as the owner of the resources. It seems, thus, that elaborating the structure of the right is much simpler in this case than in that of *in personam* rights. When designing a new *in rem* right, an important parameter to bear in mind is the minimisation of the information-cost burden imposed on third parties. Obviously, *in rem* rights involve an indefinite number of anonymous parties. Thus the holders of *in personam* rights have information on their duty holder, and may investigate past experiences before determining the form of the duty imposed. The differentiation between *in rem* and *in personam* rights, and all the intermediate categories in between, becomes relevant in particular when it comes to determining the role played by contractual agreements when they substitute entitlements or when they are complementary to them.

One interesting historical illustration of the role that contractual agreements can play in the enforcement of property rights is that of ranchers in the late nineteenth century. Because of the enforcement costs of their lease rights against outsiders, and also the difficulties in

---

76 Penner, J., *The Idea of Property in Law*, Oxford: Oxford University Press (1997), p. 30.

77 Merrill, T., Smith, H., 'Optimal Standardization in the Law of Property: The Numerus Clausus Principle', Yale LJ, Vol 110 (2000), pp. 1–70.

negotiating individually with the Cherokee tribe, ranches formed the Cherokee Strip Livestock Association in 1883. Consequently, a set of specific contracts evolved among the ranchers and between the ranchers and the tribe, to better define and enforce property rights. The contracts were signed and enforced along with the US government's recognition of Cherokee sovereignty over land.[78]

In some cases, contracts have been considered either necessary complements or equally valuable substitutes for exclusive rights. These discussions have been particularly important with regard to *sui generis* regimes. In the field of TKGR, contractual agreements have been the most direct and immediate protection scheme. It was, and still is, by means of bioprospecting agreements that the rights of TKGR holders and TKGR users are regulated. The lack of a legal entitlement covering the specific subject matter did not hinder parties engaging in bioprospecting agreements from agreeing contractual terms comparable to traditional IP licences. However, the emergence of a legal entitlement will enhance and strengthen such contractual arrangements.

5.1.4.1.4 The right to exclude and the right to property Exclusion theorists have not been able to satisfactorily describe the concept of property and the legal rules intended to protect it. However, their conclusion that property has at least one essential characteristic is valuable and provides the legal institution solid theoretical grounding.

The exclusion theory has its historical source in the words of James Madison and Thomas Jefferson. James Madison stated that property 'stands for' the domination which one man claims and exercises over the external things of the world, in exclusion of every other individual. Thomas Jefferson, in his justification as to why IPRs cannot be a subject of property, stated that an idea is 'incapable of confinement or exclusive appropriation'.[79]

The dominant theory of property has always included exclusion as one of the many essential and necessary characteristics of its legal content.[80] Grotius adopts a developmental and functional theory of property rights, investigating the conditions and goals that give rise to the need for the

---

[78] See Anderson, T., Hill, P., 'Cowboys and Contracts', J Legal Studies, Vol 31 (2002), pp. 489–514.

[79] Mossof, A., 'Who Cares What Jefferson Said About Patents? Reevaluating the Patent Privilege in Historical Context', Cornell L Rev, Vol 92 (2002), pp. 953–4.

[80] In particular in Anglo-American law.

moral concept and accompanying the institution of property.[81] He proposes a two-step process for defining the source and nature of property: firstly, an action by an individual that places him in a proper relationship with an object in the world; secondly, the social recognition of this relationship. According to Grotius, property evolves out of use rights because occupation or use necessarily turns objects into exclusive possessions. Consequently, exclusion is the analytical parameter that moves people from use rights in the state of nature to property rights in civil society.

The second step in the creation of property rights is that of social recognition of property rights, which has been a means of providing for proper and peaceful social relations. In this way, 'all agreed' to respect the abandonment of 'community ownership' and that possession acquired through occupation or use shall be retained by their owner exclusively. Consequently, the use right does not require any recognition or consent by others to be a valid entitlement; the only thing left for people to consent to is that the use of something should be transformed into an exclusive right that endures over time.

Grotius employed his theoretical framework when writing on behalf of the Dutch East India Company in order to repudiate the claim presented by the Portuguese that they owned the oceans traversed by their trade ships, as well as the island nations with which they traded. He provided that possession of movables implies seizure and possession of immovables and either the erection of buildings or some determination of boundaries, such as fencing in. The concept of possession builds upon an implicit notion of exclusion. Grotius states in his conclusions that that which cannot be occupied, or which never has been occupied, cannot be the property of anyone, because all property has arisen from occupation. In the specific case he was considering, this meant that the ocean is incapable of being occupied, which means that it is incapable of a form of exclusive possession that would give rise to property. Without the ability to exclude others physically, according to the first application of the modern concept of property, there can be no right to property. In other words, the right to property is based upon the right to exclude.

In the world of these early property theorists and modern exclusion theorists, there is a common understanding that the right to exclude is a necessary characteristic of property. An object belongs to someone in its entirety because the possessor has the right to exclude others from

---

[81] Buckle, S., *Natural Law and Theory of Property, from Grotius to Hume*, Oxford: Oxford University Press (1993), pp. 4–35.

accessing or using that thing. However, though the right to exclude was a necessary characteristic, it was not the most central one.

Aristotle defined property as 'something that is our own if it is in our power to dispose it or keep it'.[82] Although in this definition the right to exclude is implicitly invoked, the focus lies with the right to use. In fact, what was of central importance in ancient Greek society was what one did with one's property; the concept of property was defined on the basis of using something and was not about excluding others. In Roman law the concept of property reflects the integrated theory, emphasising the substantive elements of acquisition, use and disposal, while exclusion is referred to only as a secondary corollary.[83]

5.1.4.1.5 Value in property Bell and Parchomovsky,[84] proponents of a value-based approach to property, propose a combination of the theories and models presented over the years. The starting point of their approach is that 'the institution of property is designed to create and defend the value inhering in stable ownership'.[85] Property is thus set to achieve this objective by creating and protecting the relationship between a person and assets.

Bell and Parchomovsky's contribution elaborates on the previous work of central property theorists such as Demsetz,[86] Rose,[87] Barzel[88] and Shavell,[89] and assumes that the property institution has three main functions: the creation of a legal status, the definition of the legal status and, finally, the practical consequences of the violation of property rules. The stability of property law as a legal institution is decisive for its value. The value of property rights is related to the number of people who are

---

[82] Aristotle, *Politics*, trans. Ernest Barker, revised with introduction and notes by R. F. Stalley, Oxford: Oxford University Press (2009), p. 320.

[83] For a very interesting review of Aristotle's theory on property, see Mayhew, R., 'Aristotle on Property', Rev Metaphysics, Vol 46 (1993), pp. 803–31.

[84] Bell, A., Parchomovsky G., 'What Property Is', Research Paper No 04-05, Institute for Law and Economics, University of Pennsylvania Law School (February 2004).

[85] Bell, Parchomovsky (2004).

[86] Demsetz (1967).

[87] Rose, C., 'The Comedy of the Commons: Custom, Commerce, and Inherently Public Property', U Chicago L Rev, Vol 53 (1986), p. 711.

[88] Barzel, Y., *Economic Analysis of Property Rights*, Cambridge: Cambridge University Press (1989).

[89] Kaplow, L., Shavell, S., 'Property Rules versus Liability Rules' (1996), available at SSRN: http://ssrn.com/abstract=56405 or DOI: 10.2139/ssrn.56405.

aware of and respect the property system. Assets protected by property law should be limited, and only those assets for which protection of stable ownership will enhance social welfare should come under the aegis of property law. Changes in the structure of society, as well as in its objectives, will influence the assets that are apt for property law protection. Contrary to Radin,[90] Bell and Parchomovsky recognise the importance of the economic value of stable ownership for all categories of property relations, not just the nonfungible ones. In their view, value is the unifying theme for all property law.[91]

5.1.4.1.6 Relational conceptions of property The definition of property rights on the basis of interpersonal relationships has its theoretical starting point in Hegel's contribution.

Radin further developed the relational conceptions of property and introduced a fundamental distinction between personal and fungible property. Personal property is property whose 'loss causes pain that cannot be relieved by the object's replacement'. Contrarily, fungible property is that which is 'perfectly replaceable with other goods of equal market value'. While personal property is closely related to the owner's personality, fungible property is held for utilitarian purposes.[92]

Radin elaborates on the normative implications of the theoretical framework and proposes a 'two-level' property rights system that provides for differential protection to entitlements according to their classification as personal or fungible. Radin's property rights hierarchy is illustrated in her suggestions that the government should 'guarantee citizens all entitlements necessary for personhood' and ensure that the 'fungible property of some people does not overwhelm the opportunities of the rest to constitute themselves in (personal) property'.[93] According to Radin, property rights are different in nature and should be treated differently. The structure of the protection offered should be based on a careful inspection of the nature of objects subject to property rights and the roles they play in constituting the personalities of the persons claiming them.[94]

A novel 'relational' approach to property is that proposed under the human rights framework. The theories justifying IPRs have, during the

---

[90] Radin (1982).

[91] Bell and Parchomovsky (2004), p. 39. In this regard, even Barzel's analysis of the law becomes relevant.

[92] Radin (1982).

[93] Radin (1982), p. 1001.

[94] Radin (1982), p. 1009.

past two centuries, belonged either to the utilitarian or the natural rights tradition.[95] Since the time of the French Revolution, some countries have recognised certain forms of intellectual property as a category of human rights, which gave them the same protection as other property rights. French philosophy extended beyond the Lockean labour theory of property to claim that the protection of rights was a reflection of the author's personality. On the other hand, due to the fact that intellectual property was gradually treated as an extension of 'tangible' property, its protection as a 'fundamental', 'natural' or 'human' right became more and more important.

IPRs 'officially' entered the human rights framework when they were included in the Universal Declaration of Human Rights (UDHR),[96] with Article 27 of the UDHR providing that 'Everyone has the right to the protection of the moral and material interest resulting from any scientific, literary or artistic production of which he is the author'.[97] The UDHR, adopted unanimously by the UN General Assembly in 1948, provides the most authoritative statement of human rights. In its preamble, it is stated that it provides for a common standard of achievement for all peoples and nations. The first 21 articles present a series of civil and political rights such as the right to life, liberty and security of person, freedom from torture and cruel punishment, equality before law and nondiscrimination, freedom of peaceful assembly and association and freedom of thought, conscience, and religion. In addition to the traditional political and civil rights focus, the UDHR also covers a series of economic and social rights. This second category of human rights covers the right to just and favourable conditions of work, to form trade unions, to a standard of living adequate for health and wellbeing, to education, to participate in the cultural life of the community, to share in the benefits of scientific achievement and, finally, to the protection of moral and

[95] See also Gana, R., 'The Myth of Development, the Progress of Rights: Human Rights to Intellectual Property and Development', Law and Policy, Vol 18 (1996), pp. 315–54.

[96] Universal Declaration of Human Rights, GA Res 217A, UN GAOR, 3rd Session, 1st Plen Mtg, UN Doc A/810 (10 December 1948), hereinafter UDHR.

[97] The *travaux préparatoires* of the drafting committee for the UDHR operating under the aegis of the United Nations Commission on Human Rights reveal that the preceding discussions with regard to authors' rights were concerned with two major issues: firstly, the moral rights of an author to control alteration and other misuses of his creation; secondly, the right of authors and creators to remuneration for their labour.

material interests resulting from any scientific, literary or artistic production of which a person is the author.

Authors' rights were first awarded human rights status in the American Declaration on the Rights and Duties of Man.[98] According to Article 13 of the Declaration: 'every person has the right to take part in the cultural life of the community, to enjoy the arts and to participate in the benefits that result from intellectual progress, especially, scientific discoveries. He/she likewise has the right to the protection of his/her moral and material interests as regards his invention or any literary, scientific or artistic works of which he is the author.'

Article 15 of the International Covenant on Economic, Social and Cultural Rights (ICESCR) 'recognizes the rights of everyone ... to enjoy the benefits of scientific progress and its applications' and to 'benefit from the protection of the moral and material interests resulting from any scientific literary or other material interests resulting from any scientific, literary or artistic production of which he is the author'.[99] The text of Article 15 of the ICESCR lies close to Article 27 of the UDHR. Similar to the UDHR, the ICESCR includes three components: the right to culture, scientific advancement, and intellectual property.

Approaching IP as a human right gives a new perspective on its structure and applications. It would in fact embrace 'collective' ownership and would recognise the 'intrinsic value' of IP creations, which is closely related to expression of the creator's personality. What is more, IPRs would have to follow a more balanced view, taking into account the rights of the 'users' of IP and the welfare of society.[100] Article 27 of the Universal Declaration of Human Rights of 1948 includes the protection of authors' moral and material interests in their scientific, literary or artistic production as part of a list of fundamental liberties.[101] The International Covenant on Economic, Social and Cultural Rights also included a similar clause, stating that authors should benefit from the

---

98 Organization of American States, American Declaration of the Rights and Duties of Man, 2 May 1948, OEA/Ser L/V/II.23, Doc 21 rev 6.

99 International Covenant on Economic, Social, and Cultural Rights, UN GAOR, 21 at Sess, Supp, No 16 p. 49, UN Doc A/6316 (1966), hereinafter ICESCR.

100 According to Article 15 ICESCR, 'States parties are directed to ensure that everyone will be able to benefit from the protection of the moral and material interests resulting from any scientific, literary or artistic production of which he is the author'.

101 Universal Declaration of Human Rights, 8 December 1948, GA Res 217A(iii), UN Doc A/810, at 71, Art 27.

moral and material interests resulting from their works.[102] In interpreting the requirements of the norm for nondiscrimination, the United Nations Commission on the prevention of racial discrimination admonishes states to take specific steps to recognise indigenous communities' rights to own, develop, control and use their communal lands, territories and natural resources. ILO 169 maintains that indigenous peoples should be consulted even in uses of subsurface resources that normally fall under state sovereignty. Indigenous communities have the right to decide on the process of development as it affects their lives.[103] According to Article 15, the state has to consult with indigenous communities before exploiting resources pertaining to the indigenous people's lands. Furthermore, ILO 169 provides that 'peoples concerned shall ... participate in the benefits of [resource exploitation], and shall receive fair compensation for any damages which they may sustain as a result of such activities'.[104] Apart from the economic and developmental perspective, the state is under the obligation to take into account cultural, religious and social identities before engaging in developmental activities.

In the light of Article 27 of the International Covenant, the UN Human Rights Committee has recognised the imperative of indigenous peoples' participation in decisions that may affect their traditional lands. Article 3 of the Draft Declaration on issues of discrimination against indigenous peoples provides the principle of self-determination. In accordance with Article 7, indigenous communities have the collective and individual right to prevent any action which has the aim or effect of dispossessing them of their lands, territories and resources. In Article 29, it is specified that indigenous communities have the right to control genetic resources, seeds, medicines and knowledge of the fauna and flora that exist in their lands.

Paragraph 35 of the Principles and Guidelines for the protection of the heritage of indigenous communities stipulates that researchers and scholarly institutions must refrain from engaging in any study of previously not described species or cultivated varieties of plants, animals and microbes or naturally occurring pharmaceuticals without first obtaining satisfactory documentation that the specimens were acquired with the

---

[102] International Covenant on Economic, Social and Cultural Rights (ICESCR), adopted 16 December 1966, Arts 15(1)(c) and 15(1)(b), S Exec Doc D, 95-2 at 13 (1997), 993 UNTS 3, 5 (entered into force 3 January 1976).

[103] Consultations with indigenous communities should not be done on a formal basis. To serve their purpose they should allow the indigenous peoples to influence the decision-making procedures and the final outcomes.

[104] Article 15 of ILO Convention No 169.

consent of the traditional owners.[105] According to paragraph 38,[106] researchers and scholarly institutions should make every possible effort to increase indigenous peoples' access to all forms of medical, scientific and technical education and their participation in all research activities that may affect them or be to their benefit. The same requirements are applicable to industry and business.[107]

5.1.4.1.7 Utilitarianism The theoretical contributions to the evolution of property rights' definition also impacted justifications for the property rights institution. Economic analysis on classical legal concepts and institutions gradually reached the field of property law. Major contributors such as Ronald Coase and Richard Posner provided for the economic analysis of property rights on the basis of two major parameters: transaction costs and externalities.[108]

Coase's contribution refocused the discussion by showing that externalities would lead to inefficiency only when transaction costs hinder private bargaining. Where transaction costs are zero, parties would reallocate property rights to reach efficiency.

Coase was interested in using economics to explain the structure of law and thus did not contribute so much to refining the definition of property rights. Obviously, Coase did not consider property to be a distinctive right to a thing valid against the world, but rather a bundle of use rights. He focused on the resolution of discrete use conflicts, and property rights were given no significance other than as collections of use rights resulting from judicial resolutions of such conflicts.[109]

Coase actually had the opportunity to elaborate on the requirements for establishing a system of private property rights to govern the allocation

---

[105] Final Report of the Special Rapporteur, Mrs Erica-Irene Daes, in conformity with Subcommissions resolution 1993/44 and Decision 1994/105 of the Commission on Human Rights, 'Principles and Guidelines for the Protection of the Heritage of Indigenous Peoples'.

[106] Final Report of the Special Rapporteur, Mrs Erica-Irene Daes, in conformity with Subcommission's resolution 1993/44 and Decision 1994/105 of the Commission on Human Rights, 'Principles and Guidelines for the Protection of the Heritage of Indigenous Peoples'.

[107] See paras 40–5 of the Principles and Guidelines for the Protection of Heritage of Indigenous Peoples.

[108] Lands, W.M., Posner, R.A., 'An Economic Analysis of Copyright Law', in Posner, E.A. (ed), *Law and Economics*, Aldershot: Ashgate (2000), pp. 325–63.

[109] See also Hülsmann, J., 'The A Priori Foundations of Property Economics', Quarterly J Austrian Economics, Vol 7 (2004), pp. 41–68.

of resources. In his article 'The Federal Communications Commission',[110] Coase confirmed that he views property as a list of use rights. In fact, Coase claimed that giving broadcasters private property rights that can be bought and sold in a secondary market would produce more efficient allocation of the broadcast spectrum. In his attempt to meet the arguments against the appropriateness of the private property rights in the specific case, given the fact that private property rights in the electromagnetic spectrum are difficult to define and enforce, Coase claimed that privatisation should proceed not by defining exclusive rights, but by specifying certain use rights in broadcasting equipment. His conception of property as a list of uses was connected to his general view that property rights are solely a foundation for bilateral transactions.

In the post-Coase economic theories, property rights have been considered in three different ways, represented by three different schools. Firstly, 'new institutional economics' have as their main focus transaction costs in understanding economic phenomena, including the institution of property. The second school views property rights in essentially contractarian terms, while, finally, a third school builds on Calabresi and Melamed's contribution.[111]

One of the most featured representatives of this view is Barzel,[112] who claims that the world consists of a multitude of assets, each of which has multiple attributes, thus distinguishing the two sides of property rights: 'economic property' and 'legal property'. 'Economic property' was thus defined as the individual's ability, in expected terms, to consume the good directly, or indirectly through exchange. 'Legal property' includes the economic property rights that are 'recognized and enforced, in part, by the government'.[113] Barzel's 'economic right' is a very broad term and sets out to cover all relations of an individual to a certain thing.

The model of property rights proposed by Barzel presupposed that private contracting would fail to capture certain valuable attributes of assets. The legal institution of property is set up in order to address forms of protection that are not addressed by contractual relations. In fact, Barzel places property rights under the institution of contracts, stating that 'at the heart of the study of property lies the study of contracts'.[114]

---

110 Coase, R., 'The Federal Communications Commission', J Law & Economics, Vol II (October 1959), p. 1.

111 Calabresi, Melamed (1972).

112 Barzel (1989).

113 Barzel (1989), p. 4.

114 Barzel focuses exclusively on the possibilities and limitations of contractual exchange, leaving aside the *in rem* character of property rights.

The focal point of Barzel's research is not property but contract, and in fact this subordination of property to contract was harshly criticised.[115]

The second post-Coasean school concerns collectively imposed solutions to social cost problems. In this regard, Cooter considers that property is the collectively imposed allocation of use rights with respect to any particular resource.[116] Even with the property law examples he considers – government takings and nuisance disputes – Cooter regards as 'property' the allocation of use rights after a court has adjudicated a dispute and imposed the rule designed to elicit an efficient response from both parties.

Calabresi and Melamed developed a two-stage model for understanding the law of property and tort.[117] This post-Coasean school developed a theory that presents collective assignment of entitlements and contractual exchange as different steps in the analysis, while also introducing the possibility of forced exchange into the discussion. Calabresi and Melamed adopt a set of variables for assigning entitlements that is more nuanced and more focused than that presented by Coase. They claim that, when ruling on a specific case and taking into account efficiency, distributional and other justice considerations, the courts conclude as to which kind of allocation of use rights will provide the correct baseline regarding which process of contractual exchange, or who will compensate whom in the case that a forced exchange is considered more appropriate.[118] Obviously, Calabresi and Melamed's analysis does not include any consideration of the *in rem* character of property rights. In the fundamental dichotomy between property rights and liability rights, Calabresi and Melamed focus on the difference between the doctrines of specific performance and of injunctive relief. In their analysis, there is no mention of the nature, rationale and characteristics of property rights, whose main role (according to the authors) is to facilitate contractual exchange. It seems, thus, that the term 'property' covers not only property rights but also contractual rights. Although, contrary to Coase, Calabresi and Melamed deal with the accommodation of cases involving

---

[115] Merill, T., Smith, H. 'The Property/Contract Interface', Columbia L Rev, Vol 101 (2001), pp. 773–852. It was also criticised because it does not provide for a baseline or criteria to determine who contracts with whom.

[116] Cooter, R., 'Commodifying Liability', in F.H. Buckley (ed.), *The Rise and Fall of Freedom of Contract*, Durham: Duke University Press (2006), pp. 139–56.

[117] Calabresi, Melamed (1972), pp. 1089–128.

[118] Calabresi, Melamed (1972), pp. 1093–8.

a large number of affected persons, they do it in order to illustrate typical cases in which forced exchange is preferable to voluntary exchange.[119]

Taking into consideration that the 'property rights' paradigm has been defined and perceived in different ways by major representatives of the property law doctrine, there are two major challenges to the elaboration of a new legal entitlement potentially falling under the scope of property rights: the questions of which justification is applicable for the introduction of the specific property right, and what the ingredients of such a property right should be. Equally important, of course, is deciding on the appropriate model for the management of the property right.

5.1.4.2 The property rights paradigm: a uniform theory or fifty shades of grey?

Although there is a plethora of theoretical contributions regarding the origin, justification and legal content of property rights, the characteristics of the property rights institution are far from settled. Nevertheless, what seems to be clear is that whatever the origin, justification or legal content of property rights, the ways in which they are managed or enforced may differ considerably. Consequently, opting for property rights does not necessarily mean opting for private rights. Thus, even with the same entitlement as a starting point – a property right – one might still end up with a totally divergent exercise of rights.

5.1.4.2.1 Private property versus common property Legal and economic scholars have engaged in endless battles regarding the definition, development and superiority of private versus common property. In fact, common property institutions have a longer history than private property institutions.[120] Common property has, however, been considered inefficient, for three main reasons: rent dissipation,[121] transaction costs,[122] and low productivity.[123] The already blurry relationship between common

---

119 Calabresi, Melamed (1972), pp. 1089–93.

120 North, D., Thomas R., 'An Economic Theory of the Growth of the Western World', *Economic History Review*, New Series, Vol 23 (1970), pp. 1–17.

121 No one owns the resources until they are captured, and everyone is thus engaged in a race to capture as much as possible.

122 Trying to introduce rules to avoid communal owners overusing the resources entails high transaction and enforcement costs.

123 There is no motivation to work harder because there is no expectation of thus increasing private benefits. See North, Thomas (1970).

and private rights has been further clouded by a series of misconceptions and misuse and abuse of terms and concepts.[124]

Ciriacy-Wantrup and Bishop elaborated on the difference between property regimes that are open access, where no one has the right to exclude someone else from using a resource, and common property, where the members of a clearly defined group have a legal right to exclude nonmembers from using the resource in question.[125] Resources become 'open access' resources in three different cases: because of a lack of effective rules defining property rights; due to ineffective exclusion of nonowners; as a result of conscious public policies. When resources are made available under an open access regime, no one has the incentive to invest in their conservation and their future development, thus leading to misuse and overconsumption.

With regard to IPRs, the term 'public domain' is employed to describe what is free for everyone to use. The concept of the public domain was employed for the first time in jurisprudence in the US Supreme Court's 1896 ruling concerning the Singer sewing machine.[126] The Court stated that upon the expiration of a patent, the right to exploit the technology is open to the public and the technology falls into the public domain. During the 90 years that followed, the public domain was barely mentioned. The public domain was to include the leftovers of private property.

The first notable explicit reference to the legal status of the public domain was made by Lange,[127] who affirmed in the late 1970s that the public domain was a vital, affirmative entity – the publicly accessible collection of knowledge, ideas, history and expression on which creators draw in order to make their new works. It was described in large part as a repository of public knowledge. At the same time, Lange warned of the growing expansionist tendency of private rights. Oddly, the importance of the public domain and its protection, underlined by Lange, did not gain attention in legal research until approximately the mid-1980s, when Pamela Samuelson expressed her concerns for the expansion of intellectual property in new technologies and elaborated on the importance of

---

[124] Although most of these resources have been elaborated on the basis of a 'natural resources' paradigm, it is rather simple to draw IP parallels.

[125] Ciriacy-Wantrup, S., Bishop R., 'Common Property as a Concept in Natural Resources Policy' Natural Resources J, Vol 15 (1975), pp. 713–27.

[126] US Supreme Court: *Singer Mfg Co v. June Mfg Co*, 163 US 169 (1896).

[127] Lange, D.L., 'Recognizing the Public Domain', Law & Contemp Probs, Vol 147 (1981), pp. 173–8.

safeguarding and valuing the public domain; she was followed in this by a number of other prominent legal scholars.[128]

5.1.4.2.2 Common property rights Where a number of individuals have unrestricted access to a resource, that resource is managed under an 'open access' regime. Each person's objective is to maximise his own rent subject to the constraint of open access, which means that each user can only capture (and own) the output in proportion to his share of effort.

The absence of property rights leads to overuse of the asset and complete dissipation of its value.[129] Dissipation is a limiting result, however, on the assumption of homogenous users. If users are heterogeneous, dissipation under open access will be incomplete, and inframarginal (low-cost) users will earn rents. The presence of rent under open access may be an important factor in preventing the establishment of rights to open access resources, because those earning rents will have incentives to maintain the open access regime.

Common property is not equivalent to open access; it represents exclusive ownership by a group. Common property regimes have been well documented, in particular in the field of natural resources.[130] Such a property rights regime may arise out of explicit private contracting or out of custom; it may also have a legal or regulatory basis that has implicit contractual origins.[131]

Contracting to form common property effectively creates a group that has exclusive rights to the resource. Common property regimes entailing equal sharing rules and homogenous membership may contribute to the maximisation of a common property resource's present value.[132]

Semicommons property is defined as a resource that is used in common for an important purpose, but otherwise held privately. Henry Smith describes the example of the medieval open-field system, in which a field was open to common grazing during some specified months of the

---

[128] Samuelson, P., 'Preserving the Positive Functions of the Public Domain for Science' Data Science J, Vol 2 (2003), pp. 192–7.

[129] Related to Hardin's tragedy of the commons.

[130] Moretto, M., Rosato, P., 'The Use of Common Property Resources: A Dynamic Model', Fondazione Eni Enrico Mattei, (January 2002). See also Buchanan, J.M., 'Symmetric Tragedies: Commons and Anticommons', J Law & Econ, Vol 43 (2000), pp. 1–6.

[131] Eggertsson, T., *Economic Behavior and Institutions*, Cambridge, MA: Cambridge University Press (1990).

[132] Lueck, D., 'Common Property as an Egalitarian Share Contract', J Economic Behavior & Organization, Vol 25 (1994), pp. 93–108.

year but divided into privately held segments during crop-growing season.[133] This allowed for combining the benefits of certain uses better suited under the 'commons' regime, as well as the private rights regime for other adequate uses.

Information has also been granted the characterisation of 'semicommons', by Robert Heverly,[134] who extensively discusses the interaction between common and private uses of information and provides examples of the necessity of this double character. Heverly goes as far as to claim that file swapping should be allowed if there is no evidence that this will limit the private use's potential.[135] Daniel Opderdeck, meanwhile,[136] comments that the semicommons regime, as described by Smith, is equivalent to that of common pool resources and collective management. Opderdeck draws a parallel between Smith's semicommons theory and Ostrom's collective management of Turkish fisheries.[137]

On the other hand, the characteristics of the users relate to the importance of the resources for those users' wellbeing: the users must have good knowledge of how the resource is made available and the implications of their activities; they must discount the future benefits of the resource at a relatively low rate and, as they constitute a close-knit and loyal community, must have sufficient decision-making independence in establishing the rules for use of the resource; finally, they must have minimal organisational and managerial experience.

Of equal importance are the characteristics of the institution governing common resources. The following characteristics have been identified: the rights of the users must be clearly defined and there must be precise identification of the resource; the rules for use must be coherent with the local socioeconomic conditions; all users must be able to participate in the definition of the rules; the controls must be effective; sanctions must be gradual and effective; conflict solution must be rapid and efficient; and, lastly, the community holding the resource must have the right and the ability to organise itself.[138]

---

[133] Smith (2000), pp. 134–6.

[134] Heverly, R., 'The Information Semicommons', Berkeley Tech LJ, Vol 18 (2003), p. 1127.

[135] Heverly (2003), pp. 1187–9.

[136] Opderdeck, D., 'The Penguin's Genome or Coase and the Open Source Biotechnology', Harv J Law & Technology, Vol 18 (2004), pp. 168–227.

[137] Ostrom, E., *Governing the Commons: The Evolution of Institutions for Collective Action*, New York: Cambridge University Press (1990).

[138] Ostrom (1990).

Finally, the major characteristics of users' rights of common pool resources were: the right cannot be bought or sold but is acquired with the occurrence of particular conditions; the holder of the right is free to use it or not, and renunciation of use of the right does not involve any compensation; the decision to exercise the right always generates a nonrecoverable outlay; the decision to cease exercise of the right or interrupt or resume use can be taken at any time; the decision to exercise the right involves the production of a negative external factor affecting the other actual users and due to the resource subtracted by the user; and the user commits to following the rules of the community related to the use of the resource.

5.1.4.2.3 Of open access, open source and Creative Commons Apart from the central dichotomy between private property rights and commons, a number of variations in the management of rights have developed during the past few years, some of which apply in particular in the field of IPRs. Considering these alternative methods of managing resources and IPRs also provides an interesting perspective in the field of TKGR.

5.1.4.2.3.1 OPEN SOURCE The open source model has its origin in the world of computer programs. Although open source has open access as a starting point, such access is subject to a series of stringent rules and limitations.

An important characteristic of this managerial model is its rigid organisational structure. Open source projects are controlled by a limited number of project leaders that decide upon the project's orientation and goals. Participants are free to volunteer for any aspect they wish but have to respect and follow the direction of the project and not engage in counteracting activities. To this end, the open source model employs prestige expectations as well as social sanctions in the form of disapproval or even ostracism.

The rapidly growing number of internet users facilitated the acceleration of open source activities. A central development was commercial companies' contribution to open source communities. Along with the commercial interest in open source projects came enhanced flexibility of the applicable rules, as these are incorporated in the licences. The open source community developed alternative licensing mechanisms to the 'standard' licensing structure of the general public licence (GPL). The organisation that took up the dissemination of the Linux platform, Debian, developed the 'Debian Social Contract' in 1995. Under this structure, licensees had greater flexibility in deciding the status of developed software. It allowed the bundling of cooperatively developed software with proprietary code. A further development in the field was the licensing structure named 'open source definition'. Unlike the 'general public licence', this newer licence does not require all code bundled with the software to be covered under the licence agreement as well.[139] Open source projects very often target high-tech users, and offer considerable responsiveness to users' needs.

It is of course interesting to consider the incentives behind such initiatives, since they seem to defy what is considered a central parameter in the field of IPRs – the fact that creators will not invest their time and resources if they do not expect to be awarded exclusive private rights. There seem to be two specific incentives for software programmers: the first is the career-concern incentive, which covers future job offers and also shares in commercial open source-based companies; the second is the ego-gratification incentive, which originates in a desire to gain recognition from the group. Both these incentives/types are covered by a more general concept, that of 'signalling incentive'. According to the economic theory of signalling,[140] the 'signalling incentive' is stronger under three situations: (1) the more visible the performance to the relevant audience, (2) the higher the impact of the effort will be on performance, (3) the more informative the performance will be about talent.[141]

Obviously, the incentives behind open source production deviate from the traditional utilitarian view that exclusive rights are a major incentive for creativity and for the development of new products.[142] Open source structures are more and more often seen in the development of commercial software. Commercial companies increasingly appreciate open source as a potential business model, especially with regard to technology that does not represent the company's differentiation point and

---

[139] Osterloh, M., Rota, S.G., 'Open Source Software Development – Just Another Case of Collective Invention?' (March 2004), available at SSRN: http://ssrn.com/abstract=561744 or DOI: 10.2139/ssrn.561744. See also Raju, K.D., 'Is the Future of Software Development in Open Source? Proprietary vs. Open Source Software: A Cross Country Analysis', J Intellectual Property Rights, Vol 12 (2007), available at SSRN: http://ssrn.com/abstract=985237.

[140] Spence, M. 'Signaling in Retrospect and the Informational Structure of Markets', American Economic Rev, Vol 92 (2002), 434–59.

[141] Bonaccorsi, A., Rossi, C., 'Licensing Schemes in the Production and Distribution of Open Source Software: An Empirical Investigation' (2003), available at SSRN: http://ssrn.com/abstract=432641 or DOI: 10.2139/ssrn.43264.

[142] Guadamuz, Andrés, 'Legal Challenges to Open Source Licences', 2 SCRIPT-ed (2013), pp. 163–70.

can be expected to develop faster and more effectively under a commons structure.[143]

5.1.4.2.3.2 CREATIVE COMMONS Creative Commons is a nonprofit organisation founded in 2001 by Professor Lawrence Lessig, with the principal goal to expand 'the range of creative work available for others to legally build upon and share'.

Creative Commons, like the open source movement, addresses the flaws of expansionist proprietary rights on intellectual creations and of the property rights system and goes on to propose a novel managerial structure for these proprietary rights. In other words, instead of proposing that intellectual creations are placed in the public domain, it provides for a licensing platform through which owners of proprietary rights can allow for others to access and reuse their works with much more flexible terms and conditions than those provided for in the copyright system. Authors are not faced with the copyright/public domain dichotomy since Creative Commons does not really aim at creating a 'public domain'. The starting point for this alternative managerial structure is that it is possible to remedy the flaws of the copyright system without removing it, but by exercising it in an alternative way.

Creative Commons' most important contribution is the fact that it provides a common platform for a number of different groups that question the impact of copyright in creativity and access. The flexible licensing platform allows for a range of different views on ownership to coexist and find adequate representation.

The licensing platform proposed by this model includes decreasing costs as well as the removal of legal uncertainty in order to facilitate access and reuse of copyright-protected works. This is clearly reflected in the Creative Commons slogan: 'No friction, no legal doubt, no middleman'.[144]

Creative Commons offers a standardised and rather automated licensing platform. Parties to the Creative Commons licensing platform may choose between various contractual clauses in order to address the nature of the work as well as the interests of the rightholders. When the

---

[143] Von Krogh, Georg, Spaeth, Sebastian and Lakhani, Karim R., 'Community, Joining, and Specialization in Open Source Software Innovation: A Case Study', MIT Sloan Working Paper No 4413-03 (February 2003), available at SSRN: http://ssrn.com/abstract=387500 or DOI: 10.2139/ssrn.387500.

[144] Elkin-Koren, Niva, 'What Contracts Can't Do: The Limits of Private Ordering in Facilitating a Creative Commons', Fordham L Rev, Vol 74 (2005), available at SSRN: http://ssrn.com/abstract=760906.

contractual clauses are selected, the licence is made available in three separable formats. One is the legal format, the Legal Code licence, which guarantees that the agreement will be able to stand in court. The other is human-readable language, where rights and obligations originating from the contract are explained in plain language. Finally, there is the machine-readable form. This last format allows search engines to identify works covered by the determined conditions of use.[145]

Creative Commons thus proposes an innovative licensing scheme. Its goal is to develop the technological and legal platforms that will facilitate access to creative works. It achieves this by reducing transaction costs. The Creative Commons licensing platform allows authors to retain the copyright to their work while at the same time being able to license to a broader public and with more generous terms. The central objective of Creative Commons is to minimise the transaction costs that usually hinder or trouble licensing agreements, thus leading to a limited use of protected works. It is often claimed that the standardisation of the Creative Commons agreements and the multiplicity of contractual clauses covering the same protected work, and dictating the rights and obligations of the user in different 'use' environments, further increase information costs.[146] These information costs would be even higher for third parties that, when dealing with Creative Commons, would not know which uses are allowed and which remain the exclusive right of the copyright holder. Elkin-Koren concludes that while Creative Commons allows for a fine-tuning of rights, tailored to address the needs of the rightholder but also the specific nature of the protected work, the Creative Commons platform lacks standardisation and thus does not allow for a limitation of transaction costs.[147]

The Creative Commons platform is built upon the proprietary regime and derives its force from its existence. The grant of property rights on the works preserves owners' right to exclude unauthorised uses and to control the terms and conditions of authorised use, as well as the ability to collect licence fees when this is considered appropriate. Just as in the case of the open source movement, social motivation is an incitement for

---

[145] Hietanen, Herkko A., 'A License or a Contract: Analyzing the Nature of Creative Commons Licenses', NIR: Nordic Intellectual Property Law Review, forthcoming, available at SSRN: http://ssrn.com/abstract=1029366.

[146] Information costs in terms of determining the rights and obligations of parties acceding to the Creative Commons licence.

[147] Elkin-Koren (2005).

joining a Creative Commons structure.[148] The concept of Creative Commons is better understood if regarded as a social movement, a reaction against the enclosure of the public domain just like the open source movement. While the open source movement sought public acceptance in the form of support, Creative Commons takes it a step further and asks for active participation.[149]

Statistics on the actual use of Creative Commons reveal that more than 50 per cent of all licensors choose to use Attribution-ShareAlike, about 60 per cent of which licences prohibited commercial use. Among the many schemes provided by the Creative Commons platform, the most popular licence is the Attribution-Non-Commercial-ShareAlike licence. Authors have included a ShareAlike clause in the vast majority of Creative Commons contracts, which means a subsequent creator may not make a derivative work if this is not made available under an identical licence to the one covering his work.

Enforceability on third parties is crucial for the achievement of the objectives set by Creative Commons. The contractual provision setting the boundaries of Creative Commons enforcement on third parties is clearly the ShareAlike clause. The enforceability of the Creative Commons licence on the contracting parties is of course a challenge, given the fact that creative works are used, remodelled and reformulated on a constant basis.

It is important to underline that what is left outside the scope of a Creative Commons agreement is regulated by the copyright legislation. Accordingly, the author has decided that for those willing to submit to the terms and provisions of the Creative Commons licence, access and use of their works will be facilitated, while for those refraining from entering into such a licensing agreement, traditional copyright will apply. Any third party (nonparty) to the Creative Commons agreement selected

---

148 Benkler, Y. 'Coase's Penguin or, Linux and the Nature of the Firm', Yale LJ, Vol 112 (2002), pp. 369–446.

149 The ideological origin for this is Lessig's trilogy: see *Code and Other Laws of Cyberspace: The Future of Ideas and Free Culture*, New York: Basic Books (1999). Nevertheless, due to its notable ideological flexibility it has attracted a number of supporters that originate from different ideological backgrounds and it becomes thus difficult to be precise about its current theoretical framework.

by the author will thus have to abide by the requirements of copyright law.[150]

A novelty of the Creative Commons system – and a major difference between it and the open source movement – is that while the open source movement addresses a specific, rather closed group of people (programmers) that share the same social values, Creative Commons appeals to the general public. The social organisation of the open source movement has guaranteed the existence of an incentive for further creation and contribution under the same 'share regime' while at the same time functioning as a safety net against potential abuses.

Open source expresses its direct opposition to copyright and all other forms of IPRs such as patents on computer programs, while Creative Commons considers copyright not only a starting point but a *sine qua non*. They are, in practice, two property-based management regimes. Open source does not place works in the public domain or under an open access regime. Open source projects are subject to strict hierarchical organisational structures regulating how access and withdrawal of the protected material can take place. In Ostrom's example, open source participants 'own' a variation of bundles of property rights, from the right to access to the all-inclusive alienation right, depending on their position in the project's hierarchy.[151] Creative Commons, on the other hand, is nothing more than a licensing platform. The works are protected by traditional copyright, but, for a number of prespecified uses and under a set of terms and conditions predetermined by the copyright holder, the exclusive right is transformed into a liability right.

5.1.4.3.3 State property rights and mixed rights State property rights are an increasingly important category of property rights.[152] States own land, buildings and equipment. These fall under the control of governmental agencies that are ruled in their turn by various regulations and legislation. State-owned assets are managed in a variety of ways. State-owned lands, for instance, are often managed passively and are thus open for many uses. State-owned natural resources of commercial value, such as oil and coal, are usually leased to private actors that thus have

---

[150] It is, simply put, traditional copyright that applies.

[151] Krishnamurthy, S., 'An Analysis of Open Source Business Models. Making Sense of the Bazaar: Perspectives on Open Source and Free Software' in Feller, J., Fitzgerald B., Hissam, S., Lakhani, K. (eds), *Perspectives on Free and Open Source Software*, MIT Press, forthcoming. Available at SSRN: http://ssrn.com/abstract=650001.

[152] Libecap (1989).

private rights over certain attributes of the lands.[153] In some cases, state assets are assigned to individual users and thus transformed into an almost exclusive usufruct right.

Obviously, state property is very often a mixture of private property rights, common property or even open access.[154] The limited literature on state property rights concerns the analysis of natural resource agencies – those concerning federal lands and marine fisheries.[155]

Real-life mandates are quite often a combination of different layers of property rights regimes. A rancher's land may appear to be private. The right to the grass for grazing might be private but the streams running through the property may be open access for fishing or recreation; the grass might be leased from a governmental agency, with mineral rights held by another private party. The underlying oil reservoir may be governed by a unitisation contract (subject to oversight by a state oil-reservation agency) among many neighbouring ranchers, mimicking common property. Property may thus turn out to be a complex collection of rights.

Smith examined the complex regime of the common field system of medieval Europe, revealing that the lands for crops were in fact private,[156] while those for the purposes of grazing were common property. The reason for the two different regimes was that private property for crops provides incentives for investment, while a larger scale of land ownership is optimal for grazing. Ellickson analyses a number of mixed regimes involving legal and customary rights.[157]

The side effects of mixed property rights have been illustrated in the work of Michael Heller,[158] in his attempts to explain the underused storefronts in postcommunist Moscow. The unfortunate situation of 'the tragedy of the anticommons', where a bundle of property rights applies

---

153 An example is that of ski resorts that enjoy longterm leases in order to operate in stateowned lands.

154 The common characteristic of state property is limited transferability of the title of rights.

155 There is considerable economic literature investigating the economic efficiency of public land management, mostly concluding that federal lands are not particularly well managed, and that these inefficiencies are often coupled with lower environmental quality.

156 Smith (2000).

157 Ellickson, B., 'A Generalization of the Pure Theory of Public Goods' (1972), available at http://www.econ.ucla.edu/workingpapers/wp014.pdf.

158 Heller, M., 'The Tragedy of the Anticommons Property in the Transition from Marx to Markets', Harvard L Rev, Vol 111 (1996) pp. 621–88.

upon one specific subject matter, was a side-effect of a postsocialist Moscow in which property structures of the socialist regime were expected to coexist with newly introduced market-ownership rights.[159] The empty storefronts in Moscow after the political and economic transition to a market economy were the factual background to Heller's theoretical framework. Though the stores remained empty, thousands of metal kiosks filled with goods were set up.[160] Unlike in other transition economies, in Russia the metal kiosks remained for a long period of time. The underlying reason for this unfortunate situation is that the storefronts were subject to the rights of four different groups of stakeholders:[161] owners,[162] users,[163] balance-sheet holders[164] and regulators.[165] The exercise of property rights on the storefront required the authorisation of the majority of the stakeholders involved, thus forming a typical example of anticommons property.[166]

Anticommons property is defined by Heller as a property regime in which multiple owners hold effective rights of exclusion on a scarce resource.[167] The main difference between private property and anticommons property, according to Heller, is that anticommons is based on single rights and not 'bundles of rights'. An object is held in anticommons property when there are several rightholders holding different categories of rights on the object, with no hierarchy among them and with no clear conflict resolution rules. Commons property, meanwhile,

---

[159] In the case of storefronts, there was a variety of rightholders: state enterprises, research institutes, maintenance organizations that are of private or semiprivate nature, as well as local, regional and federal governmental bodies.

[160] In Poland, for instance, kiosks appeared briefly until viable property rights in commercial storefronts emerged: Heller (1996), pp. 621–8.

[161] Hardin (1968).

[162] The local government council (Duma) is the formal owner of commercial real estate and may lease or mortgage assets. The federal government, on the other hand, retains some control, such as rights to specify a sale or lease process and to define the range of possible prices.

[163] The users are often workers' collectives of the state enterprise assigned to the space.

[164] These represent an archaic Soviet form of property ownership, analogous to a trust relationship. The balance-sheet holder was a subordinate state organisation who had rights to use and dispose of property formally owned 'by the people' as state property.

[165] The regulators are the six agencies that need to approve all leases, such as the City Architect and the Land Reform Committee.

[166] Thus one single party was able to block the others from exercising their rights.

[167] Heller (1996).

relates to property that is held by a group of people who all share the same privileges of use.

Placing an object under an anticommons property regime is not necessarily detrimental to its subsequent efficient use. According to Coase's theorem,[168] in a world without transaction costs, the initial rights endowment can be rearranged and the rights transferred to the party for whom the rights in question are of most value. Coasean bargains would ultimately lead to the optimal exploitation of the object in question, which would probably be equivalent to its transfer from anticommons property to private property.

5.1.4.3 Paying when using: liability rules

While the property rights paradigm has traditionally been the dominant entitlement structure, liability rules have been employed on a complementary basis. Liability rules have been applied in situations either involving high transaction costs or characterised primarily by holdout and other strategic behaviour.

Probably the most common use of liability rules is in situations of high transaction costs. A well-known liability rule was that provided under the nineteenth-century Mill Act legislation. The liability rule of the Mill Act allowed those building mills to flood upstream land after a payment of 150 per cent of the market price and officially determined damages.[169] According to Ayres and Talley,[170] the rate set represents an attempt to estimate the average value that landowners placed on their lands. Epstein emphasises that the Mill Acts did not provide for pure liability rules.[171] According to the Mill Act, mill builders were not allowed simply to flood and pay, but had to get prior authorisation from the authorities after showing that the proposed mill was in the public interest.[172]

Other examples of liability rules may be found in the sphere of private eminent domain. According to Smith,[173] the importance of water rights and the problems that might occur because of holdouts, or other strategic tactics on the part of the landowner, justified the choice of liability rules.

---

[168] Coase (1962).

[169] Act of 3 July 1868.

[170] Ayres, Talley (1995) pp. 1029–1116.

[171] Epstein, R., *Takings: Private Property and the Power of Eminent Domain*, Cambridge, MA: Harvard University Press (1985).

[172] If it was shown that the mill was not in the public interest then the landowner could sue for an injunction and have the mill torn down.

[173] Smith (2000).

The landowner is protected by a liability rule according to which the irrigator has to compensate for the damage caused by the ditches. However, water rights do not entail a pure take-and-pay liability rule. Irrigators are subject to prior application to officials; hearings and bonds are required.

Smith refers to another important historical example of the limited replacement of property rules by liability rules: that of the regime governing miner–farmer conflicts. In mid-nineteenth-century California, goldminers were not sure where to find gold, and in their search they often entered agricultural areas. In order to address conflicts arising out of this 'double' use of lands, the California legislature passed the Indemnification Act of 1855, according to which miners were allowed to enter, search for minerals and pay for any damage caused. However, a fundamental requirement, even for this liability regime, was prior approval from a Justice of the Peace.[174]

Property rights require the intervention of the state only with regard to the formation and the determination of the beneficiary. The subsequent transfer of property rights and the price under which these shall occur are left to voluntary negotiations. Given the minimal state intervention in the field of property rights, it is interesting to investigate why and under which circumstances liability rules could be preferable.[175]

Under economic efficiency considerations, liability rules could be of interest in cases where the cost of establishing the value of an initial entitlement by negotiation is so great that even though a transfer would benefit all parties involved, this transfer simply would not happen. Calabresi and Melamed refer to the example of eminent domain in support of this hypothesis.[176] In this case, if society can remove the valuation of each tract of land from the market, decide on the value collectively and impose it, then blocking phenomena such as holdouts can be removed. Society can collectively value each individual's desire to have a park and charge him the corresponding tax accordingly. Liability rules entail the risk that the collective valuation of land misses the

---

[174] This exceptional liability rule was considered a risk for the stability of the property regime. The liability regime was finally held invalid in 1860, in the case *Gillian v. Hutchinson*, 1855 Cal State, p. 145.

[175] For the possibility to start with a property right and eventually contract into a liability rules regime, see Merges, R.P., 'Contracting into Liability Rules: Intellectual Property Rights and Collective Rights Organizations', California Law Review, Vol 84 (1996), 1293–1396.

[176] Calabresi, Melamed (1972).

'special' value an individual places on his asset; the market alternative seems even worse.[177]

Efficiency is not the only criteria for applying liability rules instead of property rights. In some cases, liability rules can serve a combination of economic efficiency goals and distributional concerns.[178]

In their article, Lewis and Reichman elaborated on the structure and evolution of a system of compensatory liability rights.[179] Their 'Green Tulip' model builds upon a model of sequential innovation.[180] In their example, Plant Breeder A develops a green tulip that has not turned out to be a commercial success. Plant Breeder B uses the know-how of Plant Breeder A and develops a red, green and white tulip, sold in large quantities to Italo-Americans. Plant Breeders C use the technology developed both by Breeder A and by Breeder B. In the case in which Plant Breeder A's know-how is protected by a compensatory liability regime, Breeder B would be able to access and use A's know-how on the green tulip, and Breeders C would be able to use Breeder A's and B's technology, in exchange for compensatory royalties.

A compensatory liability system needs to be placed into a rather specified legal framework that will regulate the use of the innovation and the compensation calculation. The terms and conditions under which enjoyment of TKGR will be possible need to be clarified. Acceptable uses might include the utilisation of an innovation's application to produce a marketable service or product, or using the innovation in the process of creating an advanced innovation. On the other hand, access to material that will lead to its being shared with third parties without any compensation being returned to the innovator might be restricted.

Another issue that needs to be regulated is the period of enjoyment of the innovation in question. Closely related to this is the question whether conditions of use will be revised after a certain period of time. It would be reasonable to claim that conditions of use should be 'softened' after a

---

[177] On the other hand, different 'beneficiaries' may place different values on certain assets, such as the Guidacres part. There is, however, homogenous taxation.

[178] In the eminent domain example, Calabresi and Melamed find that efficiency considerations are satisfied on top of distributional goals.

[179] Lewis, T., Reichman, J., 'Using Liability Rules to Stimulate Local Innovation in Developing Countries: Application to Traditional Knowledge' in Maskus, K.E., Reichman, J. (eds), *International Public Goods and Transfer of Technology under a Globalized Intellectual Property Regime*, Cambridge: Cambridge University Press (2005), pp. 337–66.

[180] Reichman, J., 'Of Green Tulips and Legal Kudzu: Repackaging Rights in Subpatentable Innovation', Vanderbilt L Rev, Vol 53 (2000), pp. 1743–98.

certain period of time, since the innovator needs more protection in the period of time directly after the release of the subject matter.

The nature of compensation and its calculation are obviously fundamental issues for the functionality of the liability system. According to Lewis and Reichman, the compensation should be higher when the innovation is used by a competitor to the innovator, for the production of a competitive product. A form of implicit complementary compensation is allowing the innovator to access any subsequent improvements made on the basis of his invention. In this case, where innovations build one upon the other, a maximum of technological development can be achieved. In other words, the compensation level will depend upon the ways in which the innovation will be used and whether the innovator will proceed to further improvements or not.[181]

Liability rules are beneficial to small-scale innovators and thus to holders of TKGR, in that they guarantee a right to compensation covering the expenses of their innovative contribution. In exchange for this compensation, innovators make their work available to others. This form of entitlement provides for the incentive to create new knowledge without putting restrictions on subsequent developers and innovators. Liability rules can be protective in nature and resemble exclusive property rights, and at the same time can allow for wide accessibility at low prices, guaranteeing research commons and follow-on innovation potentials.

They are formed in a way that places a restricted burden on the parties to the bargain and allows for a higher rate of success in the bargaining process. Negotiating exclusive property rights, on the other hand, presupposes well-informed, rational and self-interested parties that bargain to their mutual benefit, which in its turn leaves a certain space for failure.[182]

Liability rules could be compared to damages in infringement cases. The infringer has used the protected subject matter and has been put under the obligation to pay compensation, marking the transfer from a property rights regime to a liability rights regime. In infringement cases, the infringer can be deprived of the opportunity to use the property right if detected early enough. Furthermore, the court can adjudicate punitive damages in order to deter from further infringements. The transfer and use of technological know-how under a property violation scheme will

---

181 Lewis, Reichman (2005).

182 Kaplow, Shavell (1996).

thus be limited due to the injunction possibilities and the high fees the infringer might have to pay.[183]

Conflicts that occur with regard to the level of compensation and the compatibility of the protected subject matter's actual use and the prestipulated terms and conditions would be adjudicated under a form of arbitration/mediation. In that way, the transaction and litigation costs would be considerably limited.

5.1.4.4 Protecting by rewarding?

Reward systems have been presented as an alternative to IPRs even with very limited application. Taking into account the objections to a form of 'private' entitlement to TKGR, they represent a viable alternative.

The costs of traditional property rights have contributed to discussion regarding the potential to substitute the well-known system of IPRs with a government-run reward system. A number of theorists have elaborated on the paradox of IPRs entailing the grant of monopoly rights as an incentive to the creation of socially valuable information, while it is in fact this incentive that leads to the restricted access and use of the said information.[184] A reward system could provide a remedy for this paradox by offering an economic incentive for the author or inventor to generate what could be defined as desirable information or technology. Under such a system, the state rewards the author for his or her contribution, in order to make it available to the public under the cost of its dissemination.

Once the reward is awarded to the beneficiary, the innovation falls within the public domain, free for everyone else to use. Consequently, the innovation can be reproduced and distributed to anyone that is willing to pay the marginal price of production. Under such a system, consumers that were previously priced out by the monopoly prices sometimes seen under an IP system can now have access to the innovation. On the other hand, competitors can use the said innovation in their research and in production and development of new technology.[185]

---

[183] For an interesting investigation on liability rights in IP, see Kur, A., Schovsbo, J. 'Expropriation or Fair Game for All? The Gradual Dismantling of the IP Exclusivity Paradigm' in Kur, A., Levin, M. (eds), *Intellectual Property Rights in a Fair World Trade System: Proposals for Reform of TRIPS*, Cheltenham: Edward Elgar (2011), pp. 408–55.

[184] Scherer, F.M., *Industrial Market Structure and Economic Performance*, Chicago: Rand McNally & Co (1973), pp. 390–1.

[185] For an example of how such a system would function in the modern society, see Wei, M., 'Should Prizes Replace Patents? A Critique of the Medical

Innovators retain the incentive to develop technology since the rewards they will receive will be largely based upon the volume of use, which should be greater than the volume of use when rights are covered by IPRs. At the same time, an optimal level of consumption is achieved since the innovation is sold at marginal cost. Under the precondition that the reward is set to reflect the social value of the innovation, this system is much more beneficial than the IP one.

The reward system is not a merely theoretical scheme. It has been utilised in the former socialist countries as a substitute for traditional IPRs.[186] Under this regime, inventors would apply for 'certificates of authorship' and would be awarded a portion of the cost savings should an industrial application for the invention be found. In Europe, discussions concerning the replacement of the patent system with a reward system emerged in the late nineteenth century.[187] For various reasons, mostly political, the patent system prevailed.

The reward system has, however, been used as a supplement to traditional IPRs, for instance in the United States in the field of atomic energy inventions.[188] The US Atomic Energy Act of 1946 established the Patent Compensation Board to reward individuals who provided innovations involving military uses of atomic energy,[189] and who for reasons of security were excluded from the 'traditional' patent regime.

A publicly funded reward system has the objective of maximising overall social welfare by retaining incentives to create while simultaneously optimising the dissemination of information. Such a system builds on ensuring that authors and creators will have the economic incentive to continue to invest in their creativity. The public, on the other

---

Innovation Prize Act of 2005' Boston U J Science & Technology Law, Vol 13 (2007), pp. 1–23.

[186] On the use of the reward system in the Soviet Union see Hughes, F., 'Soviet Union Awards', Econ J, Vol 55 (1945), pp. 291–7; Stepanov, S., 'Increasing the Role of Innovators and Inventors in Improving Socialist Production', Problems of Econ, Vol 1 (1958), pp. 75–8.

[187] See Shavell, S., 'Reward versus Intellectual Property', J Law & Economics, Vol 44 (2001), pp. 525–47.

[188] Reisenfeld, S., 'Patent Protection and the Atomic Energy Legislation', Cal L Rev, Vol 46 (1958), pp. 40–68.

[189] Pub L No 79-585, 60 Stat 755 (codified as amended at 42 USC §§ 2011–2297g (1994)).

hand, will be able to obtain access to information where this is valued at or above its marginal cost, without having to be burdened with monopoly costs.[190]

There are certainly a number of critiques of such a system. Particularly important are, of course, the practical issues of its financing and the valuation of the awards to be distributed to authors and creators.[191] At the same time, such a system could lead to the limitation of independence in the creation of literary works and inventions and the risk of indirect censorship.[192]

One of the most problematic issues with the application of the reward system is that of its financing. The traditional IP system is autofinanced. The innovator is rewarded by means of the 'monopoly-like' prices that his IPRs allow him to charge. The reward system, on the other hand, is state-financed. Financing will thus depend on the imposition of new taxes, a practice that often gives rise to criticism not only because of the distorted work initiatives but also because of the administrative costs entailed.

Michael Polanvyi claims that the cost of taxation is paid for by means of the reduced prices consumers have to pay for innovative techniques, given the lack of 'IP monopolies'. According to Polanvyi, 'the burden would be manifestly offset, and far more than offset, by the benefits accruing to the public in the form of cheaper prices for patented articles and the general quickening of technical progress due to the free general use of inventions'.[193] There is undoubtedly a political cost to the collection of the necessary funds for this system to be put into practice.

The reward system would allow creators to work and interact in a completely different environment, since it would allow research on

---

190 For an elaboration of the positive aspects of the rewards system see Calandrillo, S., 'An Economic Analysis of Property Rights in Information: Justifications and Problems of Exclusive Rights, Incentives to Generate Information, and the Alternative of a Government-Run Reward System', Fordham Intell Prop Media & Ent LJ, Vol 9 (1998–9), pp. 301–54.

191 Scherer (1973), pp. 398–9 and Mill, J.S., *Principles of Political Economy*, ed. Ashley, W.J., London: Longmans, Green & Co ([1848] 1940), p. 932, elaborated on the problematic valuation incorporated in the reward system. The authors argue that such a system would be arbitrary and unfair, thus making it hard to argue for a substitution of the traditional IPR system.

192 Hurt, R., Schuchman, R., 'The Economic Rational of Copyright', Am Econ Rev, Vol 56 (1966), pp. 421–32.

193 Polanvyi, M., 'Patent Reform', Rev Economic Studies, Vol 11 (1944), pp. 61–9; Brian D. Wright, 'The Economics of Invention Incentives: Patents, Prizes, and Research Contracts', Am Econ Rev, Vol 73 (1983), pp. 691–707.

'dependent' inventions to a larger extent than is the case today.[194] Concurrently, legal, private and social enforcement costs necessary for the enforcement of IPRs will be omitted.[195] The valuation of the reward amount is another very important and controversial aspect of the reward system. The IP system bases the reward on the quantity of the innovative product sold and the prices the innovator was able to charge in a competitive environment. Society, and thus the state, need not interfere with the final reward awarded. Nevertheless, the amount of use of the innovation and sales of the innovative product could still be taken into consideration in the calculation of the reward. Polanvyi asserts that a stable and objective valuation mechanism is of vital importance to the success of the reward system. He underlines the need to take into account data that is endorsed by accountants in order to prevent corruption and unfairness weakening the system. According to Polanvyi's valuation method, only part of the innovation's social value needs to be returned to the innovator, taking into consideration that their achievements are partly due to the free accessibility of technology enjoyed under the reward system.[196] Polanvyi proposes that between one tenth and one third of the assessed social benefits of the protected inventions should be awarded to the creator. In that way, the reward system creates a social benefit surplus out of every new innovation.[197]

Despite the ambitious initiatives to specify the valuation mechanism under the reward system, it remains rather blurry, and contestably objective.[198] Mill argues that rewards should be arbitrary, uncertain, and

---

[194] This would stand under the precondition that rewards are established for any published investigation that leads to a practical invention.

[195] Shavell, S., van Ypersele, T., 'Rewards v. IPR', J Law Econ, Vol XLIV (2001), pp. 525–47.

[196] Under other patent reward proposals, the innovator's compensation is to be based on the inventor's expected profit. See Guell, R.C., Fischbaum, M., 'Toward an Allocative Efficiency Prescription Drug Industry', Mibank Q, Vol 73 (1995), pp. 213–30.

[197] See Mandel, G. 'Promoting Environmental Innovation with Intellectual Property Innovation: A New Basis for Patent Rewards', presentation at the Temple University Journal of Science, Technology and Environmental Law's Symposium: Environmental Technology and Innovation: Partners for Our Future (2005), Temple J Science & Envtl Law, Vol XX (2005), pp. 51–69.

[198] The valuation mechanism has been heavily criticised by defenders of the traditional IP system. See Croskery, P., 'Institutional Utilitarianism and Intellectual Property', CHI-Kent L Rev: Patent Protection and the Atomic Energy Legislation, Vol 68 (1993), pp. 631–41.

left to governmental discretion.[199] Scherer, on the other hand, questions the governmental authorities' ability to evaluate innovations.[200] To support his statement, he refers to practices of the Patent Compensation Board. Robert Goddard, the inventor of liquid rocket engines, was awarded US$1 million, while subsequent US expenditures in the area reached US$10 billion. It deserves to be noted that the Patent Compensation Board awarded that US$1 million before the extent of the invention's future utilisation had crystallised. Such experience could in fact be used to ameliorate the reward system by, for instance, periodical revision and update of the reward awarded.

Mill compares the governmental lack of information on the demand and utility of products in calculating networks with the firms' specialised knowledge and concludes that a reward system will most probably fail to capture the social value of the innovation.[201] Fudenberg and Tirole build upon Mill's reasoning and asserts that in order for the reward system to be successful, the government must be highly knowledgeable about the feasibility of various inventions and the demand for them.[202]

According to Polanvyi, innovators are able to provide data on the commercial profitability of their invention. The governmental authority in charge of the reward system will not be able to collect information about the value and utility of the invention in the same way the market will under the current IP system.

A government-run reward system has also been criticised for representing a disguised form of governmental control of research. The risk of 'rewarding' only research that has governmental 'approval' would be a return to the period in which state subsidies could determine the content and direction of arts and science. Nevertheless, one could claim that, given the safety net provided by criteria of the calculation mechanism that are as objective as possible, as well as by politically neutral and independent committees in charge of the reward system, this risk is limited if not nonexistent in a democratic society.

Unfortunately, one of the major defects of the patent system – the race to be first – does not seem to be remedied in the reward system. There is still the need to be 'first' to provide the invention in order to be awarded the reward protection. This leads to wasted duplicative, premature and

---

199 Mill (1940), section 4, p. 932.

200 Honing-Haftel, S., Martin, L., 'The Effectiveness of Reward Systems on Innovative Output: An Empirical Analysis', Small Business Economics, Vol 5 (1993), pp. 261–9.

201 Mill (1940), p. 933.

202 Fudenberg, D., Tirole, J., p. 401.

excessive investment when several innovators are working on the same invention. One possible remedy for the unfortunate effects of the race to be first would be awarding the remedy at a rather early stage of the innovation process so that the period of simultaneous investment is limited.

5.1.4.5 Liability rules or property rules?

The dilemma between property and liability was the central issue of investigation in Calabresi and Melamed's seminal 'Property Rules, Liability Rules and Inalienability', published in 1972, which has constituted the basis of a vivid academic debate.

Calabresi and Melamed proposed a number of criteria for choosing between property rules and liability rules. One of their central hypotheses was that property rules are socially preferable to liability rules when transaction costs are low. The argument in support of the hypothesis was that when transaction costs are low, an individual interested in acquiring the property of another individual should bargain for the property in order to reach a price upon which both parties agree.[203] Liability rules are presented as a second-best option, in cases with high transaction costs, where property rules are ineffective.[204] In the post-Calabresi and Melamed literature, several contributions have elaborated on the choice between property and liability rules. Kaplow and Shavell have considered the bargaining preconditions in high and low transaction cost settings.[205]

According to Kaplow and Shavell, in bargaining settings with imperfect information, neither property nor liability rules lead to an efficient outcome; nor can determination of the relative efficiency of the two rules be evaluated *a priori*.[206] The authors conclude that property rules are preferable in low transaction cost settings; however, they do this without employing the arguments of Calabresi and Melamed, but rather on the basis of 'reciprocal takings' and bad incentive effects.[207] They offer a three-step explanation of their claim:

(1) When bargaining is perfect and all negotiations are successful, according to the Coase theorem, an efficient outcome will always

---

[203] Calabresi, Melamed (1972), p. 105.

[204] Calabresi, Melamed (1972).

[205] Kaplow, Shavell (1996).

[206] This is also a point where Kaplow and Shavell contradict Melamed and Calabresi's standpoint.

[207] Reciprocal takings could be formulated in a way to entail that 'if you take my chair I will take your chair'.

be reached, regardless of the legal rule. In such circumstances, property rules and liability rules are equally efficient.

(2) When bargaining is impossible, liability rules are clearly superior to property rules. Under a liability rule, potential takers can take the entitlement and pay compensation if they value it more highly than its owner. On the other hand, under a property rule, some inefficient outcomes will occur and remain, since they cannot be corrected by bargaining, and unilateral takings are not allowed.

(3) When bargaining is possible but imperfect, inefficiency is caused by the failure of some of the bargains. If liability rules 'tie' with property rules in circumstances in which all bargains succeed, and are superior to property rules in circumstances in which all bargains fail, then they are also superior to property rules when only some negotiations end in failure.

According to this assumption, individuals will behave in strategic and opportunistic ways whenever possible. In situations where information is asymmetric, each party will attempt to misrepresent his or her private valuation of the subject matter of the bargaining process. Sellers will overstate their valuation of the good in question, while buyers will understate it. Consequently, parties may either fail to reach an agreement or reach one after a costly delay. Neither of these results is efficient. Strategic behaviour, in particular the strategic behaviour of the seller, is central in the property rules framework.

While a considerable number of scholars base their preference for liability rules on the disadvantages of bargaining with property rules, there have also been attempts to prove the opposite.[208] For this purpose, Lewinsohn-Zamir employed a bargaining scheme game: the Ultimatum Game. According to this scheme, one person (proposer) is asked to divide a sum of money between herself and another person (responder). The responder is free to either accept or refuse the sum offered. In the first case, the proposed division is applied; in the second, both players receive nothing.[209]

The application of the standard economic game-theoretic prediction is that both players will behave rationally, and thus attempt to maximise their monetary payoffs. Obviously, the proposer will expect that any

---

[208] Lewinsohn-Zamir, D., 'The Choice between Property Rules and Liability Rules Revisited: Critical Observations from Behavioral Studies', Texas L Rev, Vol 80 (2001), pp. 219–60.

[209] According to the game theory, the parties interact only once and their decisions remain anonymous.

positive share will be preferable to nothing and thus the proposer will offer the smallest unit of money. The responder will agree to the division and the proposer will retain all the gains from the transaction.

Although this is obviously the most likely outcome should one apply the economic game-theoretic model, experiments reveal other results. In the majority of the cases examined proposers offer substantial amounts, opting for an equal split of the pie, while offers that deviate substantially from 50 per cent are usually rejected. The reaction of the responders could be explained on the basis of the fact that individuals want to be treated fairly, and will thus reject such offers. Fairness considerations can obviously become more important than absolute income. The rejection of the proposer's low offer might constitute a form of educative punishment. The important role played by a sense of fairness and the importance of the educative punishment become major parameters in the bargaining process, thus undermining the assumption that individuals are to behave greedily and adopt holdout strategies.

On the other hand, the assumption that a seller will most likely opt for a holdout strategy presupposes that the seller is risk seeking. In this respect, behavioural studies have shown that sellers tend to be risk averse while buyers tend to be risk seeking. According to Tversky and Kahnman's Prospect Theory, individuals are risk averse when confronting potential gains and risk seeking when confronting potential losses.[210] In effect, sellers tend to view the transaction as a gain, focusing on how much they stand to profit from the sale. Their point of reference is their minimum reservation price, and thus any sum offered above this price will be considered a gain. Buyers, on the other hand, tend to concentrate their attention on how much they have to pay in order to purchase the good in question. Sellers' holdout behaviour will be very much limited in scope, since sellers will in principle prefer to avoid a negotiation failure and settle for some acceptable share of the profits, rather than bearing the risks necessary in order to claim a higher profit.[211]

Lewinsohn-Zamir applies the Ultimatum Game to bargaining under the scope of liability rules.[212] Lewinsohn-Zamir introduces yet another scheme, the Dictator Game, according to which one player proposes a division of some gains between herself and a second player, where the

---

[210] Kahnemann D., Tversky, A., 'Prospect Theory: An Analysis of Decision under Risk', Econometrica, Vol 47 (1979), pp. 263–74.

[211] Lewinsohn-Zamir includes a disclaimer stating that opportunistic behaviour does exist but that it is highly exaggerated. See Lewinsohn-Zamir (2001), p. 239.

[212] Lewinsohn-Zamir (2001), p. 239.

players receive whatever the dictator proposes. Experiments conducted with the Dictator Game have shown that offers were much lower than in the Ultimatum Game. The structure of liability rights resembles that of the Dictator Game, without being identical. Liability rules often entail two stages: voluntary bargaining and forced transfer. The Dictator Game structure reveals that eliminating the risk of rejection leads people to offer very little to others. Liability rules are perceived as a message from the legal system that it is acceptable to both force the transfer of the entitlement on its owner and retain all subsequent efficiency gains. Thus, liability rules might erase the 'shame' of takers when attempting to keep all the profits for themselves. At the same time, sellers can be transformed from risk averse to risk seeking, since the transaction is transformed from a transaction involving gains to one involving losses. Lewinsohn-Zamir concludes that the coercive power of the second stage is not a 'passive device', appearing whenever bargaining fails; rather, it is an active device that contributes to the failure of the bargaining process.

Hylton provided for a further elaboration of the dilemma between property and liability rules in bargaining settings with perfect information by discussing 'subjective valuations'.[213] For the purposes of his analysis, Hylton uses the example of a bicycle with an objective value (market value) of US$75. The 'subjective value' of the owner of the bicycle might exceed the market value,[214] or might be less than the market value.[215] For the purposes of this example, the value of the high-valuing victims would be set at US$85 while the value of low-valuing victims would be set at US$65. The determination of the bicycle's value in a court proceeding related to a liability rule on the bicycle would resort to the objective market value, that of US$75.

On the other hand, among the potential takers of the bicycles, there will be high-valuing takers, willing to pay US$100 for the bicycle, and low-valuing takers, valuing the bicycle at no more than US$25.[216] In a bargaining environment with high transaction costs, where parties would not have the opportunity to bargain before deciding, this would entail loss for all.

---

[213] Hylton, K., 'Property Rules and Liability Rules, Once Again', Boston University School of Law Working Paper 05-17 (September 2005).

[214] When the owner has positive associations with regard to the object in question, such as good memories.

[215] When the owner has negative associations with regard to the object in question, such as falls, flat tyres, etc.

[216] Hylton assumes that half of the victims are high-valuing and half low-valuing. The same applies for takers.

In the dilemma between property rules and liability rules, Hylton presents a number of conclusions that are even more complex and nuanced than those of Calabresi and Melamed.[217] Property rules are preferable to liability rules when transaction costs are low because they protect subjective valuations while at the same time avoiding the enforcement costs inherent to a liability rule. Property rules are preferable where potential takers seek to acquire the real or personal property of the 'victims'. Liability rules are preferable when transaction costs are high.

Finally, Hylton contributes with a further conclusion providing that property rules are equivalent to liability rules when transaction costs are high and the subjective valuations of invaders are less than those of victims. Another point of collision between Hylton on the one hand and Melamed and Calabresi on the other is eminent domain. According to Melamed and Calabresi, eminent domain was an efficient liability rule since it hindered holdouts blocking development projects. Hylton shifted the value of the eminent domain rule from holdout avoidance to tampering with incentives for expropriation.[218] The choice between property rules and liability rules entails, according to Hylton, a fundamental informative role. When the law decides to protect a specific entitlement by means of property rights, it reflects a policy that prohibits the 'taker' from engaging in a certain act. The liability rule, on the other hand, shifts the cost of the loss from the victim to the taker.

The neglected costs of obtaining and processing information that might hinder the efficient damage calculations related to a liability rights regime were discussed for the first time in Polinsky's work.[219] Polinsky posed the question 'whether the arguments favouring damage remedies are logically coherent', and concluded that in the real world 'the argument could easily go either way'. He stated that, should the court award damages that exceed the actual harm, the polluter will stop polluting even though it would be efficient for the polluter to continue, while if actual harm exceeds the damages awarded, the polluter will continue to pollute even though the pollution is, on the whole, inefficient. Consequently, a liability rule guarantees efficient results only when

---

[217] Though the basic lines of reasoning are the same as in the Melamed and Calabresi article.

[218] Hylton (2005).

[219] Polinsky, M., 'Controlling Externalities and Protecting Entitlements: Property Right, Liability Rule, and Tax-Subsidy Approaches', J Legal Stud, Vol 8 (1979), pp. 1–48.

damages are equal to actual harm. Obviously, courts do not always have information on which to base their assessments of actual harm that has occurred.

Krier and Schwab also questioned the 'conventional wisdom', stating that while conventional thinking idealistically ignores uncertainty about damages (due to assessment costs), at the same time it realistically acknowledges bargaining difficulties (due to transaction costs).[220] In the real world, both transaction costs and assessment costs are significant, and that weakens Calabresi and Melamed's argument for preference to be given to liability rules. Krier and Schwab rephrase the question, which becomes: 'which kind of rule, property or liability, promises to minimise the sum of valuation and error costs?'[221] The authors conclude that where assessment costs and transaction costs are influenced by the same factors, both property rules and liability rules will be equally inefficient in specific circumstances.

Multiparty bargaining generally presents increased transaction costs. Negotiations requiring the agreement of multiple parties, exchanges that benefit many people at once or cases in which several parties need to agree in order for an exchange to be consummated are typical high transaction cost scenarios.

On the other hand, bargaining that involves a limited (and often a specific) set of parties may entail problems of strategic behaviour. Strategic behaviour limits the accessibility of information with regard to both transaction costs and assessment costs. Liability rules have been considered the appropriate form of entitlement for situations with two parties by overcoming strategic bargaining.

In a case where two parties litigate a dispute over property rights and the bargaining is hindered by the parties' strategic behaviour, the court will have to determine value. Kaplow and Shavell concluded in this regard that liability rules can generate efficient results so long as a court can assess the value of one of the competing uses, rather than both. A court could offer an efficient solution if it evaluated the damage incurred by the plaintiff. In effect, if the defendant's use is more valuable than the harm incurred, the defendant will pay the damages and continue his/her activities. Another argument for liability rules has focused on their ability to reduce the information necessary for the courts to render efficient decisions in cases of strategic bargaining behaviour. According to Ayres

[220] Krier, J., Schwab, S., 'Property Rules and Liability Rules: The Cathedral in Another Light', NYU L Rev, Vol 70 (1995), pp. 440–83.

[221] Krier, Schwab (1995).

and Talley, liability rules can induce parties to reveal information that they might withhold under a regime of property rules, increasing the likelihood that efficient bargains will be brought into fruition.[222]

This argument claims that liability rules divide entitlements and as a result each party is uncertain whether he/she will emerge as a buyer or as a seller. Each party has a reduced incentive to misrepresent the value he or she attaches to the entitlement. On the other hand, property rules allocate the entire entitlement to a single person, and as an effect each person knows whether he/she will be the seller or the buyer, thus being able to adopt his or her own bargaining strategy.

According to Smith, liability rules reduce the incentive to collect information about productive uses of the protected subject matter. In effect, the owner of a property rule has the incentive to invest in producing that information, since 'ownership concentrates on the owner the benefits of information developed about, and bets placed upon, the value of the asset'.[223]

Smith and Merill have developed an 'exclusion strategy'[224] as the optimal procedure for allocating resources when the potential users of the resource are unidentified and large in number.[225] Most property rules typically reflect an exclusion strategy and it is argued that the property rule approach is optimal when information costs would make it unfeasible to allocate resources by contract among the many interested parties. An exclusion strategy reduces information costs by permitting the single owner to coordinate use of each resource.

The information-cost advantages of an exclusion strategy increase with the number of potential users of the contested right. When the number of contestants for a right is high, the contract solutions are impractical since any single claimant's incentive to negotiate with other claimants is low, and thus whatever agreement they reach would be subverted by the appearance of yet another claimant. An effective exclusion strategy presupposes rules that are uniform, easily identified and understood by all. Although liability rules present a number of advantages in overcoming *ex post* strategic behaviour, property rules generate considerable *ex ante* advantages. The 'owner' of a specific resource functions as a

---

222 Ayres, I. and Talley, E., 'Solomonic Bargaining: Dividing a Legal Entitlement to Facilitate Coasean Trade', Yale LJ, Vol 104 (1995), p. 1027.

223 Smith, H, 'Property and Property Rights', Yale School Legal Scholarship Repository (2004), p. 1729.

224 Merill, T., Smith, H., 'The Property/Contract Interface', Columbia L Rev, Vol 101 (2001), pp. 773–93.

225 Merill, Smith (2001).

clearing-house mechanism, since all potential users have to contact the owner of the resource in order to acquire rights. In that way, the property holder collects information about potential bidders to his right, and about the value bidders attach to the resources in questions. Consequently, the property rightholder will be in a better position to transfer the resources to the party valuing them most.

This presupposes of course that property rights are transparent, and that potential users are aware of the limits and nature of the rights, as well as the owner of the right. In real life, property rules are far from being clear. It is often very costly for potential users to collect information on the nature of rights and the owner of the rights.

The presentation of the alternative forms of entitlements, and in particular the property/liability rules dichotomy, reveals the alternatives available for the protection of TKGR. It also reveals the weaknesses of the adopted systems of protection, which so far seem to adopt a rather limited view of the alternative protection schemes, and shows that the theoretical background of the property rights paradigm – as well as its comparison to the liability rights rules – are both very fragile and, in any case, often absent in international negotiations and national and regional implementation initiatives. Review of the theoretical foundations of property, liability and reward systems is a vital starting point and a precondition for the choice of an appropriate form of protection.

6. Where traditional knowledge meets modern IPRs

6.1 PROTECTION OF TKGR: NEEDS AND EXPECTATIONS

TKGR trade gradually raised expectations of a 'green gold rush'. Bioprospecting agreements were expected to give rise to increased benefits and turn the conservation of biodiversity into an economically rational activity. Ambitions preceding the entry into force of the CBD were undoubtedly high. TKGR holders would be recognised as formal rightholders of their know-how and genetic resources and given incentives for their sustainable use and conservation. Developed countries and interested industries, meanwhile, would secure access to resources and employ traditional knowledge as valuable ethnobotanical knowledge.

It is difficult to get a representative picture of the scale of TKGR trade, since most bioprospecting agreements have been kept confidential. Bioprospecting agreements that have been published are either those that have been employed by commercial entities for public relations purposes or those that have been accused by NGOs of having a negative impact on indigenous peoples and biodiversity conservation.[1] It is, however, commonly accepted that the future of bioprospecting practices did not turn out as expected. The 'green gold rush' remained just a vision. At the same time, biodiversity conservation policies that evolved on the basis of contractual agreements did not bring about the expected results.

The benefits of TKGR trade envisioned in the pre-CBD period as well as in the aftermath of the adoption of the Convention were based on a number of optimistic assumptions. The value of TKGR for the pharmaceutical industry focused on potential incomes from the marketing of new drugs, but without taking into consideration the costs of bioprospecting. Bioprospecting costs are constantly increasing, though – especially due

[1] The INBio/Merck or Shaman agreements, for instance, where the general framework of the agreement has been published along with some provisions, but others remain unknown.

to new legal constraints and access procedures, as well as the transaction costs necessary for the conclusion of a bioprospecting agreement. At the same time, securing commercial turnover for the bioprospecting industry through the development of a successful commercial product, such as a blockbuster drug, has proved to be very rare.

Another important source of complications is the fact that the countries of origin and the indigenous communities – the holders of valuable TKGR – are often competing.[2] On the demand side, the dominant structures are still oligopolistic. TKGR holders are in a weak negotiating position and unable to assess the potential uses and benefits of bioprospecting. The asymmetry between holders and bioprospectors in the TKGR market with regard to uses, benefits and legal expertise challenges possibilities of reaching fair and mutually profitable agreements.

Examples from the bioprospecting agreements to have been concluded reveal that these can hardly live up to the requirements of a Coasean negotiation model. They are rarely concluded between rightholders and 'rightbuyers', as they often involve a number of intermediaries, such as research institutions, NGOs, universities, botanical gardens, and so on. The role of the intermediaries is often to minimise transaction costs, to save the interested parties time and effort in acquiring access to TKGR, to avoid the uncertainties of dealing with indigenous communities or institutions in developing countries or even to provide a shield from public attention. Their legal status is often very unclear to the rest of the actors in the TKGR market and creates general legal uncertainty.

Developing countries are faced with the challenge of redeeming their international obligations, in particular those originating from their WTO membership, and the need to promote and protect their own products and innovations. In this respect, the implementation of the CBD, and thus the introduction of a legal regime for the protection of TKGR, is a demanding task for two reasons. Firstly, the CBD does not provide for any more than a general framework and a list of overriding principles. This vagueness allows for considerable flexibility but at the same time deprives the implementing states of any concrete guidance. Secondly, the implementation of the CBD proceeds in parallel to the implementation of the TRIPS Agreement, which poses considerable coherence issues.

---

[2] There are in fact countries that would be classified as 'source countries', in a bioprospecting environment, that have been accused of violating fundamental human rights of indigenous communities that are holders of TKGR. It thus becomes questionable whether any benefits arising from TKGR would reach the 'true' rightholders.

When resources become scarce, resources become valuable. The increasing economic value of resources has traditionally been linked to the allocation of entitlements.[3] The turbulent legal tradition of rights allocation on lands has, to some extent, also applied to other resources such as oil, gas and sea-mineral resources. TKGR has recently been added to the list. Thus, the removal of TKGR from the realm of the public domain or *res nullius* principle and the process towards the development of a new entitlement is not a completely new phenomenon but rather an old play staged with new scenery.

Until the entry into force of the CBD, states as well as the international community had chosen to abstain from the grant of entitlements on TKGR, and thus rights and access on these resources were obviously decided on the basis of the power of the involved actors. In the absence of an international regulatory framework, indigenous communities and developing countries were unable to control and exploit their TKGR.

There could be a number of justifications for why resources and know-how previously belonging to the public domain are gradually becoming subject to extensive commodification. The sophistication of technological means and the elaboration of know-how for a more extensive exploitation of resources constitutes a typical justification parameter.[4] However, in the case of TKGR, the interest in entitlement allocation has a double source. On the one hand, the advent of biotechnology gradually extended the uses of TKGR and turned the pharmaceutical and agricultural industries' interest towards chemical substances found in nature. On the other, the patentability of biotech inventions secured such investments.

At the same time, protection of TKGR seeks to serve the purposes of protection of cultural integrity, presupposing that granting property rights guarantees the cultural protection of TK. Thus the TKGR entitlement is to enhance and protect the cultural integrity both of the TK as such, but also of the indigenous communities, original holders of the TK. The need to preserve TK cultural integrity may in fact be connected to the human rights justification of property rights, while at the same time the need to protect it *now* is related to its increasing value, for reasons presented previously in this book.

International and national regulations introduced in the post-CBD era have been reluctant to specify the characteristics of the entitlement

---

[3] Cottier, T., 'The Protection of Genetic Resources and Traditional Knowledge: Towards More Specific Rights and Obligations in World Trade Law', J Intl Econ L, Vol 1 (1998) pp. 555–84.

[4] See also Cottier (1998).

envisaged to cover TKGR. An overview of the proposals on an international level, as well as of the national legislation, reveals the lack of a fundamental discussion, which would be of utmost interest in such a turbulent field. The majority of these initiatives choose to – directly or indirectly – classify the proposed entitlement under the property paradigm.

In order to avoid misconceptions, the introduction of a new entitlement and the removal of subject matter, in this case TKGR, from the public domain should be preceded by an in-depth discussion of the roles and goals that this future entitlement will have to live up to and fulfil. Furthermore, important actors and other major characteristics of the relevant market need to be taken into consideration. Equally important, of course, is analysis of the potential side effects and weaknesses of the forthcoming new legal entitlement.

6.2 REQUIREMENTS, CONSTRAINTS AND FLEXIBILITIES IN THE INTERNATIONAL FRAMEWORK OF TKGR PROTECTION

6.2.1 Requirements, Constraints and Flexibilities Based on the International Legal Framework

6.2.1.1 A combined legal framework

In order to proceed to a thorough examination of the alternative forms of entitlement that could be applicable in the case of TKGR, it is important to consider the requirements and constraints placed on the elaboration of a TKGR entitlement by the applicable international framework.

One could not claim that the international regulatory framework is inconsistent with the principles of Coasean efficiency and Rawlsian fairness in the TKGR market. This is true both for those with a direct impact (such as the CBD) and for those with an indirect one (such as the TRIPS Agreement). However, although we find traces of both these principles in these two major conventions, it still remains unclear how they would apply in practice.[5] The CBD is the principal international agreement that provides for the legal framework ruling access to TKGR, and thus even for the 'fair and equitable sharing of the benefits' arising out of its utilisation. It is also the natural starting point for the evaluation

[5] Both Bonn Guidelines and the Nagoya Protocol have a goal of concretising the requirements of the CBD.

of available or proposed legal entitlements for the protection of TKGR. For an initial compatibility check of the provisions of the CBD it is crucially important to look into whether the CBD provides for any legal entitlements, that is, whether it creates property rights and specifies relevant rightholders.

The only right/entitlement clearly stipulated in a number of provisions of the CBD is the sovereignty of states over their genetic resources.[6] The state owns the country's genetic resources and is left with the flexibility to draft a national regime of access and benefit sharing.

Article 8(j) subjects traditional knowledge protection to national legislation, while countries are under the obligation to 'respect, preserve and maintain knowledge, innovations and practices of indigenous and local communities'. According to the same provision, countries should 'promote the wider application (of traditional knowledge) with the approval and involvement of the holders of such knowledge'. It thus could be concluded that the CBD does not pose significant limitations to the drafting of an entitlement on TKGR. Responsibility for the elaboration of new rights and protection regimes is left for national and regional implementation.

The TRIPS Agreement, on the other hand, poses certain limitations to the possibility of protecting TKGR under the realm of traditional IPR.[7] According to Article 27.1, patents shall be granted to inventions in all fields of technology, and thus also to biotechnological inventions. Article 27.3(b) requires member states to provide for the protection of plant varieties by means of either patent protection or plant variety protection. On the other hand, the patentability requirements – namely novelty and inventive step – automatically leave a considerable part of TGKR outside the scope of patentable subject matter and the Agreement does not provide for a benefit-sharing mechanism, nor does it take any regard of the 'origin' of an invention. Thus, no rightholder other than the patent holder is recognised. Apart from these two limitations, the TRIPS Agreement does not provide guidance or any major constraint in the elaboration of a legal entitlement on TKGR.

[6] The states' sovereignty over their genetic resources is stipulated in Articles 3 (principle) and 15 (access to genetic resources).

[7] Article 27.1 TRIPS Agreement.

6.2.1.2 A combined legal framework: the case of marine genetic resources

The challenges now posed by the combined legal framework of the CBD requirements and objectives and the constraints caused by the TRIPS Agreement and the general IP system are not solely inherent to TKGR. In fact, a similar interface is noted with regard to the use of marine genetic resources (MGRs), which are today considered to be a very important source of wealth, with valuable enzymes found in deep-sea species constituting the subject matter of pharmaceuticals, anticancer drugs and antiageing cosmetics. MGRs are found in the seabed, ocean floor and subsoil, beyond the limits of national jurisdiction. With more than 15,000 new molecules discovered, 700 gene patent applications submitted and a 4 per cent growth rate of new products per year, there is no doubt that the legal framework regulating access to such resources is of interest.

In the same way as TKGR, MGRs enjoy some special characteristics both with regard to where and how they are found and with regard to the applicable legal framework. MGRs are in fact found beyond the national borders of any national jurisdiction. The United Nations Convention on the Law of the Sea (LOSC)[8] constitutes the legal framework regulating access and use of MGRs. It was opened for signature as early as 1982, when very little whatsoever was known of MGRs, let alone their biotechnological applications. Access and exploitation of MGRs raises North/South disparity concerns since their lack of necessary technological means leaves developing countries deprived of opportunities to reap the benefits of MGR exploitation.

Article 136 LOSC provides that the 'area and its resources are the common heritage of mankind'. It fails, however, to explain what the legal meaning of 'common heritage' is, and what the specific obligations and rights of the parties to the Convention are. At the same time, Article 143 states that marine scientific research activities shall be carried out exclusively for the benefit of mankind as a whole, while Article 241 provides that marine scientific research activities shall not constitute the 'legal basis for any claim to any part of the marine environment or its resources'. One of the main issues with regard to LOSC has thus been whether the results of marine scientific research, and thus the inventions based on MGR, may in fact be included in patent applications, or whether patent applications are 'claims' prohibited under Article 241 LOSC. The prevailing interpretation of this article implies that IPRs were

[8] United Nations Convention on the Law of the Sea (Montego Bay, 10 December 1982, in force 16 November 1994) 1833 UNTS 396.

never considered in the drafting of LOSC and thus may not be considered to fall under Article 241. Claims according to the said article concerned physical parts of the high seas. On the other hand, applying for patent protection and developing commercial products by exploiting MGRs does not automatically mean that this is not for the benefit of mankind as a whole. The development of new drugs and even cosmetics contributes to the benefit of mankind, even if it also entails enhancing the interests of private or public actors owning the patent. In fact, taking into consideration the fact that Article 140(2) LOSC requires equitable sharing of financial and other economic benefits derived from activities in the area (high seas and deep seabed), it seems to presuppose the existence of commercial profits. Commercialisation combined with patent protection might thus be a prerequisite for the fulfilment of Article 140 LOSC and the sharing of benefits.

A key component of MGRs' legal status that differentiates them from TKGR is that the latter are in fact subject to the national sovereignty of countries of access, while the former are beyond the borders of any national jurisdiction. Thus one of the basic arguments of the CBD with regard to the fair and equitable sharing provision – that countries of origin (as well as indigenous communities) burdened with the conservation and protection of TKGR should be rewarded for their contribution – fails in the case of MGRs. This does not mean that MGRs are not worth protecting. To the contrary, the mere fact that they fall outside the national sovereignty of a state places them at risk of suffering the 'tragedy of the commons'. The need to provide for a scheme of protection for MGR biodiversity has been recognised by the EU, which has asked for a High Seas biodiversity treaty. An international regulatory scheme would need to establish a monitoring authority that would regulate access, negotiate and manage benefits. Benefits would not be received by a specific state but rather would be managed on a central level for the preservation of MGRs, in ways comparable to that of the multilateral system under the ITPGRFA. Unfortunately, the institutional framework of benefit sharing under the ITPGRFA is still at a premature stage, and in the case of LOSC, nonexistent. Of course, apart from regulating access and negotiating benefit sharing, the forthcoming system should also regulate monitoring of benefit-sharing activities.

What is more, LOSC provides for the fair and equitable sharing of the benefits derived from 'activities in the Area'.[9] The question is whether biotechnological research of MGRs is an activity performed 'on land' or

---

[9] Article 140 LOSC.

'in the Area'. The Seabed Dispute Chamber of the International Tribunal for the Law of the Sea (ITLOS) provided an interpretation of the term 'activities in the Area', stating that these cover the recovery of minerals from the seabed and their lifting to the water surface; the process by which metals are extracted from the minerals, usually conducted 'on land', is excluded from the scope of the term 'activities'. An interesting question thus arises, namely, whether the interpretation of ITLOS in fact means that research and development conducted 'on land' is exempted from the benefit-sharing obligation of LOSC.[10]

In the same way as TKGR, MGRs might be found both in the high seas and in the waters of coastal states, and thus fall under their national sovereignty. Solving the equation of ABS of resources that are found in several jurisdictions is as complicated for MGRs as it is for TKGR. In fact, where resources are found both in the high seas and under national jurisdiction, they might fall under both the CBD and LOSC concurrently.

The case of MGRs reveals that the legal status of natural resources is often subject to complicated regimes and the interface between different applicable international conventions needs to be taken into consideration in the elaboration of specific rights.

6.2.2 Requirements, Constraints and Flexibilities and the Impact of Extraterritoriality

The protection of TKGR suffers from an inherent problem of extraterritoriality. The mere fact that TKGR is accessed in one country while commercialisation and thus value-adding procedures occur in another creates certain constraints in the system to be adopted. Naturally, national legislation in access countries will never be sufficient to provide adequate protection to rightholders. After being signed, bioprospecting agreements will have to be enforced in a completely different jurisdiction than the one where they were negotiated. The legal framework providing for the regulation of these agreements and creating enforcement means is not applicable in the country of exploitation, and this entails a considerable weakness in the protection of the rights of rightholders. A major contribution of the Nagoya Protocol has been its provision of the necessary preconditions for extraterritorial enforcement of ABS legislation and bioprospecting agreements. In this respect, extraterritorial

[10] He, H., 'Limitations on Patenting Inventions on Marine Genetic Resources of Areas beyond National Jurisdiction', Intl J Marine & Coastal L, Vol 29 (2014) pp. 521–45.

enforcement has been made possible by placing the burden of control and monitoring on the member states in which commercialisation occurs.

Apart from the very important contribution of the Nagoya Protocol in this respect, extraterritorial enforcement has been an aspect of bilateral negotiations. One interesting example is the 2006 Free Trade Agreement between the US and Peru entitled 'Understanding Regarding Biodiversity and Traditional Knowledge', in which both countries recognised the importance of acquiring PIC prior to TKGR access, providing for fair and equitable sharing of the benefits and promoting quality of prior art searches of patent applications related to TKGR. Although the FTA does not go so far as to provide for the enforcement of the Peruvian TKGR and ABS legislation in the US jurisdiction, it creates obligations comparable to those provided for under the CBD. Taking into consideration the fact that the United States has not ratified the CBD, this is an important contribution.

However, the extraterritoriality dilemma under the CBD framework might in fact also cover yet another situation, namely, the regulation of access and benefit sharing of genetic resources found outside the limits of national jurisdictions. Genetic resources found in the high seas or the deep seabed are subject to a grey zone when it comes to the regulation of bioprospecting activities. This does not mean, however, that they do not represent considerable value. Aquatic resources are typical of genetic resources found outside the limits of national jurisdiction.[11]

Both the CBD and the Nagoya Protocol have considered the value of genetic resources found in territories beyond national jurisdiction and the importance of finding a way to regulate benefit sharing. The CBD provides that member states should find a way to cooperate in order to guarantee the conservation and sustainable use of such resources,[12] while the Protocol requires parties to consider establishing a multilateral benefit-sharing mechanism for resources in transboundary situations.[13]

With regard to aquatic resources, the need to provide for a regulatory framework is important, taking into account the fact that *ex situ* collections are very few, badly coordinated and offer no internal regulations

[11] One example of such uses is that of Variolin B, originating in the Antarctic sponge *Kirpatricka varialosa*, which is subject to a number of patents. See for instance US Patent No 7329666 B2, published on 12 February 2008.

[12] Article 5 CBD.

[13] Articles 10 and 11 Nagoya Protocol.

and access protocols. Thus the sole means of regulation has been private agreements, where benefit-sharing provisions are very rarely included.[14]

6.3 THE CONTRIBUTION OF REGIONAL AND NATIONAL TKGR ENTITLEMENTS: LESSONS LEARNED

The vague formulations of the CBD provisions vested national and regional initiatives with considerable flexibility and the possibility to propose adaptations and variations that take into consideration the specific regional and national needs and special characteristics of national TKGR. This leaves considerable room to manoeuvre when it comes to implementation. Unfortunately, the flexibility becomes a weakness per se, since it both deprives the contracting parties of guidance on how to comply with a general regulatory framework and neglects to set out any specific, harmonising obligations. In fact, while the CBD expresses the overarching principles and objectives of a TKGR entitlement, it fails to address its concrete structure and nature.[15]

Considering the fact that international conventions only provide for the general framework and the fundamental principles of TKGR protection, the focus lies with national implementation initiatives. States are able to decide on the specific approach to be adopted nationally and thus the nature of the equity/fairness approach to be employed. Three major 'equity and fairness' alternative approaches may be identified: procedural equity, retributive equity and distributive equity.[16]

Procedural equity concerns the fairness/equity of the procedure to be followed in decision making. It states that all stakeholders should participate directly in the decision-making process and should have the opportunity to submit their opinions. *Retributive equity* relates to *inter*

---

[14] With regards to aquatic resources see also Humphries, F., 'Technology Transfer of Aquatic Resources under the Convention on Biological Diversity and the Nagoya Protocol: "Sponging" off Patent Law Defenses', UNSW LJ, Vol 39 (2016), pp. 234–72.

[15] Guruswamy, L., 'Convention on Biological Diversity: Exposing the Flawed Foundations', Environmental Conservation, Vol 26 (1999), pp. 89–92.

[16] Pena-Neira, S., Dieperinc, C., Addink, H., 'Equitably Sharing Benefits from the Utilization of Natural Genetic Resources: The Brazilian Interpretation of the CBD', EJCL, Vol 6 (2002), pp. 1–18.

partes transactions, and requires reciprocity and balance in the obligations between two or more parties.[17] *Distributive equity* rules upon relations between the state and its people and entails that people should be rewarded for their work according to the value of their contribution to the social product, or according to the efforts or the costs that they spent for their work. Thus the application of distributive equity presupposes a level of state interference with contractual freedom.[18]

In the post-CBD era, a growing number of regional and national initiatives have been taken to support the implementation of the CBD and provide for the introduction of *sui generis* legal entitlements or other protection frameworks for TKGR. But apart from a few exceptions, the vagueness of CBD provisions has been further transposed to national and regional regulations and TKGR protection remains a blurry, complicated issue without clear entitlements and ownership structures.

In practice, TKGR as a subject matter is often ruled by a set of mixed rights. TKGR is subject to multiple layers of rights, and consequently multiple rightholders. To complicate matters further, these rights are not of the same nature and do not give rise to the same sanctions when enforced. In this set of legal rights, we find state rights, community rights and, in some cases, private property rights. In theory, access to TKGR might require access to private lands, state-owned genetic resources and indigenous peoples' traditional knowledge.

In addition, regulatory frameworks for bioprospecting activities often create a managerial TKGR environment comparable to that of Creative Commons. Just as in the case of Creative Commons, communities make TKGR available to third parties under a set of different conditions depending on the nature of the use. In a number of relevant legal national and regional regulations, when use is public research-oriented, access is possible under more favourable terms and with more limited benefit-sharing obligations compared to those applicable in commercial use access.

---

17 It is, however, difficult to assess and estimate what is 'equal'.

18 Kaplow, L. and Shavell, S., 'Fairness versus Welfare: Notes on the Pareto Principle, Preferences, and Distributive Justice', Harvard Law and Economics Discussion Paper No 411 (March 2003). Available at SSRN: http://ssrn.com/abstract=391060 or DOI: 10.2139/ssrn.391060. With regard to distributive justice, see also Honoré, A.M., 'Property, Title and Redistribution' in Mae, L., Brown, J. (eds), *Philosophy of Law*, Colchester: Wiley-Blackwell (2009), pp. 263–9.

A review of regional and national implementation initiatives provides valuable examples for consideration with regard to the protection of TKGR.

The OAU Model Law did not bring any real clarification regarding the regime of protection covering TKGR. While plant breeders' rights specify the precise nature and scope of the rights granted,[19] namely the exclusive right to sell and produce as well as the right to license the protected plant variety, no effort is made to closely define the rights of local and indigenous communities.

The OAU Model Law may provide for an extension of the subject matter related to the rights of local and indigenous communities to cover not only their traditional knowledge but also their biological resources, but apart from proclaiming the right of these communities to TKGR, the right to use their innovations and the right to share the benefits arising out of their utilisation, no further specification of the nature, scope and structure of the entitlement on TKGR is provided. Instead, the Model Law reiterates the formulations of the CBD. The same lack of precision is present in the enforcement provisions, where the violation of breeders' rights is classified as an 'infringement', while the violation of the rights of indigenous communities is sanctioned just as any other violation of administrative authorisation procedure.[20]

The Brazilian regulatory framework is a typical illustration of national implementation confirming what is stated above. The protection proposed is remarkably vague and the formulations resemble those of the CBD. While Articles 8 and 9 stipulate that the indigenous communities have the right to prevent nonauthorised third parties from using, testing, researching or making commercial use of TKGR, there is no reference as to whether the rights conferred are exclusive or not. Even if the indigenous peoples' rights include the right to receive acknowledgement of the origin of TKGR in publication, use, exploitation and dissemination, this is more reminiscent of a specific moral right of recognition. In addition, indigenous peoples have the right to prevent dissemination or forwarding of data of TKGR character, or parts thereof that relate to some form of trade-secret protection.[21]

Philippine law has introduced community IPRs for TKGR. These community rights give indigenous peoples a right to recognition of full ownership and control over projects and programs that take place in their

---

[19] See Article 26(3) of the African Model Law.

[20] The ANDEAN and ASEAN regional regulations provide for the same general framework.

[21] A similar approach is adopted by Peruvian legislation.

lands. They have a claim on prior informed consent for access to their TKGR and a right to receive royalties from its use and even to regulate entry into their lands. Here, a right of recognition is also inscribed. Publications and papers written on TKGR shall disclose indigenous peoples as the source of information. In Portuguese legislation, the choice has been made to introduce a *sui generis* exclusive right for TKGR. The legislation provides for an application and registration procedure resembling that of the patent application procedure with a specific subject matter and for a limited protection period.[22]

Thailand provides for a similar explicit legal entitlement scheme, with three escalations based on the characteristics of TKGR in question: *national formula* traditional Thai drugs are subject to state rights; *personal formula* traditional Thai drugs are subject to protection under an exclusive right similar to the traditional patent right; *general formula* traditional Thai drugs connote such TKGR that has fallen into the public domain.

Bioprospecting agreements granted under the framework of national legislation do not seem to fulfil either the equity or the efficiency requirement. The negotiating environment of bioprospecting agreements falls short of the Coasean requirements. The demand side is dominated by a few oligopolies, which have technological know-how, information as to the potential uses of TKGR, negotiating experience and raised awareness as regards legal rules and procedures. On the supply side, on the other hand, we find rightholders with fragmented rights, disputable representation structures, and limited knowledge of relevant technology, limited negotiating experience and limited understanding of the applicable legal framework. The notable disparities in the bargaining power of parties to bioprospecting agreements, as well as the oligopolistic position of bioprospectors, signify that the bioprospecting market is not a competitive market in the sense of the Coase Theorem.[23]

Bioprospecting agreements entail high transaction costs. The identification costs are non-negligent in the bioprospecting environment should one take into account the fact that for TKGR, the authorisation of a number of governmental authorities, NGOs, representatives of indigenous communities and even private parties might be required. The complicated legal status and the uncertainty with regard to ownership, in particular when the same traditional knowledge is found in a number of different

---

22 Fifty years of protection.

23 Coase, R.H., 'The Problem of Social Costs', J Law Econ, Vol 3 (1960), pp. 1–44.

jurisdictions, places costs and risks on the potential bioprospector. In such a trading environment, efficiency cannot be achieved. It lacks strong, clear and well-defined legal entitlements. Thus efficient as well as equitable bioprospecting presupposes and requires the introduction and establishment of a clear legal entitlement on TKGR.[24]

National and regional experiences with TKGR protection allow us to draw a number of interesting conclusions with regard to the difficulties and constraints involved in implementing the international legal framework. Furthermore, it confirms that the difficulties of defining the meaning and legal content of the property rights paradigm have an impact on the way these rights are formulated. In other words, there are *sui generis* rights introduced in certain jurisdictions which claim they introduced a property right, while in fact the relevant legislation stipulates and describes the typical characteristics of a liability rights regime. On the other hand, the contractual protection of TKGR has also proven to be a rather disputable choice. Experiences of bioprospecting agreements show that *in rem* protection of TKGR is unable to fulfil the equity and efficiency requirements, thus providing a very limited and problematic protection formula.[25]

An overall assessment of the different national and regional initiatives leads to the conclusion that the process of entitlement elaboration is obviously not flawless. One of the major weaknesses seems to be the lack of examination of alternatives and the impact these might have on the protection of the specific subject matter. The three major protection frameworks presented in previous parts of this study – property, liability and reward systems – will now be tested on the basis of the alternative justifications as well as with regard to their compatibility with the set objectives, in this case fairness and efficiency.

6.4 RAWLS AND COASE IN THE ELABORATION OF AN ENTITLEMENT ON TKGR

As has previously been shown, both the Coase Theorem and Rawls' Theory of Justice build upon a hypothetical model of consensus resulting

---

[24] For a very interesting discussion on the issues of territoriality of TKGR protection measures see Ubertazzi, B., 'Territorial and Universal Protection of Intangible Cultural Heritage from Misappropriation', NZ YB Intl L, Vol 8 (2010), pp. 69–106.

[25] Bioprospecting agreements have not as yet provided evidence of concrete benefits for TKGR holders. See Chapter 4.

from bargaining. Coase bases his theoretical model on a costless bargaining scheme. Rawls' consensus model, meanwhile, relates to society's constitutional framework and the recognition of human or fundamental rights,[26] as well as to principles of encouraging liberty and at the same time addressing inequalities, which are also based on a hypothetical model of consensus.[27]

A major difference between the two models is the importance of rational empathy in the Rawlsian model and its total absence in the Coase Theorem. The Rawlsian veil of ignorance presupposes that individuals will take into consideration the importance and need of a 'security net for all'. The rational individuals in Rawls' original position would opt for the most efficient use of available resources in order to create the highest expected outcome. Risk aversion will have a balancing effect. Individuals will be willing to accept a lower than expected possible outcome in order to ensure the actual outcome. Rawls' 'constructive empathy' is more than an emotion; it is, rather, a rational choice. Constructive empathy is not a result of pity and compassion but rather a strategic choice.[28]

Fairness and efficiency considerations have traditionally been kept apart. According to the Second Theorem of Welfare Economics, fairness and efficiency are separable and, as a result, separate social policies can independently achieve social goals of fairness and efficiency. The Second Theorem provides that there is no need for society to attempt to achieve both goals simultaneously. Applying the Second Theorem to the 'pollution' example would entail that entitlements are assigned, guaranteeing that the land is used efficiently without taking into account any equity or justice concerns. The 'winners' of this initial allocation will, under governmental intervention, have to 'share' the surplus with the 'losers'.[29]

---

26 See also Elkins, D., 'Responding to Rawls: Toward a Consistent and Supportable Theory of Distributive Justice', BYU J Public Law, Vol 21 (2007), pp. 267–323.

27 See Korobkin, R.B. and Ulen, T.S., 'Efficiency and Equity: What Can Be Gained by Combining Coase and Rawls?', Washington L Rev, Vol 73 (1998), pp. 329–48.

28 Individuals are thus willing to give up part of the wealth surplus in order to guarantee that their actual welfare will not fall below a specific level.

29 See also Mikhail, J., 'Law, Science, and Morality: A Review of Richard Posner's "The Problematics of Moral and Legal Theory", Stanford L Rev, Vol 54 (2002), pp. 1059–129; Georgetown Law and Economics Research Paper No 877011.

The two objectives of fairness and efficiency are obviously of paramount importance with regard to the elaboration of a legal entitlement covering TKGR.

One must not ignore the important role TKGR plays in the life of its rightholders and its close link to their spiritual and religious traditions, as well as to their survival. This special link underlines the important role of the 'moral right' perspective of a potential TKGR legal entitlement. Furthermore, the fact that the 'providers' or initial 'rightholders' of the specific subject matter are local and indigenous communities with limited means and very often acute health and nutritional problems, while on the side of the 'users' and often alleged 'free riders' we find Western-world multinationals, accentuates the importance of reestablishing equity in the specific market. This disparity between TKGR market actors thus creates extensive expectations as to the 'equity' considerations that the TKGR protection scheme would provide, and that would normally exceed its scope and applicability in effect and meaning.

Fairness and equity are principles that made their way into both the text and the spirit of the CBD. The mere existence of the Convention is the result of the will to compensate indigenous peoples and developing countries and to bring a balance in the TKGR market. As a matter of fact, one of the goals of the CBD, stated in Article 1, is the 'fair and equitable sharing of the benefits arising out of the utilisation of genetic resources'.[30] The terms 'fair' and 'equitable' were not employed as synonyms. These two terms have gained an emphasising and complementary function that connotes both to the process of providing for rights as well as to the outcome of the distribution of benefits derived from the use of biological resources as 'fair' and 'equitable'. In that way, developing countries or countries of origin were recognised a right of compensation for the development and conservation of TKGR as well as for making TKGR accessible to third parties.

Article 8(j) concerns the benefits arising from the utilisation of knowledge, innovations and practices of indigenous and local communities. Furthermore, Article 15.7 regulates the sharing of benefits arising from the results of research and development and the commercial and other use of genetic resources. Article 19.2 provides for the 'fair and equitable' access to results and benefits of biotechnologies achieved on the basis of resources provided by the party.

The equity/fairness concept is equally important in the text of the ITPGRFA. In Article 9.2, the notion of equity alone is used to specify

---

[30] Article 1 CBD concerning the objectives of the Convention.

farmers' rights to participate in the sharing of benefits, while Articles 10 and 13 integrate and differentiate the formula of 'fair and equitable' with regard to the Multilateral System of Access and Benefit Sharing. The concept of equity/fairness is often employed with regard to the relationship between the relevant players, that is, between the providers of TKGR and the purchasers of TKGR.[31] Though both the CBD and the ITPGRFA use the term 'equity', they fail to provide for its legal definition. Though 'equity' is a keyword in the discussion on TKGR protection, it is frequently used in an intuitive and nonspecific manner. It could be assumed that it relates to issues of economic and political distributive justice. This is also one of the major objectives of choosing Rawls' fairness theoretical framework, since this guides us into deciding what equity and fairness is to entail in the TKGR protection.

Efficiency, though not mentioned as explicitly in the CBD provisions, functions as an overriding principle and objective. The shift from 'commons' to 'rights' by means of the CBD is motivated by an 'efficiency argument'. The objective to 'facilitate access' and to provide for the 'sustainable use of genetic resources' incorporates an efficiency perspective. The concept of 'sustainability' itself is understood as integrating different components that define the interrelationship between humanity and nature – that is, the economic, social and ecological factors.[32] The text of the CBD, and in particular Articles 11 and 15, link conservation and sustainable use of the components of biological diversity with economic issues, such as the creation of incentives for conservation and benefit sharing.

Article 8(j) states that national legislation should 'encourage the equitable sharing of the benefits arising from the utilization' of traditional knowledge, innovations and practices. The Article provides for the 'approval and involvement of the holders of such knowledge', in that way promoting the participatory aspect of fairness. The same participatory aspect of 'fairness and equity' elements in the text can be found in Article 15 of the CBD. According to Article 15.4 and 15.5, access to genetic resources shall be granted 'on mutually agreed terms', and under the precondition of 'prior informed consent' of the country of origin.

---

[31] The term 'equity' was also of central importance in the United Nations Convention on the Law of the Sea (1982), where it was stated that 'marine resources are to be used in an equitable and efficient manner'.

[32] Biber-Klemm, S., Szymura Berglas, D., 'Problems and Goals', in Biber-Klemm, S., Cottier, T. (eds), *Rights to Plant Genetic Resources and Traditional Knowledge: Basic Issues and Perspectives*, CABI (2006), pp. 1189–1204.

Though the fundamental part of Rawls' thought employed in this thesis is the Theory of Justice, the Law of Peoples is also of interest in certain respects. The two fundamental requirements that Rawls sets out for global economic relations – the duty for assistance and the free and fair trade – are both present in the CBD provisions.[33]

The duty of assistance requires 'well-ordered peoples' (developed countries[34]) to assist burdened societies (developing countries[35]). Article 16 provides for the obligation of contracting parties to provide for/facilitate access to and transfer of technology. Furthermore, Article 19.2 CBD provides that developing countries should be provided access to the results and benefits of biotechnologies based upon genetic resources originating from the countries in question.[36] Finally, Article 20.2, 20.3 and 20.5 CBD states that developed countries shall provide developing countries with financial assistance in order for the latter to bear the costs of implementation of the Convention's provisions.

The obligation on developed countries to engage in 'free and fair trade', refraining from monopolising markets or forming cartels and even removing the defects and inequalities in the trade relations with developing countries, could be read in numerous provisions of the CBD, but are also inherent in the general spirit of the Convention. Moreover, the post-CBD international negotiations are increasingly structured under the Rawlsian model of international justice, including not only diplomatic relations between states but also a more complex regime where non-governmental actors are awarded a central role.[37] In the same way, the interest of the international community has been oriented towards the protection of rights of the less powerful, indigenous communities.

Apart from the CBD, the international agreement with direct impact on the elaboration of TKGR protection is the TRIPS Agreement. This is obviously also of relevance and influences further developments in the field of TKGR protection. While very often accused of rigidity and supporting developed countries' interests, the TRIPS Agreement, at least formally, has an inbuilt balance and equity perspective incorporated in its objectives and principles. Article 7 of the TRIPS Agreement provides that the protection and enforcement of IPRs must be carried out 'in a manner conducive to social and economic welfare, and to a balance of rights and

---

[33] Rawls, J., *A Theory of Justice*, Oxford: Clarendon Press (1972).

[34] In the CBD context.

[35] In the CBD context.

[36] That is, developing countries or another contracting party.

[37] Rawls, J., *A Theory of Justice*, revised edition, Boston: Harvard University Press (1999).

obligations', as well as 'to a mutual advantage of producers and users of technological knowledge'. Article 8.1 guarantees flexibility and equity in the national implementation of the Agreement as members may formulate and amend their laws to 'protect public health and nutrition, and to promote the public interest in sectors of vital importance'. Finally, Article 8.2 states that members may take all appropriate measures needed (consistent with the provision of the Agreement) to prevent rightholders' abuse of IPRs or the resort to practices that unreasonably restrain trade or adversely affect the international transfer of technology. In a similar way to the CBD, in Articles 66 and 67 the TRIPS Agreement provides for developed countries' assistance to developing countries in terms of technology transfer as well as financial and other assistance in the implementation process.[38]

The international agreements of relevance for TKGR protection remain silent as to the specific nature and structure of the entitlement granted, if any. The requirements of the implementation processes are: genetic resources shall be state sovereign rights; traditional knowledge shall be preserved and promoted; and at the same time, any access and use of traditional knowledge shall be subject to the prior informed consent (PIC) of its initial holders – indigenous peoples.

The IP-related obligations under the TRIPS Agreement obviously influence, even if only indirectly, the elaboration of a TKGR entitlement. The obligation to protect plant varieties, granting of patents in all fields of technology and patentability requirements per se influence further developments in the field of TKGR protection and require continuous compliance control between CBD implementation initiatives and the IP-related international obligations.

Considering the increased transaction costs in the TKGR market, it is of utmost importance to choose the right type of entitlement, the appropriate rightholders and the most efficient managerial structure. Transaction costs include lengthy procedures, multiple permits, PICs, multiple fees and overlapping procedures. Another important factor contributing to the increased transaction costs and consequently to the market failures in the field of TKGR is, of course, the limited legal certainty. The entitlement and the overarching principles and procedures

---

[38] The 'fairness and equity' perspective is also present in the ITPGRFA, which provides for the compensation of farmers who conserve the diversity of crop varieties.

surrounding it should abide by the fundamental rule of legal certainty, now a principle provided for in the Nagoya Protocol.[39]

Since TKGR is found in various forms, it could be plausible to be protected by different entitlements. It would also be recommended to employ different entitlements in intranational arrangements (relations between the state in the country of origin and the indigenous communities), as opposed to the relations between the country of origin and external bioprospectors.

Providing for a remedy to the TKGR market failures is definitely not such an uncomplicated task. The major difficulty is the variability of TKGR status and characteristics. TKGR could be a patentable invention, as for instance in the cases in which it is used almost as such in dietary products, where TKGR is used in its traditional form and application without any further research being necessary. On the other hand it could be a raw material which is attributed a certain value in traditional knowledge but is still very far from a ready-to-sell commercial product. The characteristics of TKGR, such as its link to the end commercial product, the value in the input of the associated traditional knowledge and its exclusivity, are important parameters to be taken into consideration in the choice of the appropriate entitlement.

Table 6.1 provides a classification of the different forms in which TKGR may be found. The darker the colour, the stronger the protection it could be awarded.[40]

6.4.1 Fairness and Efficiency in Property Rights for TKGR

Property rules have been considered the natural starting point for the elaboration of a remedy in the market failures of the TKGR market. National and regional regulations in the field often claim to have introduced exclusive rights to TKGR. Nevertheless, even after a number of jurisdictions have introduced some form of protection regime for TKGR, there is no clarity as to the specific status and structure of the legal entitlement introduced.

On the other hand, negotiations pertaining to international protection often start at and end with a property-based legal right. It is thus important to examine whether the structure of rights to TKGR already introduced on the national level fall under the scope of the property rights

---

[39] See paragraph 3(a) of the Nagoya Protocol.

[40] Strong protection in this respect refers to protection awarding the right-holders exclusivity and control over TKGR. An entitlement that would be appropriate would be property rights.

Table 6.1 TKGR characteristics of importance for the protection granted

TKGR status	**Characteristics of importance for the entitlement granted**	
Access mode	Ex situ	Non-commercial actors (gene banks)
		Commercial actors
	In-situ	TKGR found in one country
		TKGR found in several countries
Access Incentives	Commercial	Development of products
	Nonommercial	Non-commercial research to be at a further step transformed into commercial
		Non-commercial research related to conservation etc.
Link between genetic resources and traditional knowledge	Closely linked	Ex situ collection providing genetic resources and associated traditional knowledge
		Indigenous communities specific traditional medicinal or other use of genetic resources
	Partly linked	Traditional knowledge on the approximate value of genetic resources, though not clearly identifiable
	Not at all linked	Genetic resources found in the geographical area of the indigenous community but with no accompanying traditional knowledge.
Compatibility of TKGR with modern IPRs	TKGR kept secret	Innovative: potential for patent or plant variety protection
		Not innovative enough for traditional IPRs but with potential valuable contribution in sequential innovation
	TKGR in the public	TKGR with no potential valuable uses but still important to protect by PIC because of religious or other reasons
		TKGR in products such as food, beverages with a potential to be protected under GIs
Potential of incorporation of TKGR in end products	Incorporable as a whole	Chemical compound serving as prototype for an active compound in a pharmaceutical
		Extracts of plants used in natural cosmetics, dietary supplements etc.
	Partly incorporable	Molecule found in the plant needs to be modified in many steps to be included in product
		Function of an organism or its parts serve as a model (mimics in biotechnology)
	Not related	Genetic resources serve as research tool

Note: Similar tables are found in, Greiber et al., 'An Explanatory Guide to the Nagoya Protocol on Access to Genetic Resources and Traditional Knowledge', IUCN, Environmental Law and Policy Paper No 83, Bonn (2012), p. 7.

paradigm as a consequence, but also if property rights would provide for an efficient and equitable protection for this specific subject matter.

6.4.1.1 An entitlement under property rules paradigm: justifications

International negotiations on the elaboration of a legal entitlement or other protection framework for TKGR have been placed under the realm of IPR. However, neither the CBD nor the majority of regional or national implementation initiatives provide explicitly for the justifications leading to the introduction of a TKGR legal entitlement structured as a property right.

The property rules paradigm has been the subject matter of a mosaic of different theories and perspectives attempting to define its meaning and determine its components, scope and effects. A plausible justification for the introduction of property rights to TKGR could be that it is an expression of the indigenous peoples' 'common personality'. The application of Hegel's personality theory in the TGKR field would in fact mean that indigenous peoples, as individuals, expressed their will on genetic resources, by using them, seizing them or marking them. The expression of their will on the resources in question is decisive in the process of their self-determination, and lays the ground for their property right to TKGR.

The introduction of property rights would thus include three fundamental elements: possession of the subject matter, enjoyment and alienation.[41] In my view, a right to TKGR would fulfil these three requirements. Personality theory could indeed be employed as a justification for the introduction of property rights to TKGR, if it were not for one fundamental element of the Hegelian theory: the focus on individual, private rights. Hegel's personality theory functions as a justification for the establishment of private property rights of individuals, but not of collective rights owned by a community. The same counterarguments could apply for the rejection of the Lockean labour theory on property rights. Though TKGR is obviously a result of labour applied on genetic resources, there is no interest in removing those from the realm of common property and placing them under private property rights.[42]

These traditional naturalist theories, though not directly applicable in the case of TKGR, have laid the ground for modern relational theories.

---

[41] Knowles, D., 'Hegel on Property and Personality', Philosophical Quarterly, Vol 33 (1983), pp. 45–8.

[42] Hughes, J., 'The Philosophy of Intellectual Property', Georgetown LJ, Vol 77 (1988–9), p. 297.

Property rights classification and the diversification between fungible and personal property elaborated by Radin could be applicable in the case of TKGR. In a number of cases, traditional knowledge has been considered sacred, related to religious and spiritual ceremonies. As such, traditional knowledge could be considered 'personal' and could be subject to other provisions/regulations than the fungible TKGR – for instance, the one related to agriculture and crop conservation.[43]

Under the framework of relational theories we also find the human rights doctrine and its attempt to justify property rights.[44] Obviously, with a lack of other, more concrete justifications, human rights has become one of the most natural frameworks for the justification of granting property rights to TKGR.[45] In fact, negotiations pertaining to the recognition and protection of indigenous peoples' rights with regard to their lands, resources and cultural heritage originate from the human rights agenda. A human rights-inspired justification for property rights allows for 'collective ownership' as well as individual. Another very important aspect in the human rights framework is the importance of the 'moral right' aspect of the proposed entitlement, present both in the CBD provisions and in the national and regional regulations. A human rights justification for the rights of indigenous peoples with regard to their lands and their genetic resources has been promoted in a number of international instruments.[46]

States' obligations to demarcate and safeguard indigenous peoples' lands are stipulated in a number of relevant international and regional human rights conventions. TKGR finds a share of justification grounds in the utilitarian theories on property rights. In fact, property rights are of secondary importance; in the work of Coase as well as in the post-Coasean literature, their main role is to facilitate contractual transactions. Property rights are subordinate to contractual relations. TKGR protection,

---

[43] Radin, M., 'Property and Personhood', Stanford L Rev, Vol 34 (1982), pp. 957–1015.

[44] Schermers, H.G., 'The International Protection of the Right of Property' in Matcher, F., Petzold, H. (eds), *Protecting Human Rights: The European Dimension*, Köln: Carl Heymanns Verlag KG (1998), pp. 125–58.

[45] Coombe, R., 'Intellectual Property, Human Rights and Sovereignty: New Dilemmas in International Law Posed by the Recognition of Indigenous Knowledge and the Conservation of Biological Diversity', Ind J Global Legal Studies, Vol 6 (1998), p. 59.

[46] For an elaborate discussion on the rights of indigenous peoples in international knowledge, see Stoll, P., von Hahn, A., *Indigenous Peoples, Indigenous Knowledge and Indigenous Knowledge and Indigenous Resources in International Law*, London: Kluwer International (2003), pp. 5–43.

in particular in the jurisdictions where there is no explicit reference to exclusive rights, is provided in relation to, and as an indispensable part of, the regulation of bioprospecting agreements. In respect of the utilitarian theories, the protection of TKGR is of interest solely as a means of facilitating bioprospecting agreements.

6.4.1.2 A TKGR entitlement under the property rights paradigm: the legal content

Positivism, and in particular the contribution of Hohfeld with regard to the 'bundle of rights' character of property,[47] is much closer to the property rights structure than has been employed in the case of TKGR. The 'bundle of rights' doctrine provides for a number of layers of rights that could constitute components of a property rights institution. These rights would thus include the right to access, the right of withdrawal, the right to manage, the right to exclude and, finally, the right of alienation. Consequently, an entitlement could be classified under the property rights paradigm even in the absence of some of the abovementioned rights. Furthermore, such a property rights structure would allow different categories of property holders to retain rights in the same subject matter.

In this listing of 'bundle of rights', the right of exclusion has been awarded varying levels of importance. The dominant theory of property rights includes exclusion as the major and necessary element of property. Therefore, according to a number of property theorists, the legal entitlements provided for under national and regional TKGR regulations are not to be classified as property rules, if/where these lack the right of exclusion. On the other hand, theorists such as Blackstone consider the right of exclusion to be relevant only with regard to the relation between an owner and other individuals, and it becomes important only with regard to enforcement of property rights and not with regard to their establishment.[48]

On the whole, whether the entitlements on TKGR would be classified as property rights or not depends on the prevailing theory of the role of the right to exclusion. The *numerus clausus* principle poses limitations on the elaboration of a property right to TKGR. Contrary to the theory of a 'bundle of rights', a property right should take specific predetermined forms and consist of a limited list of components. Although national and regional protection initiatives for TKGR attempt to introduce layers of *in*

[47] Hohfeld, W., 'Fundamental Legal Conceptions as Applied in Judicial Reasoning', Yale LJ, Vol 23 (1917), pp. 16–59.

[48] Honoré (2009).

rem rights, they usually build upon and often end up creating not more than a specified structure of *in personam* rights.[49] The choice between *in rem* and *in personam* rights is one of the most interesting aspects of TKGR protection. Nominally, the right to TKGR introduced by means of national and regional legislation is an *in rem* right. However, in practice, most of the proposed entitlements could rather be characterised as intermediate situations in which the legal regime adopts contract rules, modified by rules that readdress problems of incomplete information, in that way protecting weaker parties.[50]

The value of a property right on TKGR would be dependent on its stability. Applying the theory of Bell and Parchomovsky would entail that the value of TKGR would be dependent on how many people knew about the property right and how many respect it. This stresses once more the importance of an international consensus for a property right on TKGR. Without that, in an international marketplace like that of TKGR, a property right would be of peripheral value.[51] The Nagoya Protocol, providing for an international recognition and enforcement of national ABS legislation, makes a considerable contribution to increasing TKGR value. The new possibilities of extraterritorial enforcement offered to TKGR holders by means of Nagoya will thus have an impact on the value of establishing TKGR property rights and the value of the rights themselves.

Another interesting perspective on a property right to TKGR is the fact that its primal role would be that of providing for a legal basis for bioprospecting agreements and assisting in their cumbersome enforcement. TKGR contractual arrangements are reminiscent of the illustration used in Anderson and Hill related to the importance of contracts used in order to enforce the property rights of ranches as opposed to the rights of the Cherokee tribes, and vice versa.[52] The property right on TKGR has no value per se (apart from a cultural value), since the protection of TKGR is of value in relation to the transfer of rights and licensing to bioprospectors, and not so much in excluding others. To this day, the protection of TKGR has been justified not by TKGR rightholders' interest in holding the exclusive exploitation rights for their resources

---

49 Smith, H., 'Semicommon Property Rights and Scattering in the Open Fields', J Legal Studies, Vol 29 (2000), pp. 131–69.

50 Smith (2000).

51 Bell, A., Parchomovsky, G., 'A Theory of Property', Cornell L Rev, Vol 90 (2005), pp. 531–616.

52 Anderson, T., Hill, P.J., 'Cowboys and Contracts', J Legal Studies, Vol 31 (2002), pp. 489–514.

(the rights of exclusion), but rather by receiving appropriate and enforceable remuneration for the use made by others.

Opting for the property rights paradigm allows for considerable flexibility in the legal content. Property rights in general, and IPRs in particular, may enjoy a variety of characteristics. An interesting example is that of geographical indications (GIs), often mentioned as a possibly adequate means of protecting TKGR. GIs are different from 'traditional' IPRs in that they have a much stronger 'public' character. They are not 'private' and exclusive, as other IPRs are, which in fact means that all producers from a certain geographic region, using a certain traditional recipe, are able to use the geographical indication for their products. On the other hand, GIs are not transferable. The rightholders are not able to transfer the rights to the geographical indication to third parties and receive compensation. The right to a geographical indication may not be licensed. This nontransferability is what makes it an appropriate form of protection for TKGR uses in which the rightholders (indigenous communities) proceed to the commercialisation of their resources and TK themselves. Most valuable TKGR uses are nowadays found in the field of pharmaceuticals or biotech research, and are thus of a nature that presupposes the intervention of a R&D institute or company, making GIs a less appropriate protection scheme. Nevertheless, they provide valuable experience as to the different forms IPRs might in fact adopt and reveal the flexibilities that might be exploited when drafting a TKGR-related *sui generis* right.[53]

6.4.1.3 A TKGR entitlement under the property rights paradigm: the management of rights perspective

TKGR can be regarded as a community 'good' both because it is the product of community work and innovations and because the community will benefit from it. The CBD provides for these rights of indigenous peoples and promotes the interests of the community rather than the rights of individuals. Some national and regional legislation also refers to the rights of communities and provides for special community-owned rights. The previous overview of the different theories regarding the property rights paradigm confirms that entitlements with a variation in their legal content may be classified as 'property rights'. However, even where the legal protection of TKGR is formulated as a property right, it

[53] Dagne, T., 'The Identity of Geographical Indications and Their Relation to Traditional Knowledge in Intellectual Property Law', IDEA, Vol 54 (2013–14), pp. 255–83.

predetermines neither the specific structure or the effects of such a right, nor the forms of its further management.

While it could be claimed that TKGR is a typical case of common resources, this is only true with regard to its intracommunity management. Intracommunity relations are ruled by customary law and represented on the basis of its internal hierarchical structure. The innovation process takes place under the institutional framework of the community with the contribution of all or some specific members. The nature of the contributions, the members of the community allowed to perform these contributions and the objectives of the innovative process are decided by the internal rules and on the community level. In some cases the structure and form of the innovative process in the TKGR field resembles that of the open source production projects. The end result is a product of collective work, not attributable to one individual,[54] while the interest in the ownership and the management of rights to TKGR are outside the limits of the community.[55]

Management of rights is also very important from the perspective of the bioprospectors. Their role in the fairness and efficiency of the TKGR market is, of course, vital. An interesting initiative falling under the scope of management of property rights is socially responsible licensing, a new managerial model created in order to address issues related to the public health crisis.[56] By means of that licensing model, pharmaceutical companies engage in market segmentation and price differentiation in developing countries, licensing vital pharmaceuticals to developing countries without charging any royalties.[57] The same practice has even been applied to agricultural biotechnology. Socially responsible licensing

---

[54] Opderdeck, D., 'The Penguin's Genome or Coase and the Open Source Biotechnology', Harvard J Law and Technology, Vol 18 (2004), pp. 1–80.

[55] Smith (2000).

[56] The Doha Declaration and the amendment to the TRIPS Agreement have not been efficient enough: Mimura, C., Chen J., Penhoet, B., 'Socially Responsible Licensing, Euclidean Innovation, and the Valley of Death', Stanford J Law, Science & Policy (2011), available at http://www.stanford.edu/group/sjlsp/cgi-bin/orange_web/articles/index.

[57] GlaxoSmithKline has implemented a voluntary licensing program which enables local manufacturers to produce and sell generic versions of some of its products. Since October 2001 Glaxo has signed seven licensing agreements for antiretrovirals in Kenya and South Africa. Gilead adopted this strategy too, licensing four HIV/AIDS drugs, and Crucell sells the cholera vaccine for less than a dollar per dose. See Skarp, B., 'Commercialization of University Knowledge – Aspects on Licensing and Spin-Outs', speech at European Academy of Taxes, Economics and Law, Berlin (January 2013).

fulfils the criteria of efficiency and fairness. It is also proof of the possibilities of self-regulation of the market. In this case, the pharmaceutical companies see an interest in engaging in such a voluntary system, taking into account the limited profits arising from the markets of the developing countries, on the one hand, and the positive effects of the social return, on the other. The objective – a remedy for the public health crisis – is achieved in a fair and efficient way for the parties involved. This model could also be implemented in the TKGR market, with the objective of guaranteeing the fair and equitable sharing of benefits and the prior informed consent of indigenous communities.[58]

Finding an appropriate managerial structure is of vital importance should the TKGR entitlement be placed under the scope of the property rights paradigm. Considering that TKGR rightholders tend to overestimate the value of their rights, as well as the fact that TKGR is a typical subject matter with multiple rightholders, the risk of ending up in Heller's anticommons is non-negligible.

6.4.2 Fairness and Efficiency in Establishing a Traditional Knowledge Commons

Designing a TKGR commons requires thorough consideration of the complex character of TKGR, containing a physical aspect (the biological resources) and an informational component (the genetic information as well as the traditional knowledge on potential applications).

Experience drawn from known digital information commons reveals the fundamental importance of incentive schemes that contribute to the evolution of the commons platform and which are to a large extent driven more by social motivations than by monetary rewards. Monetary awards prove to be difficult to apply in such structures since the value of each contribution is hard to determine, while at the same time clear task distribution is difficult. Another interesting aspect is that the value of resources/research results becomes apparent at a much later stage; thus, the monetary value calculated during the innovation process will be deemed to be low.

Dedeurwaerdere has analysed the institutional framework of three case studies relating to genetic resources commons in three different sectors: microbial genetic resources, plant genetic resources and animal genetic

---

[58] Skarp (2013).

resources.[59] In the field of microbial resources, the most advanced arrangement on an institutional level is that of the viral licence signed by the European Culture Collections' Organisation, which permits distribution to other collaborating institutes under the precondition that recipients use the same licence structure. This is of course a clear reminder of the open-source licence. It is important to note here that a major part of the exchange of microbiological resources is performed on an informal basis without written contracts. While these informal networks are often preferred due to limited transaction costs, they entail some major disadvantages since they fail to prove compliance with the CBD PIC and benefit-sharing requirement. The microbial commons becomes even stronger with the advent of bioinformatics such as the Straininfo bioportal, which allows the integration of knowledge generation based on decentralised efforts of more than 62 collections.

In the field of crop genetic resources, the establishment of a formal crop pool was formalised in the work of the CGIAR collections and later confirmed in the ITPGRF. The Treaty contains two alternative licensing mechanisms: either a viral licence with regard to uses of accessed material in breeding, research and education or a commercialisation licence with an exclusive licence and the payment of a fixed fee to a multilateral fund. Social incentives and a certain modular organisation are present in the field of crop genetic resources. One of the major aspects of the CGIAR network program is that it has given young scientists from more than 90 participating countries the opportunity to meet and participate in educational programs. At the same time, participating countries are given the opportunity to choose the names of the varieties they release. Such initiatives aim to strengthen the social bonds in the network and develop a feeling of coownership.[60]

Finally, with regard to farm animal breeding, 'commons' management is limited to a certain extent. Hybrid breeding is mainly performed under an exclusive access regime developed by the breeding industry. Livestock

---

[59] Dedeurwaerdere, T., 'Institutionalizing Global Genetic-Resource Commons: Towards Alternative Models for Facilitating Access in the Global Biodiversity Regime', Working Paper (12 June 2010) at papers.ssrn.com.

[60] Byerlee, D., 'Crop Improvement in the CGIAR as a Global Success Story of Open Access and International Collaboration', Int J Commons, Vol 4 (2010), pp. 452–80. See also Thornström, C.G., 'CGIAR Revising Intellectual Property Guidelines in 2000: A Non-Event with Geopolitical Boundary and Sector Transgressing Content', paper submitted on request by the Genetic Resources Policy Committee of the Consultative Group on International Agricultural Research/CGIAR, Washington, DC: World Bank (17 March 2002).

breeding presupposes a pool of animals managed in open commons. In that case, the owners of the breeding animals are allowed to use the resources for further breeding without any limitations. Such programs are obviously developed on a strictly national or regional basis. Multinational companies' increasing commercial interests pose new limitations in the commons pools, with IPRs and patents playing a major role. Even in the field of animal breeding, social values play a considerable role. Animal breeding is very important on the national agenda and breeding programs are established in order to deal with major issues such as animal health, as well as the conservation of biodiversity.

The abovementioned examples of 'commons' for genetic resources provide for certain similarities with the digital commons, such as the modularity of the structure and the dominance of nonmarket incentives. There are, on the other hand, some non-negligible differences related mainly to the specific nature of TKGR. The costs of creating a genetic resources collection are substantial compared to those of an open source society in digital knowledge commons, where in principle the only investment needed is a computer and access to the network.[61]

One of the first major initiatives seeking to establish a traditional knowledge commons is that of the traditional healers living in the Bushbuckridge area of the Mpumalamga province in South Africa. The Bushbuckridge project developed a biocultural community protocol determining the terms and conditions of access to their collectively held TKGR.[62]

This initiative represents an interpretation of Article 8(j) CBD and of the South African ABS legislation, concluding that TKGR is not the property of traditional healers – these are the mere custodians, not the owners. A central factor of this TKGR commons has been the attempt to ensure that the knowledge would be used in accordance with the customary laws. This approach to TKGR management elaborates on the fundamental perception that an extensive commodification of TKGR would gradually lead to its erosion, since it would function without any

[61] Benkler, Y., *The Wealth Networks: How Social Production Transforms Markets and Freedom*, New Haven and London: Yale University Press (2006), pp. 133–212.

[62] For an elaboration of this Commons initiative see Abrell, E., Bavikatta, K., Cocchiaro, G., 'Implementing a Traditional Knowledge Commons: Opportunities and Challenges' in de Beer J., Armstrong, C., Oguamanam, C., Schionwetter, T. (eds), *Innovation and Intellectual Property Collaborative Dynamics in Africa*, Claremont: UCT Press (2009), pp. 151–71.

respect for the value-adding chain that develops such knowledge or the ties it shares with the indigenous community developing it.[63]

Applying a commons system of TKGR management is an attractive alternative for communities that wish to exercise control over the use of their TKGR but do not wish to proceed to a case-to-case negotiation of ABS agreements. A TKGR commons would allow third parties to access and use TKGR under the terms and conditions predefined in the commons platform.

Obviously, TKGR is the result of an informal TKGR commons regime building upon the traditional forms of knowledge exchange among different indigenous communities or among members of the same community. The challenge, and the most interesting aspect of formalising the TKGR commons, concerns its enforceability by means of national and international law.[64]

In this respect, biocultural protocols could play an essential role.[65] They could function as an expression of the traditional customary laws and values and at the same time stipulate the terms and conditions regulating access of noncommercial use. Although it could be expected that the terms and conditions of different commons platforms will not be completely uniform, there are certain conditions that will figure in the majority of the TKGR commons platforms, if not in all.[66]

A major point that needs to be clarified is the definition of the term 'noncommercial use'. The definition/delimitation of this term has become

---

[63] Bavikatte, K, Jonas, H., 'Biocultural Community Protocols: A Community Approach to Ensuring the Integrity of Environmental Law and Policy', Asian Biotechnology & Development Rev, Vol 12 (2010), pp. 49–76.

[64] See also Ostrom, E., *Governing the Commons: The Evolution of Institutions for Collective Actions*, Cambridge: Cambridge University Press (1990). Another interesting approach is that of Oldham, E., 'An Access and Benefit-Sharing Commons?', Initiative for the Prevention of Biopiracy, Research Documents, Year IV, No 11 (2008), available at http://ssrn.com/abstract=1438027.

[65] For biocultural protocols and their application see Herrera, H., 'Panama Case-Study – Kuna and Embera-Wounaan Medicinal Knowledge & Access Protocols' in Song, Y. Pant, R. Li, J. Swiderska, K. Argumedo, A. Vedavathy, S. Herrera, H. Mutta, D. Munyi, P. (eds), *Protecting Community Rights over Traditional Knowledge: Key Findings and Recommendations 2005–2009*. London: International Institute for Environment and Development (2009), pp. 17–18.

[66] See also Lu, F., 'The Commons in Amazonian Context', in Nonini, D.M. (ed.), *The Global Idea of the Commons*, New York: Berghahn Books (2007), pp. 41–52. See also Scharper, S.B., Cunningham, H., 'The Genetic Commons: Resisting the Neo-Liberal Enclosure of Life' in Nonini, D.M. (ed), *The Global Idea of the Commons*, New York: Berghahn Books (2007), pp. 53–6.

much more complicated since universities, until recently the natural fora of noncommercial research, now have the right to own, patent and license inventions.[67] The biocultural protocol could thus define 'noncommercial use' on the basis of, for instance, the patent application or a published scientific article.

A researcher, a research institute or even a private entity would not have to contact and negotiate with the indigenous communities (holders of TKGR) but instead, after reading and approving the terms and conditions, would automatically acquire a PIC. Any subsequent use or further elaboration of the TKGR that could be considered commercial would have to be subject to negotiation with the TKGR holders. The procedure could be simplified even further by providing the licence in online platforms and databases. Any subsequent use of the TKGR in research would require a copy of the licence.

Such an 'automatic' licence structure would be suited for TKGR that does not require interaction with the natural environment or the indigenous communities. Should research require such interaction, there would be a need to proceed to a negotiation of an ABS agreement.

As has previously been shown, the enforceability of such agreements is very often questioned. Obviously, a major difference between a TKGR commons licence and a Creative Commons licence is that the latter bases its enforceability on the underlying copyright legislation. Since TKGR currently lacks internationally accepted *sui generis* or other IP protection, such a licence scheme will be weak. Developing extensive codes of conduct to be adopted by research institutes and universities worldwide could provide a means of indirect enforcement.

Licences may of course incorporate self-enforcement clauses such as 'break one, lose all'. Accordingly, should a researcher not comply with an accepted TKGR commons licence, the entire institution may be disqualified from accessing TKGR on the commons platform. An indirect weakness of the enforceability of TKGR commons is the burden of proof of misappropriation. The appropriate means of providing for a more effective enforceability of the TKGR commons licence is to place the burden with those accessing or using TKGR.

To provide for an illustration of the benefits of such a system, one could test its application in the case of the hoodia bioprospecting agreement. In this specific case, Phytopharm has not been able to launch

[67] In the US, in accordance with the Bayh–Dole Act (1980), universities can patent the results of state-funded research. Every research university in the US owns its own technology management office.

a commercial application of the research results, while at the same time the initial holders of TKGR have no access to the Phytopharm research. Since the benefits in the specific agreement were related to the commercialisation of end products, the bioprospecting agreement did not reward those elaborating TKGR. The initial rightholders of TKGR are thus left with no opportunity to further exploit their resources, and no possibility to negotiate with third parties. It seems that in the traditional bioprospecting model, a specific TKGR may be easily neutralised.

The Nagoya Protocol's contribution in this respect is very interesting. Its proposal, in Article 10, of the alternative of a global multilateral benefit-sharing mechanism for TKGR for which it is not possible to acquire PIC,[68] opens up space for a broader use of a TKGR commons.

6.4.3 Fairness and Efficiency in Liability Rules for TKGR

TKGR holders who share the same characteristics as the followup innovators that have invested time and resources in the development of innovative mechanisms and uses run the risk of losing the means to compensate their investment, whereas free riders are able to use the innovation without a legal framework regulating such use. At the core of TKGR development lies a form of community work in which individuals use material that is part of the public domain while making small contributions and further adjustments. There is a continuing cumulative innovative process taking place within a societal structure comparable to that of 'research commons'.

Liability rules are formed in a way that places a restricted burden on the parties to the bargain, allowing for a higher rate of success of the bargaining process. Negotiating exclusive property rights, on the other hand, presupposes well-informed, rational and self-interested parties. Liability rules have sometimes proven beneficial to small-scale innovators and could be applicable to holders of TKGR, providing the fundamental right to compensation. In exchange for this compensation, innovators make their work available to other innovators and potential users of their know-how.

Liability rules guarantee access to innovation on the basis of a predefined exchange platform. With regard to small-scale innovation, royalties will be quite limited.[69] Thus, liability rules work in the same

---

[68] A multilateral mechanism reminiscent of that stipulated in ITPGRFA.

[69] According to Lewis, T., Reichman, J., 'Using Liability Rules to Stimulate Local Innovation in Developing Countries: Application to Traditional Knowledge', in Maskus, K.E., Reichman, J. (eds), *International Public Goods and*

way as automatic licensing. There is an advantage simply in the fact that both the basic innovation and all forthcoming improvements on the innovation are open to all under liability rule provisions allowing for cooperation in the layer to layer development of technology.

Liability rules should be formed in such a way as to sanction wholesale duplication of the innovation during the period of time that follows the release of the invention to the public. According to Lewis and Reichman,[70] the period during which the innovator enjoys this reinforced protection should be equivalent to the lead time enjoyed by innovators when a product's structure and technology is not so transparent to imitators. A compensatory liability regime (CLR) would not run counter to the provisions of the TRIPS Agreement. A CLR system can, to the contrary, allow for a stronger property rights system, preventing any lowering of the patentability thresholds to accommodate the need to protect small-scale innovation, subpatentable inventions and subject matter such as the TKGR.

As has been discussed elsewhere in this book, TKGR seems to include three different stages of development. The first stage is 'raw' TKGR, which is TKGR in its pure form, kept inside the tribe's structures. In the second stage, TKGR is made available for public scientific research. The third and final stage is that in which TKGR is under commercial exploitation. In its initial state, TKGR is clearly not a protectable subject matter under IP rights. On the other hand, TKGR falling under stages two and three, as presented above, could be covered by a 'research commons' status rather than that of the public domain. Here, compensatory liability is an adequate form of protection. The duration of protection and the level of compensation should take into consideration the special character of TKGR, as well as the duration of the entire innovation process. Under the terms and during the period stipulated, TKGR holders will be awarded compensation for all commercial applications. Lewis and Reichman contemplated that those investing in the commercial or industrial application could not prevent others from investing in further applications; thus, TKGR holders would retain a right to compensation for all subsequent uses of their know-how.[71] In this respect it is also necessary to consider that some forms of TK are easier to commercialise than others. TK in artifacts is easier to commercialise directly. Such genetic resources that are embodied in pharmaceutical and biotech research need

Transfer of Technology under a Globalized Intellectual Property Regime, Cambridge: Cambridge University Press (2005), pp. 337–66.

[70] Lewis and Reichman (2005).

[71] Lewis and Reichman (2005).

the technology and know-how of pharmaceutical and biotech companies to reach customers and thus to generate income. Thus the incentive to provide access to companies and sign an access and benefit-sharing agreement is bigger, since alternative methods of commercialisation are very limited: either it is done through the intervention of a pharma company or there is no commercialisation at all. Apart from the pure technological constraints, opportunities to exploit TCEs directly are also boosted by the way the IP system works. TCEs are protected by means of copyright, where there is no need for a cumbersome registration procedure and no need for expensive fees, while technological TK could only find protection under the patent system – a complicated and expensive system of protection. Pharmaceutical research based on TKGR might in fact represent the highest value in the field of bioprospecting. It is also an area of bioprospecting that entails the highest risks in terms of holdup strategies. It is thus important to regulate at least this TKGR category.

A compensatory liability regime seems able to overcome major problematic issues related to the protection of TKGR. It facilitates access to TKGR and provides incentives for its conservation and sustainable use. Potential users of TKGR can gain access without having to enter into cumbersome negotiations, try to find the relevant rightholder or enter debate as to the value of TKGR. Furthermore, one party's access to a certain commercial application of TKGR will not exclude others interested in another commercial application. All subsequent applications and uses will return a percentage of the profits to the initial rightholders.

Though it seems that both fairness and efficiency would be safeguarded under this specific entitlement structure, liability rules might prove problematic if not modelled under a scheme similar to that proposed by Lewis and Reichman. Under 'normal' liability rules, parties wishing to engage in bioprospecting activities would not be required to ask for the authorisation or permission of the rightholders, but would proceed to access, use and compensation. Such a remedy might be unsatisfactory in cases where TKGR rightholders will wish to keep the specific subject matter 'out of the market', for religious, traditional or other reasons. Furthermore, such an alternative seems to circumvent the fundamental PIC requirement.

Nevertheless, the Mill Act (discussed at 5.1.4.3) created a liability regime that actually provided for preliminary authorisation to be acquired by the mill constructor before proceeding with the project.[72] A similar procedure could be imaginable for TKGR, where PIC may be required

[72] See section 1.4.3 in Chapter 5 of the thesis.

and environmental concerns may be discussed in relation to the specific TKGR. In the case of the Mill Act, the courts granted authorisation; in the case of TKGR the ABS Clearing House Mechanism could be used, operating under the Nagoya Protocol.

The multilateralism proposed by the ITPGRFA, presenting characteristics of a commons regime, might also be applied as a typical model of a liability regime. States are provided with a legal platform recognised on an international level, where they may submit crop genetic resources and at the same time access genetic resources on prespecified terms. The ITPGRFA thus provides the opportunity to share crops with very limited transaction costs, under a foreseeable legal regime and with an appreciated degree of transparency. In this respect the specific model resembles other IP pools.[73] The scope of this multilateral model of crop exchange could be extended to cover crop resources other than the 64 envisaged in the ITPGRFA by including *ex situ* collections of genetic resources. Although there are positive aspects to an extension of the multilateral system, such an initiative would have to consider rather complicated legal questions, related to, for instance, the legal status and ownership of resources found in *ex situ* collections before the entry into force of the CBD.

Evaluating the Multilateral System is not easy, despite its having been in place for 15 years. Apart from the fact that it only regulates access and benefit sharing of a very limited number of plant genetic resources, taking into consideration that the development of a new plant variety takes between seven to ten years to achieve, there is still very limited experience on benefit-sharing payments. The FAO has encouraged member states to make voluntary payments to the benefit-sharing fund. In fact, Norway contributes 0.1 per cent of its national seed sales to the fund. These voluntary contributions, although signs of an important trend, are currently very limited. Up to 2011, the voluntary payments accounted for a modest 13.7 per cent of the preset target for the period of July 2009 to December 2014.[74] The limited reports of benefit-sharing input under the framework of the Multilateral System have contributed to developing countries' reluctance to embrace this system and in some cases have even led to threats that they will leave the Multilateral System as a whole should the benefit-sharing system not prove to be balanced

[73] Such as, for instance, patent pools in the telecom sector.

[74] Chiarolla, C., Jugcurt, S., Outstanding Issues on Access and Benefit Sharing under the Multilateral System of the International Treaty on Plant Genetic Resources for Food and Agriculture, Zurich: Berne Declaration & Oslo Development Fund (2011).

enough.[75] The role of a multilateral system on benefit-sharing has also been pinpointed in Article 10 of the Nagoya Protocol.

The development of a system for the management of TKGR and sharing of benefits on the basis of a liability paradigm has in some cases been described as the utilisation model, or 'paying when using'. What this model entails is a pure liability regime. Users are allowed access, while rightholders may not make use of holdup strategies. Access in itself does not generate the right to benefit sharing. It is the use that creates the right to compensation, and it is thus users' responsibility to follow up and compensate in a fair and equitable way. A fundamental prerequisite for such a system is of course defining what constitutes 'use' and what does not. Is it the commercialisation, the application of IP rights, or market authorisation to put the product on the market that in fact constitutes use? The CBD remains silent in this respect. On the other hand, the Nagoya Protocol might bring some guidance. The checkpoints provided for in the Nagoya Protocol might also support a definition of the term 'utilisation'. In that case utilisation includes all acts that contribute to placing the product on the market, such as market authorisation and research funding. On the other hand, taking into consideration the fact that the Nagoya Protocol remains silent as to the role of IPRs, patent and other IP applications for registration will not be considered as use under this rationale. The Nagoya Protocol places the burden of regulation, PIC and benefit-sharing provisions on the providers of TKGR, not on the users. Although users have to be able to prove compliance, this compliance is to be tested in relation to national legislation on ABS and the provisions of bioprospecting agreements, not in relation to an internationally accepted benefit-sharing standard.[76]

6.4.4 Fairness and Efficiency in Rewarding TKGR

The CBD provisions related to TKGR protection, as well as present regional and national implementation initiatives, reiterate a number of objectives and priorities in a future legal entitlement on TKGR, namely to:

- respect, preserve and maintain TKGR;
- promote the wider application of TKGR;

---

[75] See for instance International Institute for Sustainable Development, 'ITPGR GB 3 Final', Earth Negotiations Bulletin (3 July 2009).

[76] De Jonge, B., 'Towards a Fair and Equitable ABS Regime: Is Nagoya Leading Us in the Right Direction?', Law, Environment and Development J, Vol 9 (2013), p. 241.

- encourage the equitable sharing of the benefits;
- provide for the recognition of the source of TKGR.

Sui generis rights on TKGR are very often structured under the principles of a reward system, at least in part. The state manages access to genetic resources and thus to a large extent to traditional knowledge, and decides on the terms and conditions of bioprospecting agreements. Indigenous communities, on the other hand, are attributed the right to be named as the 'source' of traditional knowledge and receive financial benefits, while also benefiting indirectly through national conservation and sustainable use projects taking place in their lands. The management of 'fair and equitable sharing of the benefits' is very often conducted on the basis of a trust fund, comparable to a reward system fund. Experience thus provides proof of the suitability of a reward-based entitlement for the protection of TKGR. The reward system would presuppose a stringent regulation of the relation between the official state of the country of origin and the indigenous communities. Necessary prerequisites for the successful application of such a system are of course respect for the rights of indigenous communities on the part of the state and the active participation of indigenous communities' representatives in decisions affecting their lands, resources and TK.

One of the major critiques of the reward system in general concerns its financing. However, while traditional reward systems are financed by means of taxation, a TKGR reward system could be financed by means of the benefits of bioprospecting agreements. The amount of the reward could increase depending on the commercial or R&D interest in the specific subject matter, the estimated commercial value and the industrial applications of the TKGR in question.

In conclusion, a reward system seems to be an attractive alternative for TKGR protection. It allows the state to concentrate and manage rights to TKGR without depriving indigenous communities of their right to compensation, while at the same time keeping transaction costs to a minimum.[77] In this respect, the contribution of the Nagoya Protocol is without a doubt considerable. However, even in the post-Nagoya era there are still certain difficulties that need to be taken into account. In order to apply the Nagoya Protocol and control compliance one has to decide who the rightholder is (which indigenous communities, which states) and what is in fact indigenous/traditional knowledge. These are, of

[77] See also Chennells, R., 'Traditional Knowledge and Benefit Sharing after the Nagoya Protocol: Three Cases from South Africa', Law, Environment and Development J, Vol 9 (2013), p. 163.

course, difficult decisions that have to be taken by national authorities with no or very limited experience in the field. Important questions that need to be answered include, for instance, for how many years should the traditional knowledge be used by the community, what happens if traditional knowledge is shared, and what happens should only some of the rightholders give their consent, not all?

The concentration of the rights to TKGR, covering its tangible and intangible aspects, would achieve a number of the objectives stipulated in the CBD, while avoiding some of the defects in the management of rights to TKGR. It would provide bioprospectors with a one-stop shop solution and thus would not burden indigenous communities with the negotiating and signing of bioprospecting agreements. National governmental agencies would thus develop the necessary expertise to successfully negotiate and enforce ABS agreements. In addition, it would considerably avoid hindrances to bioprospecting caused by the fragmentation of rights and would allow for long-term planning and management of TKGR on a state level. Such an alternative seems very attractive, but it presupposes states' respect for the rights of indigenous communities.

6.5 CONCLUDING REMARKS

Previous parts of this book have had the objective of presenting the reality – practical cases in which the lack of TKGR leads to undesirable effects such as market failure, biopiracy and hindrances to access. The mapping and analysis of relevant international conventions and treaties, both in the field of genetic resources protection and in that of IPRs, has constituted an important part of the discussion. Finally, regional and national protection initiatives have been critically analysed in order to extract valuable lessons regarding what should and should not be done in the elaboration of a future TKGR entitlement.[78] The divergent views on the theoretical framework related to the justifications, legal content and management of different entitlements reveal one of the difficulties in this, namely the lack of a uniform approach to the definition of what constitutes a property right or how common property is regulated. Another central question is what we mean by the term TKGR 'protection'. In the Western world, protection is in principle equivalent to the grant of some form of exclusive rights giving the rightholders the means

---

[78] Dagne, T., 'Protecting Traditional Knowledge in International Intellectual Property Law: Imperatives for Protection and Choice of Modalities', J Marshall Rev Intell Prop L, Vol 14 (2014), pp. 25.

to reap some form of benefit. However, protection might even concern measures for the preservation of TKGR, allowing rightholders to continue living in the traditional way that initially gave rise to the development of TK.

It is interesting to note that preservation or conservation of TK is in fact not possible (contrary to what might be the case for genetic resources), since TK is an aspect of living cultures and thus is continuously evolving and changing. Pausing TK practices in order to protect them is not even desirable if the objective is to let the practices continue to evolve. Attempting to keep culture in a static state of purity is in fact a reminder of the cultural oppressions of the colonial past. In any case, it should be up to the TK holders to decide whether their way of living, and thus their TK practices, will continue to exist, be abandoned or be mixed with the Western way of living; the Western world should not seek to make this decision.[79]

Codification (documentation of TK) might in fact contribute to preserving valuable knowledge, respecting at the same time that this must evolve or even disappear in its natural habitat. Of course, such a process needs to take into consideration the special needs and characteristics of the TK holders in question. It might be found that in some cases codification is much too disruptive for certain indigenous communities, and in these cases it should be avoided.

Despite this extensive analysis of the general legal framework on TKGR protection, it remains difficult to propose an optimal solution to the TKGR market failure. One size does not fit all, and the variations in innovative contribution and in the customary status of TKGR (sacred or not) should have an impact on the entitlement to be introduced. We are definitely moving towards a pluralist approach to the protection of TKGR, as it is not possible to provide for one form of protection fitting all TKGR scenarios. Furthermore, the 'exclusivity' of TKGR in the specific jurisdiction is also an important factor to be taken into account. When valuable TKGR is found only in a specific region, under one specific national jurisdiction, this certainly has an impact not only on its bioprospecting value but also on the choice of the appropriate entitlement with which to protect it.

It would be interesting to relate the points in the preceding discussion to the questions posed in the introductory part of the book, and attempt to answer them.

---

[79] Waldron, J., 'What Is Cosmopolitan', J Political Philosophy, Vol 8 (2000), pp. 227–32.

6.5.1 What Is the Scope and Content of the Constraints and Requirements Placed on the Elaboration of a TKGR Entitlement by Means of Binding International Agreements?

Analysing the binding International Agreements gives the discussion of elaboration of a TKGR entitlement a rather optimistic starting point. The main international treaty in the field, the CBD, stipulates the general objectives of such an entitlement: sovereign rights of states of origin over genetic resources, the fair and equitable sharing of benefits arising thereof and the protection of indigenous peoples. The CBD provides neither the means nor the character or form of the entitlement. Noncompliance with the provisions is not sanctioned and the Convention does not include a dispute settlement resolution system. The FAO legal framework, with ITPGR as a central treaty, might be used in a complementary way, but only for a limited amount of TKGR. On the other hand, analysing the impact of international IPR treaties is necessary since the future TKGR entitlement should be in compliance with the applicable IP system, if not part of it. Proposing radical changes to the IP system in order to accommodate the specific needs of TKGR protection seems a rather unrealistic approach. The introduction of a disclosure requirement will, it seems, be limited in strength, offering a monitoring of uses rather than positive protection for TKGR.

That being said, the current text of the TRIPS Agreement includes flexibilities that could accommodate, at least partly, TKGR protection considerations. The new system could include the possibility to classify TKGR as prior art, to protect it as a subpatentable invention or to propose a liability system, all of which are TRIPS-compliant alternatives.

Compatibility with the current IP system is probably the only concrete constraint to the elaboration of a TKGR entitlement. The vagueness and flexibilities left by international treaties related to TKGR protection allow for broad manoeuvring possibilities. However, on the other hand, the same flexibilities constitute a source of difficulty in the implementation process.

6.5.2 What Are the Experiences of the National and Regional Initiatives in the Elaboration of a TKGR Entitlement, Which Were the Choices Made, What Was the Outcome and to What Extent Were Available Flexibilities Taken into Account?

An internationally recognised and harmonised TKGR protection regime is obviously of major importance. In fact, the value of a TKGR entitlement is folded into its international character. The reported market failures and biopiracy cases all occur on an international level. Experiences on the national and regional levels provide useful information regarding how CBD implementation proceeds, its difficulties and potentials and the CBD entitlement's relation to the IP system. One general conclusion is that national and regional initiatives often create a system of protection without explicitly examining the overall objectives of protection and the practical implication of the set requirements. National and regional TKGR entitlements relate directly or indirectly to the national patent system, thus creating a link between the two, while at the same time the TKGR entitlement is, in the majority of cases, placed within the realm of authorities other than the national patent offices. A number of other governmental authorities are involved, the protection of TKGR being an indirect effect of a stringent system of multiple players in the area of access authorisation rather than an explicitly stipulated entitlement.

An interesting and valuable conclusion to be drawn by regional and national legislation is that TKGR can be divided into different categories, in turn to be protected in different ways. This categorisation, stated more explicitly in some cases than in others, constitutes an important starting point in the elaboration of a TKGR entitlement. Some forms of TKGR are best protected *e contrario* as 'prior art' hindrances to IP registrations, while others constitute forms of innovation to be protected by a traditional or *sui generis* right. Finally, there could be TKGR which, for religious, cultural or other reasons, should be kept outside market transactions and bioprospecting as a whole, best protected by secrecy.

6.5.3 Is There a Possibility to Proceed to a Systematisation of the Principles and Objectives to Rule the Process of the Elaboration of a New Entitlement, in this Case on TKGR?

Systematisation of principles and objectives in the elaboration of a new entitlement such as that of TKGR is of vital importance. The lack of guidance on the implementation of overarching principles and objectives in the elaboration of TKGR is illustrated in the regional and national TKGR protection initiatives as well in the bioprospecting agreements.

It seems impossible to successfully introduce a new entitlement if one is not sure of the objectives the entitlement is to fulfil. Taking into consideration the vagueness and flexibilities of the international treaties, an *ab initio* approach, where all alternative forms of protection are examined, is necessary.

The starting point of such a discussion unquestionably lies with the fundamental question of whether a new entitlement is needed and, if so, why. The instrumentalist argument, considering that TKGR holders will continue investing in their traditional innovations when they are awarded exclusive rights, has dominated the post-CBD negotiations. Taking into consideration the way traditional knowledge has evolved to date, there is a rather low probability that this incentive is so strong with regard to this specific subject matter. On the other hand, it certainly may provide an incentive to member states for the preservation of biodiversity and of the traditional lifestyles of indigenous communities, since this might be a source of revenue not only for the communities themselves but also for the member states.

Under the same instrumentalist approach we find yet another interesting argument, namely that, should TK holders be awarded a form of protection under the IP system on an international level, they will place more trust in the system as a whole and would be even more willing to make their knowledge and resources accessible. This same approach could also apply as an incentive to codify TK, according to which, if there is an efficient protection system for documented TK, TK holders will be willing to codify and publish their knowledge.

In this respect, one could in fact adopt the approach suggested by Calabresi and Melamed.[80] As a matter of fact, the evaluation of the regional and national implementation of the CBD reveals the lack of a systematic approach that would establish: (1) whether there is a need for a new legal entitlement; (2) which objectives/purposes this entitlement would satisfy; (3) the overriding principles; and (4) who the beneficiaries of the legal entitlement would be.

The lack of such a systematic and analytical approach in the national and regional TKGR-related legislation has, in a number of cases, provided for unclear and fragmented legal entitlements and numerous layers of rightholders with unspecified intrarelations.

The protection of TKGR has, to a large extent, been treated as yet another form of subpatentable/subcopyrightable intangible assets and has as such been automatically placed under the scope of the property rights system. Such a tendency is present both in the implementation initiatives and in the TKGR-related CBD and TRIPS negotiations. Property rules in the TKGR field are very often structured in different layers, imposing cumbersome procedures of access for potential users. TKGR, subject some decades ago to a 'tragedy of the commons' regime, seems to be

---

[80] Calabresi, G., Melamed, A.D., 'Property Rules, Liability Rules and Inalienability: One View of the Cathedral', Harv L Rev, Vol 85 (1972), pp. 1089–128.

suffering an emerging 'tragedy of the anticommons' similar to that illustrated by Heller.[81]

The answer to Calabresi and Melamed's first question would be: yes, the market failures in the TKGR market are such that they would require 'lifting' from the public domain. This has already been done by means of the CBD on an international convention level. The second question is more complicated. For the purposes of this book and for reasons earlier discussed, the principles/objectives of TKGR protection could in fact be fairness and efficiency. Fairness and efficiency are also the answer to the question related to the overriding principles of the system. The most problematic issue to clarify is how to provide for the practical applications of these principles, and who the beneficiaries are to be.

At first glance, property rights seem an inappropriate form of protection for the main body of TKGR. There is certainly TKGR that is closer to subpatentable innovation, attributable to specific individuals that thus benefit from a property regime such as the one envisioned in the Thai and Portuguese legislation. But in most cases, property rights-inspired entitlements on TKGR fail the efficiency and fairness test. The cumbersome procedures imposed due to the different layers of property rights granted, the unclear rules of representation of different rightholders and the weak enforcement provisions increase transaction costs to the extent that bioprospecting becomes a prohibitive endeavour.[82]

The recent developments in international negotiations and the adoption of the Nagoya Protocol confirm one concern presented in this book, namely the prohibitive transaction costs that national and regional implementation initiatives have inflicted on the TKGR market. In an attempt to limit transaction costs in TKGR trade, the Nagoya Protocol provides for an obligation to make available to the ABS Clearing House Mechanism all information of relevance to ABS on the national or regional level.[83] Another means of providing for limited transaction costs

---

[81] Heller, Michael A., 'The Tragedy of the Anticommons: Property in the Transition from Marx to Markets', Harv L Rev, Vol 111 (1998), pp. 621–88.

[82] On the tragedy of the anticommons in modern patent rights, see Domeij, B., 'Patent och innovationsprocessens avtal', NIR, Vol 2 (2012), pp. 122–40. In his article, Domeij proposes alternative means of remedying 'anticommons' effects that the patent system might inflict, such as for instance the possibility of placing patents under some kind of management structure where the patentholder can state the royalty price, thus resembling a 'creative commons structure'.

[83] Nagoya Protocol, Art 17(1)(a)(iv), providing that the information to be available should include information on legislative, administrative and policy measures on ABS and permits or their equivalent issued at the time of access as

is by using the Multilateral System introduced by means of ITPGRFA. This will of course only be of limited application, taking into consideration the limited scope of crops included.[84] Since enforcement of TK holders' rights is still, even after the positive contributions of the Nagoya Protocol, not always addressed (even if there were necessary legal means to efficiently enforce TK rights in jurisdictions of use, indigenous communities or countries of origin might not have the financial means or the expertise to pursue enforcement), codification of TGKR will contribute to enhanced accessibility and thus potentially also to broader misappropriation by third parties. The lack of accessibility of such knowledge provides an incentive for interested parties to come into contact with and negotiate ABS agreements. Isolating TK from its natural environment is not only reminiscent of colonial practices but also deprives it of its special character. At the same time, one should not undermine the extensive costs that a codification project entails if it is to be done properly. The question is who is to bear such costs, and whose interests it serves.

6.5.4 To What Extent Would the Present Objectives and Principles Assist in the Process and What Outcome Would They Have for TKGR Protection?

With the categorisation of different forms of TKGR innovation in the background, the application of present principles and objectives will be of considerable assistance in forming and managing a new entitlement. Principles and objectives will also provide guidance as to the fundamental question of whether protection/entitlement is needed or whether the market itself can solve the externalities in the long run. In this book, fairness and efficiency has been the starting point in the discussion of the choice between property rules and liability. Though the property paradigm has been chosen as the natural forum for diplomatic negotiations and academic debates, it seems that liability rules could provide for a better adapted alternative.

---

evidence of the decision to grant PIC. Even additional information such as relevant competent authorities, model contractual clauses codes of conduct and best practices may be required.

[84] M. Halewood et al, 'Implementing "Mutually Supportive" Access and Benefits Sharing Mechanisms under the Plant Treaty, Convention on Biological Diversity, and Nagoya Protocol', Law, Env & Development J, Vol 9 (2013), pp. 68–96.

Liability rules might grant a more adequate protection framework, especially in markets with high transaction costs, such as the bioprospecting market. Property rights to TKGR might hinder efficient accommodation of rights due to increased transaction costs. Access and use of TKGR may thus become subject to direct or indirect holdout strategies. On the other hand, liability deprives rightholders of the opportunity to deny access or to dictate specific rules for specific cases of access. Thus, a liability system for TKGR should presuppose an initial choice on the part of rightholders (indigenous peoples, states, etc) as to which resources will be made available under terms of 'pay after access'. A reward system could also, to some extent, be an appropriate means of protection for TKGR. Communities would be rewarded for their contribution to the elaboration and conservation of TKGR. In fact, TKGR attributed to specific individuals and presenting the same characteristics as other subpatentable innovations would find adequate protection in a *sui generis* exclusive right regime. In this respect, experiences from plant varieties that have previously tested *sui generis* rights in databases should be employed. A reward system could easily protect collective innovation and TKGR as the result of a community's traditional know-how. It could also protect that part of TKGR that would clearly otherwise be considered as part of the public domain. The Thai and Portuguese legislation has divided TKGR into different categories and provided for different forms of protection depending on their level of inventive character and their novelty.

A possible alternative could be a combination of a liability regime and a rewards system. A liability regime would be applicable on the state bioprospector level, while a reward system would apply in the relations between the state/source country and the indigenous communities. The state would thus be able to concentrate all rights to TKGR while rewarding indigenous communities for their contribution. It is obvious that the efficiency and fairness of such an approach is to a great extent dependent on the internal political situation of the state in question and the relations between the official state and its indigenous communities.

Such an alternative would provide an effective remedy to one of the national and regional TKGR protection initiatives' most important problems: overregulation. The majority of the national and regional TKGR entitlements discussed in previous parts of the book provide proof of a 'tragedy of the anticommons'. Further evidence of this concern is also found in the evaluation of bioprospecting agreements. By creating a two-level form of management of TKGR rights, one internal (state–indigenous communities–landowners) and the other external (state–bioprospector), it would be possible to provide for a more accessible system of ABS and TKGR protection.

The beneficiaries of the system will have to vary along with the variations presented by the TKGR present.[85] Naturally, indigenous communities and the country of origin are beneficiaries that could not be circumvented.

Proposing the best alternative protection system for TKGR is not an easy endeavour. It involves a multitude of rightholders whose interests are often colliding, a very special form of subject matter varying in value and degree of innovation, a demanding and highly competitive international market and a number of international, regional and national regulations with direct or indirect applicability. This book does not claim to have contributed to the elaboration of a new, ready to use TKGR entitlement. That was neither its initial goal nor its main focus.

The goal and ambition was to provide for an alternative form of reasoning in the elaboration of a new entitlement and to show that there is great value in resorting to theoretical models in order to find support for justifications, overall objectives and the principles to be fulfilled by a new entitlement. TKGR provides an excellent opportunity to test how systematisation may assist and provide guidance in the elaboration of an entitlement to be employed in a very complicated and politically loaded environment.

Providing for an alternative way of thinking when elaborating new entitlements, deviating from the usual practice of copying and pasting from other *sui generis* rights (which did not work in the first place) and allowing indepth analysis of what different forms of entitlements entail and encompass (i.e. what is a property right, what rights does it include, etc) could offer decision makers and rightholders a fresh approach to a very often autopilot-type procedure of providing for remedies to market failures by establishing exclusive rights.

And for that matter, TKGR protection is only a paradigm.

---

85 See also Table 6.1.

Bibliography

ARTICLES, REVIEWS AND OTHER DOCUMENTS

Abott, F., 'Preservation and Use of Genetic Resource Assets and the International Patent System', study for the Ministry of Foreign Affairs of Norway, Draft of March 31, 2005, rev. 1.2, Hong Kong Ministerial Revision (2005).

Adelstein, R., 'Equity and Efficiency in Markets for Ideas', Connecticut J Int Law, Vol 17 (2001–2), pp. 1–14.

Adi, B., 'Intellectual Property Rights in Biotechnology and the Fate of Poor Farmers' Agriculture', Lagos Business School, University of Tsukuba (13 January 2005), pp. 91–112.

Alston, J., Venner, R.J., 'The Effects of the US Plant Variety Protection Act on Wheat Genetic Improvement', Research Policy, Vol 31(4) (2002), pp. 527–42.

Amiott, J., 'Environment, Equality and Indigenous Peoples' Land Rights in the Inter-American Human Rights System', Envtl L (2002), pp. 873–903.

Anderson, T., Hill, P., 'The Race for Property Rights', J Law Econ, Vol 33 (1990), pp. 177–97.

Anderson, T., Hill, P., 'Cowboys and Contracts', J Legal Studies, Vol 31 (2002), pp. 489–514.

Aoki, K., 'Neocolonialism, Anticommons Property, and Biopiracy in the (Not-so-Brave) New World Order of International Intellectual Property Protection', Ind J Global Legal Studies, Vol 6 (1998), pp. 11–58.

Apreda, R., 'Underlying Counterfactual Conditionals in Rawls' "Justice as Fairness" – How the Overlapping Consensus Becomes Functional to the Original Position', Universidad del CEMA Documento de Trabajo No 238 (June 2003), pp. 1–19.

Ayres, I., Talley, E., 'Solomonic Bargaining: Dividing a Legal Entitlement to Facilitate Coasean Trade', Yale LJ, Vol 104 (1995), pp. 1027–1117.

Barbier, E.B., Aylward, B.A., 'Capturing the Pharmaceutical Value of Biodiversity in a Developing Country', Environment and Resource Economics, Vol 8(2) (1996), pp. 157–81.

Bebchuk, L.A., 'Property Rights and Liability Rules: The Ex Ante View of the Cathedral', Michigan L Rev, Vol 100 (2001), pp. 601–39.

Beitz, C.R., 'Rawls' Law of Peoples', Ethics, Vol 110(4) (July 2000), pp. 669–96.

Bell, A., Parchomovsky, G., 'What Property Is', Research Paper No 04-05, Institute for Law and Economics (February 2004), pp. 1–85.

Benkler, Y., 'Coase's Penguin, or, Linux and the Nature of the Firm', Yale LJ, Vol 112 (2002), pp. 369–446.

Blakeney, M., 'Bioprospecting and the Protection of Traditional Medicinal Knowledge of Indigenous Peoples: An Australian Perspective', European Int Prop Rev, Vol 19 (1997), pp. 296–303.

Blakeney, M., 'Ethnobotanological Knowledge and Intellectual Property of Rights of Indigenous Peoples in Australia', IP and Ethnobiology, Vol 17 (1999), pp. 15–157.

Blakeney, M., 'Protection of Plant Varieties and Farmers' Rights', European Int Property Rev, Vol 24 (2002), pp. 9–19.

Blaser, A., 'The Common Heritage in Its Infinite Variety: Space Law and the Moon in the 1990s', J Law and Technology, Vol 5 (1990), pp. 79–99.

Bordwin, H., 'The Legal and Political Implications of the International Undertaking on Plant Genetic Resources', Ecology LQ, Vol 12 (1985), pp. 1053–69.

Borris, R., 'Natural Products Research: Perspectives from a Major Pharmaceutical Company', J Ethnopharmacology, Vol 51 (1996), pp. 29–38.

Bosch-Domenech, A., Silvestre, J., 'Does Risk Aversion or Attraction Depend on Income?', Economics Letters, Vol 65 (1999), pp. 265–73.

Bosselman, K., 'Plants and Politics: The International Legal Regime Concerning Biotechnology and Biodiversity', Colorado J Int Env Law and Policy, Vol 18 (1995), pp. 111–48.

Brewer, A., 'Adam Smith's Stages of History', University of Bristol, Department of Economics, Discussion Paper No 08/601 (March 2008), pp. 1–24.

Bromley, D., 'Debunking Wholesale Enforcement of Environmental Rights', Harvard Journal of Law and Public Policy, Vol 15 (1992), pp. 311–24.

Brush, S., 'The Demise of Common Heritage and the Protection of Traditional Agricultural Knowledge', paper prepared for the Conference on Biodiversity, Biotechnology and the Protection of Traditional Knowledge, St. Louis, MO (4–5 April 2003), pp. 1–66.

Buchanan, J., Yoon, Y., 'Symmetric Tragedies: Commons and Anticommons Property', J Law Econ, Vol 29 (2000), pp. 1–13.

Byerlee, D., 'Crop Improvement in the CGIAR as a Global Success Story of Open Access and International Collaboration', Int J Commons, Vol 4(1) (2010), pp. 452–80.

Calabresi, G., 'The Decision for Accidents: An Approach to Non-Fault Allocation of Costs', Harv L Rev, Vol 78 (1965), pp. 713–45.

Calabresi, G., 'Transaction Costs, Resource Allocation and Liability Rules: A Comment', J Law Econ, Vol 67 (1968), pp. 13, 49–70.

Calabresi, G., Melamed, D., 'Property Rules, Liability Rules and Inalienability: One View of the Cathedral', Harv L Rev, Vol 85(6) (1972), pp. 1089–1128.

Calandrillo, S., 'An Economic Analysis of Property Rights in Information: Justifications and Problems of Exclusive Rights, Incentives to Generate Information, and the Alternative of a Government-Run Reward System', Fordham Intellectual Property Media & Ent LJ, Vol 9 (1998–9) pp. 301–54.

Calibrera Medaglia, J., 'Bioprospecting Partnerships in Practice: A Decade of Experiences at INBio in Costa Rica', IP Strategy Today, Vol 11 (2004), pp. 27–40.

Cameron, X., Makuch, Z., 'The UN Biodiversity Convention and the WTO TRIPS Agreement', Gland: World Wide Fund for Nature (1995).

Carbone, J., 'Back to the Future: Intellectual Property and the Rediscovery of Property Rights and Wrongs', St Louis U LJ, Vol 46 (2002), pp. 629–54.

Carvalho, N. de, 'From the Shaman's Hut to the Patent Office: How Long and Winding is the Road?' Teil 1: Revista da ABPI No 40 (1999), pp. 3–28.

Carvalho, N.P. de, 'Requiring Disclosure of the Origin of Genetic Resources and PIC in Patent Applications Without Infringing the TRIPS Agreement: The Problem and the Solution', Wash U J Law & Policy, Vol 2 (2003), pp. 371–401.

Castree, N., 'Bioprospecting: From Theory to Practice (And Back Again)', Royal Geographical Society of British Geographers, New Series, Vol 28 (2003), pp. 35–55.

Chander, A., Sunder, M., 'Is Nozick Kicking Rawls' Ass? Intellectual Property and Social Justice', UC Davis L Rev, Vol 40 (2007), pp. 563–78; UC Davis Legal Studies Research Paper No 108.

Christie, G.C., 'The Importance of Recognising the Underlying Assumptions of Legal and Moral Arguments: Of Law and Rawls', Australian J Legal Philosophy, Vol 28 (2003), pp. 39–52.

Ciriacy-Wantrup, S., Bishop, R., 'Common Property as a Concept in Natural Resources Policy', Natural Resources J, Vol 15 (October 1975), pp. 713–27.

Coase, R.H., 'The Federal Communications Commission', J Law Econ, Vol 2 (1959), pp. 1–40.
Coase, R.H., 'The Problem of Social Costs', J Law Econ, Vol 3(1) (1960), pp. 1–44.
Cocca, 'Mankind as the new Legal Subject: A New Juridical Dimension Recognized by the United Nations', *Proceedings of the 13th Colloquium on the Law of Outer Space*, Brussels (1971), pp. 211–14.
Cohen, F., 'Transcendental Nonsense and the Functional Approach', Columbia L Rev, Vol 35 (1935), pp. 809–31.
Collet, P., 'Property Rights over Biological Resources: India's Proposed Legislative Framework', J World Intellectual Property, Vol 4(2) (2001), pp. 219–22.
Columbia University School of International and Public Affairs, 'Access to Genetic Resources: an evaluation of the Development and Implementation of Recent Regulation and Access Agreements', Environmental Policy Studies, Working Paper 4, prepared for the Biodiversity Action Network (June 1999).
Coombe, R., 'Intellectual Property, Human Rights and Sovereignty: New Dilemmas in International Law Posed by the Recognition of Indigenous Knowledge and the Conservation of Biological Diversity', Indiana J Global Legal Studies, Vol 6 (1998), pp. 59–115.
Coombe, R., 'The Recognition of Indigenous Peoples and Community Traditional Knowledge in International Law', St Thomas L Rev, Vol 14 (2001), pp. 275–85.
Cooter, R., 'The Cost of Coase', J Legal Studies, Vol 11(1) (1982), pp. 1–33.
Cornish, W.R., 'European Community Directive on Database Protection', Columbia-VLA J Law & the Arts, Vol 21 (1996), pp. 1–15.
Correa, C.M., 'Biological Resources and Intellectual Property Rights', European Int Property Rev, Vol 14 (1992), pp. 154–7.
Correa, C.M., 'Sovereign and Property Rights over Plant Genetic Resources', FAO Background Study Paper No 2, Commission on Plant Genetic Resources – First Extraordinary Session (Rome, 7–11 November 1994), pp. 1–41.
Correa, C.M., 'The GATT Agreement on Trade-Related Aspects of Intellectual Property Rights: New Standards for Patent Protection', Eur Int Prop Rev, Vol 16 (1994), pp. 27–35.
Correa, C.M., 'Establishing a Disclosure of Origin Obligation in the TRIPS Agreement', Occasional Paper 12, Quaker United Nations Office (August 2003).
Correa, C.M., 'The Politics and Practicalities of a Disclosure of Origin Obligation', Occasional Paper 16, Quaker United Nations Office, Geneva (2005).

Costanza, R., D'Arge, R., Groot, R. de, Farber, S., Grasso, M., Hannon, B., Limburg, K., Naeem, S., O'Neill, R.V., Paruelo, J., Raskin, R.G., Sutton, P., Belt, M. van den, 'The Value of the World's Ecosystem Services and Natural Capital', Nature, Vol 387 (1997), pp. 253–60.

Cottier, T., 'The Protection of Genetic Resources and Traditional Knowledge: Towards More Specific Rights and Obligations in World Trade Law', J Int Econ Law, Vol 1(4) (1998), pp. 555–84.

Cottier, T., Panizzon, M., 'Legal Perspectives on Traditional Knowledge, The Case for Intellectual Property Protection', J Int Econ Law, Vol 7 (2004), pp. 371–99.

Crabb, J., 'The Environment and Values of the Legal System of Congo-Kinshasa', Wis L Rev, Vol 4 (1966), pp. 1124–34.

Croskery, P., 'Institutional Utilitarianism and Intellectual Property', Chicago-Kent L Rev, Vol 68 (1993), pp. 631–41.

Curci, J., 'The New Challenges to the International Patentability of Biotechnology: Legal Relations between the WTO Treaty on Trade-Related Aspects of Intellectual Property Rights and the Convention on Biological Diversity', Intl L & Mgmt Rev, Vol 2 (2005–6), pp. 1–42.

Dahlman, C.J., 'The Problem of Externality', J Law Econ, Vol 22 (1979), pp. 141–8.

Daly, G., 'The Coase Theorem, Assumption, Application', Economic Inquiry, Vol 12 (1974), pp. 203–13.

Dávalos, L.M., Sears, R.R., Raygorodetsky, G., Simmons, G., Cross, H., Grant, T., Putzel, L., Porzecanski, A.L., 'Regulating Access to Genetic Resources under the Convention on Biological Diversity: An Analysis of Selected Case Studies', Biodiversity and Conservation, Vol 12 (2003), pp. 1511–24.

Dagne, T., 'Protecting Traditional Knowledge in International Intellectual Property Law: Imperatives for Protection and Choice of Modalities', J Marshall Rev Intell Prop L, Vol 14 (2014), p. 25.

Demsetz, H., 'Toward a Theory of Property Rights', Am Econ Rev, Vol 57 (1967), pp. 347–59.

Demsetz, H., 'The Cost of Transacting', Quarterly J Econ, Vol 82 (1968), pp. 33–50.

Demsetz, H., 'When Does the Rule of Liability Matter?', J Legal Studies, Vol 1(1) (1972), pp. 13–28.

Domeij, B., 'Patent och innovationsprocessens avtal', NIR, Vol 2 (2012), pp. 122–40.

Donovan, E., 'Beans, the Patented Fruit: The Growing International Conflict over the Ownership of Life', Loy LA International and Comparative L Rev, Vol 25 (2002–3), pp. 117–42.

Downes, D., 'The Convention on Biological Diversity: Seeds of Green Trade?', Tulane Env LJ, Vol 163 (1994–5), pp. 163–80.

Downes, D., 'Disclosure of Origin: Time for a Reality Check?', paper presented at the ICTSD/CIEL/IDDRI/IUCN/QUNO Dialogue on Disclosure Requirements: Incorporating the CBD Principles in the TRIPS Agreement on the Road to Hong Kong, WTO Public Symposium, Geneva (21 April 2005).

Dutfield, G., 'TRIPS-Related Aspects of Traditional Knowledge', Case Western Reserve J Int L, Vol 33(2) (2001), pp. 233–49.

Dutfield, G., 'Thinking Aloud on Disclosure of Origin', Quaker United Nations Office, Occasional Paper 18 (October 2005).

Dworkin, R., 'Rawls and the Law', Fordham L Rev, Vol 72 (2003–4), pp. 1387–92.

Eisner, T., 'Prospecting for Nature's Chemical Riches', Issues in Science and Technology, Vol 6 (1990), pp. 31–34.

Ekpere, J.A., '*Sui Generis* Systems: The Case of the OAU Model Law on the Protection of the Rights of Local Communities, Farmers and Breeders and for the Regulation of Access to Biological Resources', paper presented at the International Seminar on Systems for the Protection of Traditional Knowledge, New Delhi, India (3–5 April, 2002).

Elkin-Koren, N., 'What Contracts Can't Do: The Limits of Private Ordering in Facilitating a Creative Commons', Fordham L Rev, Vol 74 (2005), pp. 376–422.

Elkins, D., 'Responding to Rawls: Toward a Consistent and Supportable Theory of Distributive Justice', BYU J Public Law, Vol 21 (2007), pp. 267–323.

Elsten, J., 'More than Enough', Univ Chicago L Rev, Vol 64 (1997), pp. 749–61.

Epstein, R.A., 'Possession as the Root of Title', GA LJ, Vol 14 (1979), pp. 1221–7.

Epstein, R.A., 'Holdouts, Externalities, and the Single Owner: One More Salute to Ronald Coase', J Law Econ, Vol 36 (1993), pp. 553–86.

Eshbach, R., 'A Global Approach to the Protection of the Environment: Balancing State Sovereignty and Global Interests', Temp Intl & Comp LJ, Vol 4 (1990), pp. 271–80.

Ewens, L., 'Seed Wars: Biotechnology, Intellectual Property and the Quest for High Yield Seeds', Int and Comp L Rev, Vol 23 (1999–2000), pp. 285–310.

Farnsworth N., Morris, R.W., 'Higher Plants – the Sleeping Giant of Drug Development', Am J Pharmacology, Vol 148 (1976), pp. 46–52.

Farrell, J., 'Information and the Coase Theorem', J Econ Perspectives, Vol 1(2) (1987), pp. 113–29.

Fidler, D., 'Neither Science nor Shamans. Globalization of Markets and Health in the Developing World', Indiana J Global Legal Studies, Vol 7 (1999), pp. 191–223.

Gámez, R., 'The Link between Biodiversity and Sustainable Development: Lessons from Inbio's Bioprospecting Program in Costa' (2003), pp. 1–15, https://www.cbd.int/financial/bensharing/costarica-absinbio.pdf.

Gámez, R., Piva A., Sittenfeld, A., Leon, E., Jimenez, J., Mirabelli, G., *Biodiversity Prospecting: Using Genetic Resources for Sustainable Development*, Washington, DC: Costa Rica Conservation Program and National Biodiversity Institute (INBio), World Resources Institute (1993).

Gana, R., 'The Myth of Development, the Progress of Rights: Human Rights to Intellectual Property and Development', Law and Policy, Vol 18(3–4) (1996), pp. 315–54.

Gardner, R., Herr, A., Ostrom, E., Walker, J.A., 'The Power and Limitations of Proportional Cutbacks in Common-Pool Resources', J Development Econ, Vol 62(2) (2000), pp. 515–33.

Gaster, J., 'The EU Council of Ministers' Common Position Concerning the Legal Protection of Databases: A First Comment', Entertainment L Rev, Vol 6(7) (1995), p. 258.

Gepts, P., 'Who Owns Biodiversity and How Should the Owners be Compensated?', Plant Physiology, Vol 134(4) (2004), pp. 1295–307.

Gervais, D., 'Intellectual Property, Trade & Development: The State of Play', Fordham L Rev (2005–6), pp. 505–34.

Geuze, M., Wager, H., 'The WTO Dispute Settlement Practice Relating to the TRIPS Agreement', J Int Econ Law, Vol 2(2) (1999), pp. 347–84.

Gibbon P., Papadopoulou, F., 'The Commodity Question: New Thinking on Old Problems', Copenhagen: UNCTAD (October 2004).

Girsberger, M., 'Transparency Measures under Patent law regarding Genetic Resources and Traditional Knowledge. Disclosure of Source and Evidence of Prior Informed Consent and Benefit-Sharing', J World Int Property, Vol 7 (2004), pp. 451–89.

Goldenberg, J., Durham, E.R., 'Amazonia and National Sovereignty', Int Env Affairs, Vol 2 (1992), p. 22.

Goldie, L., 'A General International Law Doctrine for Seabed Regimes', International Lawyer, Vol 7 (1973), pp. 796–819.

Gorove, S., 'The Concept of Common Heritage of Mankind: A Political, Moral or Legal Innovation', San Diego L Rev, Vol 9 (1972), pp. 390–402.

Greiber, T., et al, 'An Explanatory Guide to the Nagoya Protocol on Access to Genetic Resources and Traditional Knowledge', IUCN, Environmental Law and Policy Paper No 83, Bonn (2012).

Guadamuz, A., 'Legal Challenges to Open Source Licences', SCRIPT-ed, Vol 2(2) (2005), pp. 163–70.

Guell, R.C., Fischbaum, M., 'Toward Allocative Efficiency in the Prescription Drug Industry', Milbank Q, Vol 73(2) (June 1995), pp. 213–30.

Guerra, J., 'Geographical Indications, In Situ Conservation and Traditional Knowledge', ICTSD Policy Brief No 3 (November 2010).

Guntrip, E., 'The Common Heritage of Mankind: An Adequate Regime for Managing the Deep Seabed?', Melbourne J Int Law, Vol 4 (2003), pp. 376–405.

Guruswamy, L., 'Convention on Biological Diversity, Exposing the Flawed Foundations', Environmental Conservation, Vol 26(2) (1999), pp. 89–92.

Haddad, B., 'Property Rights, Ecosystem Management, and John Locke's Labour Theory of Ownership', Ecological Economics, Vol 46 (2003), pp. 19–31.

Halewood, M., et al, 'National Level of Implementation of the Multilateral System of Access and Benefit Sharing: Notes on Progress and Points of Intersection with the Convention on Biological Diversity', discussion paper presented at the workshop on the Interface between the International Treaty and the Nagoya Protocol on ABS, ABS Capacity Development Initiative, Rome (January 2013), Law, Env & Development J, Vol 9(1) (2013), p. 68.

Hardin, G., 'The Tragedy of the Commons', Science, Vol 162 (December 1968), pp. 1243–8.

Hardy, C., 'Patent Protection and Raw Materials: The Convention on Biological Diversity and its Implications for US Policy on the Development and Commercialization of Biotechnology', US Pat J Int L (1994–5), pp. 299–326.

Hedit, R., 'Maintaining Incentives for Bioprospecting: The Occasional Need for a Right to Lie', Berkeley Tech LJ, Vol 13(2) (1998), pp. 667–720.

Helfer, L.R., 'Regime Shifting: The TRIPS Agreement and the New Dynamics of International Intellectual Property Lawmaking', Yale J Int Law, Vol 29 (2004), pp. 2–81.

Heller, M.A., 'The Tragedy of the Anticommons: Property in the Transition from Marx to Markets', Harv L Rev, Vol 111 (1998), pp. 621–88.

Hendricks, B., 'Postmodern Possibility and the Convention on Biological Diversity', NYU Env LJ, Vol 5(1) (1996), pp. 1–32.

Heverly, R., 'The Information Semicommons', Berkeley Tech LJ, Vol 18 (2003), pp. 1127–89.

Hietanen, Herkko, A., 'A License or a Contract, Analyzing the Nature of Creative Commons Licenses', Nordic Int Prop LR, Vol 6 (2007), pp. 516–35.
Ho, C., 'Biopiracy and Beyond: A Consideration of Socio-Cultural Conflicts with Global Patent Policies', U Mich J Law Reform, Vol 39 (2006), pp. 433–542.
Hoffman, E., Spitzer, M., 'The Coase Theorem: Some Experimental Tests', J Law Econ, Vol 23 (1982), pp. 73–98.
Hohfeld, W., 'Fundamental Legal Conceptions as Applied in Judicial Reasoning', Yale LJ, Vol 23 (1917), pp. 16–59.
Honing-Haftel, S., Martin, L., 'The Effectiveness of Reward Systems on Innovative Output: An Empirical Analysis', Small Business Economics, Vol 5(5) (1993), pp. 261–9.
Hughes, F., 'Soviet Union Awards', Econ J, Vol 55 (1945), pp. 291–7.
Hughes, J., 'The Philosophy of Intellectual Property', Georgetown LJ, Vol 77(287) (1988–9), p. 297.
Hunter, C.J., 'Sustainable Bioprospecting: Using Private Contracts and International Legal Principles and Policies to Conserve Raw Medicinal Materials', Boston College Env Affairs L Rev, Vol 25 (1998), pp. 129–75.
Hurt, R.M., Schuchman, R.M., 'The Economic Rationale of Copyright', Am Econ Rev, Vol 56 (1996), pp. 421–32.
Hülsmann, J., 'The A Priori Foundations of Property Economics', Quarterly J Austrian Econ, Vol 7(4) (2004), pp. 41–68.
Hylton, K., 'Property Rules and Liability Rules, Once Again', Boston University School of Law Working Paper 05-17 (September 2005).
Jaffrey, P., 'Hohfeld's Power–Liability/Right–Duty Distinction in the Law of Restitution', Canadian J Law & Jurisprudence, Vol 17(2) (2004), pp. 295–313.
Janis, M.D., Kesan, J.P., 'Designing an Optimal Intellectual Property System for Plants: A US Supreme Court Debate', Nature/Biotechnology, Vol 19 (2001), pp. 981–3.
Janis, M.D., Kesan, J.P., 'Weed-Free IP: The Supreme Court, Intellectual Property Interfaces, and the Problem of Plants', Illinois Public Law and Legal Theory Research Paper No 00-07 (November 2001).
Janis, M.D., Kesan, J.P., 'US Plant Variety Protection: Sound and Fury …?', Houston Law Review, Vol 39(727) (2002), pp. 727–80; Law and Economics Papers Series, Working Paper No LE03-002.
Jurgensen, T., 'Of Plants, Patents and Breeders' Rights: Some Proposals for International Unification of Proprietary Protection of Plant Biotechnology', J Agricultural Taxation & Law, Vol 12 (1991), pp. 291–314.

Irwin, D.A., 'The GATT in Historical Perspective', Am Econ Rev, Vol 85(2) (1995), pp. 323–8.

Kahnemann, D., Tversky, A., 'Prospect Theory: An Analysis of Decision under Risk', Econometrica, Vol 47 (1979), pp. 263–74.

Kaplow, L., Shavell, S., 'Property Rules versus Liability Rules', Harv LR, Vol 109(4) (1996), pp. 713–90.

Kaplow, L., Shavell, S., 'Fairness versus Welfare: Notes on the Pareto Principle, Preferences, and Distributive Justice', Harvard Law and Economics Discussion Paper No 411 (March 2003).

Karasov, C., 'Who Reaps the Benefits of Biodiversity', Env Health Perspective, Vol 109(12) (2001), pp. 582–7.

ten Kate, K., 'Biodiversity Prospecting Partnerships', Biotechnology and Development Monitor, No 25 (1998), pp. 16–21.

ten Kate, K., Laird, S.A., 'Property Rights Issued Involving Plant Genetic Resources: Implications of Ownership for Economic Efficiency', Ecological Economics, Vol 35 (2000), pp. 75–92.

Kessler, F., 'Contracts of Adhesion – Some Thoughts about Freedom of Contract', Columbia L Rev, Vol 43(5) (1943), pp. 629–42.

Kifler, J., 'International Legal Protection of Cultural Heritage', doctoral dissertation (Juristförlaget) (1994).

King, S.R., Carlson, T.J., 'Biocultural Diversity, Biomedicine and Ethnobotany: The Experience of Shaman Pharmaceuticals', Interciencia, Vol 20(3) (1995), pp. 134–9.

Kloppenburg, J.R., 'Seed Wars: Biotechnology, Intellectual Property and the Quest for High Yield Seeds', Boston College Int & Comp L Rev, Vol 23 (1999–2000), pp. 285–310.

Knowles, D., 'Hegel on Property and Personality', Philosophical Quarterly, Vol 33 (1983), pp. 45–8.

Kordana, K.A., Tabachnick, D., Blankfein, D., 'Rawls and Contract Law', George Washington Law Review, Vol 73 (March 2005), pp. 1–62.

Korobkin, R.B., Ulen T.S., 'Efficiency and Equity: What Can Be Gained by Combining Coase and Rawls?', Washington L Rev, Vol 73 (1998), pp. 329–49.

Krier, J., Schwab, S., 'Property Rules and Liability Rules: The Cathedral in Another Light', NYU L Rev, Vol 70 (1995), pp. 440–83.

Lange, D.L., 'Recognizing the Public Domain', Law and Contemporary Problems, Vol 147 (Autumn 1981), pp. 173–8.

Lawson, C., 'Intellectual Property and the Material Transfer Agreement under the International Treaty on Plant Genetic Resources for Food and Agriculture', European Int Prop Rev, Vol 31 (2009), pp. 244–54.

Leacock, E., 'The Montagnes Hunting Territory and the Fur Trade', American Anthropologist, Vol 56, No 5, Part 2, Memoir No 78 (1992), pp. 124–35.

Leskien, D., Flitner, M., 'Intellectual Property Rights and Plant Genetic Resources: Options for a sui generis system', Issues in Genetic Resources No 6, IPGRI, Rome (1997), pp. 1–77.

Lettington, R.J.L., 'The International Undertaking on Plant Genetic Resources in the Context of TRIPs and the CBD, Bridges Between Trade and Sustainable Development', International Center for Trade and Sustainable Development, Year 5, No 6 (July–August 2001), pp. 11–13.

Levmore, S., 'The Two Stories of the Evolution of Property Rights', J Legal Studies, Vol 31(S2) (2002), pp. 423–43.

Lewinsohn Zamir, D., 'The Choice between Property Rules and Liability Rules Revisited: Critical Observations from Behavioural Studies', Texas L Rev, Vol 80(2) (2001), pp. 219–60.

Libecap, G.D., Smith, J., 'The Economic Evolution of Petroleum Property Rights in the United States', J Legal Studies, Vol 31 (2003), pp. 589–608.

Liebig, K., Alker, D., *Governing Biodiversity – Access to Genetic Resources and Approaches to Obtaining Benefits from Their Use: The Case of Philippines*, Bonn: German Development Institute (2002).

Lueck, D., 'Common Property as an Egalitarian Share Contract', J Econ Behavior & Organization, Vol 25(1) (1994), pp. 93–108.

Lueck, D., 'The Extermination and Conservation of the American Bison', J Legal Studies, Vol 31(S2) (2002), pp. 609–652.

Mandel, G., 'Promoting Environmental Innovation with Intellectual Property Innovation: A New Basis for Patent Rewards', presentation at Temple University Journal of Science, Technology and Environmental Law Symposium, Environmental Technology and Innovation: Partners for our Future, Temple J Science & Envtl Law, Vol XX (2005), pp. 51–69.

Maqueda, E., 'Something More about Humanity as a Subject of Law', *Proceedings of the 13th Colloquium on the Law of Outer Space*, Brussels (1971) 215.

Marden, E., 'The Neem Tree Patent: International Conflict over the Commodification of Life', Boston College Int & Comp L Rev, Vol 22 (1999), pp. 279–95.

Markovits, R., 'A Constructive Critique of the Traditional Definition and Use of the Concept of the Effect of a Choice of Allocative Economic Efficiency: Why the Kaldor-Hicks Test, the Coase Theorem, and Virtually All Law-and-Economics Welfare Arguments Are Wrong', U Illinois L Rev [1993], pp. 485–500.

Maskus, K.E., 'Intellectual Property and the Transfer of Green Technologies: An Essay on Economic Perspectives', WIPO Journal, Vol 1(1) (2009), pp. 133–7.

Maskus, K.E., 'Intellectual Property Rights in Agriculture and Interests of Asian-Pacific Economies', World Economy, Vol 29(6) (2006), pp. 715–42.

Maskus, K.E., Merrill, S.A. (eds), 'Patent Challenges for Standard-Setting in the Global Economy: Lessons from Information and Communications Technology', Report of the Committee on Intellectual Property Management in Standard-Setting Processes, Board on Science, Technology and Economic Policy, Washington, DC: National Research Council (2013), available at http://www.nap.edu/catalog.php?record_id=18510.

Mattix, C., 'The Debate over Bioprospecting on the Public Lands', Natural Resources and Environment, Vol 13 (1998–9), pp. 528–74.

Mayhew, R., 'Aristotle on Property', Review of Metaphysics, Vol 46(4) (1993), pp. 803–31.

Mayhew, R., The Communism of Property: A Note on Aristotle', Classical Quarterly (New Series), Vol 4(5) (1995), pp. 566–9.

McClearly, R.M., 'The International Communities' Claim to Rights in Brazilian Amazonia', Political Studies, Vol 39 (1991), pp. 691–707.

Medaglia, C., 'The Disclosure of Origin Requirement in Central America: Legal Texts, Practical Experiences and Implementation Challenges', ICTSD (June 2010), pp. 1–35.

Mekouar, A., 'A Global Instrument on Agrobiodiversity. The International Treaty on Plant Genetic Resources for Food and Agriculture', FAO Legal Papers Online No 24 (2002).

Merges, R.P., 'Contracting into Liability Rules: Intellectual Property Rights and Collective Rights Organizations', California L Rev, Vol 84(5) (1996), pp. 1293–1386.

Merill, T., Smith, H., 'Optimal Standardization in the Law of Property: The Numerus Clausus Principle', Yale LJ, Vol 110 (2000), pp. 1–70.

Merill, T., Smith, H., 'The Property/Contract Interface', Columbia L Rev, Vol 101 (2001), pp. 773–852.

Merill, T., Smith, H., 'What Happened to Property in Law and Economics?', Yale LJ, Vol 111 (2001), pp. 357–98.

Merritt, G., 'Justice as Fairness: A Commentary on Rawls' New Theory of Justice', Vand L Rev, Vol 26 (1973), pp. 665–86.

Mgbeoji, I., 'Beyond Rhetoric: State Sovereignty, Common Concern, and the Inapplicability of the Common Heritage Concept to Plant Genetic Resources', Leiden J Int L, Vol 16 (2003), pp. 821–37.

Mikhail, J., 'Rawls' Linguistic Analogy: A Study of the "Generative Grammar" Model of Moral Theory Described by John Rawls in "A

Theory of Justice"', doctoral dissertation, Cornell University (2000), Georgetown Public Law Research Paper No 766464.
Mikhail, J., 'Law, Science, and Morality: A Review of Richard Posner's "The Problematics of Moral and Legal Theory"', Stanford L Rev, Vol 54, Georgetown Law and Economics Research Paper No 877011 (2002), pp. 1059–1129.
Mimura, C., Chen J., Penhoet, B., 'Socially Responsible Licensing, Euclidean Innovation, and the Valley of Death', Stanford J Law, Science & Policy (July 2011), pp. 1–16.
Mishan, E.J., 'The Postwar Literature on Externalities: An Interpretative Essay', J Econ Literature, Vol 9(1) (1971), pp. 1–16.
Mooney, P.R., *Seeds of the Earth: A Private or Public Resource*, London: International Coalition for Development Action (1983).
Monson, J., 'From Commerce to Colonization: A History of the Rubber Trade in the Kilombero Valley of Tanzania, 1890–1914', History, Vol 21 (1993), pp. 113–30.
Moran, K., 'Mechanisms for Benefit-Sharing: Nigerian Case Study for the Convention on Biological Diversity', 4th Meeting, COP, Bratislava, Slovakia (1998).
Moran, K., King, S., Carlsson, T., 'Biodiversity Prospecting, Lessons and Practices', Ann Rev Anthropology, Vol 30 (2001), pp. 505–26.
Moretto, M., Rosato, P., 'The Use of Common Property Resources: A Dynamic Model', Fondazione Eni Enrico Mattei (Notta di Lavoro, 13 January 2002).
Morgera, E., 'Faraway So Close: A Legal Analysis of the Rising Interactions between the Convention on Biological Diversity and Climate Change Law', University of Edinburgh, Working Paper Series (2011–12).
Mossof, A., 'What Is Property? Putting the Pieces Back Together', Arizona L Rev, Vol 45 (2003), pp. 371–445.
Movik, S., 'Some Notes on Common vs Private Property Rights to Natural Resources', presented at The Commons in an Age of Global Transition: Challenges, Risks and Opportunities, Tenth Conference of the International Association for the Study of Common Property, Oaxaca, Mexico (9–13 August 2004).
Mulholland, D., Wilman, E., 'Bioprospecting and Biodiversity Contracts', Environment and Development Economics, Vol 8 (2003), pp. 417–35.
Muller, M.R., 'Disclosure of Origin and Legal Provenance: The Experience and Implementation Process in South America', ICTSD, Policy Brief No 7 (June 2010).
Mulligan, S., Stoett, P., 'A Global Bio-Prospecting Regime, Partnership or Piracy', International Journal, Vol 55 (1999–2000), pp. 224–46.

Murphy, G.J., 'Hume and Kant on the Social Contract', Philosophical Studies, Vol 33(1) (January 1978), pp. 65–79.

Nordell, P.J., 'Skyddet för funktionellt betingande utstyrslar', NIR No 5 (2005), pp. 433–63.

North, D., Thomas R.P., 'An Economic Theory of the Growth of the Western World', Economic History Review (New Series), Vol 23(1) (1970), pp. 1–17.

Oguamanam, C., 'Localizing Intellectual Property in the Globalization Epoch: The Integration of Indigenous Knowledge', paper presented at the 4th Annual Doctoral Students Conference of the Association of Pacific Rim Universities, Mexico City, Mexico (24–29 August 2003).

Oldham, E., 'An Access and Benefit-Sharing Commons?'Initiative for the Prevention of Biopiracy, Research Documents, Year IV, No 11 (2008), available at http://ssrn.com/abstract=1438027.

Opderdeck, D., 'The Penguin's Genome or Coase and the Open Source Biotechnology', Harvard J Law & Technology, Vol 18 (2004), pp. 1–80.

Parisi, F., 'The Asymmetric Coase Theorem: Dual Remedies for Unified Property', George Mason Law & Economics Research Paper No 01-13 (2001).

Parisi, F., 'Entropy in Property', Am J Comp Law, Vol 50 (2002), pp. 595–632.

Patwarhan, B., Annant Mashelkar, R., 'Traditional Medicine-Inspired Approaches to Drug Discovery: Can Ayurveda Show the Way Forward?', Drug Discovery Today, Vol 14(15–16) (2009), pp. 804–9.

Pejovic, S., 'Towards an Economic Theory of the Creation and Specification of Property Rights', Rev Social Economy, Vol 30(3) (1972), pp. 309–25.

Pena-Neira, S., Dieperinc, C., Addink, H., 'Equitably Sharing Benefits from the Utilization of Natural Genetic Resources: The Brazilian Interpretation of the CBD', Electronic J Comp Law, Vol 6(3) (October 2002), pp. 1–18.

Pogge, T.W., 'The Incoherence between Rawls' Theories of Justice', Fordham L Rev, Vol 72 (2004), pp. 1739–59.

Polanvyi, M., 'Patent Reform', Rev Econ Studies, Vol 11 (1944), pp. 61–9.

Polinsky, M., 'Controlling Externalities and Protecting Entitlements: Property Right, Liability Rule, and Tax-Subsidy Approaches', J Legal Studies, Vol 8(1) (1979), pp. 1–48.

Polski, M., 'The Institutional Economics of Biodiversity, Biological Materials, and Bioprospecting', Ecological Economics, Vol 53 (2005), pp. 543–57.

Powers, M., 'The United Nations Framework Convention on Biological Diversity: Will Biodiversity Preservation Be Enhanced through Its Provisions Concerning Biotechnology Intellectual Property Rights?', Wisconsin Int LJ, Vol 12(1) (1994), pp. 103–24.

Priya, K., 'Intellectual Property and Hegelian Justification', NJUS L Rev, Vol 1 (2008), pp. 359–66.

Rackleff, K., 'Preservation of Biological Diversity', Colorado J Int Env Law & Policy, Vol 3 (1992), pp. 429–78.

Radin, M., 'Property and Personhood', Stanford L Rev, Vol 34 (1982), pp. 957–1015.

Radin, M., Sunder, M., 'The Subject and Object of Commodification', Stanford Law School, Public Law and Legal Theory Working Paper Series, Research Paper No 97 (2004).

Ragnekar, D., 'Geographical Indications, A Review of Proposals at the TRIPS Council: Extending Article 23 to Products other than Wines and Spirits', ICTSD Issue Paper 4, June (2003).

Rai, K.A., Eisenberg, R., 'Bayh-Dole Reform and the Progress of Biomedicine', Law & Contemporary Problems, Vol 66(1) (2004), pp. 289–314.

Raju, K.D., 'Is the Future of Software Development in Open Source? Proprietary vs Open Source Software: A Cross Country Analysis', J Int Prop Rights, Vol 12(2) (March 2007), pp. 199–211.

Randall, A., 'Market Solutions to Externality Problems, Theory and Practice', Am J Agricultural Econ, Vol 54 (1972), pp. 175–8.

Rausser, G.C., Small, A.A., 'Valuing Research Leads: Bioprospecting and the Conservation of Genetic Resources', J Pol Econ, Vol 108 (2000), pp. 173–206.

Rawls, J., 'The Law of Peoples', Critical Inquiry, Vol 20(1) (1993), pp. 36–68.

Reichman, J., 'Of Green Tulips and Legal Kudzu: Repackaging Right in Subpatentable Innovation', Vand L Rev (2000), pp. 1743–98.

Reichman, J., Samuelson, P., 'Intellectual Property Rights in Data?', Vand L Rev, Vol 50 (1997), pp. 49–167.

Reidy, D.A., 'A Just Global Economy: In Defense of Rawls', J Ethics, Vol 11(2) (2007), pp. 193–236.

Reisenfeld, S., 'Patent Protection and the Atomic Energy Legislation', California L Rev, Vol 46 (1958), pp. 40–68.

Reyes, V., 'The Value of Sangre de Drago' (1996), https://www.grain.org/article/entries/313-the-value-of-sangre-de-drago.

Richerzhagen, C., Holm-Mueller, K., 'The Effectiveness of Access and Benefit Sharing in Costa Rica: Implications for National and International Regimes', Ecological Economics, Vol 53 (2005), pp. 445–60.

Ripstein, A., 'Private Order and Public Justice: Kant and Rawls', Virginia Law Review, Vol 92(7) (2006), pp. 1391–1421; University of Toronto, Legal Studies Research Paper No 894431.

Ritchie, M., 'Intellectual Property Rights and Biodiversity. The Industrialization of Natural Resources and Traditional Knowledge', St John's Legal Comment, Vol 11 (1996), pp. 431–83.

Roht-Arriaza, N., 'Of Seeds and Shamans: The Appropriation of the Scientific and Technical Knowledge of Indigenous and Local Communities', Mich J Int L, Vol 17(919) (1996), pp. 936–7.

Roos, J., 'Aboriginal Land Rights, a Continuing Social Justice Issue', Australian eJournal of Theology, Vol 8 (October 2006), pp. 1–8.

Rose, C., 'The Comedy of the Commons: Custom, Commerce, and Inherently Public Property', U Chicago L Rev, Vol 53 (1986), pp. 711–81.

Rosendal, K., 'Impacts of Overlapping International Regimes: The Case of Biodiversity', Global Governance, Vol 7(1) (2001), pp. 95–117.

Rosenthal, J., 'Equitable Sharing of Biodiversity Benefits: Agreements on Genetic Resources', National Institute of Health, International Conference on Incentive Measures for the Conservation and Sustainable Use of Biological Diversity in Cairns, Australia (25–28 March 1996).

Safrin, S., 'Hyperownership in a Time of Biotechnological Promise: The International Conflict to Control the Building Blocks of Life', Am J Int Law, Vol 98 (2004), pp. 641–85.

Samuelson, P., 'Preserving the Positive Functions of the Public Domain for Science', Data Science J, Vol 2(192) (2003), pp. 192–7.

Sandler, F., 'Music of the Village in the Global Market Place: Self-Expression, Inspiration, Appropriation or Exploitation?', doctoral dissertation, University of Michigan (2001).

Santa Cruz, M., 'Intellectual Property Provisions in European Union Trade Agreements', ICTSD Programme on IPRs and Sustainable Development, Issue Paper No 20 (June 2007).

Schillhorn, K., 'The Status and Rights of Indigenous Peoples in Australia', Heidelberg J Int L (1999), pp. 463–96.

Schlager, E., Ostrom, E., 'Property Rights Regimes and Natural Resources', Land Economics, Vol 68 (1993), pp. 249–62.

Schmitt, E.K., Moore, C.M., Krastel, P., Petersen, F., 'Natural Products as Catalysts for Innovation: A Pharmaceutical Industry Perspective', Current Opinion in Chemical Biology, Vol 15 (2011), pp. 1–8.

Schrell, A., Heide, N., 'Licensing Estonian Genes: The Human Genes Act Has Entered into Force', European Int Prop Rev [2002], pp. 337–9.

Shavell, S., 'Reward versus Intellectual Property', J Law Econ, Vol 44(2) (2001), pp. 525–47.

Siebenhuner, B., Suplie, J., 'Implementing the Access and Benefit Sharing Provisions of the CBD: A Case for Institutional Learning', Ecological Economics, Vol 53 (2005), pp. 507–22.
Siebenhuner, B., Dedeurwaerdere, T., Brousseau, E., 'Introduction and Overview to the Special Issue on Biodiversity Conservation, Access and Benefit Sharing and Traditional Knowledge', Ecological Economics, Vol 53 (2005), pp. 439–44.
Simpson, B., 'Coase v Pigou Reexamined', J Legal Stud, Vol 25(53) (1996), pp. 53–97.
Skarp, B., 'Commercialization of University Knowledge – Aspects on Licensing and Spin-Outs', speech at European Academy for Taxes, Economics and Law, Berlin (January 2013).
Smagadi, A., 'Analysis of the Objectives of the Convention on Biological Diversity: Their Interrelation and Implementation Guidance for Access and Benefit Sharing', Columbia J Env Law, Vol 16 (2006), pp. 243–84.
Smith, H., 'Semicommon Property Rights and Scattering in the Open Fields,' J Legal Studies, Vol 29(1) (2000), pp. 131–69.
Soejarto, D., 'Biodiversity Prospecting and Benefit-sharing: Perspectives from the Field', J Ethnopharmacology, Vol 51 (1994), pp. 590–9.
Song, W.Y., Pi, L.Y., Wang, G.L., Gardner, J., Holsten, T., Ronald, P.C., 'Evolution of the Rice Xa21 Disease Resistance Gene Family', Plant Cell, Vol 9(8) (1997), pp. 1279–87.
Spaulding III, N., 'Commodification and Its Discontents: Environmentalism and the Promise of Market Incentives', Stan Env LJ, Vol 16 (1979), pp. 294–311.
Sturges, M., 'Who Should Hold Property Rights on the Human Genome? An Application of the Common Heritage of Humankind', Am U Int L Rev, Vol 13 (1997–8), pp. 219–61.
Sugin, L., 'Theories of Distributive Justice and Limitations on Taxation: What Rawls Demands from Tax Systems', Fordham L Rev, Vol 72 (2004), pp. 1992–2014.
Swanson, T., Goeschl, T., 'Property Rights Issued Involving Plant Genetic Resources: Implications of Ownership for Economic Efficiency', Ecological Economics, Vol 32 (2000), pp. 75–92.
Swygert, M., Yanes, K.E., 'A Unified Theory of Justice: The Integration of Fairness into Efficiency', Washington L Rev, Vol 73(249) (1998), pp. 304–24.
Tansey, G., 'Trade, Intellectual Property, Food and Biodiversity', discussion paper commissioned by Quaker Peace & Service and Quaker United Nations Office, London and Geneva (1994).
Tejera, V., 'Tripping over Property Rights: Is It Possible to Reconcile the Convention on Biological Diversity with Article 27 of the TRIPS Agreement?', New England L Rev, Vol 33 (1998–9), pp. 967–88.

Tenenbaum, E., 'A World Park in Antarctica: The Common Heritage of Mankind', Virginia Env LJ, Vol 10 (1990), pp. 109–36.

Thompson, C.B., 'International Law of the Sea/Seed: Public Domain versus Private Commodity', Natural Resources J, Vol 44 (2004), pp. 841–66.

Thornström, C.G., 'CGIAR Revising Intellectual Property Guidelines in 2000: A Non-Event with Geopolitical Boundary and Sector Transgressing Content', paper submitted on request by the Genetic Resources Policy Committee of the Consultative Group on International Agricultural Research/CGIAR, World Bank, Washington, DC (17 March 2002).

Tinker, C., 'A "New Breed of Treaty": The United Nations Convention on Biological Diversity', Pace Env L Rev, Vol 13 (Fall 1995), pp. 1–14.

Tolan, S., 'Against the Grain: Multinational Corporations Peddling Patented Seed and Chemical Pesticides are Poised to Revolutionize India's Ancient Agricultural System. But At What Cost?', *LA Times* (10 July 1994), p. 18.

Toumanoff, P., 'A Positive Analysis of Market Failure', Kyklos, Vol 37 (1984), pp. 529–38.

Trotti, J., 'Compensation versus Colonization: A Common Heritage of Mankind Approach to the Use of Indigenous Medicine in Developing Western Pharmaceuticals', Food and Drug Law Journal, Vol 56 (2001), pp. 367–82.

Tully, S., 'The Bonn Guidelines on Access to Genetic Resources and Benefit Sharing', Reciel, Vol 12(1) (2003), pp. 84–98.

Tvedt, M.W., 'How Will a Substantive Patent Law Treaty Affect the Public Domain for Genetic Resources and Biological Material?', J Int Prop Law, Vol 8 (2004), pp. 311–42.

Ubertazzi, B., 'Territorial and Universal Protection of Intangible Cultural Heritage From Misappropriation', NZ Yearbook Int Law, Vol 8 (2010), pp. 69–106.

Umbeck, J., 'Might Makes Rights: A Theory of the Formation and Initial Distribution of Property Rights', Economic Inquiry, Vol 19, pp. 38–59, reprinted in Pejovich, S. (ed.), *The Economic Foundation of Property Rights*, Cheltenham: Edward Elgar (1997), pp. 122–43.

Vélez, E., 'Brazil's Practical Experience with Access and Benefit Sharing and the Protection of Traditional Knowledge', International Centre for Trade and Sustainable Development, Project on Genetic Resources (June 2010).

Vermeleyn, S., 'From Life Force to Slimming Aid: Exploring Views on the Commodification of Traditional Medicinal Knowledge', Applied Geography, Vol 28 (2008), pp. 224–35.

Vivas-Eugui, D., Oliva, M.J., 'Biodiversity Related Intellectual Property Provisions in Free Trade Agreements', ICTSD Natural Resources, International Trade and Sustainable Development (September 2010).

Wahlgren, P. (ed), *Intellectual Property*, Scandinavian Studies in Law Vol 42, Stockholm: Stockholm Institute for Scandinavian Law (2002), pp. 83–95.

Waldron, J., 'What Is Cosmopolitan?', J Political Philosophy, Vol 8(2) (2000), pp. 227–32

Warner, J., 'Reframing the Bioprospecting Debate', Ind J Global Legal Stud, Vol 13(2) (2006), pp. 647–58.

Weber, M., Albrow, M., 'R. Stammler's Surmounting of the Materialist Conception of History, Part II', British J Law & Society, Vol 3(1) (1976), pp. 17–43.

Wei, M., 'Should Prizes Replace Patents? A Critique of the Medical Innovation Prize Act of 2005', Boston University Journal of Science & Technology Law, Vol 13(1) (2007), pp. 1–23.

Wellisz, S., 'On External Diseconomies and the Government Assisted Invisible Hand', Economica, Vol 31 (1964), pp. 31–62.

White, M., 'The Common Heritage of Mankind', Case Western Reserve J Int Law, Vol 14 (1982), pp. 509–42.

Williamson, O., 'Transaction-Cost Economics: The Governance of Contractual Relations', J Law Econ, Vol 22 (1979), pp. 233–61.

Wolfgang, L., 'Patents on Native Technology Challenged', Science, Vol 15 (1995), p. 1506.

Wolfrun, R., 'The Principle of the Common Heritage of Mankind', Heidelberg J Int Law, Vol 43 (1983), pp. 369–82.

Wright, B.D., 'The Economics of Invention Incentives: Patents, Prizes, and Research Contracts', Am Econ Rev, Vol 73 (1983), pp. 691–707.

Zerbe, N., 'Biodiversity, Ownership, and Indigenous Knowledge: Exploring Legal Frameworks for Community, Farmers and Intellectual Property Rights in Africa', Ecological Economics, Vol 53 (2005), pp. 493–506.

BOOKS AND BOOK CHAPTERS

Abrell, E., Bavikatta, K., Cocchiaro, G., 'Implementing a Traditional Knowledge Commons: Opportunities and Challenges', in de Beer, J., Armstrong, C., Oguamanam, C., Schionwetter, T. (eds), *Innovation and Intellectual Property Collaborative Dynamics in Africa*, Claremont: UCT Press (2009), pp. 151–71.

Baker, A., Butlin, R.A., *Studies of Field Systems in the British Isles*, Cambridge: Cambridge University Press (1973).

Barton, H., 'The Impact of Contemporary Patent Law on Plant Biotechnology Research' in Eberhart, S.A., et al., *Global Genetic Resources: Access and Property Rights*, Madison: Crop Science Society of America (1998), pp. 85–97.

Barzel, Y., *Economic Analysis of Property Rights*, Cambridge: Cambridge University Press (1989).

Baslar, K., *The Concept of the Common Heritage of Mankind in International Law*, The Hague: Martinus Nijhoff Publishers/Kluwer Law International (1998).

Bavikatte, K., Jonas, H., *Biocultural Community Protocols: A Community Approach to Ensuring the Integrity of Environmental Law and Policy*, Cape Town: Natural Justice and UNEP (2009).

Becker, D., *Property Rights: Philosophic Foundations*, Boston: Routledge & Kegan Paul (2003).

Benedict, C., 'The Status and Rights of Indigenous Peoples in Canada', in *Rudolph Bernhardt Encyclopedia of Public International Law*, Vol 2, Oxford: Oxford University Press (1995), pp. 405–42.

Benkler, Y., *The Wealth Networks: How Social Production Transforms Markets and Freedom*, New Haven: Yale University Press (2006).

Biber-Klemm, S., Szymura Berglas, D., 'Problems and Goals' in Biber-Klemm, S., Cottier, T. (eds), *Rights to Plant Genetic Resources and Traditional Knowledge, Basic Issues and Perspectives*, Wallingford: CABI (2006), pp. 3–55.

Blackstone, W., *Commentaries on the Law of England*, Vol 4, facsimile edition with introductions by Katz, S.N., Chicago: University of Chicago Press (1979).

Bowman, M., 'The Nature, Development and Philosophical Foundations of the Biodiversity Concept in International Law' in Bowman, M., Redgwell, C. (eds), *International Law and the Conservation of Biological Diversity*, London: Kluwer Law International (1996), pp. 451–76.

Boyle, A., 'The Rio Convention on Biological Diversity' in Bowman, M., Redgwell, C. (eds), *International Law and the Conservation of Biological Diversity*, London: Kluwer Law International (1996), pp. 33–49.

Brockway, L.H., *Science and Colonial Expansion: The Role of the British Royal Botanic Gardens*, New York: Academic Press (1979).

Brush, S., 'Whose Knowledge, Whose Genes, Whose Rights?' in Brush, S., Stabinsky, D. (eds), *Valuing Indigenous Knowledge: Indigenous People and IPR*, Washington DC: Island Press (1996), pp. 1–25.

Buckle, S., *Natural Law and Theory of Property, from Grotius to Hume*, Oxford: Oxford University Press (1993).

Cole, D., 'New Forms of Private Property: Property Rights in Environmental Goods' in Bouckaert, B. and Geest, G. de (eds), *Encyclopedia of Law and Economics*, Vol II, Cheltenham: Edward Elgar (2000), pp. 274–311.

Conte, L., 'Shaman Pharmaceuticals' Approach to Drug Development' in Balick, M.J., Elisabetsky, E., Laird, S.A. (eds), *Medicinal Resources of the Tropical Forest: Biodiversity and its Importance to Human Health*, New York: Columbia University Press (1996), pp. 94–100.

Coombe, R., 'Protecting Cultural Industries to Promote Cultural Diversity: Dilemmas for International Policy-Making Posed by the Recognition of Traditional Knowledge', in Maskus, K.E., Reichman, J., *International Public Goods and Transfer of Technology Under a Globalised Intellectual Property Regime*, Cambridge: Cambridge University Press (2005), pp. 599–615.

Cooter, R., 'Commodifying Liability', in Buckley, F.H. (ed.), *The Rise and Fall of Freedom of Contract*, Durham and London: Duke University Press (2006), pp. 139–57.

Correa, C.M., *Intellectual Property Rights, the WTO and Developing Countries. The TRIPS Agreement and Policy Options*, London, New York and Penang: ZED Books and the Third World Network (2000).

Crosby, A.W., *The Columbian Exchange: Biological and Cultural Consequences of 1492*, Westport, CT: Greenwood Publishing Co (1972).

Cullet, P., Germann, C., Muller, A.N., Pasadilla, G., 'Intellectual Property Rights, Plant Genetic Resources and Traditional Knowledge', in Biber-Klemm, S., Cottier, T. (eds), *Rights to Plant Genetic Resources and Traditional Knowledge, Basic Issues and Perspectives*, Wallingford: CABI (2006), pp. 112–57.

Donavanik, J., 'Plant Varieties and Access Rights in Asia and the South' in *Industrial Property in the Bio-Medical Age: Challenges for Asia*, The Hague: Kluwer Law International (2003), pp. 49–73.

Dutfield, G., *Intellectual Property Rights, Trade and Biodiversity*, London: Earthscan (2000).

Eggertsson, T., *Economic Behavior and Institutions*, Cambridge, MA: Cambridge University Press (1990).

Eggertsson, T., 'Open Access versus Common Property' in Anderson, T.L., McChesney, F.S. (eds), *Property Rights: Cooperation, Conflict, and Law*, Princeton: Princeton University Press, (2003), pp. 73–89.

Ehrlich, E., *Fundamental Principles of the Sociology of Law*, Cambridge, MA: Harvard University Press (1936).

Eisermann, G., 'Pareto, Vilfredo (1848–1923)' in *International Encyclopedia of the Social & Behavioral Sciences*, Berlin: Elsevier (2001), pp. 11048–51.

Epstein, R., *Takings: Private Property and the Power of Eminent Domain*, Cambridge, MA: Harvard University Press (1985).
Farnsworth, N.R., 'Screening Plants for New Medicines' in Wilson, E.O. (ed.), *Biodiversity*, Washington DC: National Academy Press (1988), pp. 83–96.
Fudenberg, D., Tirole, J., *Game Theory*, Cambridge: MIT Press (1983).
Gertz, A., Dupont, F., 'Comté Cheese in France: Impact of a Geographical Indication on Rural Development' in Kop, P. van de, Sautier, D., Gerz, A. (eds), *Origin-Based Products: Lessons for Pro-Poor Market Development, Bulletin 372*, Amsterdam: KIT and Montpellier: CIRAD (1995), pp. 75–86.
Gervais, D., *The TRIPS Agreement. Drafting History and Analysis*, London: Sweet & Maxwell (1998).
Grey, T., 'The Disintegration of Property' in Epstein, R.A. (ed), *Liberty, Property and the Law*, Quebec City: SLS Publications (2000), pp. 233–8.
Grifo, F., Newman, D., Fairfield, S., Bhattacharya, B., Grupehof, J., 'The Origins of Prescription Drugs' in Grifo, F., Rosenthal, J. (eds), *Biodiversity and Human Health*, Washington DC: Island Press (1997), pp. 131–64.
Halewood, M., López Noriega, I., Sélim, L., 'The Global Crop Commons and Access and Benefit-Sharing Laws – Examining the Limits of International Policy Support for the Collective Pooling and Management of Plant Genetic Resources', in Halewood, M., López Noriega, I., Louafi, S. (eds), *Crop Genetic Resources as a Global Commons: Challenges in International Law and Governance*, New York: Routledge (2013), pp. 1–36.
Hanke, L., *The Spanish Struggle for Justice in the Conquest of America*, London: Oxford University Press (2002).
Hardin, G., 'Political Requirements for Preserving our Common Heritage' in Brokaw, H.P. (ed), *Wildlife and America*, Washington DC: Council on Environmental Quality (1978), pp. 310–17.
Hargrove, E., *Foundations of Environmental Ethics*, Englewood Cliffs: Prentice Hall (1989).
Hassemer, M., 'Genetic Resources', in Lewinski, S. von (ed), *Indigenous Heritage and Intellectual Property*, The Hague: Kluwer International (2004), pp. 151–217.
Hawkes, J.G., *The Diversity of Crop Plants*, Cambridge, MA: Harvard University Press (1983).
Heath, C., 'Plant Varieties, Biodiversity and Access Rights' in Heath, C., Kamperman Sanders, A., *Industrial Property in the Bio-Medical Age: Challenges for Asia*, The Hague: Kluwer Law International (2003), pp. 1–277.

Heath, C., Kamperman Sanders, A. (eds), *Intellectual Property and Free Trade Agreements*, Portland: Hart Publishing (2007).
Hegel, G.W.F., *The Philosophy of Right*, trans Knox, T.M., Cambridge: Cambridge University Press [1821] (1967).
Hensson-Apollonio, V., 'Case 10. The International Treaty on Plant Genetic Resources for Food and Agriculture: The Standard Material Transfer Agreement as Implementation of a Limited Compensatory Liability Regime' in Overwalle, G. van (ed), *Gene Patents and Collaborative Licensing Models*, Cambridge: Cambridge University Press, 2009, pp. 289–93.
Herrera, H., 'Panama Case-Study – Kuna and Embera-Wounaan Medicinal Knowledge & Access Protocols' in Song, Y. Pant, R. Li, J. Swiderska, K. Argumedo, A. Vedavathy, S. Herrera, H. Mutta, D. Munyi, P. (eds), *Protecting Community Rights over Traditional Knowledge: Key Findings and Recommendations 2005–2009*. London: International Institute for Environment and Development (2009), pp. 17–18.
Honoré, A.M., 'Ownership' in Guest, A.G., *Oxford Essays in Jurisprudence*, Oxford: Oxford University Press (1961), pp. 112–24.
Honoré, A.M., 'Property, Title and Redistribution', in Mae, L., Brown, J. (eds), *Philosophy of Law*, London: Wiley-Blackwell (2009), pp. 263–9.
Houlgate, S., *An Introduction to Hegel: Freedom, Truth and History*, 2nd edition, Oxford: Blackwell (1967).
Hugenholtz, B., 'Implementing the European Database Directive' in Kabel, J. (ed.), *Intellectual Property and Information Law: Essays in Honor of Herman Cohen Jehoram* (1998), available at https://www.ivir.nl/publicaties/download/PBH-HCJ-LIB.pdf.
Kelsen, H., *The Pure Theory*, Berkeley: University of California Press (1970).
King, S., 'Establishing Reciprocity: Biodiversity, Conservation and New Models for Cooperation between Forest Dwelling Peoples and the Pharmaceuticals Industry' in Greaves, T. (ed.), *Intellectual Property Rights for Indigenous Peoples: A Sourcebook*, Oklahoma City: Society for Applied Anthropology (1994), pp. 69–82.
Kloppenburg, J., *First the Seed – The Political Economy of Plant Biotechnology 1492–2000*, Cambridge: Cambridge University Press (1988).
Kocourek, A., *Jural Relations*, 2nd edition, Indianapolis: Bobbs-Merill Company (1928).
Kramer, M.H., *John Locke and the Origins of Private Property: Philosophical Explorations of Individualism, Community and Equality*, Cambridge: Cambridge University Press (1997).
Krishnamurthy, S., 'An Analysis of Open Source Business Models' in Feller, J., Fitzgerald, B., Hissam, S., and Lakhani, K. (eds), *Perspectives*

on Free and Open Source Software, MIT Press, forthcoming. Available at SSRN: http://ssrn.com/abstract=650001.

Kur, A., Schovsbo, J., 'Expropriation or Fair Game for All? The Gradual Dismantling of the IP Exclusivity Paradigm' in Kur, A., Levin, M. (eds), *Intellectual Property Rights in a Fair World Trade System: Proposals for Reform of TRIPS*, Cheltenham: Edward Elgar (2011), pp. 408–55.

Laird, S., 'Contracts for Biodiversity-Prospecting' in *Biodiversity Prospecting: Using Genetic Resources for Sustainable Development*, Washington, DC: World Resources Institute (1993), pp. 1–52.

Laird, S., 'Natural Products and the Commercialisation of Traditional Knowledge' in Greaves, T.C. (ed), *Intellectual Property Rights for Indigenous Peoples: A Sourcebook*, Oklahoma City, OK: Society for Applied Anthropology (1994), pp. 145–9.

Laird, S., ten Kate, K., 'Biodiversity Prospecting: The Commercial Use of Genetic Resources and the Best Practice in Benefit-Sharing' in Laird, S. (ed), *Biodiversity and Traditional Knowledge: Equitable Partnerships in Practice*, London: Earthscan Publications (2001), pp. 241–86.

Laird, S., ten Kate, K., 'Biodiversity Prospecting and Forest Conservation: Has It Lived up to Its Promise?' in Pagiola, S., Bishop, J., Landell-Mills, N. (eds.), *Selling Forest Environmental Services: Market Based Mechanisms for Conservation*, London: Earthscan (2002), pp. 151–73.

Lands, W.M., Posner, R.A., 'An Economic Analysis of Copyright Law' in Posner, E.A. (ed.) *Law and Economics*, Aldershot: Ashgate (2000), pp. 325–63.

Lesser, W., Krattiger, A., 'Valuation of Bioprospecting Samples: Approaches, Calculations and Implications for Policy-Makers' in Krattiger, A., Mahoney, R.T., Nelsen, L., et al (eds), *Intellectual Property Management in Health and Agricultural Innovation: A Handbook of Best Practices*, Oxford: MIHR and Davis: PIPRA (2007), pp. 861–77.

Lessig, L., *Code and Other Laws of Cyberspace. The Future of Ideas and Free Culture*, New York: Basic Books (1999).

Levin, M., 'Geographical Indications (GIs) in the Global Village' in Bruun, N. (ed.), *Intellectual Property Beyond Rights*, Helsinki: WSOY (2005), pp. 9–19.

Levin, M., 'The Pendulum Keeps Swinging – Present Discussions on and around the TRIPS Agreement', in Kur, A., Levin, M. (eds), *Intellectual Property Rights in a Fair World Trade System: Proposals for Reform for TRIPS*, Cheltenham: Edward Elgar (2011), pp. 3–61.

Lewis, T., Reichman, J., 'Using Liability Rules to Stimulate Local Innovation in Developing Countries: Application to Traditional Knowledge' in Maskus, K.E., Reichman, J. (eds.), *International Public Goods and Transfer of Technology Under a Globalized Intellectual Property Regime*, Cambridge: Cambridge University Press (2005), pp. 337–67.

Libecap, G.D., *Contracting for Property Rights*, New York: Cambridge University Press (1989).

Lillich, R.B., 'Global Protection of Human Rights', in Meron, T. (ed.), *Human Rights in International Law: Legal and Policy Issues*, Oxford: Clarendon Press (1984), pp. 115–70.

Llewelyn, M., 'Perspectives on Patenting Biological Material' in Heath, C., Kamperman Sanders, A. (eds), *Industrial Property in the Bio-Medical Age: Challenges for Asia*, The Hague: Kluwer Law International (2003), pp. 73–105.

Locke, J., 'Of Property' in May, L., Brown, L. (eds), *Philosophy of Law*, London: Wiley-Blackwell (2009), pp. 251–8.

Locke, J., 'Second Treatise on Civil Government: Essays by Locke, Hume, and Rousseau', in Barker, E. (ed.), *Social Contract*, New York: Oxford University Press (1962), pp. 222–44.

Locke, J., *Two Treatises of the Government*, New York: Cambridge University Press [1690] (1988).

Lu, F., 'The Commons in Amazonian Context' in Nonini, D.M. (ed), *The Global Idea of the Commons*, New York: Berghahn Books (2007), pp. 41–53.

López Noriega, I. et al, 'Assessment of Progress to Make the Multilateral System Functional: Incentives and Challenges at the Country Level' in Halewood, M., López Noriega, I., Louafi, S. (eds), *Crop Genetic Resources as Global Commons: Challenges in International Law and Governance*, New York: Routledge (2013), pp. 231–69.

Mabott, J.D., *John Locke*, London: Macmillan (1973).

Mahmoudi, S., *The Law of the Deep Seabed Mining*, Stockholm: Almquist & Wiksell International (1987).

Mahmoudi, S., 'Common Heritage of Mankind, Common Concern of Humanity', in Beurier, J.-P., Kiss, A., Mahmoudi, S. (eds), *New Technologies and Law of the Marine Environment*, London: Kluwer Law International (1990), pp. 95–109.

Maskus, K.E., *Intellectual Property Rights in the Global Economy*, Washington, DC: Institute for International Economics (2000).

Mattei, U., *Comparative Law and Economics*, Detroit: University of Michigan Press (1997).

McGown, J., *Out of Africa: Mysteries of Access and Benefit Sharing*, Washington, DC: Edmonds Institute in Cooperation with African Centre for Biosafety (2006).

Menell, P., 'Intellectual Property: General Theories' in Bouckaert, B., Geest, G. de (eds.), *Encyclopedia of Law & Economics*, Vol 2, Cheltenham: Edward Elgar (2000), pp. 129–88.

Mill, J.S., *Principles of Political Economy*, Ashley, W.J. (ed), London: Longmans, Green & Co [1848] (1940).

Mooney, P.R., *Seeds of the Earth: A Private or Public Resource*, London: International Coalition for Development Action (1983).

Moschini, G., Yerokhin, O., 'The Economic Incentive to Innovate in Plants, Patents and Plant Breeders' Rights' in Kesan, J.P. (ed.), *Agricultural Biotechnology and Intellectual Property: Seeds of Change*, Wallingford: CAB International (2007), pp. 190–203.

North, D., *The Rise of the Western World: A New Economic History*, New York: Cambridge University Press (1973).

Nozick, R., 'Locke's Theory of Acquisition' in *Philosophy of Law*, London: Wiley-Blackwell (2009), pp. 258–63.

Oldham, P., 'Biopiracy and Bioeconomy' in Glasner, P., Atkinson, P., Greenslade, H. (eds), *New Genetics, New Social Formations*, London and New York, Routledge (2007), pp. 114–34.

Ostrom, E., *Governing the Commons: The Evolution of Institutions for Collective Action*, New York: Cambridge University Press (1990).

Papadopoulou, F., 'TRIPS and Human Rights', in Kur, A., Levin, M. (eds), *Intellectual Property Rights in a Fair World Trade System, Proposals for Reform of TRIPS*, Cheltenham: Edward Elgar (2011), pp. 262–308.

Penner, J., *The Idea of Property in Law*, New York: Oxford University Press (1997).

Pettit, P.N., 'Rawls's Peoples' in Martin, R., Reidy, D. (eds), *Envisioning a New International Order: Essays on Rawls's Law of Peoples*, Oxford: Blackwell (2005), pp. 38–55.

Polinsky, A.M., *An Introduction to Law and Economics*, Boston: Little, Brown & Company (1989).

Posey, D., Dutfield, G., *Beyond Intellectual Property: Toward Traditional Resource Rights and Indigenous Peoples and Local Communities*, Ottawa: IDRC (1996).

Posner, R., *Economic Analysis of Law*, 1st edition, Boston: Little, Brown & Company (1972).

Prakash, G., *Science and the Imagination of Modern India*, Princeton: Princeton University Press (1999).

Rahmatian, A., 'A Fundamental Critique of the Law-and-Economics Analysis of Intellectual Property Rights' in Dinwoodie, G. (ed),

Methods and Perspectives in Intellectual Property, Cheltenham: Edward Elgar (2013), pp. 71–114.

Rawls, J., *A Theory of Justice*, Oxford: Clarendon Press (1972).

Rawls, J., *The Law of Peoples*, Cambridge, MA: Harvard University Press (2001).

Scharper, S.B., Cunningham, H., 'The Genetic Commons: Resisting the Neo-Liberal Enclosure of Life' in Nonini, D.M. (ed), *The Global Idea of the Commons*, New York: Berghahn Books (2007), pp. 53–66.

Schebinger, L., Swan, C., *Colonial Botany, Science, Commerce and Politics in the Early Modern World*, Philadelphia: University of Pennsylvania Press (2004).

Scherer, F.M., *Industrial Market Structure and Economic Performance*, Chicago: Rand McNally & Co (1973).

Schermers, H.G., 'The International Protection of the Right of Property', in Matcher, F., Petzold, H. (eds), *Protecting Human Rights: The European Dimension*, Köln: Carl Heymanns Verlag KG (1998), pp. 125–58.

Schovsbo, J., 'Fire and Water Make Steam. Redefining the Role of Competition Law in TRIPS' in Kur, A., Levin, M. (eds), *Intellectual Property Rights in a Fair World Trade System*, Cheltenham: Edward Elgar (2011), pp. 308–59.

Schrijver, N., 'Permanent Sovereignty over Natural Resources Versus the Common Heritage of Mankind: Complementary or Contradictory Principles of International Economic Law?' in Denters, E.M.G., Peters, P., Waart, J.I.M. de, *International Law and Development*, Cambridge: Cambridge University Press (1988), pp. 87–101.

Shelton, D., 'Describing the Elephant. International Justice and Environmental Law' in Ebbesson, J., Okowa, P. (eds.), *Environmental Law and Justice in Context*, Cambridge: Cambridge University Press (2009), pp. 55–72.

Sloane, H., 'A Voyage to the Islands [of] Madera, Barbados, Nieves, S. Christophers and Jamaica' [1707] in Schiebing, L., Swan, C., *Colonial Botany, Science, Commerce and Politics in the Early Modern World*, Philadelphia: University of Pennsylvania Press (2005), p. 352.

Stewart, T., *The GATT Uruguay Round: A Negotiating History (1986–1992)*, Boston: Kluwer Law (1993).

Stigler, J., *The Theory of Price*, New York: The Maximilian Co (1966).

Stoll, P., Hahn, A. von, *Indigenous Peoples, Indigenous Knowledge and Indigenous Resources in International Law*, New York: Kluwer International (2003).

Suganami, H., 'Grotius and International Equality', in Bull, H., Kingsbury, B., Roberts, A. (eds), *Hugo Grotius and International Relations*, Oxford: Oxford University Press (1990), pp. 221–235.

Taubmann, A., Leistner, M., 'Analysis of different areas of indigenous knowledge', in Lewinski, S. von (ed.), *Indigenous Heritage and Intellectual Property*, The Hague: Kluwer Law International (2004), pp. 59–180.
The Crucible II Group, *Seeding Solutions*, Ottawa: International Plant Genetic Resources Institute (2001).
Tuori, K., *Critical Legal Positivism*, Aldershot: Ashgate Publishing Limited (2002).
Twinning, W., 'Law, Justice and Rights: Some Implications of a Global Perspective', in Ebbesson, J., Okowa, P. (eds), *Environmental Law and Justice in Context*, Cambridge: Cambridge University Press (2009), pp. 76–98.
Walden, J., 'Intellectual Property Rights and Biodiversity' in Bowman, M., Redgwell, C. (eds), *International Law and the Conservation of Biological Diversity*, London: Kluwer Law International (1996), pp. 182–9.
Waldron, J., *The Right to Private Property*, Oxford: Oxford University Press (1988).
Weinreb, L., *Natural Law and Justice*, Cambridge, MA: Harvard University Press (1987).
Wood, T., *An Institute of the Laws of England*, London (1724), reprinted by the Lawbook Exchange referenced in the High Court of Delegates, Cambridge University Press, London [1971] (2006).
Yusuf, A., 'Technology and Genetic Resources: Is Mutually-Beneficial Access Still Possible?' in Sánchez, V., Juma, C. (eds), *Biodiplomacy: Genetic Resources and International Relations*, Nairobi: African Centre for Technology Studies Press (1994), pp. 233–40.
Zohary, D., Hopf, M., *Domestication of Plants in the Old World: The Origin and Spread of Cultivated Plants in West Asia, Europe, and the Nile Valley*, 3rd edition, Oxford University Press, New York (2000).

INTERNATIONAL CONVENTIONS AND AGREEMENTS

Antarctic Treaty, 12 UST 794, TIAS No 4780 (1 December 1959).
International Covenant on Economic, Social, and Cultural Rights, UN GAOR, 21 at Sess Supp No 16 p. 49, UN Doc A/6316 (1966).
Treaty on Principles Governing the Activities of States in the Exploration and Use of Outer Space, including the Moon and Other Celestial Bodies (27 January 1967).
Treaty on the Non-Proliferation of Nuclear Weapons, 21 UST 483, TIAS No 6839, 12 June 1968 (1970).

Vienna Convention on the Law of Treaties, United Nations, Signed at Vienna 23 May 1969, Entry into Force 27 January 1980.

Patent Cooperation Treaty, done at Washington on 19 June 1970, amended on September 28, 1979, modified on 3 February 1984 and 3 October 2001 (as in force from 1 April 2002).

Budapest Treaty on the International Recognition of the Deposit of Microorganisms for the Purposes of Patent Procedure, done at Budapest on 28 April 1977, amended on 26 September 1980.

United Nations Convention on the Law of the Sea (UNCLOS) (10 December 1982), Jamaica.

International Undertaking on Plant Genetic Resources, United Nations Food and Agriculture Organization, Resolution 8/83 (1987).

Convention concerning Indigenous and Tribal Peoples in Independent Countries, ILO Convention 169 (1989).

Convention on Biological Diversity, regarding the conservation of biodiversity, the sustainable use of its components and the fair and equitable sharing of the benefits arising thereof (1992).

Agreement on Trade-Related Aspects of Intellectual Property Rights of 15 April (1994).

Global Plan of Action for the Conservation and Sustainable Utilization of Plant Genetic Resources for Food and Agriculture, FAO (17–23 June 1996).

International Convention for the Protection of New Varieties of Plants, Paris, 2 December 1961, as Revised at Geneva on 10 November 1972, 23 October 1978 and 19 March 1991 (UPOV Doc 221(E), 1996).

International Treaty concerning the regulation of access to plant genetic resources, United Nations Food and Agriculture Organization Resolution 3/200 (2001).

WIPO, Draft Substantive Patent Law Treaty, Standing Committee on the Law of Patents, Tenth Session, SCP/10/4 (September 2003).

Nagoya Protocol on Access to Genetic Resources and Fair and Equitable Sharing of Benefits Arising from their Utilization to the Convention on Biological Diversity, 29 October 2010, 10th Conference of the Parties to the Convention on Biological Diversity, Nagoya, Japan.

EUROPEAN LEGISLATION

Convention on the Grant of European Patents (European Patent Convention) of 5 October 1973, as revised by the Act revising Article 63 EPC of 17 December 1991, and the Act revising the EPC of 29 November 2000.

Proposal for a Council Directive on the Legal Protection of Databases, COM (92)24 final, Brussels, 13 May 1992, OJ 1992 C156/4.
Proposal for a Council Decision Concerning the Conclusion of the Convention on Biological Diversity, COM(92)509 final, Brussels, 21 December 1992.
Council Regulation (EC) No. 2100/94 of July 27, 1994 on Community Plant Variety Rights.
Directive 96/9/EC of the European Parliament and of the Council on the legal protection of databases, 11 March 1996, OJ L77/20 of 27 March 1996.
Directive 98/44/EC of the European Parliament and of the Council of 6 July 1998 on the legal protection of biotechnological inventions.
Directive 2004/24/EC of the European Parliament and of the Council of 31 March 2004 amending, as regards traditional herbal medicinal products, Directive 2001/83/EC on the Community code relating to medicinal products for human use.
Council Regulation (EC) No. 509/2006 on agricultural products and foodstuffs as traditional specialties guaranteed.

NATIONAL LAW

Aboriginal Land Rights of 1976 – Native Title Act (1994).
Act 412, 31 May 2000 amending Danish Patent Act, paragraph 3; Danish Penal Code 163.
Act on Protection and Promotion of Traditional Thai Medicinal Intelligence BE 2542.
Amendment of Swiss Patent Law of 22 June 2007, RO 2008 2551, Art 49a.
American Declaration of the Rights and Duties of Man, Organization of American States, May 2, 1948, OEA/Ser. L/V/II.23, doc 21 rev 6 (1948).
Belgian Patent Law: Loi modifiant la loi du 28 mars 1984 sur les brevets d'invention, en ce qui concerne la brevetabilité des inventions biotechnologiques (28 March 1984).
Belgium: Law No 2005-04-28/33: Loi modifiant la loi du 28 mars 1984 sur les brevets d'invention, en ce qui concerne la brevetabilité des inventions biotechnologiques.
Brazil Provisional Measure No 2186-16 of 2001, Regulating Access to the Genetic Heritage, Protection of and Access to Associated Traditional Knowledge.
China: The Patent Law of 2000 and the Regulations on the Protection of Varieties of Chinese Traditional Medicine.

Chinese Patent Law Amendment (2008), Articles 5(2), 26(5).
Costa Rican Law on Wildlife Conservation, N 7317, 30 (October 1992).
Costa Rican Law No 7788 on Biodiversity (as last amended by Law No 8686 of 21 November 2008).
Danish Order on Patents and Supplementary Protection Certificates, Order No 93 (29 January 2009).
Decree Law No 118 of 2002 of Portugal.
Draft Brazilian Bill on Biodiversity Regulation.
French Patent Law of 1791.
German Seed Law, Gesetz über Sortenschutz und Saatgut von Kulturpflanzen (Saatgutgesetz) v 27.6.1953, BGBl I, 450.
India: Biological Diversity Act of 2002.
Japanese Patent Act (Act No 121 of 13 April 1959, last amended by Act No 16 of 18 April 2008).
Kenyan Forest Act (1942).
Norway: Patent Law Amendment 2004, Section 8b.
Peru Law No 27,811 of 2002 Introducing a Protection Regime for the Collective Knowledge of Indigenous Peoples Derived from Biological Resources.
Peruvian Bill, Legislative Decree No 823 (24 May 1996).
Philippines: Indigenous Peoples Rights Act of 1997.
Portugal: Decree Law No 118 of 2002 Establishing a Legal Regime of Registration, Conservation, Legal Custody and Transfer of Plant Endogenous Material.
Protection and Promotion of Traditional Thai Medicinal Intelligence Act, BE 2542 (1999).
Swedish Patent Decree Sect 5a (SFS 2004:162).
Swiss Patent Law.
Ugandan Forest Act (1942).
United States Townsend-Purnell Plant Patent Act (23 May 1930).
United States Atomic Energy Act of 1946 (Pub L No 79-585, 60 Stat 755 (codified as amended at 42 USC §§ 2011–2297g (1994)).
United States Bayh–Dole Act (Pub L 96-517 (codified as 94 Stat 3015, and in 35 USC §200-212)) (12 December 1980).
United States Patent Law.
US Patent Law, 35 USC §§1 et seq.
Title 35 of the United States Code on Patents.
Ugandan Forest Act (1942).

PATENTS

United States Plant Patent 5751, granted on 17 June 1986.
United States Patent No 5401404.
United States Patent 5401504, granted in 1995 (Turmeric).
United States Patent No 5663484.
United States Patent No 5894079.
United States Patent No 5900240, issued on 4 May 1999.
Reexamination Certificate C1, issued on 29 January 2002, cancelling claims 1–7, 10 and 14–20 of the original Basmati patent.

REGIONAL AGREEMENTS

Convention on the Grant of European Patents, European Patent Convention 5 October 1973 as revised by the Act revising Article 63 EPC of 17 December 1991 and the Act revising the EPC of 29 November 2000.
African Decree No 74/1357 (April 1974).
ASEAN Framework Agreement on Intellectual Property Cooperation (1995).
Directive No 96/9/EC of the European Parliament and of the Council of 11 March 1996 on the legal protection of databases.
Andean Community Decision No 391 of 2 July 1996 – Common Regime on Access to Genetic Resources.
Decision No 423 of 11 November 1997 – Modification to the Eighth Transitory Disposition of Decision 391: Common Regime on Access to Genetic Resources (CAN014).
European Parliament and Council Directive 98/44/EC of 6 July 1998 on the legal protection of biotechnological inventions.
Andean Community Decision No 448 of 11 December 1998 – Modification to the Eighth Transitory Disposition of Decision 391: Common Regime on Access to Genetic Resources (CAN015).
Sirte Declaration for the establishment of the African Union (9 September 1999).
African Union African Model Legislation for the Protection of the Rights of Local Communities, Farmers and Breeders, and for the Regulation of Access to Biological Resources of 2000.
ASEAN Framework Agreement on Access to Biological and Genetic Resources and Traditional Knowledge (24 February 2000).
Decision 486. Régimen Común sobre Propiedad Industrial, Lima, Perú, a los catorce días del med setiembre del año dos mil. Full text available at http://www.comunidadandina.org.

Economic Partnership Agreement, between the CARIFORUM States and the European Community, 289/II/ (2008).

CASES

Case 03-1304, *University of Rochester v. G.D. Searle & Co, Inc., Monsanto Company, Pharmacia Corporation, and Pfizer Inc.* (2004).

Ciba-Geigy/Propagating material application, T49/83 C EPOR 758.

Curry v. Audax, Case no 334492 / KG 06-176 SR District Court of Amsterdam, 9 March 2006.

Diamond v. Chakrabaty, United States Supreme Court 447 US 303, (1980).

Director-General of National Parks and Wildlife Services v. Shoalhaven City Council, NSWLEC 191, No 10376 of 1993, Land and Environment Court of New South Wales (1993).

Feist Publications, Incorporated v. Rural Telephone Service Company Incorporated, 499 US 340 (1991).

G2/07 Broccoli (2007).

G1/08 Tomato (2008).

G2/12 (pending).

International News Service v. Associated Press, 248 US 215 (1918).

Johnson v. M'Intosh, 21 US (8 Wheat) 543 (1823).

Lubrizol/Hybrid plant T320/87 (1990) OJ EPO 71.

Mabo v. Queensland, 107 ALR1 175 CLR 1; 107 ALR 1; 66 ALJR 408; (1992).

Novartis/Transgenic plant (G01/98), [2000] EPOR 303.Onco-Mouse/ Harvard, 14 July 1989 (OJ EPO 11/1989, 451; [1990] 1 EPOR 4).

Plant Genetic Systems/Glutamine synthetase inhibitors [1995] EPOR 173 at 373 (1995).

Second Decision in the case of Edmonds Institute, et al. v. Babbitt, Civ Docket No 98-561, 12/04/2000.

United Nations Human Rights Committee, *Ominayak and the Lubicon Lake Band v. Canada*, 1990, Annual Report of the Human Rights Committee, UN Doc A 45/40, Bd II AP A (1990).

Van Dale v. Romme (Dutch Supreme Court) Hoge Raad, 4 January 1991, NJ 1991, 608.

The Wik Peoples v. The State of Queensland & Ors; The Thayorre People v. The State of Queensland & Ors [1996] HCA 40.

Index